P9-ELO-431

*f*P

ALSO BY DAVE KINDRED

Around the World in 18 Holes (with Tom Callahan)

*Heroes, Fools, and Other Dreamers: A Sportswriter's
Gallery of Extraordinary People*

Glove Stories: The Collected Baseball Writings of Dave Kindred

A Year With the Cats: From Breathitt County to the White House

Basketball: The Dream Game in Kentucky

Kentucky Derby: The Chance of a Lifetime
(with Jim Bolus and Joe Hirsch)

Theismann (with Joe Theismann)

Colorado Silver Bullets: For Love of the Game

SOUND
AND FURY

Two Powerful Lives,
One Fateful Friendship

Dave Kindred

FREE PRESS

NEW YORK · LONDON · TORONTO · SYDNEY

FREE PRESS
A Division of Simon & Schuster, Inc.
1230 Avenue of the Americas
New York, NY 10020

FREE PRESS and colophon are
trademarks of Simon & Schuster, Inc.

For information regarding special discounts for bulk purchases,
please contact Simon & Schuster Special Sales at 1-800-456-6798
or business@simonandschuster.com

Manufactured in the United States of America

1   3   5   7   9   10   8   6   4   2

Library of Congress Cataloging-in-Publication Data
Control Number 2005055217

ISBN-13: 978-0-7432-6211-8
ISBN-10: 0-7432-6211-5

For
Mom
Cheryl
Sandra

CONTENTS

There are two sources of light,
The candle,
And the mirror that reflects it.
—EDITH WHARTON

AUTHOR'S NOTE

Gene Kilroy, Ali's camp business manager and friend for forty years, considered Cosell a nuisance who was lucky to have been admitted to Ali's presence. Any time we talked, he said, "Tell me again, what's Cosell doing in your book?" My best explanation for the dual biography was that the men were partners of a historic kind, and I knew them in ways that no other reporter did. I met Ali in 1966 and Cosell eleven years later. I dealt with them through the rest of their lives in professional and private circumstances. Of the dozens of Ali books that I have read, none tells the story as I knew it. As for Cosell, only he has told his story and only in scattershot memoirs.

Two advisories here. Because my reporting put me with Ali and Cosell so often, I appear in the narrative from time to time, a bit player among the action heroes. The more important advisory is the second: My experience with Ali and Cosell is the foundation of the book's narrative, its tone, and its judgments. I added reporting done in new interviews with Ali's and Cosell's friends, families, and associates as well as with authors, journalists, boxing experts, critics, and historians. I also incorporated information that I found trustworthy in books, videotapes, audio recordings, papers, news accounts, and oral histories.

In all this, my ambition was to recover Muhammad Ali from mythology and Howard Cosell from caricature. The real stories are better.

I am the greatest.
—MUHAMMAD ALI

I tell it like it is.
—HOWARD COSELL

---

*Cosell's the only guy who ever changed his name
and put on a toupee to tell it like it is.*
—JIMMY CANNON, NEW YORK SPORTSWRITER

Oh, no, if he wins, he'll think he's really God.
—KHALILAH ALI, ALI'S SECOND WIFE,
DURING ALI-FRAZIER III.

---

*How they were different.
Young and old, black and white.
Kentucky and Brooklyn, Muslim and Jew.*

*How they were alike.
In ways that could make you laugh
and make you cry.*

They Charmed and Bedeviled Us

ONE AFTERNOON IN LAS VEGAS, while in bed with Muhammad Ali, I asked him to name the members of his entourage and list their duties. He took my pencil and held my reporter's spiral notebook inches above his pretty face. In childlike block letters, he printed a dozen names. Alongside the names he wrote dollar figures in estimate of each person's weekly salary. We lay there, shoulder to shoulder, one of us wearing clothes. Here's what I thought: *Are we nuts, or what?*

Years later I told *New York Times* columnist Dave Anderson, "I was in bed with Ali."

Anderson said, "We all were."

"No," I said, "I was *in bed* with Ali."

"Oh," he said.

It happened in a hotel suite three or four days before some fight. The suite was the usual Ali Circus madhouse of perfumed women, pimp-dressed hangers-on, sycophants, con artists, sportswriters, and other reprobates. Through an open door at one side of the suite's central space, I saw Ali in bed with the sheets pulled up to his chin. On eye contact, he shouted, "My man. Louisville, come in here."

I worked for the *Courier-Journal*, his hometown newspaper, and first spent a day with him in 1966. Already famous and infamous as the heavyweight champion and loud-mouthed draft resister, he had come to Louisville to visit his parents and fight an exhibition bout for charity. I was a young reporter in my first year at the great newspaper and eager to do anything the editors asked. When one said, "Clay's in town, go find him," I did. We drove around the city, stopping now and then to do some business. My son, Jeff, four years old, rode with us, and Ali occasionally put Jeff on his lap as if he were steering the car. I thought: *a nice guy*.

Now, in his bedroom in 1973, the noise from the central suite was maddening. Ali lifted a corner of the bedsheet and said, "C'mon, get in." Over the years I had talked with him in shower stalls and toilets, in funeral homes, log cabins, mosques, and once in a Cadillac at eighty-five miles per hour on a logging road through a forest. And now—this was a reporter getting close to his subject—I took off my shoes and put myself under the sheets with the once and future heavyweight champion of the world. I wore golf slacks and a polo shirt. More than most men, if not more than most narcissists, Ali loved to show off his body. He was beautiful, six foot three and 210 pounds, with proportions so powerful and so perfectly in balance that he might have sprung to life from a Michelangelo sketch. On the off-chance that you didn't notice, he often repeated what a nurse had said on prepping his groin for hernia surgery. "She took one look," Ali said, "and she went, 'You *are* the greatest!'"

Like schoolboys on a sleepover hiding their mischief, we pulled the sheets over our heads. Ali made a tent by raising his knees. Shadows danced inside our hiding place. The suite's noise seemed distant. On my back I did an interview that ended with Ali saying, "Tell the people in Louisville this will be *noooo* contest because I am the greatest of *alllllll* times." Then I asked for my notebook back.

The strangest aspect of the undercover interview was that it wasn't strange. For Ali, it was characteristic. Whatever he wanted to do, he did it as soon as possible. *C'mon, get in.* Anything could happen around Ali and often did.

I saw him naked. I am not sure I ever saw him clearly.

Howard Cosell was in his underwear.

I sat at a breakfast table in his beach house on Long Island in Westhampton, New York. The sun streamed in over a marshland. I saw in the shadows across the room a ghostly shape that on inspection turned out to be my host shuffling barefoot from his bedroom, skeletal in a white undershirt and white boxer briefs. He was bleary-eyed. He had not yet found his toupee. As Cosell noticed me, he raised his arms and struck a bodybuilder's biceps-flexing pose. Then he spoke, and this is what he said: "A killing machine the likes of which few men have ever seen."

On this morning in September 1989, I had known Cosell for twelve years. Our relationship began the day I wrote a column in the *Washington Post* praising him as a sports-broadcasting journalist without peer. I wrote that, while his excesses invited criticism, he deserved better than to be the target of mean-spirited punks, among them a Denver bar owner who allowed patrons to throw a brick at a television set carrying Cosell's image. The day the column ran, I answered my office phone.

"David Kindred," the caller said, not bothering to identify himself, "you are a perspicacious and principled young man, and it will be my honor to meet you this next week when I am at RFK for another of these *Monday Night Football* tortures."

Sounded like Cosell.

"David, this is Howard Cosell," he said.

"Well, it sounded like you," I said.

Twelve years later, he wanted me to write his fourth memoir. We met at his place in the Hamptons. There in the kitchen, he demonstrated the complete repertoire of his domestic skills. He found the refrigerator, extracted a carton, and without injuring himself or witnesses he poured a glass full of orange juice. His sainted wife, Emmy, said, "Took forty-five years to teach him that."

Cosell that morning also pleased his daughter, Hilary. Yes, he said. Yes, a man should walk down to the beach and see the ocean on a morning this beautiful. "We'll talk," he said to me, "after we examine Hilary's beloved beach." He put himself together. Toupee. Slacks. Boating shoes. Sunglasses. Short-sleeved shirt. He was ready. "To the beach," he said. He might have been MacArthur about to wade ashore in the Philippines.

From Cosell's deck at the edge of marshy Moniebog Bay, we walked maybe a hundred yards to the beach. The Atlantic glimmered in the rising sun. The obedient father of Hilary Cosell stood at the water's edge, though not so near as to allow water to stain his shoes. He looked to the horizon. He watched a wave lap against the shore. He gave the lovely beach and the ocean's wonders thirty seconds of his time. Then he said, "Well, Hil, we saw it."

Whereupon he retraced his steps to the comfort of a deck chair shaded by an umbrella. There he talked about the book. He was certain it would make America sit up and take notice. "We will excoriate the executives in charge of network sports broadcasts," he said. "They are people without scruples, without morality, without standards, without principle, and therefore without journalism. It is far past time for someone of integrity to expose the unholy alliances between promoters, broadcasters, and the sports industry."

He was a master of excoriation. He had excoriated most everyone in his third book. I was not in favor of more excoriation. That was not the book I wanted to write. But before I could say so, Cosell was in full cry about miscreants real and imagined, past and future. At that point, I did what millions of Americans had learned to do with Howard Cosell. I gave up and I listened.

We had no choice, really, except to listen to Ali and Cosell. Across much of the last half of the twentieth century, they were major players in American sports. Had they been practitioners of traditional humility, their extraordinary talents alone would have demanded that attention be paid. But there was nothing traditional about Ali and Cosell. A thimble would have contained their humility with room left over for an elephant.

Ali's shortest poem served as the foundation for most of his wakeful thinking. It went . . .

"Me,

"Whee!"

Cosell was a lawyer and thus inoculated against such brevity. He once wrote, "Arrogant, pompous, obnoxious, vain, persecuting, distasteful, verbose, a show-off. I have been called all of these. Of course, I am."

Before Ali, sports was a slow dance. After, it was rock 'n' roll. A child of the 1950s, Ali grew up with the Temptations, Elvis, and Fats Domino. "You know who started me saying, 'I am the greatest'? Little Richard did." Ali was fifteen years old when he staked out Lloyd Price at Louisville's Top Hat Lounge to tell the singer he would be the heavyweight champion someday and, *Please, Mr. Price, tell me how to make out with girls.* When Ali beat Sonny Liston the first time, the singer Sam Cooke sat at ringside with two more of the fighter's heroes, Malcolm X and Sugar Ray Robinson.

Before Cosell, sports on television was a reverential production. After, it was a circus. He brought to his work a fan's passion, an entertainer's shtick, and (this was new) a journalist's integrity. He had no interest in creating an image of men as heroes simply because they could play a kid's game. Instead, he subjected sports to the examinations Edward R. Murrow and Walter Cronkite made of the day's news. Thirty-eight years old when he gave up the law for broadcasting, he had not yet met Ali. He was a decade and more away from *Monday Night Football*. But he announced this: He would get famous.

They should never have met. Ali and Cosell lived in parallel worlds, separated by the sociological barriers of age, race, religion, education, and geography. But greater forces were at work. Twelve-year-old Cassius Marcellus Clay, Jr. put on boxing gloves, and high school sports editor Howard Cohen wrote his first *Speaking of Sports* column. Their differences became less important than their commonalities. Ambition and talent would bend their lives to a meeting place.

For most of twenty years, the fighter and the broadcaster appeared together on national television so many times that they became a de facto comedy team, Ali & Cosell. As considerable as the sports and news considerations were to Ali and Cosell, they were also intriguing as an eccentric evolutionary step in the history of entertainment. Comedy teams could be traced to the 1840s minstrel shows featuring the Interlocutor and Mr. Bones. Then came vaudeville, America's first mass entertainment industry with two million customers a day filling four thousand theaters to see twenty-five thousand performers. Radio, movies, and television created icons: Burns and Allen, the Marx Brothers, Laurel and Hardy, Abbott and Costello, Martin and Lewis, the Smothers Brothers, the Blues Brothers Dan Akroyd and John Belushi, the ensemble comedy teams of *Seinfeld* and *Friends*.

But Ali & Cosell was different. It was real. No scripts, no rehearsals, no let's-shoot-that-scene-again. What television viewers saw was the most famous man on Earth (the pope ran second to Ali in most surveys) talking with the most famous television star in America (or maybe next to Johnny Carson). Ali & Cosell worked the way comedy teams always worked. They were their own sight gag, the handsome athlete shimmering alongside the homely fellow with the bad toupee. They sounded funny because Ali spoke simply while Cosell's language was that of a sesquipedalian trained at law and infected by grandiloquence born of pomposity. Twenty-four years younger than Cosell, Ali could represent every kid who ever flouted authority. The fighter forever titillated spectators with pantomimed threats to lift the broadcaster's hairpiece and once said, "Cosell, you're a phony, and that thing on your head comes from the tail of a pony." To a Cosell scolding of "You're being extremely truculent," the defiant child Ali replied, "Whatever 'truculent' means, if that's good, I'm that."

It made Ali & Cosell must-see TV. At the dawn of television's dominance of popular culture, they were both the creators and beneficiaries of sudden fame never before available. If blacks and Jews were marginalized by society, these two recognized that television could grant them legitimacy. Both profited from the work, for without Ali engaging his liberal social conscience, Cosell would never have found his truest voice; and without the embrace of Cosell and the American Broadcasting Company when other networks wanted nothing to do with him, Ali could have been dismissed as a cultural-fringe aberration. At each other's side, they rose on an arc of celebrity previously unknown in sports and television.

It was a bumpy ride. While violence scarred America through the 1960s, Ali preached a hateful hodge-podge of racism, religion, and black nationalism. His declarations of independence as a black man made him a symbol of pride adapted for use by groups as disparate as the separatist Nation of Islam and the integrationist Southern Christian Leadership Conference. Athletically, sociologically, and politically, Ali mattered more to his times than any other athlete who ever lived.

Only the rare journalist stood with him, though, and only Cosell did it on national television. On issues so volatile they divided America, Cosell defended Ali's right to his religion, his right to oppose induction into the army, and his right to work while appealing his conviction for refusing the draft. He did it at the risk of his reputation and his livelihood in a business—television—not famous for principled stands that might offend advertisers. He did it, too, Cosell often said, despite thousands of letters he received in which the correspondents referred to him as "a nigger-loving Jew bastard."

Mostly, Ali & Cosell worked because the men brought to their lives and to their television appearances a fascinating array of dichotomies: love and hate, racism and tolerance, fear and courage, idealism and compromise. The camera's unblinking eye testified to all that, as well as to the men's mutual respect. Cosell loved Ali, the rebel with a belief, and Ali loved Cosell, the cranky old white guy brave enough to stand with him in the storm.

———————————

A night in Baltimore. Room 428 of a hotel. A man in the hallway bangs his fist against the room door. The man is Cosell and he is shouting. From inside the room comes a raspy voice.

"Who's there?"

"Cosell."

"Go away."

Cosell beats on the door again. "Ali, it's me, Howard."

"Ain't Cosell. Tryin' to sleep."

Then comes a sentence of percussive consonants and melodramatic phrasing. "I'm warning you, nigger, you open this door, and open it now, or I will destroy it and tear you to ribbons."

The door flies open, Ali out of bed, laughing. "Cosell, get your white ass in here."

Only the inimitable, irascible Cosell could have roused Ali from bed that way. Only the inimitable, sweet-hearted Ali would answer those slurs smiling. Across a generation of tumult, they were friends, partners, and co-conspirators in an improbable dialectic that charmed and bedeviled us. One was Beauty, one was the Beast, and we never quite knew which was which.

PART ONE

Dreaming

CHAPTER ONE

"Bound Together By a Common Sympathy"

WITH HIS WIFE AT HOME in Kentucky, the brilliant and handsome Cassius Marcellus Clay so often kept the company of Russian women that husbands grew suspicious. One gentleman wanted to settle affairs with a duel. Less than eager to face Clay's famous Bowie knife, he hoped to provoke Clay into making the challenge; the offended man then would have the right to choose the weapons. At dinner, the husband unrolled his gloves and slapped Clay across the face. "In less than an eyeblink," a historian reported, "Clay threw a mace-like fist into the nose and mouth of the would-be *duelliste*. The surprise blow was delivered with such force that the man's body broke completely through a nearby table, leaving a swath of food and shattered china for several yards."

After which, Clay continued his dinner.

The name is familiar. *Cassius Marcellus Clay.* Muhammad Ali's original name was Cassius Marcellus Clay, Jr. The Clays were not related, except by history that is extraordinary, even eerie. It encourages the imagination necessary to write that Ali and Howard Cosell met before they were born.

Begin with the first Clay. As a young man at Transylvania University in Lexington, Kentucky, he had been a boxer. In the summer of 1861, as Abraham Lincoln's new minister to Russia, he was forty-nine years old, tall and strong, his brown hair streaked with gray, his handsome face only then showing the lines of a dramatic life. On July 14, a Sunday, he would present his portfolio to the court of his Imperial Majesty, Alexander II. For the occasion he dressed in the formal military uniform of a major general in the United States Army, golden epaulets and stars set on his broad shoulders. At his waist hung a silver scabbard filled with the long, broad blade of the pearl-handled Bowie knife feared by husbands and rivals on two continents. A jeweled sword bumped against his ankles.

He was a legend in American politics. John M. Harlan, a fellow Kentuckian and a justice on the U.S. Supreme Court, saw in Clay's face "a striking combination of manly beauty and strength. . . . I always had the highest regard for his integrity of character, his manliness, and his fidelity to his own convictions." That fidelity sometimes came off as orneriness. Of Clay it was said, "He would fight the wind did it blow from the South side when he wanted it to blow from the North." In his passion to end slavery, he walked alone down the center of hostile meeting rooms and at the lectern said, "For those who obey the rules of right, and the sacred truths of the Christian religion, I appeal to this book." From a carpetbag, he held high a Bible.

"To those who respect the laws of this country, this is my authority." He placed a copy of the Constitution alongside the Bible. "But to those who recognize only the law of force . . ." Here he raised two long-barreled pistols and thumped them down before turning a Bowie knife so its blade caught the room's light. " . . . for those—here is my defense."

Ambitious and brilliant, Clay might have become president had his views on slavery been expressed with less ferocity. He was the wealthy owner of twenty-five thousand acres in Kentucky and Tennessee. Convinced that slavery was an impediment to industrialization, he freed his seventeen slaves in 1844 and began a long run for the presidency calling for abolition. Though a powerful member of the nascent Republican National Committee from 1856 on, he had no chance to win his party's presidential nomination. In 1860 it went to Lincoln, who then won the presidency in a four-man race with less than 40 percent of the popular vote. Clay asked for a place in Lincoln's cabinet as secretary of war, an important appointment because a national war seemed a gunshot away. The president-elect said no, telling Clay, "I was advised that your appointment as secretary of war would have been considered a declaration of war upon the South."

War came in any case, and the president asked Clay to perform a duty he saw as critical to the Union's fate. England and France had suggested they might recognize the Confederacy as a legitimate power. Lincoln could not afford to lose Russia as well. He sent Clay to St. Petersburg with orders to keep the Russian bear happy.

On that July morning in 1861, Clay rode in an elegant carriage drawn by two bay horses to Peterhof, the tsar's country palace. There he met Alexander II, Clay's equal in stature and elegance, as described by his secretary: "He is about forty-five years of age, stoutly built, and of an exquisite figure. Very handsome, rather a round face, eyes a beautiful light blue, mustache, hair shingled, and of a dark auburn colors. Speaks 'American,' voice pleasant, and looks and walks and is, every inch a King."

Each knew the other's ambitions. The tsar wanted to reform Russia's society. He had liberalized laws oppressing Jews, and his Emancipation of the Serfs decree ended servitude for forty million peasants. Clay not only had freed his own slaves. He had badgered Lincoln to end slavery altogether. The tsar told Clay that their nations "were bound together by a common sympathy in the common cause of Emancipation."

As strong as the bonds of common cause may have been, they lasted less than twenty years. The nations soon were on opposite sides of freedom. Lincoln's Emancipation Proclamation, issued in 1863 and hailed by Clay as "the culminating act of my life's aspirations," survived the president's assassination in 1865. But the murder of Alexander II in 1881 ended Russia's progressive movement. The new tsar, Alexander III, reinstituted pogroms across his nation's lands.

By then, Clay had long since returned to his Kentucky plantation and there one of his freed slaves named a son Herman Clay. In 1912, nine years after the abolitionist's death, Herman Clay honored the old man by naming a son Cassius Marcellus Clay. That son's son was Cassius Marcellus Clay, Jr., later known as Muhammad Ali.

Millions of Jews fled Alexander III's pogroms, many going to America. Among those emigrants were Harris Cohen and his wife, Esther. In 1890 they left Poland with their infant son, Isadore. That son's son was Howard William Cohen, later known as Howard Cosell.

CHAPTER TWO

"America Was in Everybody's Mouth"

THEY SPENT THREE WEEKS on freight trains huddled among strangers. They were quarantined at seaports for two weeks. Then came two more weeks in steerage on a steamship heaving on the ocean. To travel in steerage was to suffer an immigrant's foulest degradations: darkness, oppressive heat in stale air, odors of urine and excrement, a babel of tongues. The Cohens and millions more Jews undertook journeys from the land of their ancestors to Lord knows where.

Fear was their companion. Fear at every border crossing, every port, every examination, inspection, and interrogation. Fear compounded by filthy, crowded, clamorous conditions. Fear of sickness, fear of rejection. Even fear of other Jews, for at Europe's Atlantic ports, battalions of con men, thieves, and thugs, many speaking Yiddish, preyed on immigrants who trusted them for help in lodging, food, and tickets. One steerage passenger wrote, "I wanted to escape the inferno but no sooner had I thrust my head forward from the lower bunk than someone above me vomited straight upon my head. I wiped the vomit away, dragged myself onto the deck, leaned against the railing and vomited my share into the sea, and lay down half-dead upon the deck." For this, an immigrant may have paid his last penny. In 1903 a steamship ticket from Antwerp, Belgium, to New York City cost thirty-four dollars. The trip from eastern Europe to Antwerp may have cost half again that. Before reaching immigration centers at New York's Castle Garden or Ellis Island, a family of three might have spent one hundred fifty dollars, a fortune for people already poor.

Yet life in Russia was so terrifying and the promise of the United States so appealing that from 1881 to 1914 almost two million Jews made the hellish journey from eastern Europe. "America was in everybody's mouth," the immigrant Mary Antin said. "Businessmen talked of it over their accounts . . . people who had relatives in the famous land went around reading their letters for the enlightenment of less fortunate folk . . . old folks shook their sage heads over the evening fire, and prophesied no good for those who braved the terrors of the sea and the foreign goal beyond it; all talked of it, but scarcely anyone knew one true fact about this magic land."

The Cohens arrived at Castle Garden in New York's Battery in 1890.

Nellie Rosenthal was the sixth of ten children born to Jacob and Dora Rosenthal, themselves Russian Jews who arrived at Castle Garden in 1880 and 1882. The Rosenthals settled in Worcester, Massachusetts. Jacob worked as a clothier and may have done business with a young accountant for a chain of credit clothing stores. The young man's name, Isadore Martin Cohen.

Isadore and Nellie were soon man and wife, joined in what their families considered an "arranged marriage," meaning not so much a union of lovers as a merger of class, heritage, and fortune. Pregnant at age seventeen, Nellie gave birth to her first child, Hilton, in 1914. Because Izzie's territory reached from New England to the mid-Atlantic states, the Cohens' second son, Howard William Cohen, was born in Winston-Salem, North Carolina. The date was March 25, 1918. Before Howard was a year old, the Cohens returned to Brooklyn to be near Izzie's parents. They lived in the Brownsville neighborhood, identified by a New York newspaper as "a land of sweatshops and whirring sewing machines, of strange Russian baths, of innumerable dirty and tiny shops, of cows milked directly into pitchers and pails of customers at eventide, of anarchists, of a Jewish dancing school and of a peasant market." Between 1905 and 1930, Brooklyn's Jewish population rose from one hundred thousand to more than eight hundred thousand.

The Cohens became immigrants of a different kind. Through Howard's childhood, they lived in at least six different Brooklyn apartment buildings (not always paying the electricity bill in time to keep the lights on). They sometimes moved for deals offering new tenants three months' free rent. Evictions were so common in Brooklyn through the Depression years that the writer Alfred Kazin said the most powerful experience of his childhood came "when I watched my mother, who was a dressmaker at home, leading a crowd of women to put back the furniture removed during an eviction. I never got over that and never will." He felt "a lasting sense of the powerlessness and suffering that are endemic in our society." Nellie Cohen worried that Izzie would be fired and leave the family without means to pay their rent. Because anyone with a job during the Depression went to extraordinary lengths to keep it, Isadore Cohen stayed on the road as many as fifty weeks a year. Perhaps those long absences exacerbated whatever strains came with an "arranged marriage." Irving Howe, writing of Jewish life in New York early in the twentieth century, noted that Yiddish fiction and folklore were rich with tales of wives, left alone at home by working husbands, who took in boarders, as often for pleasure as profit. "No one will ever know how many Emma Bovarys lived and died on the East Side," Howe wrote, "but if we suppose Emma to represent an eternal possibility of human nature, there must have been a good many wives like her, restless and discontented, responding to the first tremors of Jewish romanticism."

In any case, the Cohens' marriage was a melancholy union. They argued over matters small and large. Izzie loved to play the violin, but with his limited skills he repeated songs, particularly "My Hero" and "The Donkey Serenade," until the screechings moved Nellie to cry out, "Izzie, that's enough. You're driving us crazy." Money was a perennial topic, as were Nellie's ailments (she was a hypochondriac), her grousing that Izzie spent too much time caring for his parents, and Izzie's insistence on keeping a kosher home. Hearing the arguments, young Howard cringed and sought silence, only to discover there were no silent places in Brooklyn walk-up apartments. Worse, with his father out of town, he was often left alone in the apartment with his older brother. Waiting at windows to see their mother's return, they saw men bring Nellie to the building door. They would run to get into bed before she came in. There would come a time when Howard would tell his wife why he was so strict in the raising of their daughters. He would begin, "I'll tell you about my mother."

One night at his kitchen window, Howard, eleven years old and shy, believed he had fallen in love. She was a blonde of Scandinavian descent who had come into view at a kitchen window in the apartment building next door. Her name was Dorothy Schroeder.

He was never brave enough to speak when he passed Dorothy on the street; she was a gentile and not among Howard's running mates. But on this night, separated by window panes and the chasm between buildings, Howard smiled at her. To his surprise, she smiled back. He picked up a cooking pot and raised it to the window. Dorothy, bless her, answered with a pot of her own. A game of matching kitchen utensils was on.

A knife by Howard, a knife by Dorothy, a fork, a spoon. These love notes flew back and forth for fifteen minutes until the boy finally blew the girl a kiss and she answered in kind. Each night for the next two weeks, Howard returned to the trysting place, eager, maybe ready to move on from utensils and cooking ware to plates and bowls. But Dorothy did not again appear at her window. On the street, they continued to pass each other in silence.

In place of young love, Howard made do with urban adventures. In the Brooklyn of 1929, he caught the subway along Eastern Parkway, rode to the Nevins Street stop, and walked to the Paramount Theater where the two-o'clock matinee cost twenty-five cents. In later life, he loved saying aloud the names of movie and vaudeville houses: "The RKO Albee, the Brooklyn Fox, the Brooklyn Strand, Loew's Metropolitan. We saw Milton Berle, Jack Benny, Jack Oakie, Eddie Cantor. What shows we saw."

If his beloved Dodgers were home at Ebbets Field, a boy short of money for a ticket and unable to talk his way past a turnstile could scurry to Bedford Avenue, throw himself on the ground, and put an eye under the board fence to see his hero, rookie center fielder Johnny Frederick, albeit from behind and from the knees down.

At five-thirty on afternoons with the Dodgers out of town, Howard rushed to Ludell's stationery store to meet deliverymen dropping off Brooklyn's three afternoon newspapers. Because the papers often went to press before games ended, it would seem an eternity before Howard heard the final score announced on radio by the erudite Stan Lomax on his six-forty-five sports show. Lomax, a Cornell University graduate who came to radio from the *New York Journal*'s sports department, did fifteen minutes of results and commentary daily for WOR, a station started in 1922 and operating from the basement of Bamberger's Department Store in Newark, New Jersey.

Howard played baseball only once, the last kid picked: "They put me in short left field, close up to the third baseman, and Jack Storm hit a screaming liner right at me. In self-defense, I put up my hands and the ball stuck in them. I was an instant hero. The next inning I made two errors and got kicked out of the game."

Little Howie's games occasionally were interrupted by his grandfather Jacob, his mother's father, a rabbi, who marched down the street to deliver Hebrew lessons no matter his grandson's reluctance to receive them. The lessons never seemed a match for the fear Howard felt when chased home by the Irish-Catholic kids from St. Theresa's parish, all those Studs Lonigans shouting "sheenie" and taunting him as a "prick-cutter" and "Jesus killer." Howard occasionally put on a hat to attend shul with his father, but was never bar mitzvahed.

After elementary school at Brooklyn's P.S. 9, Howard wanted to attend the borough's famous high school, Erasmus. But his mother believed no boy could concentrate on schoolwork in the company of girls. So he followed his brother, Hilton, at all-boys Alexander Hamilton High. There he discovered a fondness for the sound of his voice. English teacher Joe Boland called on students to do extemporaneous speeches, and often told Howard, "Show them how to do it." Another teacher, a Miss Kaiser, suggested he read the Romantic poets Shelley, Byron, and Keats. For Miss Kaiser, he often recited Keats's "Ode to a Nightingale." Tony Bove, Hamilton's football coach, encouraged Howard in journalism by suggesting that the young man with a facility for the language work on the school newspaper, *The Ledger*. When Howard became the paper's sports editor, Bove sent him a note of congratulations that said, "You may be doing this the rest of your life." Under his senior picture in the 1936 high-school yearbook was the prophecy: "He'll be a reporter for the Brooklyn Dodgers." For *The Ledger*, Howard wrote a column, *Speaking of Sports*.

At New York University, he majored in English literature as an undergraduate before entering law school—the law not because he wanted it, but to please his father, who took out quarterly loans to pay his way. Bored by the legal reading, Howard studied little and in fact needed to study only a little. He said his recall was "photographic in its preciseness." He passed the New York State bar examination on his first try. The security and prestige of a lawyer's practice appealed to Izzie Cohen, but his son preferred an afternoon at Ebbets Field or entertainments at the Paramount and RKO Albee. A career counselor might have suggested that Howard Cohen combine his enthusiasms—language, sports, and show business—because the 1930s gave rise to radio, the new medium of mass communication.

Through the thirties, America's biggest media celebrities outside of Hollywood were Graham McNamee, Clem McCarthy, and Ted Husing. They were sports broadcasters. A rival said McNamee sounded "as though he were grinding rocks together at the same time he was talking." But McNamee on boxing, McCarthy on horse racing, and Husing on everything brought the immediate, visceral thrill of sports to listeners who once could experience a sports event only by attending or by reading about it the next day. When McCarthy broadcast the 1938 Joe Louis–Max Schmeling fight during Howard's sophomore year at NYU, ratings showed that 63.6 percent of Americans tuned in. Those millions surely included Howard Cohen, a bright, ambitious young sports fan who had already built a reputation for understanding the news business. But in 1941, fresh out of NYU and having passed the bar, he never thought of radio as an option. He seemed trapped by the law—until history intervened. On December 7, the Japanese attacked Pearl Harbor. Cohen enlisted in the army.

In Louisville, Kentucky, five weeks and three days after Pearl Harbor, Odessa Lee Grady Clay gave birth to her first child, Cassius Jr.

The reluctant lawyer and willing soldier, Howard Cohen, was not pleased with his army orders. He was assigned to Brooklyn. Commuting on New York's Sea-Beach Express, he called himself "a Sea-Beach commando." When he applied for Officer Candidate School, Izzie and Nellie protested what they thought was their son's daredevil willingness to be killed. Three months of OCS in Mississippi earned him a ticket, not to Europe or the Pacific, but back to Brooklyn and the New York Port of Embarkation.

It was the largest stateside command post in the army, with five terminals, five staging areas, and three ammunition backup points. In two and a half years at the port, Private Cohen became Major Cohen, in charge of all manpower, including fifty thousand civilians and fifteen thousand military.

The most important decision Major Cohen made had nothing to do with his army service. It came in 1943 and confirmed his willingness, perhaps eagerness, to leave behind the Jewishness that had dominated his home life and childhood without bringing joy to either. As he walked past Major Bob Lewiston's port office in Building B, he saw the major's secretary, a Women's Army Corps private—in his words, "this cute, pudgy blonde." Immediately, he entered the major's office, mostly to give the blonde time to recognize the magnitude of Major Cohen. He believed he had seen an inviting "twinkle in her eye." He asked, "Would you marry me?"

Her name was Mary Edith (Emmy) Abrams. Army regulations barring socialization between officers and enlisted personnel turned out to be the least of difficulties for the smitten parties. Abrams was a Protestant. For a Jew, marriage outside the religion was so rare in the 1940s that Izzie and Nellie Cohen could not countenance their son with a *shikse*. They refused to attend the civil-ceremony marriage at New York City Hall on June 23, 1944. Though Emmy's parents were there, Cosell characterized the marriage as "undertaken under adverse circumstances." Emmy's father, Norman Ross Abrams, a prominent New Jersey corporate executive, refused to speak to her for two years. Her mother visited the newlyweds at their studio apartment in Brooklyn Heights, but surreptitiously.

At war's end, Cohen thought his army experience in juggling a sixty-five thousand-person workforce would make him "the biggest man in industry, or labor relations." Instead, the newlyweds began a period of their lives when Howard felt, for the first time, the weight of Jewishness oppressing his professional life. He opened a law office that brought him so few clients that he, Emmy, and their infant daughter left their Brooklyn Heights apartment and moved in with his parents. "You knew, by God, that you were Jewish," he would write, "and you knew every restrictive boundary and every thoughtless slight."

His one tentative move toward broadcasting illustrated that lesson. He did an audition at WOR, the station he had listened to as a boy eager to hear Stan Lomax's sports report. He was told he did not have an announcer's voice, that his Brooklyn nasal twang was not right for the air. It was 1945. He was twenty-seven years old, a husband, father, army major, lawyer. Yet he had to take his family into his parents' apartment, a dispiriting circumstance not only because he could afford nothing else. It also closed the door to escape. Like many children of immigrant Jews, he felt the suffocating presence of his parents' past and present, the Jewishness that seemed confining, defeating, a perpetual source of discontent. His oldest daughter, Jill, would say, "His whole life, Daddy felt like a poor, Jewish boy."

These immigrants' children wanted not so much to be Jews as to be Americans. At home they heard tales of dark ordeals that involved the sufferings and deaths of Jews. They heard wailings of mourning and they saw photographs of relatives dead and they heard from their parents how lucky they were to be alive in Brooklyn. Lucky they were, but the children didn't want to be reminded of it. They preferred the fantasies and sweet coolness of the RKO Albee, Brooklyn Fox, Loew's Metropolitan. Better to sneak away to Ebbets Field than be delivered to Hebrew lessons. Movies, shows, and sports were American things that Jewish boys had as their own, symbols of the popular culture their immigrant parents did not understand. Whether stickball or punch ball, knock hockey or basketball, the games brought relief from the remembered misery at home.

For Howard Cohen, marrying a *shikse* was an act of rebellion. Another came when he changed his name from Cohen to Cosell. His older brother, Hilton, had done it first, and both said their grandfather asked them to use the family's original name, Kassell. The brothers said an immigration official could not understand their grandfather's Polish and wrote down the familiar "Cohen," the name of one of the tribes of Israel. Hilton said, "Later, when I was an accountant in a firm where there were a million Cohens, my grandfather came to *me* and said, 'Listen, "Cohen" means priest, and we're not priests. Our name should be Cosell.' So I changed it. After a while, so did Howard." It was also true that in the late 1940s, following a war in which six million Jews were exterminated, many people hid their Jewishness. Virtually no mainstream show-business people worked under names that might identify them as Jews.

Cohen or Cosell, he now knew what he wanted. Here was a man who dated the birth of his daughter, Jill, from a Dodgers game in 1945. Emmy was out of the hospital only a day or two before spending an evening on hard bleacher seats. "Emmy, on that first night, watched Luis Olmo hit two home runs," Cosell said of his wife's return from childbirth.

"My treat," she said.

By the mid-1950s, the future for a lawyer was brighter than that of a Brooklyn Jew wishing to become a sportscaster whose broadcasting resume at age thirty-four consisted of one failed audition. So Cosell became the junior partner in a law firm started by Joseph Marro, a Manhattan attorney and New York state senator. Marro, Pomper, and Cosell had a small office at 25 Broad Street in the Wall Street district. Soon, Cosell boasted of earning thirty thousand dollars a year.

As evidence he had not given up on a broadcasting career, Cosell made himself a presence at Ebbets Field, Yankee Stadium, and the Polo Grounds. On the pretext of offering legal services, he arranged lunches with athletes such as the Yankees' Phil Rizzuto and Joe Collins. It became his custom, on leaving the law office, to stop at Joe Marro's desk and ask, "Can you loan me ten dollars to take the Scooter to lunch?" Sometimes he invited the senior partners along. Marro's son, Joseph Jr., ten years old, met his hero, Mickey Mantle. Eventually, Cosell parlayed those trips and his legal expertise into representation of athletes. He helped the Giants' stars, outfielders Willie Mays and Monte Irvin, get licenses for their Willmont Liquors Store at 566 Pennsylvania Avenue in Brooklyn. In 1953 officials from Little League Baseball came to Marro, Pomper, and Cosell. The mundane work on charter language fell to Cosell, who turned it to his advantage. At the Little League World Series that summer, one broadcaster on the ABC radio network was a neophyte with a Brooklyn nasal twang. It was Howard Cosell.

Cosell gained his first measure of national attention in August 1955, not as a broadcaster but as a lawyer. He was interviewed in his office by J. G. Taylor Spink, editor and publisher of *The Sporting News*. Autocratic and reactionary, bull-voiced and indomitable, Spink commanded respect in journalism and baseball. Notice in his column, *Looping the Loops,* conferred legitimacy on its subject. Spink and Cosell talked about the lawyer's work for Irvin, Mays, Bobby Thomson, Wally Moon, Alex Grammas, and Gil Hodges. Cosell also provided an embellishment or two. The winner of a second-place medal in a city public school standing broad jump event told Spink he had been "a broad jump champion." The notes editor of the *NYU Law Review* told Spink he had been *the* editor. He was born in 1918, not 1920.

There was one remarkable moment in the interview. Cosell asked Spink to let him know whenever a major league baseball team came up for sale. "I can get up the necessary funds if the right proposition comes along," he said. He apparently had in mind tapping the resources of his father-in-law, who had moved into the Eisenhower administration as assistant postmaster general. Cosell also positioned himself as a possible adviser to Major League Baseball when he noted that Commissioner Ford Frick had ordered a national survey on the marketing of baseball. "Well, I could help that survey," Cosell said. "Up to now, I have not been asked for this help."

Spink had one question. "You know so much about the Giants. About the inside doings on the club. What's wrong with the Giants of 1955?" Cosell laughed. "You are not going to drag me into that. I have my ideas of the subject. But I am not a baseball expert. I am a lawyer, a judge of misfeasance, malfeasance of legal rights, and tax problems. But I am not going to draw a plan showing where the Giants need propping up. Nor are you going to get me to discuss Leo Durocher."

At his typewriter that week, Spink began, "Howard Cosell is not a ballplayer. He is a lawyer. But he is going places in the business of baseball." He ended the column with a reference to Cosell as "a most interesting young man."

In that winter of 1955, at Willmont liquors, a young magazine writer named Ray Robinson sat with Irvin. They were joined by a tall, thin man with vulpine looks and black hair slicked back from a widow's peak. No introductions were made, nor did the man ask permission to be there. He simply said, "I'll listen to this." Though uncomfortable with the intruder's presence and kibitzing, Robinson didn't protest, largely because Irvin seemed not to mind. At interview's end, the man shook hands with Robinson and said, "I'm Monte's lawyer, Howard Cosell."

Later, Cosell told Robinson that he was fed up with the law, that he wanted to be a radio broadcaster. Robinson soon realized that Cosell worked every angle to make that happen. If the drudgery of obtaining liquor-store licenses brought him into the orbits of baseball stars, Cosell did it. If he thought a young magazine writer could introduce him to important people, he showed up at Willmont to eavesdrop and at interview's end ask, "Ray, would you give me a lift back to New York?"

"I didn't come here by car, I don't even own a car," Robinson said. "I invite you to go back to New York by subway with me."

Over subsequent lunches, Robinson made judgments of his new best acquaintance. He thought Cosell obsessively ambitious, smart, difficult, and strident—all qualities apparent when Cosell pestered Robinson for an introduction to an NBC programming executive. Finally, as odd as it seemed to Robinson that a lawyer would think of quitting his practice, he thought it truly bizarre when Cosell told him his plans for the future: "I'm going to be the most famous sports broadcaster there is."

Robinson thought, *A mad ambition.* The voice alone, a Brooklyn Jew's in its intonations and fast-paced rhythms, rendered the idea far-fetched. In a radio era of golden voices, the more neutral the better and basso profundo preferred, who would ever put that Cosell sound on the air, let alone raise its creator to fame? Before Robinson could speak, Cosell explained his abundance of confidence.

"I can't help but go to the top," he said. "All the rest are sons of the wild jackass."

With his Little League foot in the broadcasting door, Cosell pushed. He developed a modus operandi based on his legal practice. For no fee, Cosell did tax work and provided legal counsel for top executives of the ABC network, all the while asking to expand his broadcasting work. That led to a weekly radio show called *All League Clubhouse.*

The show featured children interviewing people in sports. Cosell was the moderator. Baseball players Jackie Robinson, Harvey Kuenn, Robin Roberts, and Del Crandall were among his guests. An old Dodger who became the Pittsburgh Pirates' manager, Bobby Bragan, explained Cosell's method: "He'd call and say, 'Bobby, Cosell. Be at the studio at six.' He'd hang up. I'd be there. I'd sit at the table with the kids and answer questions that he planted with them." One week's guest was Ed Silverman, who was neither famous nor an athlete. But he did have virtues important to Cosell. Silverman was a producer, responsible for the content and form of sports-broadcasting programs. He worked with ABC radio's biggest star, Bill Stern. That relationship began when Silverman proposed writing magazine articles under Stern's byline. As he entered Stern's office, which struck Silverman as "half the length of Grand Central Station," he heard Stern shout from the far end, "I'm a whore, I want to get paid. You heard me, I'm a whore. If you use my name, I want to know what my share is."

Cosell pestered Silverman for an introduction to the great man. But Stern rejected any meeting because he considered Cosell a dilettante with an overtly Jewish voice. "He absolutely fucking hated Cosell," Silverman said. The chief executives of the three networks were Jews:

Leonard Goldenson at ABC, William Paley at CBS, and David Sarnoff at NBC. "Yet they were the worst anti-Semites in the business," said Silverman. "Announcers changed their names from Jankowski to Jones, from Schwarz to Star. You couldn't sound New York, because if you sounded New York, you were, by association, Jewish. They were pandering to the Christian majority." Stern thought Cosell, with that voice, did a disservice to any Jew who wanted to be in radio. Stern himself, a Jew whose family name was Sternberg, had created a radio voice free of ethnic tones. Even Silverman, who did interviews on Stern's program, was asked by Stern to adopt a "less foreign-sounding name." On the air, he became Ed Stevens.

Rebuffed by Stern, Cosell decided to learn the business from the producer instead of the star. He asked Silverman, "Would you take me to a fight?" Silverman's summary of Cosell's boxing knowledge in 1954: "He didn't know from shit." At Madison Square Garden, Silverman and Cosell hobnobbed with managers, promoters, writers, and show-business people. The famous boxing trainer Cus D' Amato told Cosell he had a promising young fighter by the name of Floyd Patterson. That night in '54 was the beginning of Cosell's education at the ring.

That was also the year, in a church basement in Louisville, Kentucky, when Cassius Marcellus Clay, Jr., twelve years old and eighty-nine pounds, took the first slide-steps of his boxing life.

In a hurry because he was getting no younger—thirty-eight years old in 1956, married, the father of two daughters—Cosell wanted to step up from *All League Clubhouse*. He was smart enough to know he needed professional help. He enlisted Silverman in the creation of *11:30 Clubhouse*. Done for WABC in studio 3B at the network office at 39 West Sixty-sixth Street, the show would be Cosell's entry into broadcast journalism. After two anchor candidates turned down the job, Cosell told Silverman, "There's a new young guy who's very nice. Chris Schenkel."

"I don't think he's right," Silverman said. "Chris is a sweet guy. He'll never ask the hard question."

Schenkel wanted the job badly enough to accept fifty dollars a week for five shows, eleven-thirty to midnight. But Cosell soon agreed that Schenkel wasn't right. Silverman said, "What now?"

"We do the show," Cosell said.

"We?"

"I'll be the anchor," Cosell said. "You be the producer and do the commercials."

Silverman, exhausted by his sixteen-hour moonlighting jobs, quit Cosell three weeks later. That left Cosell as the happy producer, director, writer, and anchor of his own New York radio show. Though still practicing law full time, he now thought of himself as a broadcaster. And ABC offered him twenty-five dollars a show for ten five-minute sports reports a weekend, guaranteed for six weeks.

Some men would be terrified by the prospect of replacing a thirty-thousand-dollar income with six weeks of work for fifteen hundred dollars. Some men would be cowed by the sons of the wild jackass who at the time populated the upper reaches of sports broadcasting. Some might forever hear an echo of a moment-of-anger Silverman rant: "Howard, for Christ's sake, get real. With that voice, you're never going to make it." Not Cosell.

With that ABC offer in hand, Cosell went to Emmy. Making less a declaration of intent than a request for her approval, he told his wife he had decided to leave the law. She had grown up the daughter of a corporate executive and married an army major who prospered in a Manhattan law practice. Now her husband came with a proposal to trade affluence for hardship. Cosell believed Emmy had proven her love by ignoring the anti-Semitic bias that attended their marriage. But what would she say now? Much later, Jill Cosell's son, Justin, defined his grandparents succinctly: "For all of Poppa's bluster, Gam was a thousand times tougher. Decent, kind, loving—and sharp-edged." That tough woman told her man that day, "Go ahead."

He had developed strategy and tactics that would serve him for a lifetime. At that time, top broadcasters did play-by-play of college football, horse racing, and boxing. Cosell decided, "Play-by-play, parrots can do." He would do journalism as done by newspaper reporters. He was indefatigable and ubiquitous. When the Yankee catcher Ralph Houk said, "You're like shit, you're everywhere," Cosell thanked him. One sportswriter called him "some *schnorrer* from Brooklyn whose tape recorder was always hitting me in the head." Cosell claimed he was the first sports broadcaster to carry his own tape recorder. He described it as a machine the size of a small suitcase strapped to his back. As years passed, the machine grew in size. It sometimes weighed thirty pounds, sometimes forty, always spoken of in terms suggesting its dead weight would have bent Charles Atlas double. Cosell said, "I must have looked like Edmund Hillary carrying his knapsack."

Whatever pioneering Cosell did with his tape recorder, he did it after Silverman showed him its virtues. During World War II, the U.S. Army built a primitive recorder called a Tapak. It was spring-driven and had to be wound every minute and a half. But it was cheap, which endeared it to ABC. Rather than endure the travails of mediocrity, Cosell bought his own tape recorder. The top of the line Magnemite sold for a king's ransom of three hundred thirty-five dollars. It was manufactured by the New York company Amplifier Corp. of America, 398 Broadway. It operated on three one-and-a-half-volt "A" batteries and one ninety-volt "B." Eleven inches wide, eight inches high, and five inches deep, the Magnemite had the advantage of a cast-iron flywheel; unlike the Tapak, there was no need to wind it. But the flywheel raised the reel-to-reel machine's weight—not to the forty pounds of Cosellian legend, but to seventeen pounds, still enough for Silverman to say, "Howard developed the strongest forearms in broadcasting carrying that friggin' thing around."

The tape recorder was along in the spring of 1956 when Cosell went south for baseball's spring training, but Howard wasn't carrying it. The burden fell to Ray Robinson, the sportswriter he met in Monte Irvin's liquor store. Robinson had assumed he would do interviews and writing for Cosell's radio show. That would be repayment of sorts, for Robinson had become editor of a men's magazine, *Real*, which published a column titled *Cosell's Clubhouse*. The column's raw copy came to Robinson typed on the back of Western Union papers and in need of heavy editing.

On that trip, Robinson came to think of Cosell as indomitable. He saw Cosell work around the clock. He also recognized his own purpose on the trip. He did no interviews and no writing; he carried Cosell's tape recorder, and briefcases heavy with reference books. When he also realized that he would not be paid for his work; that Cosell and ABC would not pay his expenses; that the trip would lose him money rather than earn it; that the next two weeks promised only more nights with Cosell in shared hotel rooms, Robinson returned to New York. He had been in Cosell's presence two days.

Silverman did the writing and producing that packaged Cosell's reports into a spring-training radio show they called *Baseball Sportstacular*. In that creative process, Silverman learned that despite Cosell's first-class education and inherent journalistic skills, Howard worked under a burden of insecurity, as if sure that any misstep in a world of adversaries, real and imagined, would end his career.

Silverman put the final pieces together in an editing room near midnight the day before the first *Baseball Sportstacular* broadcast. Cosell, pacing and chain-smoking cigarettes, said, "It's not going to work, Eddie, it's terrible, it's not going to work." Midnight became two in the morning. Cosell continued to smoke. "It's not going to work, I just know it. I made a terrible mistake. I shouldn't have done this." By four o'clock, Cosell seemed at the brink of a breakdown. After Silverman put music to the show, he played it for Cosell, who said, "I don't know, Eddie, I just don't know, but it's not your fault, it's mine."

The show went on at eight o'clock that night, and the next morning Cosell read a review in the show business newspaper, *Variety*. It was a rave under the headline, "A Four-Bagger for Baseball Fans." Cosell carried the good news to every ABC executive's office. Finally he stopped at Silverman's door and said, "What a great fucking show! Didn't I tell you we could do this?" For neither the first time nor the last, Cosell's behavior caused Silverman to stare in wonder. He said to the figure darkening his doorway, "Who are you? You look like the guy who was up my ass all night."

On June 26, 1959, working his first heavyweight championship fight, Cosell rushed to Floyd Patterson's corner and shouted, "Floyd! Floyd! Floyd, what happened?"

Patterson had lost by a knockout, knocked down seven times in the third round by the Swedish challenger Ingemar Johansson. "I got hit, Howard," Patterson said, and Cosell turned to the eccentric trainer, Cus D'Amato, who said, "I will tell you right now that for the first time in the history of boxing, you will see a defeated heavyweight champion win his title back."

However many professional personas Howard Cosell might come to inhabit, in this beginning he was a journalist only, the intrepid ringside reporter elbowing his way through a crowd to get the news. He had been a boy waiting for the Dodgers score in the afternoon newspapers. Now he delivered the news himself—D'Amato's prediction was the stuff of tomorrow's headlines—only he did it instantaneously and coast to coast.

Cassius Clay was seventeen years old in 1959. The national Golden Gloves and AAU 170-pound champion, he lost in the final of the Pan-American Games qualifier. He would not lose again for twelve years.

CHAPTER THREE

"You Got a Little Joe Louis There"

ON JANUARY 17, 1942, at six-thirty-five in the evening, Cassius Marcellus Clay and Odessa Lee Grady Clay became parents of a boy born in Louisville General Hospital. In a pattern to be repeated years afterward, the boy's appearance set off a commotion. Babies began crying and hollering throughout the maternity ward, and Odessa Clay thought she knew why. She had looked at an identification band on the arm of the boy delivered to her and said, "Nurse! This is not my baby! My baby's name is Clay, this baby's name is Brown. You bring me my baby, and everything'll get quiet." Sure enough, it did.

The baby weighed six pounds, seven ounces. His head was large, and doctors used forceps to pull him from his mother's womb. The instrument left a rectangular mark on his right cheek. The father had mulled over names. "I was always excited about names, big important names," he said. "I wanted a Rudolph Valentino, a Cleopatra, and a Ramona. . . . I was crazy about Rudolph Valentino. He was so handsome." But the mother remembered the day in 1932 when a girl with her called across a street to a young, handsome man with a tap dancer's physique, small and lithe.

"Cassius, you come over here," the girl said.

Cassius Marcellus Clay's courtship of Odessa Lee Grady was as quick as it was unusual. Even their friends wondered how a storm-tempered, womanizing, whiskey-eyed rogue—that was Cash—wound up with a sweet-hearted young girl who knelt down every Sunday at the neighborhood Baptist church, Mount Zion. Clay was a painter, mostly of advertising signs outside bars and stores. For twenty-five dollars and a chicken dinner, he also painted Bible scenes on church walls.

Cassius and Odessa had in common the fractured world of black people in Louisville, Kentucky, a state that had sent men to both sides of the Civil War. Odessa never knew her father and had lived with an aunt because her mother could not raise three children at once. "A pretty hard life," she called it. She worked as a domestic for money to buy clothes. Cassius's father was Herman Clay, a thick, powerful man who cleaned cuspidors for a quarter a day until he bought a truck to carry ice, coal, and wood. Herman's own father had worked as a freed man for Cassius Marcellus Clay on the abolitionist's plantation outside Richmond, Kentucky, a hundred miles east of Louisville. The Cassius Clay born in 1912 would come to say, "Yes, indeed, the original Cassius Marcellus Clay battled against slavery at all times. We proud of him. My own grandfather was brought up on the old man's land, but he was never a slave. My grandfather was *with* the old man, but not in a slave capacity, no sir! Cassius Marcellus Clay took my grandfather with him at all times."

That day in 1932 on a Louisville street, Odessa Grady told her friend, "Cassius is the most beautiful name for a man I ever heard." In the hospital ten years later, she turned her husband's vanity to her advantage. Her ruckus-raising baby became Cassius Marcellus Clay, Jr. Once he was home, Cassius Jr. found ways to spread the commotion. Early on, he climbed into the family washing machine to splash water. The more his mother tugged at him, the greater his caterwaulings. Because he balled up his little hands into fists, his mother often heard, "Well, there's another Joe Louis."

He walked at ten months, up on his toes, and his mother said that meant he would be fast on his feet. When he was a year old, if no one rocked him, he bumped his head against his chair until he fell asleep. At two, he made a habit of waking up at five o'clock in the morning to throw clothes out of a dresser drawer. He liked toys but preferred to beat on pots and pans. The child talked, shaking his head and jabbering. He stood in his bed and shook it and one morning said his first words to his mother. "Gee gee," he said. After that, she called him Gee Gee. When he learned to walk, he ran. Until he was seven years old, he ran everywhere.

The boy played basketball and softball at the Chestnut Street YMCA, where the counselor considered him "an aggressive kid" good at swimming and wrestling. After winning a marbles tournament, Cassius announced that he had "the best knuckles in Louisville." In one photograph of sixty-three YMCA children, Cassius was the only one with his mouth wide open and a hand held high. By then he had a brother a year younger, Rudolph Arnett Clay. (The father won that naming round.) The YMCA counselor, Robert Quarles, did not always know Rudolph, but had no trouble remembering Cassius: "You always knew he was around." As his seventh-grade English teacher, Penelope Fisher, talked about verbs and adjectives, the boy threw punches in the air. "That was all that was on his mind," she said. "Punch, punch, punch—and tickle the girls in front of him."

If Odessa gave Cassius Jr., her kindness and generosity, the father was the son's wellspring of manic energy and sense of theater. Old Cash was a man of many declarations, and it seemed that each was more curious than the last. Some days he draped a shawl over his shoulders and wore a tasseled hat. "A sheik," said a friend who also remembered Clay's Arab period: "At noon he used to get down off his painting ladder and in his little box he had a carpet and he'd put this carpet down and bow to the east and then bow to the west." Once, Cash explained his wide, flat nose and skin much darker than his wife's and son's by saying, "Don't I look like an Arabian? All my features are Arabian." Or he might be a Mexican under a sombrero, taking a siesta. The friend said that sometimes Clay "was a troubador, singing in the streets. People'd be trying to sleep, one, two in the morning. They'd say, 'Here comes Cassius!' He used to sing at nightclubs if they'd let him, or in the streets if they wouldn't. Love to sing!"

Mostly, he declared himself an artist. "There!" he said one day. He was in a car with Jack Olsen, a *Sports Illustrated* reporter. "That's my work right there!" He pointed to a scruffy barroom: MIXED DRINK-FOOD-COLD BEER *whiskey by the drink*. "Now I'll show you a beautiful job, an elaborate sign." JOYCE'S BARBER SHOP, *specializing in processing, shoe shine*. "Now I'll show you some big work." PACIFIC PLYWOOD PRODUCTS CO. *1299 12st. the plywood supermarket*. "Look at that work. Ain't that beautiful? That's Persian blue with white lettering." KING KARL'S THREE ROOMS OF FURNITURE. For hours on a tour of Louisville business establishments, Clay showed the full portfolio of his art. On Dumesnil Street: A.B. HARRIS M.D. DELIVERIES AND FEMALE DISORDERS.

Olsen considered Clay a clumsy amateur at best. Yet Cash talked about the work in a breathless stream of consciousness, the words mostly indecipherable, though the reporter guessed that Clay believed the paintings were evidence of genius that went unrecognized because he was a black man in the segregated South.

During the Civil War, as a major city on the Ohio River, Louisville became a market for slaves brought in by boat. Holding pens were set up on Main Street. For most of the next hundred years, racial segregation was real in Louisville. But the city praised itself for its moderation. Its power elite practiced what sociologists call "polite racism." The city's blacks won the vote after the Civil War, and its public transportation system of trolley cars was integrated in the 1870s. Still, Louisville in the 1940s and 1950s was divided residentially, financially, and socially along racial lines. Blacks could not sit at lunch counters at downtown department stores, nor could they use restrooms. They could buy clothes, but they could not try them on first. Protesters met at Quinn Chapel Church, the historic abolitionists' church at Ninth and Chestnut streets. There they planned assaults on a century of insults. They boycotted downtown stores with a "Nothing New for Easter" campaign. They counted themselves proud to be arrested for asking to buy a movie ticket.

The Clays owned a four-room house on a street of such houses in Louisville's West End, where most of the city's black families lived. Cassius Sr.'s sign painting and Odessa Clay's occasional work as a domestic made the family comfortable if not affluent. Those were the same circumstances Cash knew growing up as one of Herman Clay's twelve children: "There weren't no poor people in those days. Everybody made a pretty good living in those days. Every house in those days, when I was a boy, every house had so much food on the table that they didn't have time to put it in the icebox. They just threw the tablecloth over it."

Odessa Clay, as kindly as her husband was annoying, kept on her bedroom bureau a photograph of her father, the mulatto son of an Irishman named Grady. The faded portrait showed a man with a dignified look, light skin, long hair, and pale eyes. A pale golden color herself, she said of her father, "He looked exactly like a white man." Mrs. Clay had small features and a high, musical voice that prompted her son Cassius to call her "Bird." She explained that the baby created the space between her two front teeth: "He was in the bed with me at six months old and you know how babies stretch? And he had little muscle arms and he hit me in the mouth when he stretched and it loosened my other front tooth and I had to have both of them pulled out. So I always say his first knockout punch was in my mouth."

Like Odessa, Cash quoted neighbors saying of Cassius Jr., "You got a little Joe Louis there, sho' 'nuff, you got a little Joe Louis there." He even told folks about a certain telephone pole. Down in the West End, it was the pole that Joe Louis himself once leaned against. The father said he took his boy to lean against that pole, as if somehow the pole's splinters might transmit the Louis magic to his son.

Many a black man in America through the 1940s wanted for his son, and by extension himself, the glory of Joe Louis, an Alabama sharecropper's son and the first black heavyweight boxing champion since white men ran Jack Johnson out of the United States. Clay painted his signs and murals around town and was forever railing against the white man, especially those white policemen who came to know him on nights when whiskey had done its devil's work.

It was a small irony that the young Clay became a fighter under the guidance of a white Louisville police officer. While at a community bazaar downtown, the boy realized his bike had been stolen. It was a new, shiny, red Schwinn. He reported the theft to a policeman and promised to whip whoever took it. The traffic cop taking the report, a tough ex-cowboy from New Mexico named Joe Martin, said that if a boy made such a promise, he better be able to back it up. As it happened, Martin also worked for the city recreation department as a boxing instructor. His gym was in the basement of Columbia Auditorium downtown on Fourth Street. He invited Cassius to come by.

Then, one day, boxers in the policeman's gym heard *something*. They had never heard such a sound. It was a sharp sound rising to an angry snap. A teenager named Tom Zollinger thought, *Lash LaRue cracking his whip*. Zollinger looked around and saw a small kid hitting the heavy bag. Cassius Marcellus Clay, Jr., weighed eighty-nine pounds. The skinny little kid had made that sound. The kid was no beginner. He had been told to leave Fred Stoner's gym. Stoner was a dour, stern-faced little man, a black boxing trainer who worked near the Clays' neighborhood. He was the best fight man in town, a scientific teacher, a quiet disciplinarian. His star had been Rudell Stitch, the world's number-two-ranked welterweight the day he drowned trying to rescue a stranger. Kids came to see Stoner at the Grace Community Center. They worked in a basement room so small that Stoner lined up students shoulder to shoulder and drilled them in unison, jab, slide-step, jab, everyone moving in the same direction because collisions would cause bodies to tumble like dominoes.

Zollinger heard that this Cassius kid wanted to get fancy and there wasn't room at Stoner's for individualists. But he liked boxing too much to quit and had announced, in his father's announcing way, that he would be a champion someday. So the next Joe Louis followed a friend to the policeman's place and there made that sound against the heavy bag, the whip's-crack announcing that someone unusual had arrived. Zollinger watched how he did that thing. He saw the little kid slap the heavy bag, almost as heavy as he was, until he had hollowed out an indentation at his eye level. Then he came quickly with dozens of sharp jabs. There would be a pop-pop-pop sound. Zollinger would stop whatever he was doing. With his buddies, all quiet now, he would watch the kid make that sound they had never heard before.

The policeman's fighters also noticed that no one taught Clay anything. He just did what he wanted to do. Stoner and Martin believed there was one way to box, and one way only. Martin tried to convince Clay to box flat-footed, to slide his left foot forward as he jabbed and return the left arm to where it had begun—elbow tucked firmly to the side, fist next to the chin. It was the way ordinary men learned to fight. But Clay was not ordinary, even at twelve years old, and he knew it. He used both trainers, working afternoons at Martin's gym, being allowed back to Stoner's at nights. Martin's advantage was that he had a monopoly on providing young fighters to Louisville's television station WAVE for its Saturday night boxing program, *Tomorrow's Champions*. Before Clay's first fight on that program at age twelve, he knocked on neighborhood doors to alert everyone that he would be on television. The show's host, WAVE sportscaster Ed Kallay, considered Clay "delightful, well mannered, and courteous."

That first year, as a novice flyweight, Clay lost seven fights. But in those defeats Joe Martin saw characteristics more important than skill. He saw how badly Clay wanted to be good; he was the hardest worker ever in Martin's gym. While the policeman recognized fear in Clay's eyes, he also saw how Clay reacted to it. "All that talkin' he does," Martin said, "that's nothing but whistlin' past the graveyard. With a corn cob and a cigarette lighter, you could chase him out of town. But he never quit in the ring. Takes guts to face what you're scared of. Clay's got guts."

The gym may also have been a safe place away from home. His daddy's whiskey nights scared him. The old man would take a swing at anyone in his way. When Odessa Clay could not handle it, she called the police.

Cassius Sr. was arrested nine times for reckless driving, disorderly conduct, assault and battery, and once for "disposing of mortgaged property," which is the only line on his rap sheet that does not suggest whiskey whispering in his ear. He never did jail time, largely because the attorney Henry Sadlo, the state's boxing commissioner, had such affection for Cassius Jr. that he hauled himself out of bed at all hours to tell a judge that old Cash just needed to sleep it off.

For three or four days in the summer of 1957, Cassius Jr. did not show up at Columbia Gym. That was strange because Clay was usually first to arrive and last to leave. When he appeared with a bandage on his thigh, he told Martin he had cut his leg on a milk bottle. Martin later heard another story. A policeman had been called to the Clays' home by Mrs. Clay after a domestic quarrel, "either a cutting or a fight or something like that." When young Cassius identified himself and mentioned Martin's name, the policeman let it go. He told Mrs. Clay, "Now, look, take him to your own doctor or take him to the hospital, and if you want to, go up and take out a malicious cutting warrant." Louisville's police files held a cursory summary: "August 8, 1957—10:32 P.M., Mrs. Clay, cutting INV. [investigation] 3307 Grand. NA [no arrest]." Later that year, Cassius told Martin that he had been cut when he stepped between his daddy's knife and his mother.

Fifteen years old that summer, undefeated after losing those seven flyweight fights, young Cassius had become a prodigy in a game that stood alongside football as second to baseball among American sports fans. Boxing's premier champions in 1957 would become Hall of Famers: Floyd Patterson, Archie Moore, Sugar Ray Robinson, Carmen Basilio, Sandy Saddler. NBC's weekly *Friday Night Fights,* one element of the *Gillette Cavalcade of Sports,* broadcast nearly six hundred fights. The Cavalcade began in 1941 and when it left the air in 1964 it was the longest-running series in television history.

One afternoon in 1957, Clay called the Sheraton Hotel in downtown Louisville. He knew that the famous trainer, Angelo Dundee, was there with a fighter, Willie Pastrano. He said, "Mr. Dundee, my name is Cassius Marcellus Clay. I'm the Golden Gloves champion of Louisville, Kentucky." There followed a list of the fights he had won and the championships he intended to win, including the Olympics and the heavyweight championship of the world. "I want to talk to you and Mr. Pastrano." Here Dundee turned to Pastrano, a clever light-heavyweight, and said,

"Some nut downstairs wants to talk to us. But he sounds like he might be a nice kid. Want to talk to him?" Pastrano said, "Why not? Nothing good on television." For three hours, Clay asked the trainer and fighter how they did it. How much roadwork? How many times a day did Willie eat? How many rounds did he spar? Dundee was astonished not only by the kid's hunger for information but by the intelligence of his questions. The trainer had worked with six world champions and he had never had that animated a conversation about the craft with any of them.

Clay's curiosity also took him in search of Lloyd Price, a singer riding the success of "Stagger Lee," the first song by a black rock 'n' roll artist to lead the country in sales. Late in 1958, Price came to Louisville's Top Hat Lounge and heard a good-looking young man at the door say, "Mr. Price, I'm Cassius Marcellus Clay, Jr. I'm the Golden Gloves champion of Louisville, Kentucky. Someday I'm gonna be the heavyweight champion of the world. I love your music, and I'm gonna be famous like you."

"Kid, you're dreaming," Price said.

Each time Price came to Louisville, Clay came to the Top Hat. Clay asked questions about travel and music. He also wanted to know how to make out with girls. "Just be yourself," Price said, "and the girls will like you." Price gave the young man a couple of dollar bills. "And always have money. That's the beginning of hanging out with foxes."

Clay lost only once at the top levels of amateur boxing, at age seventeen in the 1959 Pan-American Games trials final. The defeat was to Amos Johnson, a twenty-five-year-old Marine whose left-handed style compounded Clay's difficulties. Then came the 1960 Olympic Games in Rome. The problem for Clay there was that no one ever won an Olympic gold medal without showing up—and Clay didn't want to fly. Flying frightened him so much that he once returned from San Francisco to Louisville by bus. He told Joe Martin he would go to Rome—by boat. But Martin well knew the workings of Clay's mind. Because Clay was in a hurry to get rich and famous, the trainer pointed out that a 1952 Olympics gold medal had done all that for Floyd Patterson, the current heavyweight champion. So Clay flew first to New York. There the young sports editor of *Newsweek* magazine, Dick Schaap, took him to Sugar Ray Robinson's bar in Harlem. They waited on Seventh Avenue until a purple Cadillac pulled up. "Here he comes," Clay shouted. "Here comes the great man Robinson." Schaap made the introductions and watched as the languid, sparkling Sugar Ray gave the kid an autographed picture of himself, wished him luck in the Olympics, and drifted away, better things to be done in a great man's day. Robinson's condescension did not register on Clay, who came away saying, "That Sugar Ray, he's something. Someday *I'm* going to own *two* Cadillacs—and a Ford for just getting around in."

In Rome, Clay did so much glad-handing that some athletes called him "The Mayor" of the Olympic Village. He even came across Patterson and told him, "See you in a couple years." Clay won three bouts in the 178-pound division to reach the gold-medal final. There waited Poland's Zbigniew Pietrzykowski, a three-time European champion, the 1956 bronze medalist, and, like Amos Johnson, a left-handed veteran (of 231 fights). Again puzzled by the southpaw style, Clay came to the third and final round needing to win it decisively. He put such a storm on the Pole that by round's end Pietrzykowski was helpless. The next day, Clay told American reporters that a Soviet journalist had asked how it felt to win a gold medal and know he still couldn't go home and eat with white folks. "I looked him up and down once or twice," Clay said, "and standing tall and proud, I said to him: 'Tell your readers we've got qualified people working on that problem, and I'm not worried about the outcome. To me, the U.S.A. is still the best country in the world, including yours. It may be hard to get something to eat sometimes, but anyhow I ain't fighting alligators and living in a mud hut.'"

Back in New York, Clay walked around Times Square with Dick Schaap and expressed surprise when anyone called out his name. "How'd you know?" Clay said to a passerby. "I saw you on TV," the man said. "Saw you beat that Pole in the final. Everybody knows who you are." Clay: "Really? You really know? That's wonderful." Schaap thought maybe the recognition had to do with the fact that Clay's fight had been on television two days earlier. Or maybe it was Clay's physique, "his developing light-heavyweight's build, 180 pounds spread like silk over a six-foot-two frame." There also was the blue Olympic blazer with USA embroidered on it. Then, too, the gold medal still hung around his neck. He had not taken it off since he won it. "First time I ever slept on my back," he said. "Had to, or that medal would've cut my chest."

Clay's victory thrilled him, but apparently didn't impress everyone. At year's end, for a show recapping the sports highlights of 1960, WABC sports director Howard Cosell mentioned the Olympic Games only briefly. He did not mention Cassius Clay at all.

When Clay showed up in December 1960 to work with Dundee at the Fifth Street Gym in Miami Beach, a great harrumphing came from the gym's College of Pugilistic Cardinals, those wise men who had seen the great ones sweat: Pastrano, Sugar Ray, Sonny Liston, Jake LaMotta, Kid Gavilan, Willie Pep, Emile Griffith, Sugar Ramos, Luis Rodriguez, Ralph Dupas. The scholars of the sweet science had never seen anyone fight the way Clay did and could not imagine why anyone would. He looked amateurish: He didn't block punches (he leaned away from them), he threw punches while moving (and only at the head), and he never fought on the inside. The wise men of the Fifth Street Gym reckoned he fought like a man afraid to fight. "The kid's gonna get killed," said one old trainer.

The Fifth Street Gym was a classic fighter's heaven/hellhole. Yellowing fight bills decorated the walls of the large second-story space above a drugstore at the corner of Washington Avenue and Fifth Street. The narrow stairway up was a perilous pile of weathered wood dimly lit by a bare bulb and often obstructed by the recumbent form of the previous night's wino. At ringside were two rows of spring-busted seats scrounged from a razed movie house. Two speed bags and heavy bags hung from creaking chains. A full-length mirror allowed fighters to admire themselves. The floor, mottled with blood drops, sweat, and water from spit buckets, was bare and splintering except where patches of plywood had been fitted in for repairs. Light came through two walls of grimy windows, some left open to bring in fresh air. Fighters dressed in a dark cubbyhole; they showered under an open-mouthed water spigot. In the narrow wall space between sets of windows, someone had painted boxing gloves above and below the word GYM painted in red block letters on a yellow background. It was art that Cassius Marcellus Clay, Sr., might have committed.

At the gym door, visitors passed by the skeletal figure of Emmet Sullivan, there to collect fifty cents per person. Sully mumbled. A dead cigar extended an inch or two from his toothless gums. Brown spittle flowed through the whiskers of his jowls and dripped onto a shirt collar spotted by discharges from another time. It was Ferdie Pacheco, a gym regular, who had anointed Sully, Evil Eye, Sellout Moe, and Chicky as the Pugilistic Cardinals. A physician working in a Miami ghetto, the irrepressible Pacheco had been inducted into boxing's odd little world by Dundee's brother, Chris. "Sully's main preoccupation is that someone will sneak by him without paying the tab of four bits," Pacheco said. When the writer Wilfrid Sheed thought to skirt Sully by hissing,

"Press," the tobacco-stained wretch countered, "Yeah, press your pants. Come up with the four bits, mud turtle."

The press and the Pugilistic Cardinals missed the invisible work that Dundee had done with the young Clay. Obvious as the fundamental flaws were, Dundee knew it made no sense to change them. Better to recognize Clay's strengths—size, speed, reflexes—and build from there. He was only nineteen on a day in 1961 when Ingemar Johansson's trainer made the mistake of asking for a sparring partner. The sly Dundee said, "I've got a kid who's only had four pro fights, but he'll give Ingo a good workout."

A kid nineteen? In with a twenty-eight-year-old veteran who had won and lost the heavyweight championship in fights with Floyd Patterson? Their third fight would happen in three weeks, and now, in the Fifth Street Gym, Johansson needed some work.

"Hey, Cash," Dundee shouted, "get your ass over here. Wanna go three rounds with the Swede?"

Fresh and eager, Clay practically sang in response. "Do Ah wanna go three rounds with the Swede, do Ah wanna go three rounds with the Swede? Ah'm gonna be dancin' with Ingemar Johansson . . ."

First round: Clay, never getting hit, his jabs snapping Johansson's head, the older man plodding after a teenager. Second round: another shutout, accompanied by Clay shouting, "I should be fighting Patterson, not you, sucker. I'm the next heavyweight champion of the world. Here I am, sucker. Come and get me, sucker." There was no third round. (Johansson's trainer called it off in hopes that his man could piece together his self-esteem. Maybe he couldn't. On March 13, 1961, Patterson knocked him out in the sixth round.)

What the College of Pugilistic Cardinals missed most egregiously was Clay's confidence. The weight of his self-assurance may have been best measured by a photographer with no experience in sports. Flip Schulke had covered Martin Luther King, Jr., and the civil rights movement. In 1961 *Sports Illustrated* and *Life* asked Schulke to go to Miami Beach and photograph the young boxer Cassius Clay, who had made news by announcing he would become the youngest heavyweight champion ever.

They started out shopping. On the magazine's expense account, Schulke thought to upgrade Clay's meager wardrobe. But Burdine's, a major department store in Miami, refused to let him try on clothes. When Schulke demanded an explanation, the store manager said, "It's policy, Negroes can't try on clothes."

"Listen," Schulke said, "this man won an Olympic gold medal."

"Yes?" the manager said.

Clay interrupted. "Don't worry about it, Flip. I don't want to make a mess here. It's like this in Louisville, too. Let's go to the black section."

For a generation to come, Clay's face turned to cameras as flowers answer to the sun. It started with Schulke, whose practiced eye examined the kid's face and found it perfect. It wasn't so much the physical beauty of it, though there certainly was that. Unlike some faces with features so odd they achieve a striking look, Clay's was a gathering of all-stars. He had Asian-prince eyes, almond-shaped, the irises brown under shining black brows. Genetics had done him more than one favor. It left the hard, lean darkness with his father and gave him his mother's softness, a golden aura, even her cupid's-bow lips. Schulke saw sweetness, a twinkle always dancing in the kid's eyes.

They were together five days, shooting and talking. When Schulke said Clay might be more kindly received if he didn't talk so much and so loudly, the photographer heard an explanation he had not expected. "Look at Gorgeous George," Clay said, naming the perfumed villain of 1950s professional wrestling, notorious for delivering orations on his own beauty and invincibility.

"You're not going to put on a wig and cape like him, are you?" Schulke said.

"No, no, the idea is to make the press mad at me. If they think I'm crazy, they're going to write about me. Gorgeous George isn't even a good wrestler and he fills auditoriums. And I'm a good boxer. Think what I'll get."

Schulke thought, *Bright!* Clay also was clever enough to con the worldly photographer into an extraordinary photo session. "I want to get into *Life*," Clay told Schulke, "and I've got an idea that's right up your alley." Schulke had told him about shooting underwater pictures of a water skier. Clay said an old trainer had taught him to throw punches underwater because the water acted like a weight against the fist. With scuba tank and underwater camera, Schulke shot Clay standing on the pool bottom in a fighter's pose, left foot forward, knees bent, fists up, chin tucked. *Life* ran four pages of the photographs, Clay underwater, bubbles coming from his nostrils, water flowing over his fists. Only when the magazine was in his hands did Clay tell Schulke that he had never trained underwater at all, that, in fact, he was afraid of water, that he had done it just to get into *Life*. This time Schulke thought, *I never had a clue. Bright? He's a genius. And he's nineteen!*

The Clay of Miami Beach was also an ascetic. No easy thing, considering he lived cheek to cheek with temptation. Pacheco said Ali's hotel, the Mary Elizabeth, "was to the world of the corrupt what St. Peter's represents to Catholics. The rooms were filled with whores, johns, pimps, boosters, grifters, con men, and addicts." But Clay didn't drink, didn't smoke, and didn't chase. To all those shake dancers who lusted after the fresh young kid from Kentucky, he said no because he believed what wizened old men told him, that sex interfered with training. And he was a man on a mission. He would be the Heavyweight Champion of the Whole Wide World! His belief in that destiny was so genuine that people in the ghetto protected him, from himself as much as anything.

"He was their giant toy, their baby," Pacheco wrote later. "Pimps trying to fix him up with foxy ladies would be taken aside and told to lay off 'the Champ.' 'Man's got to have pussy,' the pimp would grouse as he pulled away his whore. 'Man mus' be a sissy,' the rejected hussy would hiss." That last possibility excited the many homosexuals of Mary Elizabeth, but soon even they gave up pursuit of the sweet thing.

One night before a fight, in his hotel room, Clay talked with Jack Olsen, the *Sports Illustrated* reporter: "The hardest part of the training is the loneliness. I just sit here like an animal in a box at night. I can't go out on the street and mix with the folks out there 'cause they wouldn't be out there if they was up to any good. . . . Here I am, just nineteen, surrounded by showgirls, whiskey, and sissies, and nobody watching me. All this temptation and me trying to train to be a boxer. It's something to think about." He had done two of three things he planned: win the Olympics, buy a Cadillac; next, the heavyweight title. "I'd be plain silly to give in to temptation now."

He was helped in that denial by a force new in his life. As early as 1959, at age seventeen, he brushed against the sect known as the Nation of Islam. His father's sister, a grade-school teacher named Mary Turner, noticed that Clay came back to Louisville from the 1960 Golden Gloves tournament in Chicago with a 45-rpm recording of a song written and sung by the Muslim minister Louis X. Farrakhan. The title summarized the Nation's ideology: "The White Man's Heaven Is the Black Man's Hell." His aunt said Clay listened to the song "over and over" until he was "brainwashed, hypnotized." She did not like the way he looked at her. She thought, *They musta fed him something before he came back this way!*

Until 1961, Clay's knowledge and understanding of the Nation consisted of that disembodied voice on a record and a passing notice of the NOI newspaper, *Muhammad Speaks*. Then he met a man on the street, Sam Saxon, a NOI minister selling the newspaper and recruiting new members for the religion. He called himself "Cap'n Sam" and when Clay said, "I'm Cassius Clay, I'm gonna be the next heavyweight champion of the world," Saxon replied, "I know you, man. I followed you to the Olympics." Back in Clay's room, looking at his scrapbook, Cap'n Sam had an epiphany: "I knew if I could put the truth to him, he'd be great, so I invited him to our next meeting at the mosque."

The Nation was a heretical branch of Islam established in 1930 in Detroit by W. D. Fard, an ex-convict who anointed himself the messenger of Allah. Fard pronounced blacks to be the Asiatic "Original People" whose ancestors ruled the earth trillions of years ago. Advocating black separatism as a means of establishing pride and discipline, he suggested African-Americans emigrate or risk extermination. His unique contribution to the Nation was racial chauvinism declaring blacks righteous and whites evil. Fard accounted for that difference with the story of Yacub, a god who rebelled against his fellow black men. To prevent revolution, the king of Mecca gave Yacub and his 59,999 followers safe passage to an island and the wealth to build a new civilization. There Yacub set in motion six hundred years of genetic engineering designed to create a race of pale-skinned, blond-haired, blue-eyed devils who would wreak havoc on blacks. Fard also taught that a mothership hovering in space would lift to salvation 144,000 believers who would otherwise be lost in the destruction of Earth; the years first mentioned for that event were 1966 and 1970.

It all made sense to the young Clay, who had been unwittingly prepared for Cap'n Sam's sales pitch by his delusional fantasist father. For years Clay had heard from Cash of the black man's greatness and the white man's devilry. The father's belligerence helped create in the son the sense of martyrdom endemic in the Nation's members, maybe 40,000 blacks from low economic levels. After Cap'n Sam began recruiting the charismatic Clay for the attention he could bring to his little-known sect, the deal was closed by Malcolm X.

The most famous of the Nation's preachers, Malcolm X was irresistible, to reckon by the poet Maya Angelou's recollection of meeting him in her political-activist youth: "His aura was too bright and his masculine force affected me physically. A hot desert storm eddied around him and rushed to me, making my skin contract, and my pores slam shut. He approached, and all my brain would do for me was record his coming. I had never been so affected by a human presence . . . His voice was black baritone and musical. . . . Up close he was a great red arch through which one could pass to eternity. His hair was the color of burning embers and his eyes pierced."

Clay responded at a lower temperature than the poet had. But he also enjoyed the minister's presence: "Malcolm was very intelligent, with a good sense of humor, a wise man. When he talked, he held me spellbound for hours." Most likely they had met in 1962. Malcolm X was thirty-seven years old, Clay twenty. They became confidants. Their relationship, it seemed, would last a long time.

CHAPTER FOUR

"Liston Is a Tramp, I'm the Champ!"

IN NEW YORK BEFORE THE ELEVENTH fight of his professional career, Cassius Clay took a train from the city to Albany. The legislature had invited him up to testify at hearings on a bill to abolish boxing in the state. Organized crime had made the sport its newest revenue stream. On a bitter cold day, February 4, 1962, ice covered the sidewalks and provided Clay's metaphor. "Boxing is at the winter of its year," he said. "In the time when there were great fighters like Dempsey and Joe Louis, nobody talked against it. When there are not great fighters, people lose interest. It's a question of time."

He pointed through a window. "In winter, leaves are not on trees, the grass and flowers are dead, the mind is thinking of chili and hot foods. Time is why. But the Earth rotates around the sun in 365 days and in that *time* there are winter, fall, spring, and summer. *Time* makes those flowers jump out of the ground. The trees get leaves, you see people walking the dogs, time changes their mind. They don't want that chili but popsicles and ice cream—the mind changes into light clothes."

This was the Cassius Clay who had bedazzled Flip Schulke. The man-child knew what he wanted—the heavyweight championship. He also knew how to get it—make so much noise that his inferiors could not ignore him. Two weeks past his twentieth birthday, he presented himself to New York lawmakers as a fresh and bright alternative to the day's dark world of boxing. "Time, it takes time," he said. "Will man ever get to the moon? In time he will. Will I be the next champ? Time will tell. In boxing's winter, people lose interest, but I am here to liven things

45

up. On March 13, I will be fighting at the Garden, and it will be a total sellout."

A spectator at the proceedings, *The New Yorker*'s boxing scholar, A. J. Liebling, made note of what happened next for Clay: "A legislator of distrustful aspect asked him if all his seventeen victories had been on the level, and Mr. Clay said pertly, 'They say it take a crook to tell a crook.' When he stepped down, a faint odor of *hubris*, like Lilac Végétal, lingered behind."

Others had seen nothing in Clay but the theatrics of the Gorgeous George who sprinkled golden hairpins among his fans. Liebling saw more. Perhaps *The New Yorker*'s man intended his suggestion of hubris only as a whimsical comment on the heavyweight poet's behavior. It yet remained a warning. Arrogance that blinds a man's judgment is dangerous, especially for fighters with years of judgments to make on matters personal and professional. Liebling left the thought of hubris unexamined, but it was there to be read in years that would shape Clay.

On the train ride back to New York, the young *Sports Illustrated* reporter, Frank Deford, was Clay's audience for a loud disquisition on spacemen who operated a mothership hovering over Earth until time to rescue a certain number of believers. Deford had no idea what the kid was talking about. He thought, *A real fruitcake. Very amusing, but nutty.*

Later that month, after Clay's victory over Sonny Banks, Liebling wrote words that would define Clay's style forever. He spoke of "the butterfly Cassius" whose busy hands were "stinging like bees." A gym rat and aspiring writer named Drew (Bundini) Brown, Jr., may have put down his *New Yorker* and made a journal note about this butterfly that stung like a bee. What's certain is that Bundini, then working for Sugar Ray Robinson, met Clay sometime in the next year. It's also certain that Bundini first put the lyrics to the image: "Float like a butterfly, sting like a bee! Rumble, young man, rumble!"

Cosell and Clay met in July 1962. Because Clay had made such noise, and because a guy working in both radio and television needs material, Cosell thought, *What the hell, I'll talk to him.* Cosell asked about the next heavyweight championship fight, Floyd Patterson defending against Sonny Liston. "Which man do you see as the winner, Cassius?" Cosell asked.

"Well, Howie, Patterson is the more scientific fighter, and as you know I'm a scientific fighter myself, so I have to say Patterson."

"But isn't Liston's power more than enough to offset Patterson's finesse?"

"Yes, sir. I agree with that. It might be one punch, and all over. Liston by a knockout early."

Cosell said, "Cassius, they both can't win. Which is it?"

"Me! Give me both them bums, same night, I whup 'em both."

Most of the day's sports journalists, given to portraying Joe DiMaggio's sullen silences as exemplars of class and dignity, would have ignored the kid. But Howard Cosell was as revolutionary in broadcasting as Clay was in boxing. For Cosell, the radio microphone was more than a journalist's tool. It was also part of the show business that had entranced him from his days in Brooklyn's vaudeville and movie houses. What could be better than a fighter who supplied both news and entertainment?

In the summer of 1963, undefeated in nineteen fights, his most recent victory a fifth-round knockout of British veteran Henry Cooper, Clay did his second interview with Cosell and insisted he was ready to fight for the championship, by then in Liston's possession. He said, "I want the big, ugly bear."

"Cooper knocked you down," Cosell said. "What's Liston gonna do to you?"

"Noooo contest," Clay said. "Not a chance."

Boxing's wise men discounted Clay. From the Fifth Street Gym to Gleason's in New York, they saw a kid who did everything wrong. He reminded them of no great fighter, certainly not the textbook stylist, Gene Tunney, or Jack Dempsey, a mauler. Joe Louis's defense was an arsenal of jabs stronger than Clay's hooks. Rocky Marciano waged battles of attrition never to Clay's liking. Jersey Joe Walcott and Ezzard Charles killed bodies. Floyd Patterson was the ultimate creation of Cus D'Amato's art, a defensive specialist with quick hands. If anyone thought Clay was the one fighter in a lifetime who could do everything wrong and make it right, that prescient observer's name likely was Cassius Marcellus Clay.

Bigger than all those champions, Ali moved with a little man's speed and acrobatic agility. No heavyweight threw as many punches as quickly and as accurately from as many angles. No one, big or small, ever seemed as insistent on not getting hit. He made more technical mistakes in one round than Sugar Ray and Willie Pep made in ten. But the mistakes didn't matter. Instincts and reflexes bordering on the preternatural moved him out of harm's way. How else to explain a man who draws his head back from a punch precisely the saving distance? He stayed calm because he had seen it all in thousands of rounds. For him, action moved in slow motion. He knew things. A shoulder's twitch put him on alert before the opponent decided to punch, and he'd be gone, leaving the poor man to search for the damn kid who wouldn't stand still and fight.

He was a genius. It wasn't his hands or his feet. Light-heavyweight champion Jose Torres said, "Watch his brains." The frustration of chasing him, the inability to touch that unprotected chin, the confusion caused by his snake-lick jab snapping against your face—it wore a guy out mentally as much as physically. There also was Clay's conversation during the fight. *Is that all you got, sucker?* The hell of it was, during all this Clay also would rain fists on you. *Sports Illustrated* did a photo shoot to capture his hand speed. From sixteen and a half inches away, his jab landed against a balsa board in 0.19 seconds. The magazine reported, "His fist actually covered the distance in four/one-hundredths of a second, about the period of a blink of the eye." Editors timed a six-punch combination in 2.15 seconds. Two jabs, a hook, a right to the body, another hook, a finishing right. Imagine. Count one thousand one, one thousand two. You have been hit six times by a two-hundred-pound professional fighter who never misses.

Those early critics who saw only the mistakes identified his defense as a fatal flaw. They insisted that anyone pulling his head back eventually makes a mistake and pays for it. Clay had been knocked down twice already, by Banks and by Cooper. Though he rose to knock out both men and become the number one challenger for Liston's title, his ability to take a punch was in doubt. The argument was not if he could beat Liston. Almost no one gave him a chance. Most observers shuddered in agreement with Liston's sentiment: "If they ever make the fight, I'll be locked up for murder." They mainly debated if Liston might be the greatest heavyweight ever. To look upon his dead-eyed face atop a bull's shoulders was to feel an urge to flee. He had done hard time in a federal penitentiary for work performed as muscle for the mob. Charles (Sonny) Liston was one bad-ass thug.

So what did Clay do? The sweet-hearted son of a church lady, in violation of all common sense, taunted Liston. He went to Las Vegas, where Liston trained for a second title fight with Patterson. As Liston played craps in a casino, Clay stood against a wall. The unfolding scene moved Harold Conrad to awe as few things could do. He was a New York boxing publicist, out of the Damon Runyon canon, a cheery cynic, tall, lean, and dapper, silk scarf bunched at his throat. Conrad saw Liston losing at craps and growing meaner with every unrewarding roll. There was a silence over the table, lest anyone disturb the mean-tempered sumbitch. That silence was ended by Clay's shouting.

"Look at that big, ugly bear. He can't even shoot craps."

Liston glared at him, picked up the dice, and rolled again. Another craps.

"Look at the big, ugly bear. He can't do nothing right."

Liston dropped the dice, walked over to Clay, and said, "Listen, you nigger faggot. If you don't get out of here in ten seconds, I'm gonna pull that big tongue out of your mouth and stick it up your ass." Joe Martin had said you could run Clay out of town with a corn cob and a cigarette lighter. Maybe so. For sure, a Sonny Liston threat would run him out of a casino. When Harold Conrad saw Clay turn and quick-step to the nearest exit, he made a judgment. *Clay's scared shitless.*

Whatever the texture of his fright, Clay showed up at ringside on July 23, 1963. As Liston and Patterson warmed up, Clay bounded through the ropes and bowed ceremoniously to Patterson, the fellow Olympic champion whom he had met in Rome three years earlier. Turning to Liston, Clay opened his eyes wide and his mouth wider. He raised his hands in mock surrender and scurried from the ring as if in fear for the future placement of his tongue. Patterson laughed. From Liston, not so much as a smile. He was not there to play games with a faggot. He was there to hurt somebody.

Liston needed two minutes and ten seconds to again leave Patterson in a sad lump. The ending produced a rush of officials, cornermen, and hangers-on into the ring. By custom, duty, and for the pure thrill of it, Howard Cosell shouldered his way into the bedlam. There he pursued the high, holy truth of what the hell happened. Cornermen snapped open smelling salts under Patterson's nose. "I'm over him," Cosell told his radio and television audience. Out of respect for Patterson, the D'Amato creation who had become his friend, Cosell spoke softly to filter from his voice the adrenaline-rush excitement that attends a lights-out end of fights. "And Floyd knows exactly where he is and who I am. And, Floyd, it was amazing it happened again so suddenly, wasn't it?"

The rematch had lasted four seconds longer than the first fight when Liston sent Patterson skulking into the night, driving alone from Chicago to New York, disguised by a beard he bought in anticipation of defeat. Now, hearing Cosell's question, Patterson said, "Yes, it was," before Cosell asked, "What went wrong?"

"Well, I didn't fight the type of fight that I had planned on fighting, for one thing. I didn't move enough. I gambled with him, to trade punches, which was my biggest mistake, I think."

"When did you decide to make that gamble? When you got through to him the left?"

"Yes."

"You decided that from there on in, that maybe you could finish him off?"

"That's right."

"What happens now, Floyd? Is this it? Is this the end of boxing?"

"Pretty hard to say, Howard. I haven't really made up my mind yet."

Then Cosell did the good journalist's thing of asking a hard question, only to do the friend's act of softening it before Patterson could answer: "Are you going to go away the way you did the last time? I don't think you've done anything to be ashamed of."

Patterson knew better. "Oh, well," he said. "It's the first round again."

"Listen, Floyd, I'm not going to bother you anymore. Compose yourself, collect yourself. You're a sportsman. Good luck to you."

That night in Las Vegas, television still was so new that Cosell could work as reporter, friend, and avuncular adviser. "Let's go ahead and get Sonny Liston." He reported what he saw next. "There's a big mob still around him. Cassius Clay now in the ring. Sonny is still over in the other corner of the ring being kissed by children. . . ."

Cassius Clay now in the ring.

Finally, their talents and ambitions had brought Cosell and Clay into the same ring at the same time. Cosell was forty-five years old, in his fourth year on fight broadcasts, and he worked with confidence born of competence.

"Here comes the champ, here he comes," Cosell said. "Sonny, it was almost an exact duplicate of the last one."

"Well, I said to the fans, when I was coming up for the fight, I was going to make this look like a rerun."

"A workmanlike performance. What's next, Sonny? Are you going to fight the noisome one, Cassius Clay?"

Even as Cosell stood with Liston, another voice could be heard at some distance from the ABC mike. "The fight was a disgrace!" It was Clay's voice.

Liston answered the question. "Well, I'm going to take them as they list them."

"As they list them? And if they list Clay, it'll be Clay . . ."

"That's right." And, small in the background, Clay again, "Liston is a tramp, I'm the champ!"

"All right, Sonny boy," Cosell said. "Go back to the dressing room, we'll see you there. That's the story from the ring."

Clay's voice, one more time: "Don't make me wait, I'll whup him in eight!"

No more waiting. A Liston-Clay fight was set for February 1964, and Clay came to New York to promote it. He sat in a television studio dressing room with Jack Paar, host of the *Tonight* show. Clay seemed shy, unsure, even happy to confess that, no, sir, he was not always bold and brash. "Naw," he said. "I just put that on, to make 'em mad, so they hate me. They hate me and come see me."

Paar said, "What if you lose? You could lose, couldn't you?"

Now Clay told Paar exactly how much Liston frightened him. "I lose, I'll say to Liston, 'You're the greatest, you're the Champ.' I'll kneel right down. Then I'll take the first plane out of the country. I'll even go to another planet. I'm too great to lose. If Liston even dreamed he beat me, he'd call up and apologize."

That night on Paar's show, as the sequined Liberace tickled the keys of a white, candelabra-bedecked piano, Clay recited poetry from a newly released comedy album, *I Am the Greatest*. His reputation as a poet had come from childish dreck such as:

> *This guy must be done.*
> *I'll stop him in one.*

And:

When you come to the fight,
Don't block the aisle and don't block the door
I'll say it again, I've said it before.
Archie Moore will fall in four.

Notwithstanding those lame lines, the comedy album was sensational—because Clay didn't write it. Gary Belkin did. The album was Belkin's baby from the start. The veteran gag writer for Sid Caesar and Carol Burnett had heard about the charismatic young fighter who charmed everyone by reciting his poetry. He thought it would be fun, and profitable, to put together an album. But when they met, Belkin realized Clay knew only elementary doggerel. Worse, Clay could barely read or write. "A functional illiterate," was Belkin's unhappy verdict. He was on his own. Other than the Liebling/Bundini phrase, "Float like a butterfly, sting like a bee," Belkin wrote the entire album.

Clay rehearsed two weeks with actors and an orchestra, then did the recording before a studio audience. Belkin's major poem, thirty-two lines, was a prophecy of what Clay would do in an eighth round against Liston. Clay was nervous but drew up all the boyish enthusiasm and impish glee that he had ever invested in his own pale doggerel.

Clay comes out to meet Liston
And Liston starts to retreat
But if he goes back any farther
He'll end up in a ringside seat.
Clay swings with his left,
Clay swings with a right,
Look at young Cassius
Carry the fight.
Liston keeps backing
But there's not enough room
It's a matter of time.
There, Clay lowers the boom.
Now Clay lands a right,
What a beautiful swing,
The punch raises Liston
Clear out of the ring.
Liston's still rising

And the ref wears a frown,
For he can't start counting,
Till Sonny comes down.
Now Liston disappears from view.
The crowd is getting frantic,
But our radar stations have picked him up
He's somewheres over the Atlantic.
Who would have thought
When they came to the fight
That they'd witness the launching
Of a human satellite?
Yes, the crowd did not dream
When they put down their money
That they would see
A total eclipse of the Sonny!

Howard Cosell expected no such eclipse. In a radio commentary, he said Clay had no chance, that the kid's braggadocio might disguise his fear but it would not help once he came near Liston. As Cosell walked into the Fifth Street Gym on February 24, 1964, he realized that his words had preceded him. He heard Clay direct at him a litany of feigned lamentation.

"I'm gonna—just gonna collapse when I get in the ring against that big, ugly bear!" Then, mocking Cosell's words, he said, "There is no way, no way that young Cassius can fight that man . . . he is a terror."

Cosell thought, for the first time, that Clay might not be afraid, a thought confirmed as truth when they recorded an interview that day. More than thirty hours before the fight, Cosell asked Clay to tape a bit that would not be used on air until the next night. This was Cosell, the director, working with Clay, the actor: "I want you to assume that you're about to leave the dressing room, You start walking toward the ring. What do you think your mental processes will be as you make that walk?"

Clay began in a whisper into Cosell's microphone. "I'm leaving the dressing room, about to go against the big, ugly bear. This terrible man. Cassius Clay is frightened. Cassius Clay is ready to run. I keep walking toward the ring and, all the time, even while I'm so frightened that I'm almost afraid to look at him with that terrible look he gives you, I'm thinking . . ."

Then, a shout . . .

"YOU POOR OLD MAN!"

As much fun as that was, it did not serve Cosell's needs for network radio. He asked Clay to do it again, seriously this time. Clay recorded new words:

"Sonny Liston is scared. Sonny Liston's scared to death. Today at the weigh-in, he was so nervous he couldn't even get on the scales. I could see defeat in his eyes. He was wary. He's afraid. That's his gimmick, scaring people at the weigh-ins. But I got him today. My prediction still stands at round eight."

As Clay spoke, the weigh-in was twenty-four hours away. The fight was thirty-six hours away.

Cosell said, "Cassius, are you scared, really?"

"No, I'm always nervous," Clay said. "I can't tell a lie, to hear the roar of the crowd, to feel the pressure . . . but once I throw the first punch, I'll be all right."

Either by Clay's plan—*Today at the weigh-in,* he had said the day before—or by spontaneous combustion, the weigh-in created a level of anxiety never before achieved in boxing. At ten-thirty on the morning of February 25, Clay momentarily stopped in the weigh-in room at Miami Beach Convention Center. Inscribed in red on his blue denim jacket: "Bear Huntin'." Clay and Bundini Brown shouted in each other's face: "Float like a butterfly, sting like a bee! Rumble, young man, rumble! Aaaarrgggghhh!" Clay banged the floor with an ornately carved cane given to him by Malcolm X. "I'm the champ! I'm ready to rumble! Tell Sonny I'm here! He ain't no champ! Round eight to prove I'm great! Bring that big, ugly bear on."

Thirty-nine minutes later, after a warning that he would be fined for further demonstrations, Clay reappeared in a white terry cloth robe alongside Liston. He seemed to go into hysteria, or suffer a seizure that caused him to thrash while screaming, "I'm ready to rumble now. I can beat you anytime, chump! Somebody's gonna die at ringside tonight. You're scared, chump! You ain't no giant! I'm gonna eat you alive!" Angelo Dundee, a Louisville sponsor named Bill Faversham, and Sugar Ray Robinson held on to Clay, trying to calm him down. As Clay seemed to try throwing everyone off him so he could get to Liston, the *Sports Illustrated* reporter Mort Sharnik saw him wink at Sugar Ray.

The Miami boxing commission fined Clay two thousand five hundred dollars on the spot, and the examining doctor pronounced him "emotionally unbalanced, scared to death, and liable to crack up before he enters the ring." The author Norman Mailer, a fight fan, also offered a diagnosis: "Hell, he's close to dementia now."

But, as promised, in fact before he threw the first punch, Clay was all right. Cosell realized as much during preliminaries when Clay stood at the back of the Miami Beach Convention Center and watched his kid brother, Rudy Clay, in the first fight of his own professional career.

"What was all that this morning, the weigh-in?" Cosell said.

Clay smiled. "I wanted Liston to know I was crazy. Only a fool isn't scared of a crazy man. You'll see tonight."

Had Cosell thought beyond the ring, he might have known that Clay was involved in politics more frightening than any fight. Clay's guests in Miami Beach included the Nation of Islam's most notorious leader, Malcolm X. As a wedding anniversary gift, Clay had asked Malcolm X to bring along his wife, Betty, and their four daughters. It was a curious invitation, given the tenor of the times. The nation's wounds from the assassination of John F. Kennedy were just three months old. Malcolm X had violated Elijah Muhammad's direct order that the Nation's ministers make no public statement on it. Instead, ten days after JFK's murder, Malcolm X characterized the killing as a case of the violent reaping of the violence the administration had sown in Vietnam, the Congo, and Cuba. "Being an old farm boy myself," he said, "chickens coming home to roost never did make me sad; they've always made me glad." For those remarks, Muhammad suspended Malcolm X as a minister for ninety days. He also ordered his followers to have no contact with the minister, and, four days before the Liston fight, told Clay that "all good Muslims should stay away from Malcolm."

Malcolm X and Elijah were in the early stages of a conflict that could turn bloody. It began in 1963 when the minister confronted his spiritual superior with knowledge of his nine illegitimate children, a profound transgression against the Nation's puritanical dogma. Now Malcolm X saw his suspension as the beginning of Elijah Muhammad's retribution. He also knew the Black Muslims exacted real retribution. Within two weeks of JFK's assassination, Malcolm X heard that he himself was targeted for execution, that a mosque official told brothers: "If you knew what the minister did, you'd go out and kill him yourself." Malcolm X told his biographer, Alex Haley, "As any official in the Nation of Islam would instantly have known, any death-talk for me could have been approved of—if not actually initiated—by only one man."

Yet he was at Clay's side in Miami Beach. He stayed there until the fight promoters persuaded him that his presence hurt ticket sales and they would cancel the fight unless he left town. He left briefly, then returned on fight night and sat at ringside—in a seat numbered seven, "my favorite number"—with Sugar Ray Robinson and rock 'n' roll singer Sam Cooke. Earlier, he had met with Clay and told him: "This fight is the *truth*. It's the Cross and the Crescent fighting in a prize ring—for the first time. It's a modern Crusades—a Christian and a Muslim facing each other with television to beam it off Telstar for the whole world to see what happens! Do you think Allah has brought about all this intending for you to leave the ring as anything but the champion?" Malcolm X believed that Liston was "about to meet one of the most awesome frights that ever can confront any person—one who worships Allah, and who is completely without fear."

With half the arena's fifteen thousand seats empty, ABC's blow-by-blow announcer Les Keiter worked from Section S, Row A, Seat 13. Alongside him was Cosell, his fight broadcast partner for five years. Keiter's voice caught the excitement, high, crisp, quick, as in round one: "Clay is moving clockwise. Clay keeps dancing. Clay just laughs at Liston. . . . Clay is inviting murder with his hands down. . . . Clay doesn't seem awed by Liston. . . . In the first two minutes, it's been Cassius Clay doing what the experts said he could not get away with doing. It's Clay so far. . . . Clay's eyes look like doorknobs, they're so wide open."

Liston's people did not like what they had seen. In the dressing room beforehand, the champion was confident because he believed Clay's performance at the weigh-in had been caused by absolute fear. Cornerman Milt Bailey realized Liston couldn't catch Clay and knew his man was in trouble.

Round three, Keiter: "Clay lands a left and right that hurt Liston. He has Liston's eye cut open. This may be the upset of the century. . . . Liston's eye is badly cut. . . . Clay forces Liston to miss a right hand. . . . Now it's Clay out of breath. Liston is throwing caution to the winds. . . . Now Clay is exclusively on his bicycle moving backwards now. He's making Liston look very awkward. Liston's eyes look like he's been in a meat-grinder."

After the third round, Cosell said, "Words don't make a fight. Fists do.

Clay is making the fight tonight with his fists. We're surprised. So is everybody else in this arena, including the top sportswriters in the nation."

Then, after the fourth, Cosell noticed a commotion in Clay's corner and said, "Something is the matter with Cassius Clay as we're getting ready for the fifth round, and he is having trouble with his eyes. Something on Liston's gloves." Coming back to his corner, Clay shouted to trainer Angelo Dundee, "I can't see! My eyes! Cut the gloves off! We're going home!"

The stinging in Clay's eyes may have come from a liniment on Liston's body or from coagulant used to stop his bleeding. In any case, with his man winning the fight, Dundee told Clay, "Forget the bullshit. This is for the championship. Sit down." Dundee rubbed a towel across Clay's eyes, rinsed them with a sponge, slid the mouthpiece in, and said, "This is the big one, Daddy. Stay away from him. Run!"

Clay did not sit and demand again that the fight be stopped. He rose from his stool and felt Dundee's hand pushing him forward. He then did what Dundee told him to do, and more.

Keiter, round five: "Clay is blinking. That could be fatal. He still blinks like he can't see. . . . Clay is backing away halfheartedly. Clay is blinking, blinking. . . . Liston's close to finishing it now. Clay is only halfheartedly side-wheeling away. Liston is still throwing dynamite. . . . Now Liston's left eye is closing again. Clay is taunting Liston with his left. He's just laying it on Liston's nose."

No one could question Clay's courage. He could barely see and he was in the ring with Sonny Liston. For a minute and a half, he improvised a blind man's defense. He pawed with his left at the blur of Liston to measure the distance, to stop Liston's advance, to confuse him. When his eyes cleared, Clay fought Liston evenly.

Keiter, round six: "Who's going to run out of gas? It's a shock to most experts already. Clay's eyes are wide open like doorknobs again. It's Clay coming on again. He may be out to finish Sonny now. The champion of the world is being harassed by Clay now. . . . The big question is, what's the matter with Sonny Liston now? He looks all right, but he's not throwing any punches. It's Liston backpedaling away. Clay is doing the stalking now."

After the sixth, Cosell looked across the ring at Liston on his stool, there tended by two cornermen, one dabbing at the cut under the left eye. Cosell said, "Sonny looks like he's just about had it." Then he saw more. "Now . . . wait a minute. WAIT A MINUTE! Sonny Liston is not coming out! Sonny Liston is NOT COMING OUT! He is OUT! The winner and the new heavyweight champion of the world is Cassius Clay! Les, I'm going up in the ring!" Cosell clambered over ABC's broadcasting equipment, hauled himself onto the ring apron, and bent between the ropes; he carried a stick microphone tethered to a hundred-foot cord.

Keiter told listeners, "Sonny Liston is sitting on his stool. Has not moved. Nobody's said a word. Clay was the first to realize it. He came running out of his corner, waving his arms, all over the ring, waving his arms."

Buffeted by Clay's celebrants, Cosell shouldered his way into the madhouse. He called out, "Cassius, Cassius!" And there began Cosell's first interview of the champion Clay, who answered with manic shoutings heard at ringside and on radio coast-to-coast: "I AM THE GREATEST! I AM THE KING OF THE WORLD!"

Cosell said, "Tell the truth, Cassius—"

"I UPSET THE WORLD!"

"—did you believe it would happen this way?"

"I told him if he wants to go to heaven, I'll get him in seven. I AM THE KING! I AM THE KING! I AM THE KING!"

"What made him so easy for you?"

"I'm too fast. He was scared."

"Who gave you your plan, Angie Dundee?"

"No. Myself."

"Was there any single point where you knew you had him?"

"I knew I had him in the first round. Almighty God was with me. I want everybody to bear witness. I am the greatest! I shook up the world! I'm the greatest thing that ever lived. I don't have a mark on my face, and I upset Sonny Liston, and I just turned twenty-two years old. I must be the greatest. I showed the world, I talk to God every day. I shook up the world. I'm the king of the world! I'm pretty! I'm a bad man! I shook up the world. You must listen to me. I am the greatest! I can't be beat!"

"What happened to your eyes coming into the fourth?"

"He had liniment on his hands and gloves. I couldn't see all that round."

Cosell was ready to leave Clay and go to Liston. "My congratulations to you," he said, and then realized he could not move because the microphone cord would not move with him. So he said, "Let go of the mike, Cassius."

As Cosell went to Liston's corner, Clay continued his manic raving. "It's no fix when his eye's closed. That wasn't no fix. I didn't stop it. I want everybody to know, I AM THE GREATEST! I AM THE KING OF THE WORLD!"

Clay must have known that the cry of fix would go up, for Liston was more than a fighter. He was boxing's darkness of the soul made flesh. He had been taken from a penitentiary and sent to do vengeance. This pretty boy whips him? But fixes were customary in those times when organized crime ran the fights. And in Miami Beach, the world championship his, Sonny Liston quit. Sat on his stool. No heavyweight champion had quit since Jess Willard in 1919, and Willard's face had been caved in by Dempsey. Look at the fight the way a Liston biographer, Nick Tosches, did a generation later. Liston delivered "none of the awesome power that in the past had felled man after man." In the fifth, Clay could not see and yet had no trouble evading Liston's punches, "which seemed at times designed not so much to hit Clay as to punctuate the air of his blind bob and weave." That was the round in which Clay touched a glove against Liston's nose and Liston "never struck or swatted that arm away." Then Liston quit and Tosches imagined Liston's soulmates in cellblocks of the Jefferson City penitentiary snarling: "The son of a bitch had thrown the fucking heavyweight championship of the motherfucking world. Shit, some reckoned: a thief for a penny, a thief for a pound."

Later came news that Liston's bosses had paid fifty thousand dollars for rights to Clay's first fight after Liston. Odd to buy the next fight of a kid about to be eaten alive. A Liston bodyguard, Lowell Powell, told Tosches a story that spoke of a fix. Powell had told Liston, "Sonny, I'm gonna put some more money on you," only to hear, "Don't . . . two heavyweights out there, you can't tell who will win." After Liston quit, Powell said, "Sonny, why you let me lose my last penny on a fight and you knew you were gonna lose it? You could've at least pulled my coat." Liston said, "With your big mouth, we'd both be wearing concrete suits." Word came to Tosches that members of Liston's camp got down three hundred thousand dollars on Clay at seven-to-one for a two-point-one-million-dollar payday. Also came the hearsay evidence of what ought to be a line in a blues song, Liston's sad words, "I did what they told me to do."

These sinister, sensational explanations never gained credibility, largely becasue they ignored the obvious truth that Clay, the better fighter by all measures that night, simply beat the hell out of Liston. Cosell certainly saw no fix. He saw Liston suddenly old, not the thirty-two he claimed, maybe even older than the thirty-six on a public record. Cosell thought the bleeding did it, that Liston for the first time tasted his own blood and the blood washed away the lie of age even as it left revealed the truth that bullies live in fear. Crossing the ring to Liston on his stool, Cosell now said, "Sonny, I hate to bother you in a moment like this. But you've been a great champion and you fought tonight. Can you tell us in your own words exactly what happened, Sonny?"

"My shoulder feel like it's broke," Liston said. "I don't know what's wrong with it."

"All right," Cosell told his radio audience, "they're putting the robe on Sonny Liston right now. Sonny, if given another shot at this boy, who has been so amazing, do you think you can do to him what you did to Patterson?"

"I don't know. I'll have to think about it."

"Thank you, Sonny, and good luck to you, anyway."

Then, wrapping up: "That's the history as we have it now in this incredible ring. They are booing Sonny Liston. You heard the story of his shoulder, what he says happened to it. Cassius is standing in the ring. He's taking his bows. Joe Louis suddenly next to him, and it was Joe who said Liston could fight anybody in any era. This is, without a doubt, no need to pour it on, one of the most astonishing upsets in the whole chronicle of boxing."

CHAPTER FIVE

"The Black Man's White Man"

THE MAN RUNNING ABC Sports in 1964, Tom Moore, was a beefy son of cracker-country Mississippi, a huntin', fishin', good ol' boy who came to the sports division from advertising sales by way of his earlier work down home. "The Mississippi cemetery lot salesman," Cosell called him. They had been at odds for five years because Moore kept Cosell off the network "for being too New York, too loud, too pushy, too all the qualities that made Cosell Cosell," as Roone Arledge later put it. "Howard thought anti-Semitism was the actual root of his banning."

Where Cosell the attorney claimed earnings of thirty thousand dollars a year in the mid-1950s, a decade later the local-level broadcaster earned an income of "next to nothing." But with the hunger of an outsider desperate to belong, Cosell created his own path to the network using whatever tools he could invent, whatever leverage he could apply. The magazine writer Ray Robinson, even after resigning from his role as Cosell's pack mule in spring training, came to parties at the Cosells' place: "Howard had already accumulated the friendship of a lot of big-name people—Frank Gifford among them, and the president of Mount Holyoke College—these interesting connections long before he became a household word." The great newspaper columnist W. C. Heinz, and his wife loved evenings with the Cosells: "The ladies took turns making meat loaf, and Howard did play-by-play of 'The Great Meat Loaf Contest.'"

Ed Silverman saw the parties as thinly veiled business transactions: "Emmy was a very charming lady and pretty good cook. So Howard would invite over ballplayers in town with no place to go. Ballplayers found a guy in sports communications who treated them as human beings, as family. Or Howard would take them out, buy a steak, five bucks in those days, a lot of money. But Howard was making a lot more than the players' five, eight thousand dollars a year. The quid pro quo was, if in a year or two these guys were stars, they'd be accessible to him."

His neighbors in Peter Cooper Village were the actors John Forsythe, Karl Malden, Tony Randall, and James Whitmore. "My voice is not a broadcaster's," Cosell said later. "But it has identifiability. What I did was make an unwanted voice an asset by understanding voice variety. Forsythe's problem was he sounded like Henry Fonda. So he studied voice and told me about 'voice variety.' I realized how effective it would be in the courtroom. And when I went into broadcasting, I used it accordingly. No lessons, just my own intelligence."

Cosell's voice moved New York quickly. He hammered consonants and followed the harshness with abrupt slides into hushed tones, each movement a signal of his feeling for the subject at hand. He could read a note to the milkman in a way that let listeners know his great and abiding disappointment in being left two quarts rather than three. Cosell's staccato rhythms were so eccentric as to demand a listener's attention, but to say the voice succeeded because it cut through the clutter of broadcasting's neutral sounds was insufficient to define it. The critic Ron Powers would call it "one of television's most inspired creations—a voice that was virtually a finished character in and of itself." If the voice, directed to a few people in a room, was too much—its melodrama shamefully obvious— it became, on the air, a perfect answer to the hyperbolic demands of television.

Cosell did five daily radio spots six days a week in addition to Channel 7 sports reports, fight coverage, and two radio interview shows, *Speaking of Everything* and *Self Portrait*. Channel 7's news anchor, Murphy Martin, never saw Cosell prepare copy to be read from a prompter. "Copy?" Cosell once said. "I need no *copy*. I am a fucking genius! It is all right *here*," accompanied by an index finger tapping his right temple. To the anchor's praise, Cosell's thanks took the form of a peer's good-natured barb: "Martin, you have the innate ability to languish forever in impoverished anonymity." Followed by a flick of his cigarette's ashes.

Because Moore wouldn't allow him on the network, Cosell found another way to gain national attention. He became a producer of documentaries. More than any work he had yet done, those documentaries and other one-hour specials created his reputation as a complete journalist. Cosell was at heart a social crusader. The common thread running through his career of commentary and reporting would be outrage against injustice. What Woody Guthrie achieved in protest songs and Clifford Odets in plays, Cosell did in journalism. Early in his radio career, he produced a series of one-hour network shows portraying International Olympic Committee chairman Avery Brundage as a poseur whose games were exercises in political and financial hypocrisy. Almost daily through 1956, Cosell assailed Walter O'Malley for the owner's transparent plans to extract the Dodgers from Brooklyn. He was a father who took his eight-year-old daughter Hilary and their Irish setter walking in the woods and passed the time by explaining the U.S. Army's march against its own veterans in the Bonus Army of 1932. He brought to the work the skills, common sense, and emotional judgment necessary to show athletes as human beings rather than cartoon figures—not to mention a directing/producing manner that was utterly Cosellian.

In a 1965 television profile of the new Yankees manager, *Johnny Keane: The Yankee from Texas,* narrator Horace McMahon and Keane were instructed to walk down steps outside a Catholic church with the actor saying, "You studied for the priesthood once, didn't you, John?"

Instead, McMahon said, "You go to mass every Sunday, John?" Keane said, "Yeah, yeah, we like to go." McMahon asked, "Where do you go?" Keane answered, "Well, we like to go . . ." McMahon: "Did you like the homily today?" Writer-producer Jerry Izenberg watched the pair descend the long staircase and waited to hear his script's priesthood question. McMahon and Keane then began a discussion of Catholic church architecture. At which point Izenberg saw a dark figure fly into the camera shot, take the church steps two at a time, and hurtle toward the actor and the baseball man. He identified the dark figure as "this Jewish avenging angel." It was Cosell. Sweeping down on the churchmen. Screaming, "What the fuck is going on here? I am not making a commercial for the Vatican!"

Cosell believed that social issues could be reported through the prism of sports. He found a kindred spirit in Izenberg, a sportswriter from the stable of the legendary editor Stanley Woodward at the *New York Herald-Tribune.* Both men saw the beauty and cultural significance of sports. Because the civil rights movement dominated America's domestic political agenda in the 1960s, Izenberg proposed a documentary on the football program at Grambling College in Louisiana. For twenty years, the historically all-black school had sent players to the National Football League.

"Howard, there has never been an all-black show on television except

Green Pastures," Izenberg said. "Do Grambling and you'll be a pioneer." That pitch appealed to Cosell's social conscience, his maverick tendencies, and his lust for attention. Cosell would do narration laid over the finished production as reported and filmed by Izenberg and his one-camera crew. But problems started immediately. Grambling itself was under siege. Dissident students occupied the administration building. For three days, as sporadic fires sent smoke over the campus, Izenberg and his crew moved among law enforcement agents. They filmed the high-stepping Grambling marching band. They filmed a player's mother in her one-room sharecropper's cabin, chickens on the porch, the woman maybe forty years old and looking eighty. Though spoken with great dignity, her words were mumbles: "I'm so proud, I'm so prouda my Henry." Henry's picture was on a nightstand by her bed.

Meanwhile, Cosell, out of harm's way in New York, called his man on the scene to say, "Jerry, this is a sociological document. We need to show how badly these people live. No sidewalks, puddles of water on the dirt streets."

"Howard," replied Izenberg, "they don't live that badly, most of them. It's not the eighteenth century. And it is fucking September in Louisiana. They have not had rain here for two months. If you want me to go and piss on Main Street, I will do it and then have the cameraman film the puddle. Now leave me alone until this gets done."

On Izenberg's return, Cosell's hired director saw in the unedited film a naked football player in a locker room. He framed the image with his thumbs and said, "We can do something with that. Did you see Fellini's last film?" Izenberg replied, "Are you nuts? It's a guy in a locker room with his dick hanging out and you're talking Fellini? Howard, it's either me or him."

Because the documentary was Izenberg's creation, Cosell sent the Felliniophile packing. The sternest test of Cosell's will came after his sales staff noticed only one white face in the film and declared it impossible to sell. Cosell drew himself up tall. "I can see now that I have got to save this show. I cannot put this on the air with my name on it. Jerry, that old woman is unintelligible. I want her out of the show. That band, cut it in half. I've made a list of things that must be done. Then you'll see amazing television."

Izenberg said, "Give me the fucking list, leave me alone, and don't ever call me again after this show." There followed three days and three nights during which Izenberg and his film editor hunkered down in a dirty little hole somewhere in the city. They drank too much. They ordered in pizza. Women arrived. What Izenberg did not do was look at Cosell's list of proposed changes. "Touch that film," he told his editor, "and I'll break both your arms." On the fourth day, Cosell called. Izenberg said, "Howard, you must be a mind reader. We have worked three straight days. We just finished the last cut. Come on over."

The three men sat in a dark little room to watch *Grambling: 100 Yards to Glory*. At its end, Cosell turned to Izenberg, every aspect of his face reflecting triumph. "Now that is television," he said. "I did some damned rescue job here."

"Yes, you did," said the weary Izenberg.

The documentary legitimized Grambling football and moved the Yankees' president, Michael Burke, to schedule an annual game for Grambling at Yankee Stadium. More important for Cosell, the documentary succeeded without revealing his doubts, equivocations, and fears on matters of race; in fact, the work was a lesson in race relations. Izenberg believed it defined Cosell's reputation from there forward: "He became the black man's white man."

The first Cosell documentary, *Run to Daylight*, drew a portrait of the Green Bay Packers' coach, Vince Lombardi, as neither the martinet nor tyrant of popular caricature but a complex figure, a sentimental authoritarian who had created his time's dominant team. He was so respected by players that even the Packers' playboy halfback, Paul Hornung, rushed away from Cosell to catch a team bus.

"But I thought," Cosell said, "you were giving me a lift."

"Didn't you listen?" Hornung said. "The coach wants everyone in the bus in five minutes. I'll be in the bus. If he said everyone walks to practice, I walk. If he says everyone runs to practice, I run. If he says everyone swims the Fox River to practice, I swim the damned river."

Work on the documentary produced a nickname for Cosell when he heard Lombardi refer to him as "Coach." "What Howard didn't know," said W. C. Heinz, his writer on the piece, "was that Lombardi was terrible at names and called everybody 'Coach.' Instead, so hungry for praise was Howard in those days, he thought Lombardi had certified him as a football genius." The documentary's second salutary effect was that it pleased

Cosell's harshest critic. Tom Moore said, "You're a helluva producer," and asked him to be involved in producing a show for the network's newest division, ABC Sports. "I want you to get with Roone Arledge."

Roone Pinckney Arledge was twenty-nine years old, and as surprised as anyone that he had become the first boss of ABC Sports. The son of a Long Island lawyer, a graduate of Columbia University, Arledge had always had plans. He would do big things, important things, things that had never been done before. So far, as of the summer of 1964, he had produced a show starring a ventriloquist's hand puppet named Lamb Chop. Then he tried to sell a program he had created, *For Men Only*, a television version of men's magazines. He had shown it to several prospects before inviting in Ed Scherick, a disheveled New Yorker with a television production company called Sports Programs, Inc. He watched Arledge's pilot and said, "I don't have any use for this. But I'd like to meet the guy who produced it."

Arledge said, "That'd be me."

"Ever produce sports?" Scherick said.

"Sure," said Arledge, whose sports production résumé consisted entirely of one segment on the WRCA Citywide Marbles Tournament.

"Come over to my office tomorrow. We'll talk."

The next day Arledge took a cab from NBC's headquarters at 30 Rockefeller Center to a seedy neighborhood on Forty-second Street off Times Square. Scherick's office was a two-room disaster area that suggested a bookie joint in distress. As Arledge took a seat, careful to avoid a protruding spring, he noticed photographs of athletes on the walls.

"Who's that?" Scherick said, pointing to a baseball player sliding home.

"Willie Mays."

"And that?" A pitcher winding up.

"Sal Maglie. 'The Barber.' Best there is."

"Why do they call him 'The Barber'?"

"Because he likes to give batters 'close shaves.'"

Scherick next administered a test of Arledge's appreciation for derring-do. He told a story in which he was the hero. He said that just that past winter, acting on behalf of ABC—the "Almost Broadcasting Company" he had spirited away from mighty NBC one of television's most valuable sports programming packages, the rights to NCAA football.

It began with intelligence gathering. Scherick learned that NBC's man always came to the NCAA auction with two envelopes, one with a low bid, usually 10 percent above the current contract, the other with a sure-to-win bid in case a lesser network dared to enter the competition. Scherick thought he might beat NBC's low bid, but knew he could not match a blow-away number. He needed to persuade NBC's man that there were no other bidders in the room and it was safe to submit the low bid. He needed a courier who could pass for invisible. As it happened, he had just the man, one Stanton Frankle, plucked from an ABC control room because his physical attributes included a plainness suggestive of wallpaper.

As a safeguard against disaster, Scherick sent a second faceless man behind Frankle. "I explained to this man that if he should see Stanton Frankle fall injured in the streets, he should let Frankle lie where he fell and proceed on to the consummation of his mission." Scherick's instructions to Frankle included an order to wait for the NBC man to make his bid. "When, and only when, he removes his fingers from his envelope, you are to come forward and say, 'I represent ABC,' and place your envelope on the table. Now go, and Godspeed."

So it was that ABC won a two-year contract with the NCAA at a cost of $6,251,114. Arledge asked, "Why the eleven hundred and fourteen dollars?"

Scherick smiled. "I didn't want to seem chintzy," he said, especially since the money had come, in a way, from NBC itself. Because of boxing's scandals, NBC had dropped *Friday Night Fights*. The fight sponsor, the Gillette razor blade company, then jumped to ABC. Gillette's money went for the NCAA rights.

Next, Scherick intended to create ABC's own sports division. That was why he was hired, and why he wanted to hire Arledge, who in Scherick's tale had heard a siren's song of romance, possibility, and high-stakes adventure.

"It's a deal," the kid said.

Scherick asked the new kid to write him up a memo on how he would produce college football games. "Make it detailed," he said. "And, remember, this is television. Don't be afraid to hype." At home that weekend, Arledge took a beer from his refrigerator, sat at a typewriter, and wrote words that changed his life, Cosell's, and the very nature of television sports. The memo began, "Heretofore, television has done a remarkable job of bringing the game to the viewer—now we are going to take the viewer to the game!! We will utilize every production technique that has been learned in producing variety shows, in covering political conventions, in shooting travel and adventure series to heighten the viewer's feeling of actually sitting in the stands and participating personally in the excitement and color of walking through a college campus to the stadium to watch the big game. . . ."

Arledge envisioned cameras on jeeps, on mike booms, on helicopters, "anything necessary to get the complete story of the game." He wanted to see "impact shots . . . a coach's face as a man drops a pass in the clear—a pretty cheerleader just after her hero has scored a touchdown— a coed who brings her infant baby to the game in her arms . . . two romantic students sharing a blanket late in the game on a cold day . . . all the excitement, wonder, jubilation and despair that make this America's Number One sports spectacle and a human drama to match bullfights and heavyweight championship fights in intensity.

"In short—WE ARE GOING TO ADD SHOW BUSINESS TO SPORTS!"

He would tell the story of the school, the town, the region in which the game is played. He would have cameras on tailgaters arriving early. He would introduce players in "their normal street attire. These are enthusiastic college kids—the pride of America, not hard-bitten old pros—and we want everyone to know this." He would put microphones on referees.

These were visionary ideas and Arledge reveled in them. He wrote for two hours before ending the memo to Scherick: "The personal satisfaction in such an undertaking will be great. We will be setting the standards that everyone will be talking about and that others in the industry will spend years trying to equal."

When Tom Moore told Cosell to see Arledge, the men had never met. But Arledge had heard that voice the night of June 20, 1960, at New York's Polo Grounds. Heavyweight champion Ingemar Johansson said he would not enter the ring if promoters introduced Sonny Liston in prefight ceremonies. What the Swede had against organized crime's favorite thug, no one knew. But Johansson was insistent. Ingo would not bring his Toonder and Lightning into the ring if that man shared the space. The word went out that someone should tell Liston.

Because it was the rare fool who chose to disturb Liston, an ABC executives did what executives do. He said, "Hey, kid, come here, we got a job for you." The sacrificial messenger was redheaded, freckle-faced, and newly on board from NBC where he had produced that hand-puppet show done by a rabbi's daughter. It was Arledge's third day on the new job, and as he stood before Liston he had reason to wonder if there would be a fourth day. A derby hat a size too small teetered atop Liston's massive, shaved skull. The kid put out his hand in greeting, only to draw it back when he noticed that Liston's hands were the size and texture of frying pans.

He said, "Mister . . . ah . . . Liston."

"Yeah." The voice was that of a big, ugly bear.

"Well, sir," the kid said, "it seems we have a small problem."

Each word describing the smallness of the problem enlarged it until tendrils of smoke could he seen under Liston's derby. Arledge then scurried to the safety of his seat on the far side of the ring. There he listened to ABC's radio broadcast and heard a distinctive voice, singsong and nasal, that of the movie comedian Eddie Bracken. He wondered aloud what Eddie Bracken was doing at the microphone on an ABC fight. No, no, someone said, that's not Bracken. It's that smart-ass from WABC, Howard Cosell.

Arledge came to recognize Cosell as this "strange creature who'd wandered the nation's locker rooms with a thirty-pound tape recorder strapped to his back, interviewing anyone who'd talk to him." First amused and later intrigued by the creature's productivity, Arledge felt the stirrings of "acquisitive lust." He also noticed Cosell's command of the medium, as confirmed on Christmas Eve of 1964. His Channel 7 guest was Tracy Stallard, previously famous as the Boston Red Sox pitcher who gave up Roger Maris's sixty-first home run in 1961. Stallard believed they were in a commercial break. They weren't. Pictures and words went on the air live as Stallard said, "So, Howard, do I bullshit you first, or do you bullshit me?" Cosell patted Stallard on the shoulder and said, "Any more good words for the people of New England?" Stallard rose and left the set, silently.

Arledge decided to use Cosell in a low-profile spot doing pregame interviews on one of ABC's losers, weekend baseball. This time he called in Cosell and explained how he intended to sneak him onto the baseball show with intentions to make him an integral part of the network. Cosell realized his years in limbo were over. At last he had a real shot at those wild jackasses. Grateful and congenitally unable to say anything indicating how grateful he was, Cosell instead said, "Roone, we are today witnessing an occurrence on the scale of Philo T. Farnsworth's invention of the cathode ray tube: the television rebirth of an acknowledged genius. You are to be congratulated, young man, on your sagacity."

"Howard," Arledge said, "cut the crap."

They laughed like hell.

Cosell's life was at full tide. Law practice long behind him, fully committed to journalism, at last in the good graces of his bosses, he moved to the upper tier of sports broadcasting in 1966. He did daily radio and television reports and his weekly interview show in addition to regular work on Arledge's baby, *ABC's Wide World of Sports*. At age forty-eight, he had arrived.

CHAPTER SIX

"I Don't Have to Be What You Want Me to Be"

THE NIGHT OF FEBRUARY 25, 1964, as Sonny Liston lay in wounded silence on a hospital's metal examining table, Cassius Clay sat in a motel room eating ice cream and drinking milk. It was hard to tell which man was in more trouble.

Under a harsh light, the swellings and bleedings of Liston's face persuaded the only reporter there that the fight had been legitimate. Mort Sharnik of *Sports Illustrated* watched doctors do X-rays of Liston's shoulder and stitch together a gash under his left eye. "That's not the guy I was supposed to fight," Liston said. "That guy could punch." Sharnik thought Liston looked like the loneliest person on Earth. He saw no fix. He saw an old man who was beaten, shamed by it, and quit.

A fighter who quits on his stool does it for a good reason that his courage no longer can hide. Once courage fails, the fighter's life in the ring is over. The only question is, when? For Sonny Liston, sad-eyed on that cold, bare, metal table, the answer seemed to be sooner than later. For Clay, brilliant in the ring, the questions were of a different kind. Who, really, was this phenomenon? Why in Miami Beach, home to so many Jews, did he associate with Malcolm X, who in 1960 said, "In America, the Jews sap the very life-blood of the so-called Negroes to maintain the state of Israel . . ."? What was this dance with the Black Muslim minister, a dance dared near the twin fires of public condemnation and Elijah Muhammad's wrath?

In keeping with the eccentric rhythms of a day and night filled with mystifications, Clay chose to stay away from a victory party. Instead, he went to the Hampton House Motel, across Biscayne Bay in Miami, there to visit with Malcolm X and Jim Brown, the Cleveland Browns football star. The new champion took a short nap on Malcolm X's bed, then returned to his little rental house on the mainland in low-rent North Miami.

The next morning, talking to reporters, Clay said winning the championship had changed his attitude. "All I have to be is a nice, clean gentleman," he said. "I'm through talking." The *New York Times'* neophyte boxing writer, Robert Lipsyte, was fascinated as the thoughtful, polite young fighter promised he would defend the title against all contenders. As the conversation became repetitive, sportswriters folded their notebooks and drifted away. Only then did a straggler ask a question born of Clay's relationship with Malcolm X and phrased with the curious wording borrowed from the 1950s-era Communist witch hunts.

Was Clay "a card-carrying member of the Black Muslims?"

" 'Card-carrying,' what does that mean?" Clay said. Then he was off on a shouted soliloquy: He was baptized at twelve, but was no longer a Christian. He believed in Allah. He didn't want to live in a white neighborhood or marry a white woman. He wanted to be with his own kind. Lions are with lions, tigers with tigers, bluebirds with bluebirds. That's human nature, to be with your own kind.

Reporters had embraced the reality that the loud-mouth Clay would not be Joe Louis. But this was weird, this Nation of Islam stuff, its radical separatism, its hateful babble about blue-eyed devils, the bizarre demand by Elijah Muhammad for his own nation carved out of Mississippi, Louisiana, and Alabama. Still fresh in the public's mind, Clay's mentor and friend Malcolm X had been connected with an alleged plot to assassinate the new president, Lyndon Johnson. On January 14, news organizations reported that the FBI wanted to question Malcolm X about a Black Muslim plan to kill LBJ. Two days later, Hoover's agents called it a mistake and cited an unemployed handyman for "filing a false report." No matter that the original media reports likely were FBI fictions designed to discredit Malcolm X; he stood suspected by millions who trusted their government. Now Clay heard questions about Malcolm X, about civil rights, about integration. Though it was unlikely that any reporter there knew Nation of Islam tenets, they challenged Clay's acceptance of the ideology.

Finally, exasperated, Clay said, "I don't have to be what you want me to be. I'm free to be who I want."

When reporters wanted more a day later, he gave them more: *Black*

Muslims, that's a name invented by the press. The real name is Islam, which means peace. More than 750 million people believe in it. I'm one of them. I can't be a Christian, not when colored people are getting blowed up. I don't want to be washed down sewers, or hit by stones, or chewed by dogs. The Nation of Islam doesn't want to take over the United States. It is no hate group. Followers of Allah are the sweetest people in the world. They don't carry knives. They don't tote weapons. They pray five times a day. Muslims only want to live in peace with their own kind.

To some listeners, those words rang false. Only twenty days earlier, Clay's father had reported death threats from Black Muslims in reprisal for his claim that the sect had "brainwashed" his son. In Chicago, though, Clay's tutorial pleased Elijah Muhammad. "I'm so glad that Cassius Clay admits he's a Muslim," Muhammad said. "He was able, by confessing that Allah was the God and by following Muhammad, to whip a much tougher man . . . Clay has confidence in Allah, and in me as his only messenger."

That was hypocrisy. It was also political machination. Before the fight, Muhammad had ordered his ministers to disavow interest in Clay; he preached against sports as "wicked," and he believed Clay's certain defeat would disgrace the Nation. But now he knew Clay was vital to his self-interest; the champion's celebrity would bring the Nation a financial windfall and attention disproportionate to its size. Elijah Muhammad also knew what only he and Malcolm X knew. On January 2, he had suspended Malcolm X indefinitely, a certain prelude to excommunication. He could not now afford to allow Clay to leave the Nation and join Malcolm X in a rival organization. On January 7, the Messenger made a veiled reference to killing Malcolm X. "It is time," he said on an FBI-wiretapped phone call to an associate, "to close his eyes."

So began an internecine struggle for Clay's loyalty. So began the Elijah Muhammad jihad against Malcolm X.

The Messenger was infuriated to see Malcolm X and Clay together in New York the week after the fight. Newspapers tracked their movements. February 29: In Times Square, Clay noted that Malcolm X signed more autographs than he did. *"He is the greatest."* March 1: Malcolm X was in the *Amsterdam News* offices when Clay said he had taken the name "Cassius X." March 2: Clay told reporters that what they had heard from him on the Nation was nothing next to what they would hear from Malcolm X soon. March 4: With Malcolm X, Clay met United Nations delegates from four African countries and announced that he would visit Africa and Asia. He said, "My companion on my world tour will be Minister Malcolm X." March 5: On a second visit to the UN, Clay told a reporter that his name was Cassius X Clay.

March 5 was also the day the U.S. government announced that its Selective Service system would expedite a second test of Clay's fitness for military duty. "I tried my hardest to pass" the first time, Clay told reporters, but he couldn't do the math. Almost unnoticed was his reply to a question suggesting he might request exemption as a conscientious objector. "I don't like that name," he said. "It sounds ugly—like I wouldn't want to be called. I'd need two hours on the radio—with a national hookup—to explain my position." Actually, the explanation would have been easily done. Malcolm X did it in 1953 (only to be rejected for military duty on mental grounds). There was also the example of Elijah Muhammad's son, Wallace Dean Muhammad (who spent three years in prison for refusing to report in 1957 after his conscientious objector claim was denied).

Malcolm X's appearances with Clay were open defiances of Elijah Muhammad's authority. As to why Clay persisted in friendship with a Nation outcast, it was possible that Malcolm X had convinced him the suspension would be lifted at any moment. Clay may have hoped to broker peace between his mentors, or he may have bought into Malcolm X's plans and dared Muhammad to confront them. The simplest explanation: Clay was a twenty-two-year-old self-absorbed athlete with no political skills whose opinions generally reflected those of the most recent person to flatter him.

Elijah Muhammad demonstrated the truth of the simplest explanation. With a series of moves against Malcolm X and toward Clay, he split the pair. On March 5 he publicly announced Malcolm X's suspension to be "indefinite." That night, he also did a radio broadcast and made a phone call. He announced that he would give Cassius Clay an "original" name. "This Clay name has no divine meaning," Muhammad said. "I hope he will accept being called by a better name." Some days earlier, Muhammad had tried to persuade Clay to accept the new name, but Clay preferred Cassius X Clay, because he loved the sound of "Cassius" and felt he did not deserve the honor. This time Muhammad prevailed, and Cassius Marcellus Clay, Jr., no longer existed. He became Muhammad Ali. In the Nation, a name change was given to fewer than 1 percent of members; even Malcolm X had not been renamed. "Muhammad" signifies "one worthy of praise." "Ali" was a military general and the third caliph after the death of his cousin, the Prophet Muhammad.

That same night, Muhammad called Ali. He passed along a stern father's advice. If Ali ever wanted to become a minister in the Nation, he should end contact with the suspended Malcolm X. The chastened Ali promised to do that.

Malcolm X believed the gift of a holy name was a political ploy practiced on the naïve Ali to ensure his loyalty. He was sure of it when he tried to call Ali at his hotel, only to be told the fighter wasn't there. On the March 8 *Today* television show, Malcolm X said he had left the Nation because of its leader's moral bankruptcy. He would start his own organization. The *New York Times* put the story on its front page. The next day, Malcolm called Ali eight times without reaching him. Instead, a lieutenant to Herbert Muhammad, Elijah's son, called Malcolm with the news that Herbert was now Ali's manager, and that Ali would make the African trip alone.

Ali never explained his move away from Malcolm X. It came about so abruptly, however, as to leave only one conclusion. Elijah Muhammad had ordered it, and the son of an abusive father had no taste for a confrontation with his spiritual father, a man who had shown a willingness to order physical retaliation against those who disobeyed him. At least twice, Ali had spoken to journalists about his unwillingness to cross the messenger. He said to George Plimpton, "Man, you just don't buck Mr. Muhammad." Alex Haley, working with Malcolm X on his autobiography, asked Ali what caused the rift in his relationship with the minister. Evenly, Ali said, "You just don't buck Mr. Muhammad and get away with it. I don't want to talk about him no more."

When Haley reported Ali's words to him, Malcolm X was hurt. "I felt like a big brother to him," Malcolm X said. "I'm not against him now. He's a fine young man. Smart. He just let himself be used, led astray." As sad as it was to realize he had lost Ali's friendship, Malcolm X knew the political reality was worse. He knew that Elijah Muhammad could now move against him without fear of alienating the new heavyweight champion of the world.

On March 11, 1964, two days after his rebuff of Malcolm X, the young man newly named Muhammad Ali sat in a WHAS radio studio in

Louisville. For an hour, in his warmest, most appealing voice, he answered questions from listeners calling in.

A timid voice, a boy's: "Cassius?"

"Cassius speaking." He spoke with the precision of an elocutionist.

Cassius speaking? The Nation's internal wars were invisible to mainstream Americans. But the Clay-to-Ali name change drew attention. This was not an actor or athlete changing his name for commercial reasons. Archibald Leach became Cary Grant, Joe Barrow became Joe Louis, Walker Smith, Jr., became Sugar Ray Robinson, Howard Cohen became Howard Cosell. But *Muhammad Ali* was different. It was alien. It was further rejection of everything familiar to Americans. For some people, it was more evidence that the man had become an enemy of the state in league with sinister forces preaching racist hate. Those people refused to accept the name, and Ali immediately decided he would not compromise. In his second week as Muhammad Ali, he walked out of a Luis Rodriguez–Holly Mims fight at Madison Square Garden rather than allow himself to be introduced as Cassius Clay.

But here, in his hometown, he was okay with Cassius.

The boy calling in said, "I lost five dollars on your last fight, Cassius."

Almost singing, Ali said, "I told you, if you want to lose your money, be a fool and bet on Sonny."

The next caller's mention of Sonny Liston gave the show's host, Milton Metz, reason to tell listeners that Ali earlier had spoken of Liston. It was recent news that Liston had been arrested in Denver on charges of speeding, resisting arrest, and carrying a lethal weapon, a handgun. "Cassius, if you don't mind," Metz said, "would you say what you had in mind?" Here Ali didn't sound anything like the Ali who had raised raucous commotions. Instead, he tried for the voice of a kindly elder expressing compassion for a poor fellow tangled up in life's difficulties.

"Sonny Liston, before he was champion, he was in the same predicament. Took a lot of money to build him up and to present him to the public as a human being and not just an old savage animal as they seemed to be painting a picture of him at that time. And the championship was really the only thing that made him feel like a man, gave him dignity, made him feel like a citizen. And I guess as soon as he lost the championship, he lost all confidence in trying to do the right thing and just went back out to his old self again. And what he really need is somebody to tell him that the world haven't come to an end yet, and when you're as famous a person like Sonny Liston and I, it's hard to even go out when you're famous and to receive peace from the public. And a fellow like Liston who let a lot of people down and who received such a tough loss, well, it's really hard for him to show his face. He just go out of his head."

Metz asked if Ali would like to see Liston again. "Out of the ring, I mean."

"Yeah, I believe I'll pay Liston a little visit. Call him up and let him know I'm coming and spend a week or so with him, talk to him, and let him know that I'm all right with him, it wasn't nothing but a bout, we still buddies. And show him a lot of things in life, correct a lot of his mistakes. Because I can do it. I've never been in no trouble. I dodge all trouble and all violence, and I've never been in no trouble. I go everywhere, I talk to everybody, I go in all types neighborhoods and all types nightclubs, meet everybody, never been in one minute's trouble because I know how to conduct and handle myself. I know how to adjust myself to any type civilization or nature or culture. Sonny Liston needs somebody really to take patience with him and advise him. By me beating him and being the heavyweight champion, maybe I can influence him a little."

None of this was true. Liston had called him a nigger faggot, and threatened to pull his tongue out and stick it up his ass. Ali himself had portrayed Liston as an animal, a big, ugly bear, and mocked his boxing ability as well as his intelligence, character, and courage. They had never been friends. Yet here was Ali saying, *We still buddies.*

He said so because on that day in that place he was playing yet another role as Muhammad Ali. In Malcolm X's presence, he was the protégé. For Elijah Muhammad, he was the obedient acolyte to the supreme being. Now, for the WHAS audience and Milton Metz, he played the charming hometown hero reaching out to his fallen rival. In a disorienting world that expanded daily and exponentially, Ali's soliloquies on Liston provided clues to a pattern of behavior that gave him comfort. He was not so much a man in search of self-identity as he was a child looking to be loved. He told people what they wanted to hear. Folks listening on hometown radio did not want a Nation of Islam rant. They wanted their homeboy polite, courteous, soft-spoken. He gave them that Muhammad Ali, as when a caller suggested that less boasting and more humility were in order.

"Well, you keep this in your books," Ali said, and then did a happy recitative: "A wise man can act a fool, but a fool cannot act a wise man."

Caller, unsure: "Uh-huh."

Metz to Ali: "That's pretty good. Where's that quotation come from?"

"Oh, that's something I figured out."

"Sounds like Shakespeare."

Ali laughed. "Might be. I heard it somewhere."

A man whose name he did not want to use on the air in Louisville had said it in Miami two weeks earlier. He told a reporter that people underestimated Clay's mind: "He fools them. One forgets that though a clown never imitates a wise man, the wise man can imitate the clown." The man was Malcolm X.

Two months later, with Ali and Malcolm X on separate trips rather than a joint "world tour," coincidence brought them together in Ghana. The strained meeting on a city street would be their last.

Shortly after arrival in Africa on May 17, 1964, Ali shouted to his new manager, Elijah Muhammad's son, "Hey, Herbert, when's the man coming to take us diamond hunting? I heard they got a lake somewhere so full of diamonds you just wade in and feel around." Most of what he knew about Africa involved lions, tigers, and Tarzan movies.

When a Ghanaian said there was no such lake, the disappointed but resolute Ali said, "I'm still going to go diamond hunting, wherever they hunt them here." He also spoke of visiting the United Arab Republic. "Why, that's a Muslim country, you know. I'm going to get me four wives and take them back home and put them in a house I'm going to build that will cost one hundred thousand dollars. It'll be like a castle and I'll have a throne room for my heavyweight crown. One of my wives—Abigail—will sit beside me feeding me grapes. Another one—Susie—will be rubbing olive oil over my beautiful muscles. Cecilia will be shining my shoes. And then there'll be Peaches. I don't know yet what she'll do. Sing or play music, maybe."

Establishing the future, Ali returned to the present. He presented himself to people who had gathered in the street to be near the famous American boxer.

"Who's the king?" Ali shouted.

"You are," came the reply. "You are."

"Louder. Now, who's the greatest?"

A roar: "You are."

Malcolm X's trip began quietly with his hajj, the pilgrimage to Mecca that every orthodox Muslim is expected to make. He made it because once he decided that Elijah Muhammad was a false prophet, he saw the Nation's tenets were distortions of Islam. As Martin Luther King, Jr., had written a declaration of belief from a Birmingham jail, Malcolm X now wrote a thousand-word letter home to assistants at his new mosque in Harlem. He added a note asking that the letter be distributed to the press.

"During the past eleven days here in the Muslim world," he wrote, "I have eaten from the same plate, drunk from the same glass, and slept in the same bed (or on the same rug)—while praying to the *same God*—with fellow Muslims, whose eyes were the bluest of blue, whose hair was the blondest of blond, and whose skin was the whitest of white. And in the *words* and in the *actions* and in the *deeds* of the 'white' Muslims, I felt the same sincerity that I felt among the black African Muslims of Nigeria, Sudan, and Ghana."

Malcolm X moved on to Africa where he was often mistaken for Ali; newspapers had printed a picture of them together at the United Nations. "Even children knew of him," Malcolm said, "and loved him there in the Muslim world. By popular demand, the cinemas throughout Africa and Asia had shown his fight. At that moment in young Cassius' career, he had captured the imagination and the support of the whole dark world."

Malcolm X made news with a consistent message to the media and national leaders; he said the 22 million African-Americans in the United States could become a positive force for African independence while, in turn, African nations could press for an end to America's racial discrimination. "Just as the American Jew is in political, economic, and cultural harmony with world Jewry," Malcolm X said in Nigeria, he was "convinced that it was time for all Afro-Americans to join the world's Pan-Africanists."

In Ghana, a newspaper story said, "Malcolm X's name is almost as familiar to Ghanaians as the Southern dogs, fire hoses, cattle prods, people sticks, and the ugly, hate-contorted white faces . . ." Another called him "the first Afro-American leader of national standing to make an independent trip to Africa since Dr. W.E.B. Du Bois came to Ghana." Ghana's president Kwame Nkrumah received Malcolm as if he were a head of state.

While Malcolm X made his last day's political rounds in Accra, Ali arrived to a reception at the airport. Ali met Nkrumah, then flew to Kumasi where he fought an exhibition. Most remarkable, the fighter and a friend, Osman Karriem, drove into the barren countryside beyond Accra and heard a sound like the beating of drums. Karriem realized the sound was the voices of people along the road shouting, "Ali! Ali!"

Ali sat there, silent, his name on the air, fascinated that such a thing could happen to him in a land so far from home. Karriem said, "I saw the birth of a new human being. It was like Cassius Clay came to an end and Muhammad Ali emerged."

The morning of Ali's second day in Accra, Malcolm X stood outside the Ambassador Hotel with expatriate Americans. He wore a traditional Ghanaian robe and carried a walking stick. As Ali came out of the hotel, a moment of recognition connected the men. Malcolm X shouted, "Brother Muhammad. Brother Muhammad." When Ali stopped, Malcolm X said, "Brother, I still love you, and you are still the greatest." On Malcolm X's face was a sad smile.

Ali was stern. "You left the Honorable Elijah Muhammad. That was the wrong thing to do, Brother Malcolm." One expatriate, Maya Angelou, thought Ali looked disappointed, sad, and hurt. Then Ali walked away. Angelou saw Malcolm X's shoulders sag as he said, "I've lost a lot. A lot. Almost too much." When a friend asked if the incident surprised him, Malcolm X answered only by saying of Ali, "He is young. The Honorable Elijah Muhammad is his prophet and his father, I understand. Be kind to him for his sake, and mine. He has a place in my heart."

Later that day, Ali spoke derisively of Malcolm X. "Man, did you get a look at him? Dressed in that funny white robe and wearin' a beard and walking with that cane that looked like a prophet's stick? Man, he's gone. He's gone so far out he's out completely." Then he curried favor with Elijah Muhammad's son. He said to Herbert, "Doesn't that just go to show that Elijah is the most powerful? Nobody listens to that Malcolm anymore."

Betrayed as Malcolm X had felt on discovering Elijah Muhammad's immorality, Ali's rejection hurt him more personally. He sent Ali a telegram: "Because a billion of our people in Africa, Arabia, and Asia love you blindly, you must now be forever aware of your tremendous responsibilities to them. You must never say or do anything that will permit your enemies to distort the beautiful image you have here among our people."

On Malcolm X's return to New York's newly named John F. Kennedy Airport on May 21, he saw so many reporters and photographers—maybe sixty—that he wondered what celebrity had been on his flight. He was news because of his unexplained split from Elijah Muhammad, his journey through Africa, and the increasing racial turmoil in Harlem and across America. He had become the symbol of a racial movement that pursued equality "by any means necessary," as he had once said.

It was time, Malcolm X decided, to give the reporters real news. He said blacks "needed to quit thinking what the white man had taught him—which was that the black man had no alternative except to beg for his so-called 'civil rights.'" The American black man "needed to recognize that he had a strong, airtight case to take the United States before the United Nations on a formal accusation of 'denial of human rights.'" If Angola and South Africa were precedent cases, he said, "then there would be no easy way that the U.S. could escape being censured, right on its own home ground."

Never before had he sought a political solution to racial oppression. Malcolm X's proposal for an international movement to condemn the United States was evidence of the changes produced in him by the hajj and his African journey, as was the conciliatory tone of his "Letter from Mecca." Malcolm X said he no longer condemned all whites: "I never will be guilty of that again—as I know now that some white people are truly sincere, that some truly are capable of being brotherly toward a black man. The true Islam has shown me that a blanket indictment of all white people is as wrong as when whites make blanket indictments against blacks."

At home in Phoenix, Arizona, Elijah Muhammad came to see Malcolm X as a threat to his authority and empire of affluence built with money taken from the Nation's treasury. On June 28 at a Nation meeting in New York, Elijah Muhammad's son Elijah Jr. said, "Malcolm should have been killed by now. All you have to do is go there and clap on the walls until the walls come down and then cut out the nigger's tongue and put it in an envelope and sent it to me. And I'll stamp it 'approved' and give it to the Messenger."

Ali moved from Ghana to Nigeria and then to Egypt, where the geographically challenged traveler told his hosts, "I've learned from our spiritual leader, Elijah Muhammad, that all civilizations began here in Asia." As he sat in the Cairo Hilton lobby, he held the hand of a nine-year-old girl named Nirvana. He said, "I haven't been treated this good nowhere. See this little girl? I couldn't hold her in America. There were thousands of people in the street waiting to see me. People hug you and men kiss you. I don't worry about my color. I'm free over here. I don't have to get bit by no dogs, I don't have to follow no Martin Luther King. They treat me like in white America they'd treat a white champ."

He told the Egyptians that the U.S. government someday would get tired of dealing. Then "the government itself is gonna say, 'Okay, Elijah, you can have 'em. We don't know what to do with 'em. They're layin' on our sidewalks, marryin' our daughters, comin' in to our suburbs. You take 'em.'" Until then, Ali figured it would be more of the same. "How's it gonna look when I come back to my hometown and I get treated like an animal?"

In June 1964, shortly after Malcolm X's return, Ali was back in the United States. Like Malcolm X, he had come home changed. He had been a figure of respect and honor in Africa; at home, although many Americans found him a refreshing departure from boxing's dark side, he remained the object of mainstream insult. But where Malcolm X answered insult by proposing that the United Nations address black Americans' grievances, Ali didn't bother with thought. He cried out, "I'm not no American, I'm a black man."

Never a statesman, always boyish, Ali sit in a Harlem restaurant with the *Times'* Robert Lipsyte and asked, "Hey, you know what happened on the way to Egypt? I sat with the pilot, that's right, the pilot of a big jet plane, and he talked to me about boxing while I drove the plane, and I sat behind a wheel, too, and whenever he turned his wheel, my wheel turned, too, and I could sit there and pretend I was driving the plane."

As he wolfed down navy-bean pie, Ali checked out the waitresses and whispered to Lipsyte, "When I get married, it's gonna be a pretty little Muslim girl, seventeen years old, I can teach her my ways. A virgin, a girl ain't no one touched."

In Egypt, Ali had spied a waitress and announced he would marry her, only to hear Herbert Muhammad intercede with a promise to introduce him to a young woman in Chicago. Herbert, a professional portrait photographer, produced a picture of Sonji Roi. On July 3 in Chicago, Ali met her. Sonji Roi was indeed beautiful. But she was not Muslim, was not seventeen, was not a virgin, and there was nothing Ali could teach her about anything. She was twenty-three, a mother, a cocktail waitress, a model, and, in the words of a Nation minister, "two cents slick." That night, Ali asked her to marry him. Herbert Muhammad, who had intended Roi only as a one-night plaything, sputtered, "Man, you don't marry this girl. She works at a cocktail place wearing one of those little bunny things on her behind. You don't want to marry no girl like this."

On August 14, 1964, Ali married Sonji Roi before a justice of the peace in Gary, Indiana.

By October 1964, certain that his execution was planned, Malcolm X sat with his back to the walls of public places, even in Nairobi, Kenya, when meeting with two black Americans in Dr. King's movement, John Lewis and Don Harris.

Lewis admitted to surprise on meeting Malcolm X, whom he had known only by reputation as the fire-breathing Nation of Islam separatist. This transformed Malcolm X said, "Don't give up. This is an ongoing struggle. People are changing. And there are people all over the world supporting you." Lewis believed that Malcolm X's "overwhelming reception in Africa by blacks, whites, Asians, and Arabs alike had pushed him toward believing that people could come together."

In his hotel room that day, Lewis sensed a fearful disquiet in Malcolm X. How his killing would be done, why, from whom the order had come—Malcolm X told Lewis he knew none of that. He knew only that somebody wanted him killed, the latest news of a death threat reported to him just two weeks earlier—reported by a man in Muhammad Ali's training camp.

The man's name was Leon 4X Ameer. Small and grim, thirty years old, an ex-Marine, Ameer worked as the karate instructor to the Black Muslim muscle known as Fruit of Islam. He had been Malcolm X's bodyguard. In the fall of 1964, as Ali trained for a rematch with Liston, Ameer served as the champion's press secretary.

Ameer knew of the threat because he had been called to Chicago in late September for a meeting of FOI warriors capable of killing. For eight hours, Elijah Muhammad ranted about the dangers the Nation faced—dangers to its very existence—from members who now chose to be aligned with Malcolm X. He called Malcolm X "the greatest hypocrite the

NOI has ever seen," and said, "He must be stopped." The Messenger said apostates were to be beaten or murdered. Ameer made three decisions. He would leave the Nation, join Malcolm X's movement, and tell Malcolm X what he knew. The Nation's plan for Malcolm X was an open secret. The December 4 issue of *Muhammad Speaks* carried a cartoon that showed a cemetery with headstones marked "Judas," "Brutus," and "Benedict Arnold." Above a bed of bones was a stone with the name "Malcolm: Little Red." Little Red was Malcolm X's nickname. The cartoon showed his decapitated head bouncing through the cemetery.

Ameer's connection to Malcolm X now put him on the Nation's list of traitors. On Christmas Day, FOI enforcers led by Clarence 2X Gill—a fearsome bruiser who had been Muhammad Ali's most obvious bodyguard—beat Ameer senseless in the lobby of Boston's Sherry Biltmore Hotel. That night, on his return from a hospital to his sixth-floor suite, Ameer was beaten again, dragged into a bathtub, and left there bleeding. He was in a coma for three days, in the hospital for two weeks. His injuries included a fractured skull, broken ribs, and a perforated eardrum.

Hoping that publicity would protect him from further assault, Ameer called a press conference in Harlem's Theresa Hotel on January 9, 1965. He denounced the Nation as a racist organization and claimed that his friend, Muhammad Ali, was "beginning to have grave doubts" about the Nation's leaders. As he feared for his own life after the two beatings, he now was afraid Ali might be injured or killed in "Black Muslim in-fighting." He called Ali "a victim of circumstances" and said, "Clay is being used to woo young men and women into the Muslim fold. He is a dedicated young man who believes in the spiritual movement of the Muslims, but the truth is that the spiritual sense of the organization is just about dead and a strong ruthless structure has taken over."

Ali gave Ameer the back of his hand. In the same hotel that day, Ali said, "Ameer's nothing to me. He was welcomed as a friend so long as he was a registered Muslim, but not anymore. And he was never my press secretary. I do my own press work and publicity." Four days later, at a Fruit of Islam party, Ali moved from denouncing Ameer to denouncing Malcolm X: "Malcolm believed the white press which referred to him as the number two man, and became disillusioned."

The next day, Ali grew angry. At a press conference, Bob Lipsyte raised questions about Ameer and his accusations. Ali said, "Ah-meer? Little fellow? I think I remember a little fellow who hung around camp, a little fellow who liked to go downstairs and get me papers." Lipsyte waited for more. Ali accommodated him: "Now I hear he's telling lies, saying he was my press secretary." Ali then shrugged, the end of it.

But Lipsyte persisted, and Ali had had enough. "Any fool Negro got the nerve to buck us, you want to make him a star. Jim Brown said something about the Muslims and they made him a movie star. Ameer was caught with a young girl. He had a wife and nine children. That man stole eight hundred dollars, he was a karate man and he come down on three officials and he got what he deserved."

Lipsyte asked about other people who had disappeared from Ali's entourage. They were "weak believers out to get what they could," Ali said. "God burned their brain and made them go crazy."

"Is Ameer justified in being afraid for his life?" Lipsyte asked.

Ali answered with a virulence that was startling, as if he had never cared about Malcolm X and Ameer: "They think everyone out to kill them because they know they deserve to be killed for what they did."

Intrigued by Ameer's troubles and revelations, Lipsyte met him for a series of interviews. The karate man still complained of headaches and dizziness produced by the beatings; he told Lipsyte he "could feel the clot swelling and moving inside his head." Because the *Times* sports editors showed no interest in Ameer's story, Lipsyte pitched the idea to *Look* magazine only to find no deal there, either. Like Malcolm X, Ameer had grown disenchanted with the Nation's politics and its distortions of Islam. Like Malcolm, he had lost faith in Elijah Muhammad, an old man in freefall to madness: impregnating his teenage secretaries, courting radical-right white leaders, endorsing violence as remedy for dissent. Like Malcolm X, he considered his own murder inevitable. Ameer believed that his death and the death of Malcolm X would have an effect on Muhammad Ali. Their murders, he told Lipsyte, "would keep Ali in line as long as the Nation could use him."

As a wedding anniversary present the year before, the young and sparkling Cassius Clay had invited Malcolm X, his wife, Betty Shabazz, and their four daughters to Miami Beach. Now, early in February 1965, the Nation of Islam disciple given the name Muhammad Ali walked into

Harlem's Theresa Hotel. Just inside the door, he saw Betty Shabazz, who wanted an answer. "You see what you're doing to my husband, don't you?" she said.

Ali raised his hands. "I haven't done anything. I'm not doing anything to him." Ali had made his choice. He was with Elijah Muhammad. Whatever the Messenger proposed, Ali accepted. When the Messenger chose death for those members that he believed were dangerous to him and the Nation, Ali agreed they "deserve to be killed."

On February 19, Malcolm X told photojournalist Gordon Parks, "It's a time for martyrs now. And if I am to be one, it will be in the cause of brotherhood. That's the only thing that can save this country. I've learned it the hard way—but I've learned it." Parks asked Malcolm X if killers were really after him. "It's as true as we are standing here," Malcolm X said. "They've tried it twice in the last two weeks." When Parks asked about police protection, Malcolm X laughed. "Brother, nobody can protect you from a Muslim but a Muslim—or someone trained in Muslim tactics. I know. I invented many of those tactics." He told Parks he had regrets. "I did many things as a Muslim that I'm sorry for now. I was a zombie then—like all Muslims—I was hypnotized, pointed in a certain direction and told to march. Well, I guess a man's entitled to make a fool of himself if he's ready to pay the cost. It cost me twelve years."

Malcolm X checked out of the New York Hilton Hotel at 9:00 A.M. February 21 and drove uptown to Harlem's Audubon Ballroom. Chairs had been set up for a crowd of four hundred. Malcolm X was to talk about his Organization for Afro-American Unity. Shortly after three o'clock that afternoon, his assistant, Benjamin X, told the crowd, "And now, without further remarks, I present to you one who is willing to put himself on the line for you, a man who would give his life for you—I want you to hear, listen, to understand—one who is a *Trojan* for the black man."

"*Asalaikum*, brothers and sisters," Malcolm X said, taking the lectern on stage. The crowd responded, "*Asalaikum salaam.*" Then, a disturbance. Eight rows back. A man's voice, raised in anger. And Malcolm X saying, "Let's cool it, brothers."

Next, gunshots. One witness called it a firing squad. Others said they saw two men, one with a shotgun, the other with a revolver in each hand. Another witness saw a man firing a gun from under his coat as he ran backward from the stage. Malcolm X put a hand to his chest and fell back, knocking over two chairs. Betty Shabazz and her four daughters were there, invited at the last minute by Malcolm X, who first had asked his wife to stay at home. At the sound of gunfire, she threw herself over her daughters. Then she ran to the stage, crying. "My husband! They're killing my husband!" Malcolm X's white shirt had been torn open by people trying to stop the bleeding from the shotgun blast. His wife looked down at his bare chest. "They killed him!"

At three-thirty that afternoon, doctors abandoned efforts to resuscitate Malcolm X.

There was no sign that Malcolm X's assassination saddened Ali. Five days after the murder, Ali sat on the dais with Elijah Muhammad when the Messenger convened the Nation's annual Savior's Day convention in Chicago. That day Muhammad said of Malcolm X, "He criticized, he criticized, he criticized . . . Malcolm got what he preached . . . he was a star as long as he was with me. Now he is a man, his body on the way to the middle of the earth. . . . We didn't want to kill Malcolm and didn't try to kill Malcolm. They know I didn't harm Malcolm. They know I loved him. His foolish teaching brought him to his own end." Ali joined in the laughter and cheering of the four thousand faithful who looked up at the Messenger and the champion seated regally behind a phalanx of Fruit of Islam bodyguards.

Nor was Ali disturbed by the news that his one-time press secretary, Leon 4X Ameer, had died March 12 in his Sherry Biltmore hotel suite. Ameer's death, likely the result of trauma associated with his Christmas Day beating, came nine days after *Muhammad Speaks* identified him as part of a Malcolm X "vengeance" squad "headed for Chicago to assassinate the great Islamic leader, the Honorable Elijah Muhammad."

Ali's public indifference was epitomized when a reporter asked if he had heard the rumors about Malcolm X's people planning an attempt on his life, maybe even during the rematch with Liston. Ali said, "What people? Malcolm ain't got no people." Jerry Izenberg, then a columnist at the *Newark Star-Ledger*, thought, *You son of a bitch. One minute, Malcolm is great, and then all of a sudden he's nobody because somebody tells you he's nobody.*

On April 1, 1965, the deaths in his wake, a lighthearted Ali boarded a bus. To avoid flying, he had bought an old bus. He called it the Little Red

Bus. On its roof line, his father had painted in script letters *World Heavy-weight Champion.* He was planning to drive from Miami to Chicopee Falls, Massachusetts, where he would train for the rematch with Liston. Ali had invited four journalists to join him and a dozen members of his camp.

As the group was about to leave, Sonji Ali called out, "Ali, you see about my dry cleaning?"

"All sent," the husband said.

"How about my shoes at the shop?"

"Done."

"Then take out the garbage," she said.

Silence.

"Ali, don't you go off out of here without taking out that garbage," Sonji Ali said.

"Woman, I ain't taking out no garbage."

"You're going to take out that garbage before you leave."

"Woman, the champion of the world don't carry no garbage."

One sportswriter, Edwin Pope of the *Miami Herald,* heard a tone of finality in Sonji Ali's next sentence: "I'm telling you, Ali, you'd better not . . ."

As to what happened then, Pope made a note. *Champ submits. Sonji beautiful.*

Murder and beatings were not passengers on the Little Red Bus. They had been left behind, the way Ali left most things behind. He was a child, unburdened by what he had done, unafraid of the consequences of what he would do. He was twenty-three years old. He drove the bus in Miami traffic with one hand as he looked over his shoulder to do commentary on the good luck of his passengers: "Just think, the whole world would love to be on this bus with me, but they ain't, and you are. We're going to breathe fresh air and look at pretty trees and eat that chicken and you can interview me while I'm driving my beautiful bus along at the cruising speed of eighty-five." Everyone should eat a bunch of that fried chicken brought on board, "'Cause we ain't stoppin' in Georgia. We flyin' over Georgia."

By the way, he said, anybody got gas money? "You," Ali said, pointing at a man slumping down in his seat, the better to avoid the pinch, "you with the glasses. What's your name?"

"Pope."

"Pope, loan me a hundred dollars."

A parsimonious prince of prose, Pope said, "When you going to pay me back?"

"When we get to Chicopee Falls."

"Don't worry about it," Pope said. "No use both of us worrying."

Be a trip you'll tell your grandchildren about, is the way Muhammad Ali put it in explaining the blessings of the four white men. Be an educational experience, as when Ali plopped himself down on an empty seat alongside a reporter and explained that the Nation of Islam expected the world to blow up. Looks like 1970, he said. The mothership up in the sky, operated by men who never smile, would circle the world at eighteen thousand miles per hour until time to blow everything up by dropping bombs that would burrow a mile deep into the earth before exploding. These truths were revealed to Elijah Muhammad by Wallace Fard, whose frayed picture Ali carried in his wallet. Earth's blowing up wouldn't kill everybody. Eight to ten days before the big bang, notice would be given to the righteous by way of notes in Arabic dropped from the mothership, which would hover until 144,000 Negroes were carried up to salvation. Ali said he had seen the mothership many times, and if it was clear on this night, everybody on the bus could see it by looking out the windows.

One journalist on board, George Plimpton, thought Ali might have been seeing Venus or Jupiter, but he kept the thought to himself rather than interrupt Ali's new monologue, this one on the creation of Earth.

The original black man lived on the moon until a great scientist became enraged that he couldn't get people to speak the same language. He caused an enormous explosion that sent most of the moon spinning into space where it became the planet Earth. Some people survived the trip, including the evil genius Yacub, who spent six hundred years breeding blackness out of original man. When Yacub had created 59,999 white people, the whole bunch was cast out of Paradise. Ever since, the white man has been the black man's devil. Plimpton noticed that at every mention of Yacub, Ali's voice became a conspiratorial whisper, as if to speak the name was a dangerous, spooky thing to do.

Dangerous enough, Ali said, to be driving from Florida up into Georgia, Edwin Pope's home state. He sat beside Pope and said, "I ain't letting you Georgia Baptists get me."

"I'm not Baptist," Pope said.

"Sure you're Baptist. Everybody from Georgia is a Baptist."

"I'm a Presbyterian."

"No, you ain't, you're one of them Georgia Baptists."

Pope had to smile. He couldn't work up any dander about the kid. Yacub and the mothership were too much, but did Ali really believe it? Pope didn't know and figured nobody knew, least of all the kid. Ali conjured up images of the white-man devil, but there he was bumping along backwoods roads in a bus with four middle-aged white journalists. They weren't fifty miles out of Miami when Pope realized that Ali made color disappear on the bus. Black and white, the nineteen men were just guys. Pope even thought, *It's like Ali feels God has played a trick by making some people black and some people white, and he thinks he can make it all right. There's nothing murderous or malicious about him, not what you'd expect from somebody indoctrinated by the Black Muslims. Innocence is more like it.*

Plimpton recorded one of the innocent's jokes. "This cat had him a car, a special-built car, that do hundred and eighty and which he use to agitate the cops—they come after him on this three-hundred-mile-long stretch of highway and he just *toy* with them. But this one time, this cop he keep up to him. When he do hundred, the cop do the same. So he shove her up to hundred thirty, but the cop holds on. He let her out to a hundred *fifty* and the cop is still stuck to him, the siren goin', and so, this cat he shoves her down to the floor, a hundred *eighty,* and man, he don't budge an *inch* from that cop. So, he give up and pull over t' the side of the road. He say, 'You take me to jail, you do *anything* to me, but first allow me one look under the *hood* of yo' car.' So you know what he find under the hood of that car? He look under there an' he find six niggers wearing *sneakers."*

It was dark and they were still in Florida, driving on U.S. Route 17 through a pine forest coming to the Georgia border, when Bundini Brown said, "Let's stop and eat. I empty."

Bundini—pronounced "Boo-dini"—called himself Ali's assistant trainer. He had worked for Sugar Ray Robinson as master of the logistical details of a fighter's craft. Whatever Robinson needed done outside the ring, Brown did it. For Ali the past year and a half, he had done that—and more. He was Ali's emotional soulmate, eccentric and expressive, a black street-smart hustler so important to the champion that he ignored Brown's Star of David pendant, his marriage to a white Jew, and his habit of referring to God as "Shorty."

At a middle-of-nowhere town called Yulee, the bus driver pulled in to a truck stop where a little neon light hung against a restaurant window.

In the Deep South, at night, on the road, in the spring of 1965, black Americans seldom frequented truck-stop restaurants. As Bundini Brown left the bus, Ali's brother, Rudy, now a Muslim who took the name Rahaman, told Plimpton, "You're going watch a man face reality—that's what you're goin' to see."

Ali said he wasn't going in. "I might not be welcome, and, besides, I don't believe in forcing integration." He taunted Brown. "You go ahead, though, Jackie Robinson."

The four white journalists and Brown took stool seats at the restaurant counter. A manager said, "I'm sorry. We have a place out back. Separate facilities. The food's just the same." One of the journalists, Bud Collins of the *Boston Globe,* no doubt aware that the 1964 Civil Rights Act was enacted for just such circumstances, said, "Isn't this discrimination against the law?"

"Not in this county," the manager said.

"Isn't this county in the United States?"

"Not yet."

Brown said, "The heavyweight champion of the world, and he can't get nothing to eat here." And, "I fought for my country, but I can't get nothin' to eat here like a white man." From the restaurant door, Ali shouted, "You fool. What's the matter with you—you damn *fool!* I tol' you to be a Muslim. Then you don' go places where you're not wanted. You clear out of this place, nigger. You ain't wanted here, can't you *see?* They don't want you, nigger." His hands on Brown's denim jacket, Ali jerked him out of the restaurant and pushed him toward the bus, all the while shouting, "I'm *glad,* Bundini! I'm glad! You got *showed,* Bundini, you got *showed.*"

"Leave me alone," Brown said.

"Don't you know when you not *wanted?* Face reality and dance!"

The beleaguered Brown said, "I'm good enough to eat here. I'm a free man. If a man is a puppet, go tell Henry Ford to give him a nose and an eyeball and a new heart. God made me. Not Henry Ford. No slave chains around my heart."

As the bus left Yulee, Ali's voice was the only sound as he leaned over a seat to get at Brown. "Uncle Tom! Tom! Tom! Tom!" He pushed a red pillow against Brown's face. "This teach you a lesson, Bundini!" He shoved Brown's head down. "You bow your head, Bundini."

"Leave me alone! My head don' belong between my knees. It's up in the stars. I'm free. I keep trying. If I find a waterhole is dry, I go on and find another."

"You *shamed* yourself back there!"

"*They* were ashamed."

"What good did that do," Ali said, "except to shame you?"

"That man, that manager, he'll sleep on it. He may be no better, but he'll think on it, and he'll be ashamed. I dropped a little medicine in that place."

Ali would have none of it. "Tom! Tom! Tom! You belong to your white master."

Now Bundini Brown began to cry. Plimpton saw his face as a perfect reflection of the mask of tragedy. Ali softened. He wiped away Brown's tears with the red pillow and thought to make his friend laugh. "Hey, Bundini, what sort of crackers was they back in that restaurant?"

Brown didn't answer. "I'll tell you what kind of crackers. They was not Georgia crackers, they was soda crackers. And if they're soda crackers, that makes you a graham cracker. That's what you are—a *graham cracker.*"

Brown asked why they had to take the bus. Why couldn't they fly and skip all this trouble? "Les' just train and fight—none of the other stuff," he said.

"Don't fly over it, Bundini," Ali said. "You fight it out, Bundini, like your aunts and uncles have to do."

That was odd. Fight it out? Only five minutes earlier, Ali wanted nothing to do with any fight for fairness in Yulee, Florida. His instinct had been to avoid the confrontation. Thirty miles north on U.S. 17, when Brown saw another roadside restaurant and said he was still empty, Ali gave in. "We'll stop. This is Georgia, Bundini. You haven't been *showed*?" This time the sparring partners joined the journalists and Brown as they left the bus. Rahaman Ali called after them, "You facing reality, Bundini—reality." It was Brunswick, Georgia. The assembled group's numbers and nature made them a forbidding crew, a dozen road-weary men, eight of them black, muscled, and tattooed. They moved slowly through the restaurant. Customers stopped their forks in midair. The bus riders kept moving, waiting for a sign that they had not yet entered the United States. They took seats around a long table and heard a waitress say, "You all look *hungry.*" She handed them menus.

Bundini Brown, who had served his country, who was no puppet, who had no slave chains around his heart, began to giggle. "My," he said, "no one mind if I sit at the head of the table?" He pointed out the window to Ali, Rahaman, and the other Muslims. "I'm goin' to eat three steaks standin' up so's they can see." After a while, seeing no confrontation, Ali came in to the restaurant. Bundini greeted him with smug satisfaction. "What you doin' here?" Bundini said. "This place only for integrators. Soda *and* graham crackers."

When Ali's coffee came, he said, "Bundini, I'm goin' to integrate the coffee."

He poured cream into it.

"One of these days," Bundini said to his boss, "we're goin' to find out which one of us is crazy. I think it's you."

No longer empty, Ali and his traveling circus moved north.

They were seven weeks away from Sonny Liston in Lewiston, Maine.

CHAPTER SEVEN

"I Ain't Got Nothing Against Them Viet Cong"

WITH INSOUCIANCE BORN OF YOUTH, beauty, and damned near all the cockiness God ever gave a twenty-three-year-old athlete, Ali strolled into view of the ABC camera. He was wrapped in a white robe. At ringside, waiting to do his first national television interview with the new champion, Howard Cosell came to attention. It was May 22, 1965, at the Schine Inn, a roadside motel near Chicopee Falls. The Liston fight was three days off.

"Howard Cosell," Ali said, "the world's greatest newscaster. How ya feelin'?"

Originally scheduled for Boston in November 1964, the rematch was postponed by Ali's emergency surgery to repair a hernia. Promoters then backed out when closed-circuit television outlets reported possible boycotts of any fight involving Ali. He had twice failed to qualify for 1-A status. Though he had not said he wouldn't go into the army, he had come to be known as a draft dodger. With no big city eager to embrace Ali, the fight found a home in Lewiston, Maine, a depressed mill town that made available its high-school hockey arena.

"You're very kind, champ," Cosell said, "but let's get to cases. People are saying this is just an act, that deep inside you are scared, that Liston is better trained for this fight."

"If it's an act," Ali said, "just look at my record and see, have the other fights been acts?"

Silence from Cosell.

"Have they been acts?" Ali asked again.

"Not so far."

"Well, what makes you think I've been acting?"

Whereupon Ali turned to roar open-mouthed at Bundini Brown, "Aaaaarrrhh," and walked away from the laughing Cosell, who said, "And with that final stage of the act, we leave the heavyweight champion of the world, Muhammad Ali, or Cassius Clay, if you will."

The moment was entertaining. Egomaniacs at play: no heavyweight champion ever expressed self-adoration so openly, and no broadcaster ever so clearly was his subject's accomplice in mischief. ABC's cameras so loved Ali's face that they stayed fixed on it in full-frame close-ups and left Cosell's voice disembodied. Anyone who believed in modesty as a virtue and pride as a sin must have worried for the very souls of Muhammad Ali and Howard Cosell.

Others worried for their lives because of reports that a carload of black gunmen was on its way from New York to deliver vengeance in Malcolm X's name. The shooters would kill Ali, who had abandoned Malcolm X in his time of peril and need. The debonair publicist Harold Conrad invoked the name of Jack Ruby, who a year and a half earlier had put a bullet into the stomach of JFK's killer, Lee Harvey Oswald: "People wanted to see another Ruby. If they thought there'd be an assassination in the ring, you could sell a million tickets." The columnist Jimmy Cannon wrote that plainclothes police officers said some of Malcolm X's hotbloods were "missing from their usual haunts." At roadblocks, blacks were searched. Some sportswriters believed it might not be a good idea to be at ringside. As in Las Vegas two years earlier when Liston threatened Ali in a casino, Conrad looked upon Ali in Maine and again decided: "He was scared shitless."

No death car delivered killers to Maine, or at least the killers never did their work. The fight went off without a hitch, except that the fight itself achieved the near impossible feat of being more bizarre than the first. Ali knocked Liston down in the first round with a short right-hand punch to the top of his head. As Liston reclined on the canvas, Ali demanded he get up and fight or people would think it was another fix. Of the estimated 2,500 witnesses in half-filled St. Dominic's Arena, most agreed with Ali. They chanted, "Fix . . . Fix . . . Fix."

Cosell saw Liston leave the ring and remarked on the beaten man's "look of absolute relief." At a press conference, Cosell bulled his way to the stage alongside Ali, who said the decisive punch had been "the anchor punch" once used by Jack Johnson, who "took it to the graveyard with him." He said he learned it from Stepin Fetchit, the sixty-year-old actor. "It's a snap punch," Ali said. "You can't see it, but if you hit by it, you all be knocked out."

Cosell reported a scene of "bedlam, chaos, and confusion." A man could practice law forever without hearing that Stepin Fetchit resurrected Jack Johnson's anchor punch from the graveyard for use by a Black Muslim against the forehead of a mob leg-breaker who took it as signal to find a soft place to lie down. At Ali's mention of Stepin Fetchit, Cosell said nothing. Stepin Fetchit? Whose life's work in Hollywood had been the exploitation and perpetuation of a stereotype of black men as subservient, ignorant, and cowardly? Yes, that Stepin Fetchit stood alongside Ali, the living symbol of black defiance and aspiration. Cosell finally retrieved the ability to speak. "If boxing can survive this," he said, "it can survive anything."

Sonji Ali had slipped the curly-headed kid from Boston five dollars to smuggle cigarettes to her hotel room in Auburn, Maine. Mike Marley was thirteen years old, a latchkey kid whose divorced parents only sometimes knew his whereabouts. He was the founder and president of the International Cassius Clay Fan Club. He advertised in one of the boxing magazines, charging five dollars for a membership and a monthly newsletter entitled *The Louisville Lip*. The *Lip* featured stories by nine sportswriters (Marley under nine noms de plume). He was in Maine because Ali had given him two ringside tickets. They had met in Boston when the kid went to Ali's hotel, used a house phone to ask for Cassius Clay, and next heard the fighter say, "Hello."

Rather than introduce himself, the kid did Ali's voice as he had learned it from a record album, "I am the greatest! I want the big, ugly bear. If he wants to go to heaven, he will fall in seven!"

"Hey, you a white boy," Ali said, "or a little colored boy?"

"I happen to be white," Marley said, "and if that matters, I can hang up right now."

"No, don't hang up, man. You're that kid that's been sending me all those letters with the fan club. Come see me at the hotel tomorrow."

Next thing the kid knew, he was at a press conference with Ali's arm around him. He told reporters he started the Cassius Clay Fan Club for three reasons: "Number one, his fighting ability. Number two, personality. Most of all, his *humility.*"

Marley solved the problem of how a prepubescent boy gets from Boston to Maine by asking around until a man said, "Come with us, kid. I'm Diamond Jim. These are my ladies." Marley had the back seat of the Eldorado Cadillac to himself. The ladies rode up front with Diamond Jim. When someone told the kid he had ridden all that way with a pimp and his prostitutes, young Mike Marley's adult education began.

The night of the fight, Marley hung near ringside, a kid with a ticket but too thrilled to sit down. He didn't see the knockout punch, but he caught up to Bundini Brown in the victory melee and soon enough the kid who rode to Maine in a pimp's Cadillac was on a school bus with Muhammad Ali and his entourage returning to their hotel in Auburn. Marley had never seen so many people so happy. Ali began singing a song his friend Sam Cooke had done. He sang "Stand by Me."

That night in the hotel courtyard, Jerry Izenberg saw Ali carrying on in celebration with Nation members and men from his fight camp. From a second-floor balcony, Sonji Ali leaned over a railing and called to Ali, "Come upstairs." The men said they didn't want him to leave. Two or three sat on the stairs and didn't move. Izenberg thought, *There's a tug of war going on.* It went on for five minutes, Ali starting to move, the men asking by their body language that he stay with them. Finally, Ali looked up at his wife and said, "Go to bed."

Less than a month later, on June 23, Ali wanted out of the marriage. He first sought a money-saving annulment on grounds that his wife had reneged on promises to adhere to tenets of his religion. He wound up with a divorce that gave her fifteen thousand dollars a year for ten years. Ali sent Sonji a note saying, "You traded heaven for hell, baby." Sonji Ali agreed that there had been a trade, only it had been a trade of marriage for life. She later told Bob Lipstye that the Nation of Islam had stolen her man's mind and spirit. "I wasn't going to take on all the Muslims," she said. "If I had, I'd probably have ended up dead."

To create starshine of his own, Cosell transformed himself in the aftermath of the Lewiston fight from professional broadcaster to a new kind of media creature. He became a journalist/carnival barker reporting the news even as he invited rubes inside the tent to see a new kind of heavyweight champion. That was clear two days before Ali's second defense of the title, against Floyd Patterson on November 22, 1965. As Ali walked into Cosell's camera shot, he said, "Well, if it's not the wonderful, miraculous, gifted one, Howard Cosell, how ya feelin'?"

"You're very kind, Muhammad," Cosell said. "It's interesting to watch you work out, m'boy. I hope that you're ready to hit Patterson with a punch that everybody in the house can see."

Journalists may "hope" for an outcome, but they do not announce it. Shills do both. Shills also stoop to race-based controversy to create attention. Patterson already had infuriated Ali by saying he wanted to regain the championship for Christianity. Now Cosell said to Ali, "Privately, you've confided that Patterson has been 'the white hope' to the country. Do you still believe that?"

"That's right," Ali said to Cosell. "He's a technicolor white hope."

For twelve rounds, Ali beat Patterson so badly that Cosell, in his postfight journalist persona, asked why Ali punished a man who during the fight had incurred a back injury. "I want to know why," Cosell said, "you weren't more aggressive when you had the boy so bombed out? . . . You carried the boy."

"Well, yes, I would say so. . . . I boxed him, but I didn't throw it too hard. I'd rather for you to talk about me carrying a man than killing him."

The truth was, Ali had tortured Patterson for his denigration of the Nation of Islam. Cosell touched that indirectly with a comment to Ali on religion: "People feel you've provided a very bad image for boxing because of your religion, very honestly, it's the minority group you belong to."

Ali said, "That couldn't be a bad image because most fighters in the past, in Jack Johnson and Jack Dempsey days, you see the fighters come in bars with two blondes on each arm, run the bars, be training on drinking beer, and many in all types of scandals and morals and all type. I'm not a person who's involved in none of these. I'm strictly a religion person who professes belief in the religion of Islam that is recognized by four hundred million people or more, and I don't see why this would make me bad. I'm not into the racial disturbance you see today, such as force myself on people, leading marches. I don't see where I'm such a bad champion."

"You don't see where some people could accuse the Muslim group of being a hate group?" Cosell said.

"No, sir. No, sir."

"You've never seen any evidence of this?"

"You haven't, either. You can't find nowhere in history, or the present, when you can be justified in saying the followers of the Most Honorable Elijah Muhammad is a hate group. We are the victims of hate. Black people in America are the victims of hate. We cannot be taught to hate. If a person can be here for four hundred years, suffering what the American so-called Negroes have suffered—the murders that was just committed in the South, and thirty or forty of our people were just shot down in the streets of Los Angeles by army equipment and war equipment—I don't think you can call us haters because we want to separate from these people who are continuing in doing this. This is just good. A man's a fool if he don't want to."

Shamefully, the broadcaster who boasted of his journalistic bona fides only listened to Ali's monologue defending Elijah Muhammad and portraying the Nation of Islam as a peace-loving group. Cosell could have questioned Ali on Malcolm X's assassination and Leon 4X Ameer's death. He might have asked how Ali could espouse faith in a religious sect that appeared to sanction savage beating and murder.

Instead, Cosell asked nothing. He ended the interview by playfully touching a fist against Ali's chin and delivering a shill's set-up line, "Documentarily, in your opinion, you are the greatest. Is that true?"

"Howie, you're the greatest, also," Ali said.

Cosell thanked him, smiled, well pleased, and said, "I guess we get arguments from a lot of people on both statements."

Two months later, Bob Lipsyte interrupted his vacation in the Florida Keys to spend an afternoon with Ali. It was February 17, 1966. He found Ali in a lawn chair under a palm tree by his small, gray cement house in North Miami. Children were coming home from school. Ali called out to one, "Hey, little girl in the high-school sweater, you not gonna pass me by today."

"Hi, Cassius, how you been?"

"Fine. Whatcha learn in school today?"

A phone call inside the house took Ali away from the children gathered on the lawn. When he came back, Ali was angry, bewildered. "Why me? I can't understand it," he said. "How did they do this to me—the heavyweight champion of the world?"

A reporter had asked Ali's reaction to a government decision that made him eligible to be drafted by the U.S. Army. Once, Ali had been ready to serve. The *Louisville Courier-Journal* of March 24, 1963, reported that Ali "expected to be called up next year for armed forces duty. He is inclined, now, to serve for two years and get it over with, rather than take a six-month hitch and attend Reserve meetings once a week for some years." But early in 1964, the month before the first Liston fight, Ali failed the army's mental examination and was classified 1-Y, unfit for military duty. He scored sixteen when a passing mark was thirty. He couldn't handle questions such as: "A shopkeeper divided a number by 3.5 when the number should have been multiplied by 4.5. His answer is 3. What should the correct answer be? (a) 5.25 (b) 10.50 (c) 15.75 (d) 47.25."

Retested two months later, under observation to see if he had failed on purpose, he again was classified 1-Y. "I said I was the greatest, not the smartest," he told reporters. After the test, he lay on a couch at home in Louisville and told *Courier-Journal* reporter Larry Boeck, "That test was tough. But I did my best—I don't want anybody to think I'm crazy." Math eluded him. "One went like this: There are twelve bushels of apples. They cost ten dollars each. You buy them, but before you do, you take out a third of apples out of each bushel. How much do you pay for the apples? After scratching around ten or fifteen minutes, I think I got the answer. But then a guy came by, took that test out of my hand, and gave me another one. When I looked down on the test he took from me, there still was a long row of questions I didn't answer."

Now that test didn't matter. With war in Vietnam raging, the government said standards had been lowered to bring in more soldiers. A score of fifteen made a candidate 1-A. As Lipsyte watched, television trucks arrived at Ali's little rental house in North Miami. Ali once shouted, "I've got a question. For two years the government caused me international embarrassment, letting people think I was a nut. Sure it bothered me, and my mother and father suffered, and now they jump up and make me 1-A without even an official notification or a test. Why did they let me be considered a nut, an illiterate, for two years?"

An interviewer's suggestion that Ali might be called to service within weeks set him off again. "How can they do this without another test to see if I'm any wiser or worser than last time? Why are they so anxious, why are they gunning for me? All those thousands of young men who are 1-A in Louisville, and I don't think they need but thirty, and they have to go to two-year-old files to seek me out."

Lipsyte heard Ali humming Bob Dylan's "Blowin' in the Wind," a song with a lyric asking, "Yes, 'n' how many deaths will it take till he knows/That too many people have died?" Nation bodyguards and friends rattled Ali's cage with dire descriptions of the army's racial discrimination. One said Ali wouldn't get through basic training because some fat cracker sergeant gonna blow him up on the hand-grenade range. Ali got busy thinking up reasons he shouldn't have to go. "They are going to draft me because I am a Muslim," he said. All those baseball, football, basketball players—and they pick on the *only* heavyweight champion? He called President Lyndon B. Johnson a wise man. "Maybe he will see what is happening and call up a few people and change this." Ali said he was always asked why he wouldn't fight for his country. "I want to say I have been fighting for my country for six years. In the ring." He said that from his fight earnings he paid fifteen million dollars in taxes, enough to pay two thousand soldiers and buy two jet bombers.

The longer he ranted, the bigger the numbers became. "Why are they so anxious to pay me eighty dollars a month when the government is in trouble financially? I think it costs them twelve million dollars a day to stay in Vietnam. I buy a lot of bullets, at least three jet bombers a year, and pay the salary of fifty thousand fighting men with the money they take from me after my fights." Soon enough, practically every reporter who ever wanted to ask Ali a question about Vietnam showed up in the yard.

How do you feel about the war in Vietnam?

"I don't know nothing about Vietnam."

Do you know where Vietnam is?

"It's out there somewhere. I don't know."

Are you a hawk? . . . Are you a dove? . . . Is it a just war?

Questions piled up with no answers. Either Ali didn't want to say what he thought, or he didn't know what he thought. One reporter sensed that Ali simply had no clue about the war although it had been on every front page and every newscast every day for the past year and a half. So he asked Ali, "What do you think about the Viet Cong?"

The fighter knew he didn't want to go to Vietnam, wherever it was.

Taking him into the army wasn't fair, not after they'd already told everybody he was too dumb. Now, all day, reporters kept asking what he thought about the army and about Vietnam. He didn't know what he thought. Only they wouldn't stop asking. Now they wanted to know—what? What he thought about the Viet Cong? Lipsyte suspected a government vendetta to punish Ali for transgressions against the Establishment. Otherwise, after two years, why suddenly reclassify him 1-A? Lipsyte thought, *It's all coming down on him. He's being fucked over. He doesn't know if he'll ever box again. Some cracker sergeant might blow him up first. This isn't boxing or the mothership. This is serious shit.* And someone asked, again, what about the Viet Cong?

Lipsyte saw Ali tired and exasperated, angry and betrayed, finally blurting out an answer, "I ain't got nothing against them Viet Cong."

On March 29, 1966, Ali was asked if he would follow other young men of draft age moving to Canada out of the Selective Service's reach. "People can't chase me out of my birth country," he said. "I believe what I believe, and you know what that is. If I have to go to jail, I'll do it, but I'm not leaving my country to live in Canada."

Jerry Izenberg asked, "How do you think it will come out?"

"Who knows?" Ali said. "Look what they done to sweet baby Jesus."

Ali appealed the draft reclassification on grounds that he was a conscientious objector. On August 23, 1966, a special officer appointed by the U.S. Department of Justice conducted a hearing. Judge Lawrence Grauman, a veteran of Kentucky courts, heard testimony from Ali, his lawyer, his parents, Odessa and Cassius Clay, Sr., a Nation of Islam representative, and four Louisville residents who had long associations with Ali. Judge Grauman also had a report from the Federal Bureau of Investigation and thirty-four signed witness statements.

"Mrs. Clay is a Baptist," the judge's report said, "and appears to be a conscientious, sincere person who is much disturbed by her son's affiliation with the Muslim faith. She testified that her son had stated that he would die for his religion." Cassius Sr. said the same thing. One witness testified to Ali's sincerity, but in the FBI report the same witness was also skeptical of Ali's conviction on anything and said he would not be surprised "if a year from now the registrant becomes disenchanted with the Muslims and voluntarily joins the United States Marines."

Ali told Judge Grauman, "Sir, I said earlier and I'd like to again make that plain, it would be no trouble for me to go into the Armed Services, boxing exhibitions in Vietnam or traveling the country at the expense of the Government or living the easy life and not having to get out in the mud and fight and shoot. If it wasn't against my conscience to do it, I would easily do it. I wouldn't raise all this court stuff and I wouldn't go through all of this and lose the millions that I gave up and my image with the American public that I would say is completely dead and ruined because of us in here now. I wouldn't jeopardize my life walking the streets of the South and all of America with no bodyguard if I wasn't sincere in every bit of what the Holy Qur'an and the teachings of the Honorable Elijah Muhammad tell us and it is that we are not to participate in wars on the side of nonbelievers, and this is a Christian country and this is not a Muslim country. We are not, according to the Holy Qur'an, to even as much as aid in passing a cup of water to the wounded. I mean, this is the Holy Qur'an, and as I said earlier, this is not me talking to get the draft board or to dodge nothing. This is there before I was born and it will be there when I'm dead and we believe in not only part of it, but all of it."

Grauman's decision was a surprise. He reported to Justice: "After very thorough consideration, the Hearing Officer is of the opinion that the registrant (Ali) is not a hypocrite or a faker with reference to his conscientious objection claim. The Hearing Officer is constrained to the view that the registrant is sincere in objecting, on religious grounds, to participation in war in any form."

Cosell and Ali were in this together. In May 1966, Cosell began an interview, "Muhammad Ali, also known as Cassius Clay . . ." Ali stopped him. "Howard, are you going to do that to me, too?" Taken aback, Cosell said, "You are quite right. I apologize. Muhammad Ali is your name. You're entitled to that." He would not question him on some real issues. But he would use the man's chosen name. He had chosen sides, if implicitly, in those arguments about race, religion, politics, and war that were dividing Americans' opinions on Ali.

In February 1967, Cosell came as near to expressing those opinions on the air as he ever would. It happened during an interview that was as unprecedented as the men themselves, at once combative and comic. They were to review Ali's recent fifteen-round victory over number-one challenger Ernie Terrell. As he had done to Patterson, Ali punished Terrell for criticizing his religion and opposition to the Vietnam War. He also called him Clay. Though Ali quickly caused Terrell's eyes to swell nearly shut, he had no interest in ending the fight. As he threw the occasional uncontested punch, he shouted at the blinded fighter, "What's my name? What's my name?"

The performance provoked newspaper columnists into vitriolic attacks. Ali, sitting with Cosell on *Wide World of Sports,* said he talked to Terrell because "my blood was hot, and I'm a warrior, I'm a fighter. Kinda hard to hold me down when I get hot."

No, Cosell said, it was more than that, it was "your behavior pattern . . . the cruelty in your eyes, the malice in your voice."

"I'm out to be cruel, that's what the boxing game is about," Ali said. "He's out to beat me. I'm out to beat him. And as far as the fight being cruel, the referee has authority to stop it if it's so cruel, the judges have the authority to stop it if it's so cruel, the doctor who was in the corner after each round has the authority to stop it if it's so cruel. If I had stopped it, it wouldn't be legal. I would have lost."

Cosell started a question with the condescending preamble, "You are not a stupid boy . . ."

Ali interrupted. "Thank you, Howard. You're not as dumb as you look." Then: "If you defended me like you usually do, you will catch criticism, too."

Cosell said, "I have never defended you," a curious thing to be said by a man who had put himself on Ali's side a dozen times. And he added, "I have never gone against you."

"This time," Ali said, "you haven't said nothing."

"I think the pictures speak for themselves."

Ali continued. "And I think I understand why."

Ali's implication was that Cosell had caved in to that segment of the public that reviled Ali for his religion and his refusal to accept the draft. That accusation hurt Cosell, who stumbled awkwardly through his next three sentences. He said to Ali, "I don't see that a man's privacy of worship and his right to his own religion or a man's utilization of due process with regard to his military posture before the government—I don't see that they're involved. And nobody has said they're involved. The press hasn't said they are."

Cleverly and subtly, Ali had raised the issues without saying the words. Cosell, feeling attacked on principle, could not let it pass. In his clumsy way, Cosell affirmed on national television for the first time his belief that Ali had the right to his religion and the right to legal defense against the draft.

Ali then said, "All I have to say is, if I'm going to be judged by the press, mostly white people, not the Negro, then I think if I'm going to be judged for talking to a man, you would be awful awful guilty for the things you've been doing every day and have been doing every day for four hundred years to the so-called Negro in America."

Cosell, still defending himself, said, "The test of a man's courage is not necessarily his willingness to support you. Do you understand that?"

Yes, and Ali also understood that it was time to get funny on whether or not he understood Cosell. "Well, I'm trying to. Your words are so large. I didn't finish, go to college, and I don't understand the meaning of the big words you're talking."

"Yes, but as I said, you're not a stupid boy." Then he, too, changed the subject. "Now, one final question. I'm not sure there's anybody left for you to fight."

Ali's eyes twinkled. "You."

Cosell smiled. "That may come about someday."

"Stay in shape."

A month later, at a Madison Square Garden weigh-in, Cosell remarked on Ali's confidence going into a fight against Zora Folley. Ali the ticket-seller snapped, "I'm always confident, my image is being confident, why you trying to make it look like something new for? I'm always confident I can whip all of 'em."

Cosell laughed. "You're being extremely truculent."

Not missing a beat, Ali said, "Whatever 'truculent' means, if that's good, I'm that."

The U.S. Justice Department ignored its special-hearing officer's finding and recommended that the Louisville draft board deny Ali's appeal. The word from Justice came over the signature of T. Oscar Smith, Chief—Conscientious Objector Section. The order to report for induction came to Ali shortly before he fought Zora Folley in New York on March 22, 1967.

For Gordon Davidson, the lawyer representing the eleven-man Louisville Sponsoring Group that guided Ali's early career, proof of his sincerity came that week. Angelo Dundee had called Davidson with the news that Ali intended to refuse induction. "My God," Davidson said, "don't do anything until I can get there." Ali's hotel suite was filled with Fruit of Islam bodyguards in black suits, bow ties, and stone faces. The fighter, the lawyer, and Dundee went to a back bedroom where Davidson said to Ali, "Look, we've never interfered in your personal life. And we're not doing it now. But I feel both as a lawyer and a friend of yours, that before you make this decision, let me point out a few things. On my desk right now, there must be a million dollars' worth of contracts. Endorsements, public appearances. But they're going to be pulled if you do this. Plus, who knows what it'll do to your boxing career?"

Davidson said arrangements had been made with the National Guard, the Army reserve, the Coast Guard, and the Naval Reserve for him to fulfill his military obligation without facing combat. "Even if you go in the army," Davidson told Ali, "you're going to do a Joe Louis. Do exhibitions for the troops. You'll do this good stuff, like Joe Louis, DiMaggio, the movie stars. Muhammad, nobody's going to shoot at you."

Ali thanked him. "But I gotta tell you, Gordon, I'm not gonna go. My religion won't allow it."

Davidson added it up. Ali had refused respectable alternatives. Walked away from a million dollars. Gave up the heavyweight championship and however many more millions that meant. Faced five years in a federal penitentiary. Was ready to be the most reviled celebrity in America. "Well, okay," Davidson said. "That's it."

That week at Madison Square Garden, Ali sat for a radio interview with a twenty-year-old student from Columbia University. Thomas Hauser used a reel-to-reel recorder to tape interviews for his show, *Personalities in Sports*, carried on the school's student station, WKCR. He asked Ali, "What will you do if your final appeals fall through and you're drafted? Will you then resist going into the army?"

Ali said, "I haven't been drafted yet. My appeals haven't run out. . . . So it wouldn't be respectful to make a decision or say anything on this radio show. But the world knows that I am a Muslim. The world knows that I'm a sincere follower to death of Elijah Muhammad. And we say five times a day in our prayers, 'My prayers, my sacrifices, my life, and my death are all for Allah.' I repeat, 'My prayers, my sacrifices, my life, and my death are all for Allah.' This is what I sincerely believe. I've upheld my faith through the past years. I gave up one of the prettiest Negro women in the country; cost me $150,000 in alimony. This was all controversy and publicity before the draft started. The white businessmen of Louisville, Kentucky, will tell you that I've turned down eight million dollars in movie contracts, recordings, promotions, and advertisements because of my faith. So I don't see why I should break the rules of my faith now."

As for the "eight million dollars" turned down: The lawyer Davidson put the number at one million, with another two million not turned down but lost because of Ali's connection to the Black Muslims. As for the rules of his faith, they seemed uncertain. Ali insisted they precluded participation in war unless declared by Allah. But the August 26, 1966, edition of *Muhammad Speaks* reported: "We do not believe this nation should force us to take part in such wars, for we have nothing to gain from it unless America agrees to give us the necessary territory wherein we may have something to fight for."

Elijah Muhammad himself was a draft resister during World War II. But he never made a religious claim against military duty. He simply refused to fight a war for the white-devil Americans. FBI surveillance also suggested that Muhammad collaborated with Japanese warlords inside the United States. He was arrested and indicted on sedition charges as well as for failure to register for the draft. FBI agents reported that they traced Muhammad to his mother's house in Chicago and found him under her bed inside a rolled-up carpet.

Just after eleven o'clock the night before he fought Folley, Ali asked Sugar Ray Robinson to come to his hotel. There was something in Ali's voice. So the man he called "the king, the master, my idol" stopped by Loew's Midtown Motor Inn, on Eighth Avenue across from the old Madison Square Garden. Ali told Sugar Ray, "It's the Army."

"What about the Army?"

"They want me—soon."

"I know that," Robinson said.

"But I can't go."

"You've got to go."

"No," Ali said. "Elijah Muhammad told me that I can't go."

"What do you mean, you *can't* go?"

Ali sat on the room's bed, eyes down. "That's what he told me."

"I don't care what Muhammad told you," Robinson said. He told Ali he'd go to jail, lose the championship, would never fight again. "Do you realize that you're forfeiting your entire career?"

"Well, Muhammad told me."

Robinson said it would be Ali alone going to jail, not the Muslim leaders. "You must live by the law," he said.

"But I'm afraid, Ray, I'm real afraid."

"Afraid of what? Afraid of the Muslims if you don't do what they told you?"

No answer came from Ali, and Robinson said, "Now, look, Cassius. I told you what I think. That's all I can do for you." As Robinson left, he shook hands with Ali. He saw tears in the kid's eyes.

April 26, 1967, was a gray, damp morning in Chicago, two days before Ali was to be in Houston for his induction into the army. He sat with Bob Lipsyte in the coffee shop of the Lake Motel. "I don't want to go to jail," Ali said, "but I've got to live the life my conscience and my God tell me to. What does it profit me to be the wellest-liked man in America who sold out everybody?"

He envisioned—and feared—widespread repercussions from his decision. "My case is just revealing so much, shaking the black man's confidence in the white liberals. But I'm taking no credit as a leader. They're not going to make no Malcolm X out of me. If they make you a leader, they can catch you up."

Lipsyte's friend, the journalist Nicholas von Hoffman, wondered why Ali didn't just do the celebrity tour of duty, "give exhibitions and teach physical fitness."

"What can you give me, America, for turning down my religion? You want me to do what the white man says and go fight a war against some people I don't know nothing about, get some freedom for some other people when my own can't get theirs here?"

The more people, mostly white men, who stopped by Ali's table to wish him well, the lighter his mood became, even playful, his voice deep now: "Ah-lee will return. My ghost will haunt all arenas. The people will watch the fights and they will whisper, 'Hey, Ali could whip that guy.' . . . 'You think so?' . . . 'Sure.' . . . 'No, he couldn't.' . . . Twenty-five years old now. Make my comeback at twenty-eight. That's not old. Whip 'em all—if I get good food in jail."

He recited a new poem:

Two thousand years from now,
Muhammad Ali, Muhammad Ali,
He roamed the Western Hemisphere,
He was courageous and strong,
He called the round when the clown hit the ground,
Tell little children whatever they believe,
Stand up like Muhammad Ali.

The next day he flew to Houston.

The Ali story had outgrown sports. Now it belonged to the front pages and the network news divisions. ABC sent diplomatic correspondent John Scali to Houston to cover Ali's appearance at the armed forces induction center. Working with Cosell, Scali was to produce a special titled, *The Champ: Count Me Out.* Cosell's assignment: Take a film crew, live with Ali through the process, and return to New York with the footage.

The night of April 27, 1967, Cosell for the first time found Ali unwilling to be interviewed. The broadcaster talked his way into Ali's room at Houston's Hotel America, where Ali lay in bed watching Johnny Carson's television show. "What are you going to do, Champ?" Cosell asked. "You going to refuse to take the step?" *Take the step.* When called for service at an induction center, draftees stepped across a yellow line indicating acceptance of military duty.

"Can't tell you a thing," Ali said. "I'm under orders not to talk to nobody. I only let you into the room because it's you."

For Cosell, refusal was the beginning of negotiation. "But I have a camera crew and I have to spend the whole day with you. I must have assurances that you will talk to me."

"I'm under orders. Talk to nobody. You won't get a word out of me."

Cosell became Cosell by getting a million words out of Muhammad Ali. He believed Ali was unable to remain silent. He said, "What if I get a crew over here right now, Champ? Just shoot you on the night before—"

"No, absolutely no. Not a word."

He did persuade Ali to call Herbert Muhammad. When Cosell divined that the conversation was going against him, he took the phone himself and said, "Herbert, I think . . ."

Herbert stopped him. "Absolutely not, not a single word. It's Elijah's dictates and that's it."

From Chicago, the Messenger had ordered Ali's silence. Cosell knew defeat when he saw it. "See you tomorrow," he said. Ali nodded. Not a word.

The media had been all over the case, often presenting speculation as fact, even in the *New York Times*. The newspaper of record's sports columnist, Arthur Daley, wrote that Ali "has been so thoroughly brainwashed that he now believes what he says even if the words are put into his mouth by the Muslims."

Because nothing of consequence happened to high-profile members of the Nation of Islam without Elijah Muhammad's approval, it was reasonable to think Ali had refused the draft for the same reason he refused to speak to Cosell. It was "Elijah's dictates." Even as Herbert Muhammad insisted to the media that his father had not ordered Ali's decision, privately he reminded Ali that Elijah had gone to jail rather than serve in the army during World War II. The FBI's story that it came to arrest the Messenger and found him wrapped in a carpet under his mother's bed—Herbert didn't pass that along to Ali.

Ali's mother called from Louisville and said, "Gee Gee, do the right thing. If I were you, I would go ahead and take the step. If I were you, I would join the army. Do you understand me, son?"

"Mama, I love you," he said. "Whatever I do, Mama, remember I love you."

She began to cry, and Ali said he would call back when it was done.

By April 1967, thirteen thousand Americans had been killed in Vietnam. Thirty thousand men a month were drafted. On the morning of April 28 in Houston, at 701 Jacinto Avenue, Ali left a taxi and hurried toward a federal building and the U.S. Armed Forces Examining and Entrance Station.

From behind, Ali heard that familiar voice.

"Are you going to take the step, Muhammad?"

It was Cosell, microphone raised.

Again. "Are you going—to take—the step?"

Ali smiled. "Howard Cosell—why don't *you* take the step?"

Cosell said, "I did. In 1942."

The morning Ali and Cosell did their act on the federal building steps, a general of the army told the U.S. Senate Foreign Relations Committee, "American forces will prevail in Vietnam over the Communist aggressor." The day before, that same general, William Westmoreland, commander of U.S. forces in Vietnam, complained that protesters and "unpatriotic acts at home" encouraged the enemy to keep fighting. The general did not mention the truth that the Vietnamese led by Ho Chi Minh needed no encouragement. By then they had been waging guerrilla war against assorted opponents for almost twenty years. Ho had defined the nature and accurately predicted the outcome of an earlier conflict with France's colonial forces: "If ever the tiger [his army] pauses, the elephant [France] will impale him on his mighty tusks. But the tiger will not pause, and the elephant will die of exhaustion and loss of blood." Like Muhammad Ali in the ring, Ho Chi Minh in war was as yet undefeated.

Ali came to Room 1B in the federal building where Lieutenant Steven S. Dunkley stood at a rostrum with American flags behind him. "Attention," the lieutenant called out to forty-six men, "you are about to be inducted into the Armed Forces of the United States, in the Army, the Navy, the Air Force or the Marine Corps. . . . You will take one step forward as your name and service are called and such step will constitute your induction into the Armed Forces indicated."

Jason Adams, Army, stepped forward, as did Luis Cerrato, Army, and then Dunkley said, "Cassius Clay—Army."

When Ali did not move, the lieutenant ordered all other draftees from the room and said, "Cassius Clay, will you please step forward and be inducted into the Armed Forces of the United States."

Again, he did not move.

He was told: *Refusal is a criminal act. You could go to jail for five years. There could be a ten-thousand-dollar fine. Do you want a second chance?*

"Thank you, sir, but I don't need it."

To fulfill the legal requirements of the moment, the induction officer one more time invited the draftee to step forward. Ali still did not move, and an officer said, "Please give us in writing your reason for refusal."

Ali wrote, "I refuse to be inducted into the armed forces of the United States because I claim to be exempt as a minister of the religion of Islam."

Boxing officials already had made noises about taking away the heavy-weight championship. Ali knew, too, that of the many ways he had offended mainstream America, refusing military duty in a time of war was the least defensible. That offense was made more profound by Ali's claim of conscientious objection. Who could believe that? He was a member of the Nation of Islam, a cult whose most charismatic figure, Malcolm X, had preached violence, had celebrated Kennedy's assassination, and had died by violence that was condoned by the sect's leader, Elijah Muhammad. Besides, Ali was no Zen Buddhist meditating in search of peace; he was a professional prizefighter paid to scramble other men's brains. Conscientious objection based on his work as a minister was seen as legal gobbledygook invented only because he could not gain exemption for political and personal reasons. The political reason: He refused the draft in protest of the white-man devil's racism that denied freedom to black Americans. His personal reason was more coldly practical, suggested once as he waited to go on Jack Paar's *Tonight* show and asked Vietnam veterans there that night, "How bad it hurt when bullets hit you?"

As Ali left the courthouse that day, he again heard that voice.

"Look, Muhammad," Cosell said, "I want to drive back to the hotel with you." He would acquiesce in not doing an interview of Ali, but they would sit together and he would read on the air a statement from Ali.

"You'll get me in terrible trouble," Ali said.

"It's just ridiculous for you to go on this way."

Ali said, "I'll do it."

In the lobby of Ali's hotel, the fighter sat stone-faced alongside Cosell as the broadcaster read from a statement written by lawyers in Ali's name.

" . . . I strongly object to the fact that so many newspapers have given the American public and the world the impression that I have only two alternatives in taking this stand: Either I go to jail or go in the army. There is another alternative and that alternative is justice. If justice prevails, if my constitutional rights are upheld, I will be forced to go neither to the army nor jail. In the end, I am confident that justice will come my way for the truth must eventually prevail.

"I am looking forward to immediately continuing my profession. As to the threat voiced by certain elements to strip me of my title, this is merely a continuation of the same artificially induced prejudice and discrimination . . ."

When Cosell finished reading, he asked Ali, "Is there anything else you want to say at this time?"

"No."

"You're satisfied that this is a fair representation of your position?"

"Yes."

It was the shortest Ali-Cosell interview ever. Two words from the fighter.

Then, off-camera, Ali said, "I may have talked too much."

"If you did, Muhammad, it will be one helluva scoop."

The New York State Athletic Commission immediately announced that it had "unanimously decided to suspend Clay's boxing license indefinitely and to withdraw recognition of him as World Heavyweight Champion." New York chairman Edwin Dooley said Ali's "refusal to enter the service is regarded by the Commission to be detrimental to the best interests of boxing." Immediately, other boxing commissions fell in line.

Boxing's sudden claim to purity would have been laughable had it not been illegal. The sport's officials took away Ali's right to work, a naked violation of the U.S. Constitution's Fourteenth Amendment protection against the loss of life, liberty, or property without due process of law. In Ali's case, due process hadn't been started, let alone exhausted.

Back in his hotel room, Ali made a telephone call to Louisville.

"Mama," he said, "I'm all right. I did what I had to do. I sure am looking forward to coming home to eat some of your cooking."

That day, six men met for drinks at the Lion's Head bar in New York's Greenwich Village. They were Jack Newfield, a *Village Voice* reporter; novelists Norman Mailer and Frederick Exley; Jimmy Breslin, the *New York Post* columnist; Pete Hamill, of the *New York Daily News;* and George Plimpton, editor of the *Paris Review* and an Ali specialist for *Sports Illustrated.* One man present called it a gathering of "left-wing writers, alcoholics, and other bohemians." Naturally, they were in Ali's corner.

"Injustice on an historical scale," Newfield declared. No champion had ever lost his title except in the ring. The New York commission's move against Ali smacked of racism, xenophobia, jingoism, religious persecution, and political retribution. Plimpton's position expressed at the bar:

"Forget the war. We're all against it. It's just wrong to punish Ali for having the courage to take a stand." He also pointed out that the action was illegal: "Without so much as a hearing, Ali was dispossessed of what is his."

What this ad hoc Ali committee could do, its members had no idea. They knew only it needed to be done dramatically. Fair coverage of Ali and sympathetic support had come from Bob Lipsyte of the *Times*, Larry Merchant and Jerry Izenberg of the *New York Post*, and Stan Isaacs at Long Island's *Newsday*. But newspapermen might write for months without effect beyond the narrow borders of their circulation areas.

We need a national voice, someone said.

Someone else said, *How about Cosell?*

George, you know him, don't you?

The winter before, Plimpton had been a guest on Cosell's radio show, *Speaking of Everything*. The topic was *Paper Lion*, Plimpton's book about his participation in training camp and in an exhibition game with the Detroit Lions of the National Football League. Cosell declared it "literature of a salutary kind never before committed in the name of football." As the Ali committee's emissary to the West Sixty-sixth Street offices of ABC, Plimpton found Cosell in his little office seated at a desk with his back to a window. Plimpton began to explain his mission: "Ali has been unjustly treated and we believe voices should be raised . . ."

Here, Cosell put up a hand. "Let me articulate my position," he said. "Georgie-boy, I'd be *shot*, sitting right here in this armchair, by some crazed redneck sharpshooter over there in that building . . ." He motioned over his shoulder. His voice rose, as if broadcasting the assassination. " . . . if I deigned to say over the airwaves that Muhammad Ali should be completely absolved and allowed to return to the ring. I'd be *shot*—right through that window!"

Now, softly: "My sympathies are obviously with Muhammad. He has no greater friend among the whites . . ." The voice again rising: " . . . but the time, at this stage in this country's popular feeling, is not correct for such an act on my part."

"But, Howard, no one's going to shoot you from that building," Plimpton said. "That's the Bankers Trust."

"To begin with," Cosell said, "it's *not* the Bankers Trust. And secondly, I know whereof I speak. I would be *shot*, and right through this window. There is a time and place for everything, and this is not it. I am referring, of course, to the matter of Muhammad Ali's reinstatement, not to being shot from what you so incorrectly refer to as the Bankers Trust."

Jack Newfield had suggested contacting Cosell because he was "famous, powerful, television." It turned out that those were the reasons Cosell would not help. The idea of participation in an organized endorsement of Ali caused Cosell great anxiety. It might put his reputation and career at risk. He was a New York media star heard dozens of times weekly on local radio and television. His coverage of Ali for *Wide World of Sports* gave him a national profile. Yet Howard Cosell, né Howard Cohen, saw himself on the precipice of professional peril, a short step, or push, from plummeting into the abyss of anonymity. Being Cosell, he expressed his fear, even his cowardice, by insisting that he was a portrait in utter and indomitable courage.

"What more could I do, Georgie-boy, than what I have already done?" Cosell said. "I have consistently referred to him as Muhammad Ali, not Cassius Clay, and that is contribution to his cause greater than any made by any other journalist. In the end, this is a matter for adjudication by the courts, not by journalists, not even by those of us practiced at the law. You and your little committee are embarked on a quixotic journey against giants. It is certain to be as frustrating as it will be fruitless."

Reporting to the Lion's Head literati, Plimpton said Cosell rejected their invitation on the grounds that the committee's ideas were "absurd, amateurish, and impractical." And there was the matter of the Bankers Trust sniper.

PART TWO

Climbing

CHAPTER EIGHT

"We Don't Want to Live With the White Man"

THE MORNING AFTER HER SON refused to take the step, I found Odessa Clay in the yard behind the house Ali had bought for her and Cash in Louisville. She was hanging out clothes, towels, and sheets on a sagging rope line. She said she was tired and not feeling well and didn't want to talk about it. "Maybe tomorrow," she said, and I knew she wouldn't talk then. There was too much sadness in her sweet face.

I drove to 1823 West Broadway, an address where Louisville's white downtown merged with the black residential neighborhoods of the West End. There the fighter's father had opened a sign shop and art gallery. I found Cash sitting on the street curb, his legs under a pickup truck. On the truck's passenger-side door, he used red paint to fill in stenciled lines that spelled out RAY'S PLUMBING AND ROTO-ROOTER SERVICE. The first thing he said to me was, "Wouldn't you have done the same thing?"

I had expected the rogue to blame "them damned Muslims," his epithet for Elijah Muhammad and the Nation of Islam. Instead, he said, "I tried to talk Cassius out of the Muslim stuff at first. But it didn't do any good. Anyway, who am I to judge another man's religion? Maybe God sent those people. Maybe Cassius is the Messiah. Who can say? I was raised a Methodist. But now I go to all churches—Catholic, Presbyterian, Christian, all of them. I followed my mother's lead when I was a kid. Did what she told me and figured I'd be all right. Cassius doesn't listen, but then he's twenty-one. He has his religion and he lives by it. What he does now is up to him. Who am I say it isn't right?" Besides, he said, "No

119

young man just starting out wants to get killed—right? Some of them even leave America to avoid the draft. They go to Canada."

The *Courier-Journal* didn't send a reporter to Houston for the induction ceremony. It ran an Associated Press report on the front page. My four-hundred-word story appeared on the fourth sports page under the headline, "Cassius Sr. Won't Condemn Son."

Like almost everyone of my generation who met Ali, I was mesmerized. I was also confused. I knew little about the Nation of Islam, let alone why Ali embraced it. In my presence, he had been funny, courteous, kind, and charming. But now, on Broadway, I heard his father say the damndest thing. *Maybe Cassius is the Messiah.* Neither did I know what to make of Ali's religious rants. I had questions, such as: *He believes a big-headed scientist bred the white race to bedevil blacks? And a bomber mothership hovering over Earth will pull up 154,000 disciples on the last day? And Mississippi, Alabama, and Louisiana ought to be given to the Nation for the establishment of its own sovereign state? Separation of the races, now and forever?* The less I heard, the better I liked it. The problem was, he wouldn't shut up.

On June 20, 1967, a jury found Ali guilty of refusing the draft. During the jury's twenty-one minutes of deliberation, Ali sat in silence, subdued, doodling on a yellow legal pad. After the verdict was announced, he told the judge, "I'd appreciate it if the court would give me my sentence now instead of waiting and stalling." The law allowed a sentence of up to five years and a ten-thousand-dollar fine. U.S. Attorney Mort Susman told Judge Joe Ingraham the government would not object to a lesser sentence. He noted that Ali had no criminal record, and said that Ali's membership in the Nation of Islam began his troubles: "This tragedy and the loss of his title can be traced to that," largely because the Nation was "as much political as it is religious."

Despite that, Ingraham imposed the maximum sentence. He also ordered Ali's passport revoked, a routine procedure following conviction for a felony. But the passport was critical for an athlete who in 1966 fought four times outside the United States. Now, while free on appeal, Ali could not fight in the United States because every state boxing commission shut him out, and without a passport he could not fight abroad.

Later, after a hearing on the passport issue, Ali managed to make the five-year sentence the basis for a joke. He said he had imagined what it would be like in prison. In a deep, theatrically masculine voice, he spoke as if being interviewed: "Yes, I accept my punishment, and I will serve my time like the man I am." Now, he said, it's five years later and the same interviewer asks if he will fight again. This time Ali's answer came in a high, winsome twitter. He added the slightest swish of a wrist to the words: "Well, honey, I can't rightly say at this moment . . ."

On that yellow legal pad in the courtroom, Ali had drawn an airplane crashing into a mountain.

On August 17, 1967, Ali married a woman he had met in 1960 when she was a girl ten years old attending the Nation of Islam school in Chicago. Though Belinda Boyd heard her classmates cheer the Olympic champion Cassius Clay, the precocious fourth-grader lectured him: "Clay? Is that like dirt and mud? You don't know who you are." She had learned well her lessons on slavemaster names. They met again when she was sixteen, six feet tall, a worker in a Nation bakery, the strikingly beautiful daughter of a black army veteran and a Native American woman. Long since divorced from the anti-Muslim Sonji, Ali on their first date told Belinda they would get married. This time she cheered.

She told friends it was "a Cinderella story," that she and Muhammad were the Nation's version of royalty. She also said she had been instrumental in Ali's refusal to join the army: "Elijah Muhammad didn't tell him not to take the step forward. We were conscientious objectors. We didn't fight American wars. I was seventeen and I knew better than that. The Vietnamese didn't put names on us, didn't put chains on us, didn't harm us. Why fight people who didn't do anything to us? Ali, by hearing that, made his own decision." Belinda Ali had not seen Ali's legal-pad doodlings of a plane crash. But she soon lived the metaphor. Ali's fight purses had been divvied up so many ways that he did well to keep 10 percent. Money went to the Nation, to Herbert Muhammad, to Angelo Dundee, and to anyone who put a hand out to a young man who cared less about money than about pleasing people, even people who deserved no pleasing, even people naked in their larcenous intent. Before long, the royal couple dipped into Belinda's savings, fourteen thousand dollars set aside for college.

Money was only part of Ali's problems. What he needed most was what he had always needed: attention. One night in 1968, Belinda lay sleeping on a couch. She heard a noise and called out, "Ali?" It was two in the morning. "Ali, is that you?"

The heavyweight champion in exile stood above her with a man at his side.

"Look," Ali said. "Wyatt Earp!"

That night, somewhere in Chicago, Ali had met actor Hugh O'Brian, famous as television's version of Tombstone's gun-slingin' marshal. Presented with Marshal Earp, Belinda Ali said six words. They were, "What the hell? Let me sleep."

Ali's camp business manager, Gene Kilroy, had an idea to bring Ali notice and money. Kilroy and booking agent Richard Fulton set up a speaking tour. Appearances at Temple and Cheney universities in Pennsylvania earned Ali one thousand five hundred dollars. The idea was inspired in that it usually took Ali to predominantly white colleges where audiences likely would be friendly to anyone critical of both the Vietnam War and the draft. Young people distrusting their government wanted to hear from Ali, the antihero. They heard this on the war in Vietnam:

"I'm not going to help nobody get somethin' my Negroes don't have. If I'm gonna die, I'll die now, right here, fightin' you. If I'm gonna die. You my enemy. My enemy's the white people. Not the Viet Cong, the Chinese, Japanese. You my foes when I want freedom. You my foes when I want justice. You my foes when I want equality. You won't even stand up for me in America for my religious beliefs and you want me to go somewhere and fight but you won't even stand up for me here at home."

To Ali, all the bad stuff coming down on blacks was caused by white folks' devilry—though he insisted he did not hate them for it. "I don't hate nobody and I ain't lynched nobody. We Muslims don't hate the white man. It's like we don't hate a tiger; but we know that a tiger's nature is not compatible with people's nature since tigers love to eat people. So we don't want to live with tigers. It's the same with the white man. The white race attacks black people. They don't ask what's our religion, what's our belief? They just start whupping heads. They don't ask you, are you Catholic, are you a Baptist, are you a Black Muslim, are you a Martin Luther King follower, are you with Whitney Young? They just go whop, whop, whop! So we don't want to live with the white man; that's all."

In 1968, the second year of his exile, Ali said he did not need money: "Don't drink, don't smoke, don't go nowhere, don't go running with women. I take my wife out and we eat ice cream. My wife is such a good cook I never go to a restaurant. I give her twenty dollars for a whole week and it's enough for her. We can eat on three dollars a day. Look out there at that little robin pecking and eating. The Lord feeds the birds and the animals. If the Lord has this power, will the Lord let His servant starve, let a man who is doing His word go hungry? I'm not worried. The Lord will provide."

The Lord, perhaps, moved Ali to ask a New York radio interviewer for ten dollars that fall. Julius Lester said, "Don't have my wallet on me." He worked for WBAI, a small, listener-supported station, and had hurried over to the New York Hilton when someone told him Ali was in town. As the men met and moved through the lobby, no one seemed to recognize Ali. The radio man thought that odd, but no more odd than what came next.

Leaving an elevator, Ali shadow-boxed down a hallway to his room, exhaling mightily with each punch, as if to remind Lester, and perhaps himself, that here, in exile, hitting up a stranger for ten dollars, still the heavyweight champion of the world, was Muhammad Ali. They sat in Ali's small hotel room, the shades drawn, a bed unmade. Another man watched from a dark corner. He was not introduced. He did not speak. Ali was somber in talking about fruitless plans to resume his boxing career on Indian reservations, which were lands outside the jurisdiction of the U.S. government. When Ali turned to Nation of Islam rhetoric, he became so insistent and aggressive that Lester years later would say, "Ali tried to convert me."

Part sermon, part harangue, and part sociological claptrap, Ali's monologue began with commentary on money and respect, moved to the brainwashing of the public that he saw as self-evident in the naming of angel food and devil's food cake, and ended with a diatribe in opposition to interracial marriage. It was Ali talking to another black man in stern tones seldom heard from him among whites. Lester tape-recorded it for use on his radio show the next night, Ali saying:

"This is our trouble today. All the so-called Negroes worry about is money. He's like the white man now. He'll blow up his mama for some money. Sell out his people for some money. That's why we're nowhere today because all the big Negroes with money are up on the hill with the white folks, riding with the white folks, going to church with the white folks, *marrying* the white folks, shufflin' and tommin' and lovin' white folks. And they forget all about the brother down there in Harlem. His rent's due, living in a bad home, standin' on a corner, nobody know him, nobody want him, and he rides by in his limousine, 'Well, let them niggers make it like me. I can't take no chance on losin' my money.'

"Once we become followers of the Honorable Elijah Muhammad, the flesh and blood of our people is more important than the white man's money. Money don't mean nothin' to the white man if you're black. Live in five-hundred-dollar house or five-hundred-thousand-dollar house, you still a *nigger*. Adam Clayton Powell, a big black man, bumped him off in your face unjustly. Martin Luther King, a big black man, bumped him off in your face unjustly. Muhammad Ali, the biggest black man in all history of boxing, they bumped me off unjustly in your face.

"So, excuse the expression, money ain't worth a damn thing when it comes to wanting to be a man. And I'm proud to say that I am the first man in the history of all America, athlete and entertainer-wise, who gave up all the white man's money, looked the white man in the eye, and told him the truth, and stayed with his people. I'm just so happy. I go to bed happy, I wake up happy, and I'll go to jail for ten years happy. And it'll always be said, 'There's one that didn't compromise.'

"So they'll have to say that I'm the first black man that took a stand and didn't get weak and go back. But I hope and pray that I'll be one black man that they can look at and say, 'He never had a white woman. Never chased a white woman! Turned down all ten million dollars in commercials, royalties. Turned down the world heavyweight title.' 'Where is he at?' 'There he is, over there sittin' on the garbage can with the wine heads. He don't have to be over there. There he is talking to the prostitute. There he is pickin' up the brother out of the alley, taking him to the Muslim temple. There he is selling the prostitute a Muslim newspaper. Ain't that something. He really don't have to do it.'

"See, they have to look at me now greater than just in a boxing ring. 'Good fighter, boy.' White man got all the money, two Negroes cut each other up, they can't talk, and they pat 'em on the back. 'Good fight, boy.' 'Great fight, boy.' 'Good show, boy.' 'Good dancin', boy.' They can't look at me like that. See, I get all respect because of the Honorable Elijah Muhammad.

"So, all these so-called Negroes listening to this show, I hope you learned something from this. Damn the money when it comes to your mama's freedom. You're so quick to go to Vietnam and fight and shoot and kill somebody you don't know, fightin' so they can be free, and you come home and you get your head busted. So if I gotta die, if I gotta sacrifice, if I gotta suffer, let it be for my black brothers and sisters, let it be for my mama and not somebody ten thousand miles from here."

Lester came to the Hilton with questions. He had asked one. Now he said, "One more question. What do you see wrong with black men and white women?"

"The Honorable Elijah Muhammad says that God created us in nations, families, and tribes. Some people he made white, some he made black, some he made brown, yellow, and red. And I'm sure the divine supreme being didn't make a mistake in his creation. The Honorable Elijah Muhammad teaches that God, Allah, put all of these people in separate countries and nations to themselves. We find Chinese in China, we find Mexicans in Mexico, we find Israelis in Israel, Egyptians in Egypt, Pakistanis in Pakistan, Syrians in Syria, Ghanaians in Ghana, Nigerians in Nigeria, Algerians in Algeria, Ethiopians in Ethiopia, Arabians in Arabia. Beautiful.

"Now, every man want a son to look like himself. Any white man listening to this show and any white woman listening to this show in his or her right white mind don't want little black girls and little black boys coming to marry their sons and daughters and in return introducing their grandchildren as little half-brown, kinky-haired Negroes. It's a shame, it's a disgrace. Find a black baby in a white neighborhood, exile the whole family. Not going to happen, we don't want it, either. Don't want to mix up our beautiful black blood with no white folks. Too much in us now. Weakens us now. A strong cup of coffee is black. To make it weak, put some cream in it.

"No black man listening to this show and no black woman in his or her right black mind wants little white boys and white girls coming to marry their sons and daughters and introducing their grandchildren as little half-green-eyed blond-head white folks. Black people are beautiful. We have beautiful sons. Our little brown girls are so beautiful. Black girls are so beautiful. And we should not want to mix up our blood with our four-hundred-year-old enemies of freedom, justice, and equality who lynched and burned and assassinated and castrated and raped us for four hundred years.

"We are the onliest people on Earth who want to marry and love white folks and we should be the last because we've been the one who've been oppressed, denied freedom, justice, and equality. We are sick. We are brainwashed because this here white Jesus who looks like the white woman, same hair, blond hair, blue eyes. We see the Lord's Supper, all white folks. All the angels in heaven, all white folks. Tarzan, king of the jungle, he's white. White Owl cigars. We've been brainwashed. White Swan soap. White Cloud tissue paper. White Rain hair rinse. White Tornado floor wax. White Plus toothpaste. Angel food cake is white, devil's food cake is chocolate. Can't go to heaven unless you walk on the Milky White Way. When you get there, you gotta be washed in lamb blood and be white as snow before you get in. You go look at King Kong at the movies. Big ol' gorilla out of Africa, fourteen stories high, he's running up and down the Empire State Building, fightin' guns and bullets just to keep a white woman in his arms. You have been brainwashed.

"The black woman is the most beautiful. She has lips where a white woman don't. She don't need lipstick. She's got complexion. She's got beautiful black hair. She's got beautiful black eyes and not animal green and blue eyes. We are the original people, God taught the Honorable Elijah Muhammad. We are the best. Why are we seeking to lose our blood through racial integration? It's the worst thing we can do. Now the Honorable Elijah Muhammad teaches us that integration means self-destruction and that means death and nothing less.

"So on those grounds we are justified in saying that we should respect and protect our women and keep the white man out of our neighborhoods on Fridays, Saturdays, and Sunday nights. That's what you do when you integrate. You're giving the white man the legal right to carry your women to the hotel or the motel, give all kinds of diseases, don't want to marry her, just want to use her. I travel from coast to coast every day. I know all the pimps and players. I know what I'm saying is right and you do, too, and the white folks listening know this is right. Muhammad is bold and he makes us bold and we gonna tell it. We'll never be respected if we don't respect our women because the woman is the field which produces your nation. If you don't protect your field, you'll produce a bad nation. It's suicide to want a white woman."

Here, worn down and worn out, Lester ended the show. "This is Julius Lester and I've been talking to the heavyweight champion and Muslim minister Muhammad Ali. Thank you."

———

Ali knew no one had gone to jail for the murder of Emmett Till. He also knew what his daddy thought of the police. But he didn't know the intricacies of the Supreme Court deliberations. This was big. This was the United States government promising to lock him up. He might never fight again. Prospects were ominous. After Ali's conviction in 1967, the Fifth Circuit Court of Appeals affirmed it. The last appeal was to the U.S. Supreme Court—and rarely did the high court consider appeals from circuit court rulings. If the justices said no, Ali's legal journey was over. They did in fact say no at a meeting in March 1969. The vote was eight to one against hearing *United States of America* v. *Cassius Marsellus* [*sic*] *Clay*. Only William Brennan wanted to hear it.

Ali would go to prison.

But, wait.

The fight doctor, Ferdie Pacheco, believed Ali to be a charmed figure. He had seen Ali do foolish things that worked to his advantage. The doctor called it "Ali's luck." Now there came a breathtaking example. Within a week of the Supreme Court's vote against hearing the case, the Justice Department admitted it had done wiretaps in violation of a year-old law. As it happened, Ali had been recorded five times. The contents of those wiretaps should have been in evidence at Ali's original trial, but had never been disclosed. So the Supreme Court delayed announcing its vote against Ali. It ordered Federal District Court Judge Joe Ingraham to conduct a hearing on whether evidence gathered in the wiretaps played any part in Ali's conviction.

At that hearing on June 6, 1968, government agents testified in a way that reinforced suspicions by Ali supporters that the government was out to get him. First, an Ali lawyer testified that one wiretapped conversation contained proof of Ali's religious orientation; he said a forty-five-minute conversation between Ali and Dr. Martin Luther King, Jr., included references to the fighter's religious activities. In answer, an FBI agent said that recording had been destroyed and there was no transcript of it. Then T. Oscar Smith, the Justice Department official who recommended that the Louisville draft board deny Ali's conscientious objector claim, testified that he had never heard of the wiretaps. This after an FBI agent in Phoenix said he had sent two such conversations to the bureau office in Louisville, home of Ali's draft board.

The next day, Ingraham ruled that Ali's conviction and sentence would stand. So, once again, Ali's lawyers would appeal to the Supreme Court

in a case that had become so entwined in racial politics that neither Ali
nor the government could admit their true motivations. Instead, the
combatants engaged in a complex charade.

Ali's case was never about religion. As Belinda Ali said, "We didn't
fight American wars." But Ali could not refuse the draft on those
grounds; thus, the claim to be a conscientious objector. At the same time,
the government could not imprison Ali for his political beliefs. But once
he claimed conscientious objector status, the Justice Department certainly could pursue him relentlessly. The case was a dance of proxies; as
Ali used religion to cover his politics, the government used the draft laws
to practice its politics.

To Americans opposed to the war, the only important thing was that
the world's most famous man refused to serve. In Louisville, one of the
nation's most famous civil rights and antiwar activists, Anne Braden,
paid close attention. Her son, Jimmy, was eleven years old when he won
a school chess tournament, the victory coming shortly after Ali won a
gold medal in the 1960 Olympic Games. Jimmy Braden called home to let
his mother know, "I am the greatest! I am the greatest!" Anne Braden
never thought Ali's opposition was based on conscientious objection.
She said, "It was an evil war, and he wasn't going to support it. Why he
took his position didn't matter. People in our movements just really admired him. He inspired other people to take the same position."

In the fall of 1969, Ali walked to the Alvin Theater in New York. He had
been invited to opening night of a play about a black heavyweight champion of the early twentieth century. *The Great White Hope*'s story was of
Jack Johnson's martyrdom by white America. Above the theater marquee
Ali saw a giant poster. It showed a black man with a shaved skull. He lay
in bed with a white woman. "So that's Jack Johnson," Ali said to his friend
and photographer Howard Bingham. "That was a b-a-a-a-d nigger!"

Fifty years before, Johnson had raised six kinds of hell. He had been arrested on morals charges and fled to Europe to avoid prison. On stage
that night in 1969, the actor James Earl Jones opened the play as Johnson
telling sportswriters why he smiled so much in the ring: "Ah like whoever
ah'm hitting to see ah'm still his friend." Jones played Johnson as an un-
inhibited individualist hounded and persecuted by racists, forced to fight
in Europe, scraping by on whatever money he could make however he

could make it. Ali nudged Bingham: "Hey! This play is about me. Take out the interracial love stuff and Jack Johnson is the original *me*." One scene stayed with Ali. Because Johnson's exile to Europe left him destitute, sharks closed in. Boxing promoters proposed that he return to the United States. They imposed one condition: He would lose the heavyweight championship to a white man, Jess Willard. Johnson finally said, "Come get me, here I is."

After the play, Ali told Jones he wanted to go on stage and say those words. When the audience had left, Ali filled the empty theater with his voice: "Here I is! Here I is!"

The fighter said the play was about him, and Jones said, "That's the whole point."

"Only one thing is bothering me," Ali said.

"What?"

"Just what are they gonna do fifty years from now when they gotta write a play about me?"

Johnson lost to Willard on a knockout in the twenty-sixth round. He never fought seriously again. He served his time in Leavenworth's federal prison, a year and a day. Notorious for high-speed driving, Johnson died at age sixty-eight from injuries sustained when he lost control of his Lincoln Zephyr and crashed into a power pole.

"I wish I knew how it was gonna turn out," Ali said.

Millions of Americans believed their government's move against Ali was motivated, nourished, and sustained by a political, racial, and personal bias. By the time Ali walked onto the Alvin Theater stage and spoke Jack Johnson's words, the nation had endured a decade of savagery. President Lyndon B. Johnson decided he would not seek a second election to the office that for forty years had been his life's ambition. His successor, Richard M. Nixon, promised to bring home the U.S. troops. On November 15, 1969, eleven months into Nixon's presidency, more than a quarter-million protesters gathered in the nation's capital, the largest antiwar demonstration yet, to remind him that his promise had not been kept.

It now seemed less important to put Ali in prison. He led no organization, gathered no followers, made no appearances at protest rallies, advocated no armed rebellion, presented no national security threat. Because of his celebrity, Ali became a symbol of protest, but a symbol outside the mainstream, an unquestioning member of a religious sect found to be toothless. The longer Ali was out of the ring, the more his star dimmed. College appearances throughout 1969 brought him some attention and provided money to pay bills; small consolations to a man accustomed to international fame and unlimited cash. Once so famous that the sound of his voice identified him, he remained famous enough to be invited onto the television quiz show *What's My Line?* as a Mystery Guest (paid $450), but not so famous that the blindfolded panelists could guess who he was.

The newspaperman Bob Lipsyte returned from that show with Ali and saw another small humiliation. When Ali couldn't open the door to his hotel room, an assistant manager explained that it was locked until the bill was paid. The New York Hilton wanted fifty-three dollars and nine cents. "When you're the champ, they never make you pay right away." Ali told Lipsyte, who found the scene outrageous, especially as Ali, undisturbed and courteous, signed autographs for the manager and a hotel detective. "It's only when you're down and busted they want their money up front. That's the way of the world."

Ali scraped up ten thousand dollars for doing scenes in a hagiographic documentary, *A/K/A Cassius Clay*. He also filmed a "computer" fight against the old heavyweight champ, Rocky Marciano. In thirteen years of retirement, the Rock had lost his hair, gained fifty pounds, and become forty-six years old. A crash diet, toupee, and one-minute rounds with extensive rest periods made it possible to film Marciano in the ring with the twenty-seven-year-old Ali. As shown in the United States, Marciano won the fight with a thirteenth-round knockout; in Europe, Ali beat Marciano bloody.

Then he became a Broadway musical star. Really. None of this empty-stage shouting he did with James Earl Jones. Costumed in an Afro wig and a beard, he appeared as the title character in the musical, *Buck White*.

After sixteen preview performances, the show opened December 2 and closed four days later. Reviewers were kind to Ali, among them Broadway's most influential, Clive Barnes of the *New York Times*. He wrote, "How is Mr. Clay? He emerges as a modest naturally appealing man. He sings with a pleasant slightly impersonal voice, acts without embarrassment, and moves with innate dignity. He does himself proud."

The allusion to the constraints of a script fit his life as well; he could not do what he wanted to do. Even as he denied wanting to fight, clearly he wanted to fight. Nothing more significant than the arrival of a new Cadillac moved him to a speech on the subject. "See my new limousine?" he said to one of those Midtown New York crowds that materialized whenever he set foot on a street. "They think they can bring me to my knees by taking away my title, and by not letting me fight in this country, and by taking my passport so I can't get to the three million worth of fight contracts that are waiting for me overseas.

"Shoot! I ain't worked for two years and I ain't been Tommin' to no-body and here I'm buying limousines—the president of the United States ain't got no better one. Just look at it! Ain't it purty? Y'all go and tell everybody that Muhammad Ali ain't licked yet. I don't care if I never get another fight. I say, damn the fights and damn all the money. A man's got to stand up for what he believes, and I'm standin' up for my people, even if I have to go to jail."

He always meant what he said when he said it. What he said before, that didn't matter. What he would say later, that didn't matter. At this moment, there by the gray Cadillac limousine, talking to those people, he absolutely meant that he didn't care if he ever fought again.

But, of course, his minions criss-crossed the nation in search of a ju-risdiction that would license him. He was a fighter. He wanted his title back.

It now belonged to Joe Frazier. He had moved from South Carolina poverty to Philadelphia butcher houses to recognition as Ali's num-ber-one challenger. In Ali's absence, Frazier had been elevated to the championship by acclamation. He solidified his claim to the title with a knockout victory over Jimmy Ellis, Ali's boyhood friend and sparring partner who had won an eight-man elimination tourna-ment.

Ali was Ahab now, in pursuit of the great whale, Frazier. He did a drawing for *Jock*, a sports magazine, that depicted two fighters, one la-beled "Ali," the other "Joe Frazier." Ali's drawing showed "Frazier" falling to the canvas in "Round 9." In a word bubble above "Ali," the artist Ali printed in crude block letters with eccentric punctuation, "He, was not the champ, he was a tramp."

There was growing sentiment that Ali's major transgression in refus-ing the draft was in his timing. Budd Schulberg wrote, "Just as we had premature antifascists in the middle thirties whose opposition to Hitler,

Mussolini, and Franco brought them ridicule and ostracism . . . so Ali was made to suffer the prematurity of a stand taken in '66 that was no longer scandalizing." By November of 1969, thirty-one months after Ali said he had no quarrel with the Viet Cong, polls showed that more than 50 percent of Americans wanted out of the war. *Esquire* magazine photographed a dozen men in a boxing ring, among them Cosell, Schulberg, Truman Capote, George Plimpton, and James Earl Jones. They stood under the cover line, *Muhammad Ali deserves the right to defend his title.* Inside, Irwin Shaw argued that anyone convicted of a crime and appealing that conviction is by law allowed to work at his trade, yet Ali was not. Worse, Ali was drafted while "no halfback or a pitcher or even a Boxing Commissioner has fallen in action or even heard a shot fired in anger." To the ordinary American, then, "especially the black American, it must seem that one man has been singled out and hounded down where hundreds of his more cautious colleagues have been allowed to drift off into safety."

Shaw saw an America riven by misconduct. "The credibility gap continues to exist between government and governed. In plain words, we believe that we are being lied to. . . . In the era of the fix, the payoff, the payola, the lobby, the secret deal, the double-talk, Muhammad Ali would seem to have a right to bitterness as he stands confronted with the full lonely majesty of the law. Against this background consider us as we struggle futilely with our most desperate problem. Black and white grow further apart. Day by day, the wound grows uglier. Do we do anything toward healing that wound by insisting on the last full pound of flesh from Muhammad Ali?"

The solution to Ali's problems was obvious: Fight again. But the publicist Harold Conrad visited twenty-two states and found none willing to license Ali. Herbert Muhammad's deal with an Indian reservation in Arizona came undone when a tribal council member said "it would desecrate the land some of our brave boys have walked on," among them the Medal of Honor winner Ira Hayes, a Marine who helped raise the American flag at Iwo Jima. When a news report early in April 1969 suggested Ali might fight in Texas, Cosell tracked him down near Dallas.

"Yeah, I'd go back if the money was right," Ali told Cosell. "I have a lot of bills to pay."

That was not news. The news came two days later. Elijah Muhammad had seen Cosell's show and with a phone call stopped the presses of *Muhammad Speaks*. He ordered a front-page editorial that ran under the headline: WE TELL THE WORLD WE'RE NOT WITH MUHAMMAD ALI. Over his signature, Elijah Muhammad wrote:

"Muhammad Ali is out of the circle of the brotherhood of the followers of Islam under the leadership and teaching of Elijah Muhammad for one year. He cannot speak to, visit with, or be seen with any Muslim or take part in any Muslim religious activity. Mr. Muhammad Ali plainly acted the fool. Any man or woman who comes to Allah and then puts his hopes and trust in the enemy of Allah for survival is underestimating the power of Allah to help them. Mr. Muhammad Ali has sporting blood. Mr. Muhammad Ali desires to do that which the Holy Qur'an teaches him against. Mr. Muhammad Ali wants a place in this sports world. He loves it."

Because the suspension produced so many questions, Muhammad used the next week's newspaper to spell out particulars: Ali had disregarded Allah's power; chosen to go with the white man when deferred from army duty; fought for the entertainment of the white man; risked killing an opponent for a "leetle money"; forgotten he was respected around the world only because the Messenger had named him "Muhammad Ali," and "made a complete fool of himself for accepting the sport which Allah (God) condemns."

Throughout the indictment, Muhammad followed each mention of Ali's name with Cassius Clay in parentheses, reminding him that he was again to be known by his slavemaster name: "If I take Muhammad Ali (CASSIUS CLAY) down as being worthy of the respect of the Islamic world, do you think they would still respect him. NO!"

Muhammad ended the mad diatribe with this: "LET THIS BE A LESSON TO YOU WHO ARE WEAK IN THE FAITH."

Only the unthinking believed a word of it. What, the Messenger only now noticed that Ali made money fighting for the white man? Ali had defended his championship nine times since announcing his connection to the Nation. Muhammad's son Herbert was the fighter's manager. But, yes, some things had changed. While fighting, Ali had given hundreds of thousands of dollars to the Nation. As the heavyweight champion and international celebrity, he brought visibility that helped in recruiting members. Now the money well was dry. Now Ali's star had dimmed. Now the concept of Black Power drew members. Now, using the Cosell interview as pretext, the political intriguer Elijah Muhammad put his foot on Ali's throat.

Ali's reaction to the suspension provided all the evidence anyone would need of his subservience to Muhammad. Where Malcolm X had rebelled against the Messenger—and paid with his life—Ali meekly accepted the punishment. He even borrowed from the Messenger's indictment to criticize himself: "I made a fool of myself when I said that I'd return to boxing to pay my bills. I'm glad he awakened me. I'll take my punishment like a man and when my year's suspension is over, I hope he'll accept me back."

Early in the suspension, Cosell saw Ali. Before Cosell could say anything, Ali shook his head.

"Can't talk to you no more," he said, "not without Elijah's permission."

Still under suspension, Ali found balm for his wounds in an unlikely way in an unlikely place. A black legislator and a Jewish mayor produced a license to fight. Ali would return in the heart of the Confederacy, in a state with an avowed segregationist governor, in a city where a patrician mayor of the 1960s earlier had suggested the race problem might be solved by shipping blacks back to Africa. On October 26, 1970, after forty-three months out of the ring, Ali came back in Atlanta, Georgia. For the first time, he would fight a man younger than himself. Jerry Quarry, twenty-five years old, had lost only four times in forty-six fights and was ranked the number one challenger for Frazier's title.

What a scene it was. The Hyatt-Regency Hotel, where the fight crowd gathered, stood twenty-three stories tall on Peachtree Street with an odd structure at the top, a bulbous room, either a revolving restaurant or UFO parked there. The hotel was architect John Portman's vision of the future, its lobby the size of two football fields, its atrium open to the top floor, glass-walled elevators rising like rocketships past the parapet-like corridors from which guests looked down the vast open shaft to upturned faces far below. Somehow, a flower-petal canopy floated above the lobby bar.

In that lobby, fans wore ermine-trimmed hats with brims drooping to their shoulders. They outfitted themselves in purple velvet and golden silk. Mink coats came to their ankles above pointy purple suede shoes. Those were the men. They all came to Atlanta; pimps and platoons of plumed and pleasing ladies to Atlanta in yellow Rolls-Royces and psychedelic Stutz Bearcats with curlicue fenders and hoodlum tires, "every black man and woman in America who could scratch up the change," as Budd Schulberg put it, "high rollers from the biggest floating crap games in the land." It was a dreamscape of America's black Mafia and black intellectual elite drawn to this city famous for William Tecumseh Sherman's fire, for Scarlett and Rhett and a way of life gone with the wind, celebrities Bill Cosby and Sidney Poitier and Harry Belafonte and the Supremes and Mr. T, all drawn to Atlanta by Muhammad Ali, the great-grandson of slaves, both carrier and repository of black pride. A Rhodes scholar, Stan Sanders, a survivor of both Watts and Yale Law School, said to Schulberg, "You know the day will come when our sons will be asking us, 'Daddy, where were you on the night they let Muhammad Ali come back to the ring?'"

Three days before the fight, I watched Ali work out in a rams

le building once used for pro wrestling, fallen into such disrepair it had been retrofitted for square dancing with plastic wagon-wheel chandeliers and a faux saloon bar. The hall smelled of wet bar rags. Ali's entrance changed the feel of the place. He walked in slowly, his entourage streaming behind. He wore a yellow shirt hanging out over gray pants that covered dirt-browned roadwork boots. "Oh, God," a young woman said to Ali, "you're beautiful." Ali looked and said, "Oooooh, Lord. Ooooh, my."

For five rounds of sparring, he allowed himself to be hit in the ribs. "It's like the astronauts goin' to the moon," he explained. He sat in the ring answering reporters' questions. "Before they let the astronauts go to the moon, they make 'em practice—just in case. That's what I'm doin' takin' all those shots to the body. I'm not lookin' to get hit with no shots like that. I don't expect I will get hit like that. But just in case—I have to let that man pound on me for fifteen minutes. I'm gonna be ready."

What was more important in the fight, money or principle? "The money. I'm not a kid no more. I've got a wife and three beautiful little children to support, I'm interested in buyin' 'em a nice house, I'm interested in security same as any of you. Of course, principle is important, too. They took my title away and gave it to Frazier. If I can get by the second-best in six weeks, then I'm ready to give Frazier a chance."

Ever been afraid? "I'm nervous, not afraid. People comin' from all over the world—Russia—tryin' to contact me. All comin' to see two guys jumpin' around in a ring. If I lose, I gotta leave the country—*that's* what makes me nervous." He saw a tall black man. "Elgin Baylor, come here. Elgin, come see me. Elgin Baylor, hey, Elgin." Only it wasn't Elgin Baylor, it was another basketball star, Walt Bellamy of the Atlanta Hawks. "Sorry, folks," Ali said, "all them spook basketball players look alike." The men shook hands, Ali at six foot three looking up at Bellamy, six foot eleven. "If *he* could fight, that would scare me!"

The afternoon of the fight, at a hideaway cabin a half-hour out of town, Ali and his noisy acolytes watched Jack Johnson fight films on a bedsheet tacked to a wall. Maybe twenty people raised havoc, the phone ringing constantly, Willis Reed calling, Hank Aaron, Willie Mays, Gale Sayers, none Muslims, none separatists, all brothers to Ali. "Like old times," Schulberg said, "only bigger and better." Then Ali picked up the phone again, whooped, and ordered quiet. With a ring announcer's stentorian tones, he said, "He's on his way out . . . the Reverend Jesse Jackson . . . my own head nigger! . . . The baddest nigger of them all!"

On arrival, Jackson declaimed over the noise, "If he loses tonight, it will mean, symbolically, that the forces of blind patriotism are right, that dissent is wrong; that protest means you don't love the country. This fight is Love-it-or-leave-it vs. Love-it-and-change-it. They tried to railroad him. They refused to accept his testimony about his religious convictions. They took away his right to practice his profession. They tried to break him in body and in mind. Martin Luther King used to say, 'Truth crushed to the earth will rise again.' That's the black ethos. And it's happening here in Georgia of all places, and against a white man."

Back at the Hyatt Regency, before the players and their powdered ladies left for the arena, the boxing writer and broadcaster Bert Sugar stood among the hotel lobby's raucous crowd. There was Ali in one of the glass rocketship elevators. As the elevator rose, Sugar lifted his eyes to follow Ali's ascension. He called the moment spine-tingling and spoke of resurrection.

That night, as Ali stepped into the ring, Bundini Brown shouted, "Ghost in the house! Ghost in the house!" He meant Jack Johnson's ghost, given form by Muhammad Ali. Through the three rounds necessary for Ali to cut Quarry's eye eleven stitches wide, Brown shouted, "Jack Johnson's heah! Jack Johnson's heah!" Quarry had been ranked number one among heavyweight contenders, yet was no match for an Ali with six weeks of training after three years and seven months away. I walked from ringside with Schulberg, who said, "Good, good. May have gone back a step, but good."

From Elijah Muhammad there came no protest that Ali had again made *a complete fool of himself for accepting the sport which Allah (God) condemns.* On December 7, Ali returned to Madison Square Garden. He regained his license to fight when the National Association for the Advancement of Colored People filed suit against the New York State Athletic Commission. The NAACP's lawyers argued that the commission's actions in denying Ali a license had been a violation of his Fourteenth Amendment rights (as Cosell so often had declared). The lawyers also showed that the commission had licensed dozens of felons, including men convicted of murder and military desertion. District Judge Walter Mansfield called the commission's denial "astonishing."

Against the Argentine bull named Oscar Bonavena, Ali won on a knockout in the fifteenth round. Afterward, I stood with other reporters as Ali lay on a rubbing table in a small dressing room. His faithful, silent Cuban masseur Luis Sarria rubbed Ali's bruised body. Only reporters near the table could hear Ali, who sounded more the loser than the loudmouth who promised a ninth-round knockout.

As it happened, Bonavena nearly won it in the ninth. A series of punches had Ali in trouble: "No pain. It's like an electric shock. I was in a daze. An electric shock. Zzzzz. Going right through me. I always wondered what it would be like to be in a daze. I always wondered what I would do." He draped himself over Bonavena. "I had to stay on him, so I could let the daze clear up. . . . If I am anything but supreme, the press gets on me. They expect me to be super at all times. I told everybody Bonavena was a good fighter, probably the best I've ever fought."

The next week, I went to Ali's new home outside Philadelphia to spend time with him away from crowds, to see him at rest, maybe with his wife and children. For the five or six hours I was there, Belinda Ali stayed in another room, unheard, never seen. "She's a good Muslim woman," Ali said. "She knows the man is in charge." We sat in a living room that was testimony to his need for gratification that was instant and constant. The walls were mirrors, floor to ceiling, and he spoke less often to me than to his reflection, Narcissus at the pool. There were twenty-two telephones in the ten-room house. He held in his arms one of his four-month-old twin daughters, perhaps Rasheeda, maybe Jamillah; he couldn't tell them apart. When Rasheeda (or Jamillah) yawned, Ali said, "Shut your mouth. Leave the talkin' to Daddy."

He touched the girl's lips. "I wish they were boys. It won't be no time before some fellow marries them and takes them away from me. Boys, they stick around longer." I asked if he would want his son, Muhammad Jr., to fight. "Naw."

"Why not? You've done all right."

"I'm one in millions," he said.

We talked about the Quarry fight. "It showed me I wasn't in really tip-top shape. But he didn't hit me in the face once in three rounds, and he was a fast man, tricky with a good left. And I cut him quicker, cut him deeper, cut him in a new place, one that had never been cut before." Both Quarry and Bonavena had been steps toward a championship fight with Joe Frazier, and Ali was eager. "With Frazier, I'll be able to dance more. Bonavena, you never knew where he was coming from. He didn't do anything but run into me and then start throwing those roundhouse punches. Hit me on the back of the neck, on the ears, in the throat, below the belt, everywhere. But Frazier tries to box. He sticks that left jab out there. He's always coming in. He'll be easy, Joe Frazier will."

I must have raised an eyebrow.

"I will defy the critics again. No one has written what I have done so far. I had ten title fights before they took away my title. A man is supposed to be going downhill after ten title fights, they take so much out of him. Then I was away three and a half years, and I weighed 240 pounds, and on six weeks' notice—six weeks' notice!—I fought Jerry Quarry and beat him worse than Joe Frazier did.

"Then I fought Bonavena, who had knocked Frazier down twice and had never been knocked down in twenty-five rounds with Frazier—and I knocked him out in the fifteenth round when I was supposed to be in trouble against a strong man like Bonavena. But I knocked him out, something that had never been done before. And the press, they write that I'm just another fighter."

Ali was restless. "Want to go for a ride?" he said. He opened a door and shouted, "Cash, come on." Up from a lower level came his father, Cassius Clay, Sr. Fifteen minutes later, Ali had parked his Rolls-Royce on the street in front of a Philadelphia rowhouse funeral home. The three of us looked into an open coffin. There were five or six rows of wooden chairs on a gray linoleum floor. The room's only lights were bare bulbs in floor lamps at either end of the coffin. The harsh lights played against Ali's face each time he tilted his head to look at the dead man, killed by an off-duty policeman after pulling a knife in an argument during a closed-circuit telecast of the Ali-Bonavena fight.

Ali had read about it. "What was his name?" he asked the funeral home director.

"He was Leslie Scott," Harrison Byrd said.

"Have a family?"

"Two children about grown."

"How about his wife? She take it pretty hard?"

"Very, very hard. She took it hard."

Ali put his hands on the coffin's edge.

"What's he feel like?" the heavyweight champion asked. "Is he hard?"

"Like clay," his father said. "Putty. Not hard."

Ali touched the dead man. With his right index finger, he pushed against the body, testing it, first on the thigh, then between the thumb and fingers, finally on the cheek.

"Cold," he said. "His cheek is hard."

"Sometimes," his father said, "they put cotton in their cheeks."

"They do?" He stared. "He was a big man."

"'Bout your size."

"Yeah."

Ali traced lightly over the coffin with his fingertips. "Life is pitiful. One second, this man is alive. He's arguing that I'm a better fighter than Joe Frazier. The next second, he's dead." Ali walked away. "I ain't worth dying for," he said.

CHAPTER NINE

"Tel-e-VISION!"

I SAW COSELL IN PERSON for the first time at the 1967 World Series. Before I saw him, I heard him. I stood in a single-file line of sportswriters against the crumbling bricks of Fenway Park, waiting for admittance to the Red Sox clubhouse. I was at my first World Series, thrilled to be in the line right behind the *New York Daily News* columnist, Dick Young, a newspapering legend. I was about to learn that gentlemanly behavior was not a requirement for journalistic fame. Young also heard Cosell, and it made him angry. Then he became more than angry. He levitated in righteous rage. He bellowed expletives and obscenities. His carotid arteries ran hot. I watched, awed. To understand how one man's voice can be the catalyst for another man's paroxysm of vitriol, it is necessary to know three things: Young's place in sportswriting history, his competitive relationship with Cosell, and that time's changing nature of the media in sports.

Sportswriters once wrote only what they saw on the field. Young changed that. He invented the clubhouse interview. In the late 1940s, covering the Brooklyn Dodgers, he descended from the press box to the players' lair and, chin out, demanded from athletes an explanation for every act of commission and omission. Both Young and Cosell worked for WABC on its broadcasts of New York Jets football games. They had separate and distinct duties, never sharing air time, largely because they despised each other. No one knew if that enmity came about despite their commonalities or because of them; both were Brooklyn Jews whose ambitions and obsessions were shaped by Depression-era childhoods. Most intolerably, from Young's point of view, Cosell had become a national television star. Like many newspaper people of his time, Young considered television a superficial medium unworthy of respect. As early as 1956, when televised sports was little more than a novelty, Young wrote a *SPORT* article entitled, "How Television Is Ruining Sports." It was a polemic denouncing television, the devil incarnate, for tempting college football officials to start games at unholy hours, some even at night.

Now, on this October day in 1967, with the surly impatience of a man who believed he had earned a proprietary interest in every baseball clubhouse, Young first chafed at being forced to wait outside a closed door. He shouted, "Get somebody from the Red Sox. Get us in there." Then I heard that voice. It shouted one word, then repeated that word twice more. The word was shouted so theatrically, with an accent on the last syllable, that it seemed both an announcement of great moment and a command that inferior beings should get the hell out of the way. Turning to my left, I saw the man who had shouted the word. Cosell.

With a cameraman and sound man scurrying in his wake, Cosell swept past me, past the sputtering Young, past the stationary herd of sportswriters waiting in line. Cosell walked straight to the Red Sox clubhouse door. He rapped on it. It opened. He disappeared behind the door. All the while, Young ranted because he heard Cosell say that word and he saw Cosell sashay past us and he saw what he never thought he would see, a baseball clubhouse open for television interviews and closed to newspapermen, closed even to the very man who invented newspapermen digging for clubhouse quotes.

The word Cosell shouted was . . .

"Tel-e-vision!"

"Tel-e-vision!"

"Tel-e-VISION!"

It was as if Howard Cosell believed he *was* television.

Newspaper reporters could get huffy, but they knew Cosell had a point. He might not be television, but his bosses at ABC were—certainly in sports. Before the 1960s, television selected events for broadcast that sports fans had proven they wanted to see: college football, the National Football League, Major League Baseball, heavyweight championship fights. Then along came Ed Scherick, Tom Moore, and Roone Arledge. ABC's adventurers were the first executives in network television to understand—maybe they made a lucky guess—that the allure of television was more powerful than the games themselves. If they put a game on TV, any game, people would buy in.

In 1960 ABC bankrolled the new American Football League, a rival to the powerful NFL. In 1961 the network created *Wide World of Sports,* a weekly series often originating in faraway places and featuring unusual events performed by athletes mostly unknown. Those moves changed both television and sports. The ABC-AFL partnership showed that a professional sports league expected to survive on television advertising money. That expectation prompted entrepreneurs to create the American Basketball Association, the World Hockey Association, and the World Football League. Existing leagues expanded into new markets where stadiums had been raised. Established teams used the threat of leaving town to persuade their cities to build them new ballparks as well. Sports in America once had been almost an exclusive club, perhaps not with secret handshakes and unwritten oaths but with knowledge and interest limited to those who worked at it. In the 1960s, the club's doors were thrown open to every American with a television set.

ABC Sports came to mirror a nation in revolution. Early in the decade, half the population was under thirty years of age, then half under twenty-seven, finally half under twenty-five with 40 percent under seventeen, and those under eighteen increasing four times as fast as the rest of the population. The youth culture was clamorous at best, riotous at worst. Sports fans of a generation past were accustomed to modesty from their heroes. Now came Joe Namath's autobiography, *I Can't Wait Until Tomorrow . . . 'Cause I Get Better-Looking Every Day.* He also did a television commercial aimed at women, Namath mischievously sexy on a bearskin rug, his famously damaged legs in pantyhose. One imagines Bronko Nagurski, the old bruiser in Minnesota, his TV tuned in to an AFL game. One imagines Bronko seeing a quarterback in pantyhose. One imagines Nagurski fainting away.

As if in step with the tumult of the civil rights movement, there arrived an extraordinary group of black athletes who raised the level of their sports: Willie Mays, Hank Aaron, Roberto Clemente, Jim Brown, Bill Russell, Wilt Chamberlain, Oscar Robertson, O. J. Simpson, Joe Frazier, Muhammad Ali. In 1966, for the first time in college basketball history, a team with an all-black starting five (Texas Western) won the NCAA championship (by defeating all-white Kentucky).

Death was the decade's shadow. The war in Vietnam burned itself into Americans' hearts. Cosell's overheated ravings to George Plimpton of a gunman aiming at him from another building had their origins in cold murder. As assassins killed John F. Kennedy and Malcolm X, a man with a rifle killed Martin Luther King, Jr., in April 1968. In June '68, a man with a revolver killed Robert F. Kennedy.

The day of RFK's death, Cosell refused to announce the sports scores on his radio shows. Instead, he eulogized Kennedy. The *Los Angeles Times* sports columnist Jim Murray also ignored sports that day, arguing that any American with a public forum should speak out against the nation's madness. Cosell also explained his position:

"All I tried to do in a time of national disgrace, which is more frequently recurring with assassinations becoming commonplace, was find some adequacy within myself for what I do, which is so dreadfully unimportant in the whole human spectrum. Because when things like this happen, honestly, I don't think it's important what pinch-hitter Gil Hodges selects or how the Mets made out the prior night. And if people can get that sense of values instead of living every day for the immediacy of their own enjoyment without regard for national catastrophe, then I'm making a contribution that has meaning. I make no contribution when I give ball scores."

Three months after Kennedy's killing, the real world again insinuated itself into sports. Again, ABC Sports, Arledge, and Cosell were there. Ten days before the 1968 Olympics were to begin in Mexico City, nearly ten thousand people gathered to protest the nation's expenditures on games when millions of Mexicans lived in poverty. Gunfire from soldiers and police killed more than two hundred protesters. Against that backdrop, Arledge had decided that ABC would make the Mexico City Olympics the most ambitious project in television history.

He commanded fifty tons of equipment, forty miles of cable, fifty cameras, and four hundred fifty producers, directors, and crew members for forty-four hours of same-day coverage. An Arledge lieutenant, Dick Ebersol, had gone around the world gathering biographical information on 1,600 athletes to provide story lines that for the first time humanized Olympians. It was a dramatic technique that had made *Wide World of Sports* compelling television, and there came a moment in Mexico City when it made ABC's coverage unforgettable.

Late in the games, the black American sprinters Tommie Smith and

John Carlos finished first and third at two hundred meters. They were protégés of the black activist Harry Edwards, a professor at San Jose State. Once an athlete himself, Edwards had helped organized protests by athletes at thirty-seven white-dominated universities; they demanded more black coaches, cheerleaders, and trainers. Early in 1968 he created the Olympic Project for Human Rights (OPHR). At a press conference alongside Martin Luther King, Jr., and Floyd McKissick of the Congress of Racial Equality (CORE), Edwards proposed a boycott of the Mexico City games unless certain demands were met. Those demands included barring South Africa and Rhodesia from the Olympics, the hiring of black coaches and officials on the U.S. team, and the end of Avery Brundage's reign as the ultimate Olympic stiff-neck. The first of OPHR's demands was the reinstatement of Muhammad Ali as heavyweight champion. Lost in political exile, his passport taken up, unable to work at his profession, Ali became a symbol. Edwards called him "the warrior saint in the revolt of the black athlete in America."

No boycott developed, but Arledge expected *something*. His instructions to his ace reporter, Cosell: "Do your thing. I don't want any newsman beating us on any story."

Then, there it was, the *something*. As Smith and Carlos stepped onto the victory stand to receive their gold and bronze Olympic medals, they were barefoot. Their heads were bowed. Each wore one black glove. As Arledge watched the scene on a control-room monitor, he shouted to directors and camera operators: "Get in there!" He wanted close-up pictures of Smith and Carlos. He said, "This is Black Power!" In a city where people had been killed by government action during peaceful protests, in a time when black Americans protested institutionalized racism, Arledge was prepared. He recognized the social and political significance of the Smith-Carlos scene. Rather than turn ABC's camera away to preserve the IOC's pretension that politics played no part in the Olympics, Arledge shouted again, "Get in on them!"

The medal ceremony began with the gold medalist's national anthem. Smith and Carlos would not look at the American flag. They bowed their heads and thrust black-gloved fists overhead, holding the pose of defiance throughout "The Star-Spangled Banner." Then, without a word to the media, Smith and Carlos disappeared into the night—with Cosell in pursuit. He learned that the U.S. Olympic Committee had banished the pair from the athletes' village. He worked every source he had, sports-writers, officials, friends of the men. Nothing. Then Hayes Jones, a 1964 Olympic gold medalist working as an ABC commentator, told Cosell that Smith and Carlos had moved to Mexico City's Diplomat Hotel. It was then eight in the morning. Cosell had not slept when he made a call to Smith's room. Smith said he would not talk. Yet Cosell inveigled an invitation to come on up. ("You ever tried to tell Howard no?" Arledge said.) Smith told him, "You'd think I committed murder. All I did was what I've been doing all along, call the attention of the world to the way the blacks are treated in America. There's nothing new about this."

"It's new when you do it at a world forum," Cosell said. "I think you should state what you did and why you did it. Then at least some people might understand." Finally, Smith joined Cosell for the kind of news-making interview once the exclusive province of print journalists. Cosell asked, "Tell me, Tommie, what did you mean, symbolically, by the bowed head, the shoeless feet, the outstretched fist?"

"The fist to show Black Power, the strength and unity of black people. The shoeless feet to show the anguish of black people through all the years. The bowed head because the words of the anthem were not being applied to blacks."

Cosell asked, "Are you proud to be an American?"

"I am proud to be a black American," Smith said.

Jerry Izenberg had called Cosell "the black man's white man." Now, in Mexico City, Cosell stood with Tommie Smith. He understood the black athletes' complaints because he, like them, had lived with prejudice. He had known oppression. He had been told he wasn't wanted, wasn't al-lowed. To succeed, he had pushed open doors closed in his face. The night after his interview with Smith, Cosell stood in the lobby of the El Presidente Hotel. A car passed by the door, stopped, and came back to let out John Carlos. He shook Cosell's hand and said, "We're grateful for your fair treatment." With that, he vanished.

Another moment defined the enthusiasm underlying Cosell's work. It came during the decathlon's fifteen-hundred-meter run, the last of the event's ten disciplines contested over two days.

He knew Bill Toomey's story. A childhood injury left the twenty-nine-year-old schoolteacher with a withered right hand. Never a world-class athlete at any single event, Toomey combined strength, speed, versatility, and will to excel in the decathlon. "You, sir," King Olav of Sweden had said to Jim Thorpe, the 1912 decathlon gold medalist, "are the greatest athlete in the world." That title was implicit in every Olympic decathlon, and Toomey had survived the bad hand, near-fatal hepatitis, a shattered kneecap, and mononucleosis to reach Mexico City.

Now, to win the gold, he had to win the fifteen hundred. Late that afternoon, Cosell went into the athletes' restroom in the Olympic stadium. There he saw Toomey on the floor, exhausted. Cosell gave him no chance. But a half-hour later, Toomey was on the track. It was dusk. Wind had come up. Rain fell. Cosell thought the race would never end, four laps, and on the fourth, out of the final turn, here came one man alone, Toomey.

Cosell was fifty years old. Though he was not reporting the event, he later wrote that he was in the stadium and "cheering like a damned kid." He explained: "It wasn't the victory. It was Bill Toomey—his whole life, what he had gone through to achieve what he had just done. This is the essence of what is great in sports, a complete manifestation of the sheer magnificence of the human spirit. What a man can do if he but wills it."

Howard Cosell's declamations would have been teeth-rattling intrusions in the deferential productions of NBC and CBS. But in the Arledge revolution, Cosell was the perfect soldier. His reporter's instincts, broadcaster's skills, and open need, even lust, for attention carried him to the center of every story. NBC and CBS broadcast games as solemn events. Not Arledge, whose defining words in the Scherick memo were these: "human drama." Cosell understood that. As an NYU undergraduate, he had been a literature major for whom the Stendahl novel *The Red and the Black*, the story of a young Parisian seeking social justice, was a transforming influence. He could, and did, while interviewing Muhammad Ali, cite John Keats's poetry. To Cosell the games were secondary to the stories they encapsulated. And when Cosell found the drama—Bill Toomey rising from exhaustion—the discovery animated him. There was truth in the sportswriter Larry Merchant's caricature of the Cosell method: "He makes the world of fun and games sound like the Nuremberg trials." But at his best, Cosell brought such passion to his work that his thrill became the listener's thrill.

————————

Already aglow with confidence, Cassius Clay at age fifteen posed with his first trainer, the Louisville police officer Joe Martin. (LOUISVILLE COURIER-JOURNAL PHOTO)

Howard Cosell with his wife, Emmy, in New York in 1954, when he was still a frustrated attorney hoping to break into broadcasting. (COURTESY OF JUSTIN COSELL)

Clay's first world championship came at the 1960 Olympics in Rome, where he stood tall for the gold medal ceremony. (AP/WIDE WORLD PHOTOS)

The year they met, 1966, the author had his notebook at the ready as Ali warmed up for an exhibition in his hometown, Louisville. (COURTESY OF C. THOMAS HARDIN)

Ali always drew a crowd of reporters. The one in a fedora is Howard Cosell.
(AP/WIDE WORLD PHOTOS)

After defeating Sonny Liston for the heavyweight championship in February 1964, Ali spent a week in New York City accompanied by Malcolm X. (AP/WIDE WORLD PHOTOS)

Ali and Cosell, here on the set of ABC's *Wide World of Sports*, became a frequent television act, beginning in the mid-1960s. (©ABC PHOTO ARCHIVES)

As Ali made an impassioned speech at a 1968 Savior's Day convention of the Nation of Islam, his rapt listeners included The Messenger himself, Elijah Muhammad. (AP/WIDE WORLD PHOTOS)

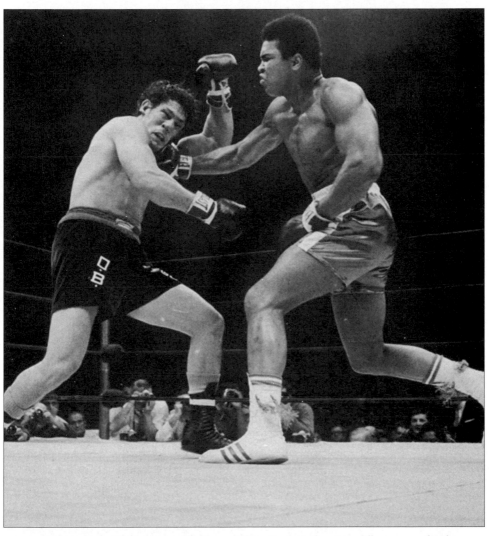

Ali brought athleticism, strength, and ferocity into the ring. All were on display here as he delivered a right hand to Oscar Bonavena's face in December 1970. (AP/WIDE WORLD PHOTOS)

Ali would do anything for a camera. In 1974 he climbed atop a rock at his boxing camp in the Pennsylvania mountains. Thus, the Colossus of Deer Lake. (COURTESY OF GENE KILROY)

In the 1970s, Cosell created an ABC franchise with *Monday Night Football* and maintained an uneasy relationship with co-announcers Don Meredith, left, and Frank Gifford. (©ABC PHOTO ARCHIVES)

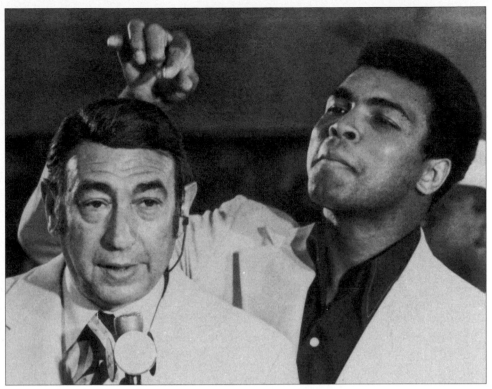

There is no record of Ali even touching Cosell's hairpiece. But he often threatened to liberate it. Here they work together on a 1972 ABC telecast from West Point. (AP/WIDE WORLD PHOTOS)

Mighty athlete that he was, Cosell landed a right hand on Ali's jaw in 1984. (AP/WIDE WORLD PHOTOS)

Two of the world's most famous religious figures, Ali and Jimmy Swaggart, came together in Ali's home in 1987. (COURTESY OF VICTOR SOLANO)

In retirement, Ali came to depend on his wife, Lonnie, for guidance in his professional affairs. They made a promotional trip to Dubai in 1987. (COURTESY OF LARRY J. KOLB)

The lion in winter with his soulmate, Emmy. It was 1988. (COURTESY OF JUSTIN COSELL)

With his lighting of the Olympic Games flame in 1996, Ali rose from the shadows of his middle life into the bright lights of the world stage he once dominated. (AP/WIDE WORLD PHOTOS)

Victor Solano was a Los Angeles teenager when he sparred with Ali. Thirty-five years later, in March 2005, they were old friends connected by memories. (COURTESY OF VICTOR SOLANO)

By the time they last met at a public function, in 1992, Ali and Cosell had transformed their show-biz act into a warm friendship. (AP/WIDE WORLD PHOTOS)

Avery Brundage surely had more on his mind than Howard Cosell when he said of the 1968 Olympics, "Warped mentalities and cracked personalities seemed to be everywhere, and impossible to eliminate." The *Warren* (Ohio) *Tribune*, left no doubt of its targets. With the Black Power controversy raging, the newspaper printed a full-page, black-bordered broadside with the headline: "SHAME ON HOWARD COSELL—AND SHAME ON ABC." Yet Cosell and Arledge returned home triumphant, having done "some of the best damned television in the history of the medium" (to quote Cosell). The good work included journalism seldom seen on sports television and never seen at all when challenged by its contractual partners, as in Mexico City.

It had been fourteen years since the restless, kibitzing lawyer Howard Cosell declared to Ray Robinson, *I can't help but go to the top.* Now he had done it. He was no longer the boxing guy basking in the reflected glory of Muhammad Ali. A year after Mexico City, Arledge called Cosell a "genuine celebrity . . . insecure, insomniac, self-involved—but, I thought, well worth the trouble." Such was Cosell's presence that he had become an American icon, at once recognizable as the nagging conscience of American sports and a self-caricaturing performer on network television. He even came to Woody Allen's mind.

The comedian and movie director asked Cosell to narrate the opening scene of *Bananas,* a farce about a Latin American revolution. The scene was a parody of *Wide World of Sports* with Cosell narrating an assassination on live television. "This is tremendous," he says, his ABC microphone in hand as he stands at the Capitol steps waiting for El Presidente to be shot. "The atmosphere heavy, uncertain, overtones of ugliness. A reminder in a way of how it was in March of 1964 in Miami Beach when Clay met Liston for the first time and nobody was certain how it would turn out." When shots are fired, Cosell shouts, "It's over. It's all over for El Presidente!" He pushes his way through the crowd. "Will you people let me through! This is American television! American television!" Kneeling at the fallen leader's side, he asks, "Sir, you've been shot. When did you know it was over?" No answer. So Cosell leaves the beaten man bleeding on the steps and goes to the new dictator to ask if he is worried about his next opponent, the rebels in the far hills. By movie's end, Cosell sits on a bed's edge to narrate live TV coverage of the wedding-night sex performed by the film's protagonists, Fielding and Nancy Mellish, invisible in their exertions under the covers. When Cosell sees those covers quiver one last time and fall still, he shouts, "It's over!" And he interviews the breathless couple.

Then came *Monday Night Football*, Roone Arledge's revolutionary baby, an NFL game broadcast in prime time on a weeknight. The deal had been made between ABC and the NFL when Arledge said to NFL Commissioner Pete Rozelle, ever so casually, "What would you think if I put Howard in the booth?"

"*Cosell?*" Rozelle laughed. "Why don't you just dig up Attila the Hun?"

Cosell recognized the Monday night telecast as the logical next step in his career. He knew the gossip: Arledge wanted his friend, the Giants football legend Frank Gifford, in the booth, but Gifford was under contract to CBS; Gifford recommended Don Meredith, the thirty-two-year-old quarterback who had abruptly retired from the Cowboys that year, saying, "If it ain't fun, it ain't worth doing." Cosell also heard his own name, and dearly wanted the job, but his calls to Arledge went unreturned. (After Mexico City, Arledge hired an answering service for his home phone to deflect Cosell's all-hours harangues, pleadings, and bloviations.)

On an afternoon in June 1970, Arledge finally called Cosell. He caught him at Jimmy Weston's restaurant in Midtown Manhattan at the end of a liquid lunch consisting of a martini or three, "my silver bullets," as Cosell called them. "Get over here as soon as you can," Arledge said. "There's something I need to talk to you about."

"Ahhhh," Cosell said. "From the desperation of your tone, I can only conclude that the bon vivant who is Roone Pinckney Arledge is beseeching me to rescue the trifle he's devised for Monday evenings. Am I not correct?"

"As always, Howard."

"And you no doubt expect me to shoulder this Stygian burden without additional compensation."

"Yes, Howard, I do."

"I accept."

One night shortly before *Monday Night Football*'s debut, the men shared a limousine ride home. Always the agitator, with a drink in his hand, Cosell said to his boss, "I suppose that in a strange way it matters to you whether this succeeds or not."

Arledge said, "Yes, Howard, it does. And it better damn well matter to you."

Monday night, September 21, 1970. Cleveland, Ohio. The Browns of Leroy Kelly, the Jets of Joe Willie Namath. A record crowd at the old stadium by Lake Erie, 85,703 people . . .

And that voice . . .

"It is a hot . . . sultry . . . almost windless night here at Municipal Stadium . . ."

Cosell's voice was subdued, almost languid, as if oppressed by the night air, deliberately understated to leave room for wisecracks to come with Meredith. The country boy from Mount Vernon, Texas, wasn't sure he could do this TV stuff. But Cosell had mastered the dynamics of a comedy act alongside Muhammad Ali. He told Meredith, "You'll wear the white hat, I'll wear the black hat."

Cosell the reporter was on top of the game, just as he had promised the press before the game when he said, "With the intelligent viewers I'll destroy the parrots in the cages who have been providing us with their tired litany for years." Using information gleaned from Namath, he pointed out the Jets' dominance of a rookie defensive lineman. Cosell also alerted viewers that Cleveland quarterback Bill Nelsen would take advantage of a Jets safety—because Nelsen had told the reporter just that. When Leroy Kelly rushed for only forty-four yards in twenty-six carries, Cosell said the Browns' star had not been "a compelling factor." An obvious comment, except that obvious negatives were seldom heard on national sports broadcasts. However, even a parrot might have avoided one Cosellian declaration. He said, "As long as Cleveland keeps possession, Namath can't score." Meredith's white hat all but glowed as the old Cowboy said, "Ya got a point there, Ha'hrd." And when Cleveland wide receiver Fair Hooker caught a Nelsen pass, Meredith asked his broadcast partners, "Isn't Fair Hooker a great name?"

"I pass," said, play-by-play man, Keith Jackson.

In a moment without precedent, Cosell sat mute.

"Fair Hooker," Meredith said. "I haven't met one yet."

It had been a competitive game. There was no friction in the three-man booth. The production finished with a take of Namath on the sidelines, unmoving, head bowed, hands on hips, a study in defeat, the embodiment of the human drama that Arledge saw in sports. ABC was pleased, but some critics savaged the show, one bemoaning Cosell's "retching prattle," another calling him "the master of the verbal cheap shot," yet another noting his "towering ignorance of football." The *New York Times* said Cosell's "parochial partisanship for the Jets was grating enough, but his miscalls of what happened on the field suggested that boxing is his bag."

Sacks of mail came to Arledge, who later wrote, "More than one in three Americans who'd turned on a television had watched *Monday Night Football*, and, in Howard Cosell, they'd found the man they loved to hate." Asked by a reporter if the controversy worried him, Arledge said, "*Worried?* That's exactly what I'm looking for." *Newsweek*'s Pete Axthelm acknowledged to all that "Cosell is, well, Cosell. Authoritative, energetic, Olympian in his proclamation. He grates on some, but his perception far outstrips that of anyone else in the business."

Not that Henry Ford II agreed. On Tuesday morning, Ford called Leonard Goldenson. Network chairmen of the board, ABC's Goldenson among them, take phone calls from advertisers who spend tens of millions of dollars on their air. Nobody threw more money at ABC than the Ford Motor Company, whose owner now told Goldenson, "I listened to that gab between Don Meredith and Howard Cosell last night. I couldn't concentrate on the football. Take that guy Cosell off." Arledge wouldn't do it. He argued to Goldenson that in another month Cosell's value would be clear. He dared not mention the Ford call to Cosell, already in a sulk from reading press reviews. Arledge called in director Chet Forte to replay the tape and asked, "What do you think?"

Forte said, "I don't think he's done a fucking thing wrong." Then he called Cosell to report that he and Arledge thought he had done well, no matter the critical mail. "More than half of it, Howard," he said, "doesn't even relate to the telecast. It's about you and Muhammad Ali." Cosell believed that whatever the letters said, they meant: *Get that nigger-loving Jew bastard off the air. Football is an* American *game.*

When Arledge, during the second week's game, barked a reprimand to Cosell through his earpiece, the petulant star refused to say another word. He had no idea that his immediate future was dependent on pleasing Arledge, Goldenson, ABC president Elton Rule, and the grandson of the man who put America on wheels—and not necessarily in that order. By coincidence, *Monday Night Football*'s third game was played in Detroit, Henry Ford II's town. Cosell moped under what he called "a good case of the blues." At dinner with Jackson and Meredith the night before the game, Cosell said, "I'm not coming back." Jackson vowed to quit, too. Not Meredith, who said, "The ol' Cowboy, he's coming back. I got nothing better to do that pays me so much." The three then did their best telecast, a Lions-Bears game with ratings that matched NBC specials with Bob Hope and Jack Paar. Arledge told Cosell, "Keep that up and there's no way they can touch you." By "they," he meant the critics, most writing for sports sections. Cosell called them "one-hundred-and-eighty-dollar-a-week mediocrities."

The next morning, Henry Ford was again on the phone to Goldenson, only this time offering an apology: "Despite my complaints on opening night, I like that patter that's going on between Cosell and Meredith. I'm enjoying that along with the game, and I want to withdraw my objections."

Because Cosell had never known that his job was in jeopardy, he didn't know he had rescued it. He had no reason, then, to feel good on arrival in Minnesota for ABC's game six. Indeed, he declared himself to have reached a nadir. His persecutors were relentless. He saw enemies everywhere. He had felt eyes on him even in the ABC offices in New York. Now those ankle-nibbling mediocrities of the sporting press had taken to calling him the "voice you love to hate." They also denigrated his work because he "never played the game."

It was a simple little game. The same game you played in the streets. Send the tall guy out against a short guy, a fast guy against a slow guy. And now they hated him because he wouldn't cover the game as if it had been invented by Enrico Fermi and refined by Wernher von Braun? Throughout the day, Cosell behaved badly. He later wrote: "Let's face it. I had become a pain in the ass." Arledge ordered him to quit it. "You've got everybody unnerved, everybody, the way you're acting," he said. The game, Los Angeles and Minnesota, had championship implications. "If you want to quit after this game—fine. If you want to talk it over tomorrow—fine. But give us all a break and do your thing tonight." That telecast went well, but if Cosell had come to Minnesota feeling things could hardly get worse, he was wrong. Three weeks later in Philadelphia, on a freezing night in an open press box, he had trouble enunciating sentences. Arledge asked Forte, "What the hell is the matter with Howard?"

By halftime Cosell slurred *Philadelphia* into *Phuldulpha*. Before the second half began, Cosell left the stadium and took a taxi to New York, a ninety-two-dollar fare. He did his radio show before the next day's dawn and, when apprised of news stories saying he was drunk in Philadelphia, he denied it. He told Arledge he had suffered "toxic vertigo, an infection in the inner ear that causes loss of balance and, sometimes, thickness of speech." ABC Sports' publicist Irv Brodsky defended Cosell: "Oh, I've seen him drink, and I've seen him drink a lot. But I have never seen him drunk." Arledge acknowledged that Cosell had had one drink before the game, and, like Brodsky, he supported the network star's explanation of sudden illness.

Arledge cared only for Cosell's preservation, because *Monday Night Football* had become a national phenomenon. The critic Ron Powers believed the show's success began with its juxtaposition against the time's terrible realities of assassination, racial turmoil, and the war in Vietnam: "*Monday Night Football* offered a benevolent vision of the possible; it offered a game played against chaos and death, against entropy. It offered a kind of 'reality' without the consequences of reality. It intensified the passions of mythic conflict, but it withheld the horror and guilt of America's exposure to living-room war: the images of torn bodies, the grief over slain, wasted heroes. On *Monday Night Football*, the heroes arose again and again from the brilliant green field in their gleaming helmets that caught the stadiums' fiery floodlights, and director Chet Forte's twelve probing, peering, insistent cameras zoomed in and in for lingering portraits of their handsome, charged faces."

Or maybe, as Arledge insisted, it was a *game*. It was more than okay to have fun, it was obligatory. So when Forte's cameras caught a shot of veteran quarterback/carouser Sonny Jurgensen's geriatric paunch, Meredith said, "Now there is an example of what clean living can do for you." Cosell and *MNF*'s audience had enjoyed the Cowboys losing, 38–0, especially with Meredith feeling his buddies' pain. "Dadgum it," the old 'Boys quarterback said of a muffed punt. "Things like that get the Cowboys in a hole." Cosell exploited every moan, once saying, "I wish the viewers could see Don Meredith right now. He's upset, gritting his teeth. It may make a better picture than the game." Cowboys fans in the Cotton Bowl looked to the broadcasting booth and chanted, "We want Meredith, we want Meredith." But Dandy Don demurred: "I'm not going down there. Not on a night like this."

Of the twenty-two new shows in 1970, *Monday Night Football* ranked third behind *The Flip Wilson Show* and *The Mary Tyler Moore Show*. On a typical Monday night minute, 31 percent of all televisions turned on were tuned in to *MNF.* Cosell was delighted. He had experienced thirteen weeks of anxiety, doubt, daring, confidence, and triumph to emerge as a national celebrity. He had done Channel 7's local sports reports for twelve years, but no more. He said he was free at last "to do other things outside of the confining dimensions of sport." As offers for television appearances came in, he acknowledged the wonder of it all: "The tall figure with the ferretlike face, having passed the fifty-year milestone, would debut in prime-time situation comedies. . . . I was wanted in Hollywood."

Few sweeter words could have been uttered by a poor, Jewish boy from Brooklyn who had been entranced by motion pictures in grand old movie houses. *The Partridge Family,* starring Shirley Jones, cast him as an investigative reporter who helped save the whales. He played a biology teacher for *Nanny and the Professor,* quarterbacking the faculty football team to defeat at the hands of a team of students twelve years old and younger.

After *MNF*'s last game, show business agent Jim Mahoney gave Cosell and Emmy a ride to the airport. Before Cosell entered the car, he heard a passerby shout, "Hey, Howie baby. Were you really drunk in Philadelphia?" Mahoney laughed with Cosell and said, "They bum-rapped you the whole damned season, and they wound up making a star out of you. *Monday Night Football* is the biggest hit in the country." This, Cosell thought, from Sinatra's agent.

CHAPTER TEN

"*You'll Never Really Know Him*"

ELIJAH MUHAMMAD'S SUSPENSION of Ali, trumpeted with such vehemence in *Muhammad Speaks,* never really began and never was officially ended. Never did Ali give up his honorific name and revert to Clay, as Elijah ordered. Not a word of reproach was said when Ali returned to the ring against Quarry and Bonavena, though the Messenger had inveighed against the evils of sports. Herbert Muhammad, Elijah's son, remained the chief executive of Ali the Money Machine, and it required no cynicism to say that Ali's trespasses were forgiven when a fight with Joe Frazier in March of 1971 promised a payday of $2.5 million, much of which would find its way into the Nation's bank accounts.

On a day in January of that year, Cosell and Emmy were poolside at Miami's Americana Hotel when they heard a familiar voice.

That voice . . . Muhammad Ali, in full cry: "Where is he?"

Cosell raised himself up from his chaise longue.

"Where's that white fella who gives me so much trouble? Where's Cosell?" He had created a rhyme. "When I'm finished with Frazier, at the sound of the bell . . ." Quickly now . . . "I'll jump through the ropes—and take care of Cosell!"

The act had been big before, but not this big, Ali again a fighter, Cosell a household curse, both men famous and infamous, each magnified by the other's presence. Now Ali had an idea for a field trip in Miami, as he said to Emmy, "I want your husband. I want to take him with me. I want to show him it's only fifteen minutes from heaven to hell."

"Take him," Emmy said, somewhat more cheerily than her husband would have liked. "He's yours."

When Cosell protested the dragooning, Ali said, "I know what you've been saying about me. 'He's not in shape, his speed is gone.' I'm gonna take care of you today." They drove across the Seventy-ninth Street Causeway into Miami. "I'm gonna take you to the ghetto to meet my people," Ali said. "You'll see what life is really like."

"I've seen Harlem and I've seen Watts," Cosell said. "It won't be news to me."

"Listen," Ali said, "there's something else I want to talk to you about. It's that football business you're involved in. And this guy who works with you. What's his name? Dandy? I think you're making too much of him. You gotta remember, we're the number one act in sports." There was reason to doubt that. Ali had returned to the ring only three months earlier after three and a half years gone. To a new set of fans, Ali was an old-timer who had come back to fight Quarry and Bonavena. Maybe he was good enough to handle Frazier, maybe not. Meanwhile, in its first season, *Monday Night Football* had become the hottest item in popular culture, with "Humble Howard" and "Dandy Don" its stars. Still, the flash of Ali's insecurity surprised Cosell.

"You're a nut," Cosell said, and Ali, happy with that affirmation, drove on to a pool parlor in one of Miami's black neighborhoods, there herding Cosell into the shadows and announcing, "Here he is! Here's the white guy who gives me all that trouble on television!" Cosell heard more. Like, *Come here, boys, it's our turn to give him trouble.* And, *We been waiting for this, ain't we, boys?* The players gathered around Cosell, whose trips to Harlem and Watts may not have included personal confrontation with men moving in cool darkness and carrying pool cues in service of the most famous black man on Earth. He told Ali, "Knock it off. These guys might take you seriously."

Ali threw an arm around Cosell's shoulder. "I'm only kidding," he told the pool shooters. "He's my friend." Leaving, Ali whispered into Cosell's ear. "Call me 'nigger.'"

"No way. I may have a few years left."

Next stop, a barber shop, where Ali put Cosell into a chair and shouted to the crowd, "Let's give Howard a haircut. Howard needs a haircut bad, don't he?"

Not really, though he did not have on his toupee. "Lay off me, Muhammad," Cosell said. He squirmed to get out of the chair. "I have little enough hair as it is." Back at the Americana, Emmy asked Howard, "What did Muhammad want?"

"It was strange," he said. "Somehow he felt he wanted to be with me. Maybe because he's coming up to the fight of his life, and because we've been together so long. Maybe because he feels kind of lonely, with so many writers picking Frazier. And he did want me to see the ghetto, where he had hung out when he first came down here."

He also told her about Ali's mention of Don Meredith. Emmy said, "Is he worried that will change what you think of him?"

"More like he was being demoted."

Emmy didn't know what to make of that. "As long as you know him," she said, "you'll never really know him."

As Cosell did not truly know Ali, Ali never knew Cosell. Theirs was a partnership more than a friendship. They had met nine years earlier and would be in each other's company until one or the other left the stage. "But Cosell was not our friend," Gene Kilroy said. "We were never in his house, he was never in ours. He just used Muhammad." In truth, both men were so self-absorbed as to be blind to the other's needs except as those needs met their own. Psychologists have found narcissists to be people wounded in childhood, abandoned psychically by their parents, as both Cosell and Ali were. Abandoned, they become the Albert Camus character whom the novelist has say, "It is not true, after all, that I never loved. I conceived at least one great love in my life, of which I was always the object."

On the important questions in Ali's life, Cosell was invisible. In his four memoirs, Cosell never takes a position pro or con on Ali's opposition to the Vietnam War, or on the war itself, for that matter. Never does he address the political question in Ali's draft case, that is, did the U.S. government single out Ali for induction to silence him? Nowhere is there evidence that Cosell, the nonobservant Jew, made a judgment of the Nation of Islam ideology espoused by Ali. Voluble on a thousand subjects, Cosell never addressed these, at least not in his memoirs and not in interviews. Most likely, he ran silent on his radio shows as well, or the answers would have found their way into screaming headlines: "Cosell Accuses Uncle Sam of Persecuting His Pal Ali!" "Cosell Calls Black Muslims Hate-Mongers!" "Ex-Army Major Cosell Says Vietnam War an 'Utter Mistake.'"

No such headlines were written because Cosell never broached those issues. "Mr. Middle of the Road," Jerry Izenberg called him. Cosell did a clever high-wire act. He portrayed himself as a brother in arms standing with Ali. In fact, he never defended a single Ali position on race, politics, or religion. He defended the fighter's rights to hold those positions. That was a good and brave thing to do in a time when many people's rights were taken from them. But it was a different thing from agreeing with Ali's philosophies and ideologies. Cosell's defense was a narrow constructionist's that excused him from ever taking a stand on the volatile issues of Ali's life.

He moved toward Ali on Vietnam, not because of Ali but because he had engaged in debate with a political protester near his heart: his younger daughter, Hilary. The talk began in 1967 when she was a fourteen-year-old freshman at Fox Lane High School in Bedford, New York. During her high-school years, Hilary organized antiwar walkouts, vigils, protests, and bus trips to demonstrations in Washington, D.C. "One of the hardest things an overprotective father like Dad ever did," she said, "was kiss me good-bye as I went off to D.C. yet again. He was terrified I'd be seriously injured or killed by violence. But he knew it was right, and important, so he waved good-bye. Hell, he raised me to do it. He set the example." Still, a major in the U.S. Army during World War II was not easily persuaded that an American war was senseless. The H. Cosells, Howard and Hilary, engaged in what she called "mandatory eight-count, three-knockdown rule fights about the war." The debate ranged beyond Ali and student radicals and foreign policy. The father and daughter dealt with what they saw as the injustice of a war fought by blacks and poor whites unable to flee to Canada or create deferments. In the end, Hilary said, "reason, intellect, the history of Nam after WWII, and the utter futility and waste of the war turned my father against it."

Better than anyone, perhaps, Hilary Cosell, who later worked in sports broadcasting herself, understood her father's position on Ali and the draft. Howard may never have said publicly that the government used the draft to punish Ali, but Hilary believed his silence spoke loudly: "Because it was so patently clear that Muhammad was drafted because of his color, persona, and politics, there was no need to state the obvious."

Nor did she think it necessary that her father offer an opinion on Ali's acceptance of Nation of Islam ideology. "Dad was a humanist, not a separatist," Hilary said. "As a Jew, he saw separatist ideology as a negative, destructive doctrine in theory and in practice. He saw the tenets of civil

disobedience, of Dr. King, of Freedom Riders and voter registration, uni-
fication and inclusion and equality, as the key. At the same time, he understood where Muhammad, Malcolm X, and the Black Muslims were
coming from. So while he didn't personally 'like' it or believe that in the
end it was going to serve a great purpose for black Americans, he respected Muhammad's choice and beliefs, even though he didn't agree
with them."

Cosell's reluctance to enter those dark waters betrayed his personal insecurities in a profession notorious for the insecurity of its practitioners.
He feared that taking a position either way on Ali's thinking would hurt
him professionally, either with ABC's corporate hierarchy or with Ali
himself. He created and sustained the image of his moral superiority on
the slender thread of defending Ali's rights without defending Ali's
ideas—even to construction workers on Fifty-second Street in New York.

"Hey, Cosell," one shouted to him in February 1971, a month before
Ali fought Frazier. Even then, the Ali-Cosell connection was so well established that the Coach's customary walk from ABC's offices for lunch
at Manuche's restaurant was done with Ali's shadow at his side. The construction worker shouted so his buddies could hear, "Hey, Cosell, what's
with you and that black son of a bitch Clay? That traitor should never be
allowed to fight."

As the hard-hats gathered around him, Cosell spoke to the leader,
rough-cut and beer-bellied. "Now wait a minute, Johnny. I know how we
can settle this. Clay is just around the corner at the Hilton. We can go
over there right now, and you can lay that son of a bitch low."

"You serious?"

"Look at your body. You can handle him. I'm with you all the way. He's
around the corner in room nineteen-ten. He's up there right now. We'll
go over—you bring the other guys along—and you can have a piece of
him. You can whip his ass."

Here his buddies bought in to Cosell's fun. "Yeah, Johnny," one said.
"C'mon, Johnny. Let's go."

The big man raised his hands for quiet. "Hell's the matter with you
guys? You crazy? The guy's a professional fighter. Gimme a hammer, I'll
go over there. Maybe."

Two weeks later, apprised of Johnny's interest, Ali joined Cosell for a
stroll along Fifty-second Street to the construction site.

"Johnny," Cosell said, "I want you to meet Muhammad Ali. You know, the black son-of-a-bitch traitor." Behind him, straining forward, Ali assumed his most ferocious, hold-me-back-Howard pose.

"Now, wait a minute, Champ," Johnny said. "Howie, you gotta understand, ya know?"

Ali growled. "Did you call me a black son-of-a-bitch traitor?"

"Kiddin', Champ. Just kiddin', ya know?"

Now Ali laughed. It took only five more minutes of Ali's charm, and the hard-hats were no longer ready to fight him. They, too, wanted a piece of Joe Frazier.

PART THREE

At the Top

CHAPTER ELEVEN

"God Knows the World
Wants Me to Win"

FERDIE PACHECO LIKED TO BET on Ali's fights. The morning of March 8, 1971, his wife said, "Don't bet this one."

The fight doctor listened to Luisita. She had often seen in dreams what she would see in life. She came from a family with claims to psychic powers, descendants of Plains Indians with Spanish blood. This morning, twelve hours before Ali would stand in against Joe Frazier, Pacheco asked his wife, "Why not bet?" She explained that she had awakened from a dream that she saw as through a telescope. She saw Ali in red trunks with reds tassels at his shoetops. It was late in the fight. She saw Ali's legs in the air. She saw the red tassels flying.

The doctor said, "Not to worry. He wears only white."

For almost four years, Ali had done none of the athletic work necessary to be a prizefighter. He had sparred a few rounds with British contender Joe Bugner, but he did it with no sense of sharpening his skills; he did it for the hundred dollars a round spending money. He ran occasionally to lose weight because his vanity demanded it. But he was in his physical prime, twenty-eight years old, and he believed that if someone gave him a license, he could be ready the next day.

Six weeks' training for Quarry were enough, and the fight cost him so little in energy that another six weeks put him ready for Oscar Bonavena, a fight that left him bruised and exhausted. Two fights against top heavyweights in three months after forty-three months away should have been followed by a long, recuperative rest. Instead, Ali agreed to fight Frazier three months later. He did not want anyone to believe that Frazier was the rightful champion. Also, there was on the table an offer of the biggest payday in sports history, $2.5 million to each fighter.

Ali's return in Atlanta had been less a fight than a resurrection celebrated by acolytes and idolators who saw in him what they wished to see in themselves. He was bold and beautiful, and damned if he couldn't do whatever he said he could. He did it to Sonny Liston. Now Liston was gone, dead with needle tracks in his arm, dead in Las Vegas, maybe murdered. Ali told the U.S. government he wouldn't go to its war, and he didn't, and he said they could put him in prison, and in almost four years they hadn't been able to do it. Good men gone. John F. Kennedy, Malcolm X, Martin Luther King, Robert F. Kennedy. Gone, and here was Muhammad Ali, gone all that time, chosen for persecution, banished, excommunicated, left for psychically dead, and yet there he was, in Atlanta, next door to MLK's daddy's church, alive again.

His athletic gifts were diminished. Once he had been ineffable. He liked to say he danced. What he did, moving in the ring, was more than a dance, for dancers touch the floor, and Cassius Clay floated, a leaf on the air. Lifted by a sudden breeze, a leaf rises silently and comes down in a new spot, only to move again, in a new direction, quicker, turned on its side and showing another color. Cassius Clay moved that way. The way he moved, that was the art of it. Every so often he stopped to hit somebody in the face. Yes. There was that. But somehow, in the most brutal sport, the only sport that rewards you for doing injury to your opponent's brain, Cassius Clay seemed less a fighter than an artist.

Muhammad Ali was no longer Cassius Clay. Against Quarry and Bonavena, he moved with greater elegance and grace than most fighters could imagine. For maybe a minute of each round in those fights, he did an impression of the 1964 Clay who had rendered Liston incompetent. He did the impression well, and there were those who believed that when it *really* mattered, he could turn it up a notch. Yes, with more work in the gym, asking more of himself in the ring, he could be what he once was. I believed that in the way others believed everything he said. It was a level of belief that had nothing to do with reality. He had been an athlete unlike any other, and that's the Ali I wanted, the Ali who stole my reason. I knew the truth when I saw him in Madison Square Garden against the Argentine bull Bonavena. He was no longer Clay. He was Ali. He was still great. But it just wasn't the same. He had come down from preternatural to extraordinary.

And now he had to fight Joe Frazier.

In Ali's absence, Frazier had walked through the heavyweight division, and now he needed to deal with Ali. The king had returned from exile and wanted back the title taken from him unjustly; no other heavyweight champion had ever lost the title except in the ring. Even in exile, Ali insisted that he was the true champion, addressing that insistence to all people everywhere, for he was certain now, as always, that his every thought, word, and movement entranced the world. "I think," he said to the London sports journalist Hugh McIlvanney, "I must have the most populous face on earth, exceptin' maybe Nixon's. And maybe even more than his." McIlvanney liked that word, "populous," he said, "for no one who looks into Ali's face can expect to see one man. He dreams himself anew each morning."

Both Frazier and Ali came to March 8 undefeated. One a puncher, the other a boxer. One a man, the other a symbol. One spoke softly when spoken to, the other shouted at all hours. One quoted the Bible, the other the Qur'an. Ali at six foot three was four inches taller and at 215 pounds was ten pounds heavier. He had turned twenty-nine, and Frazier was twenty-seven. Both were black and proud of it, and yet Ali, with malice, cruelty, and something approaching sadism, rained insults on Frazier relentlessly, his unforgivable intent nothing less than the transformation of a proud black warrior into a feckless white hope.

Ali: "The only people rooting for Joe Frazier are white people in suits, Alabama sheriffs, and members of the Ku Klux Klan. I'm fighting for the little man in the ghetto. . . . Joe Frazier is too ugly to be champ. Joe Frazier is too dumb to be champ. The heavyweight champion should be smart and pretty like me. . . . Frazier's no real champion. Nobody wants to talk to him. Oh, maybe Nixon will call him if he wins. I don't think he'll call me. But 98 percent of my people are for me. They identify with my struggle. Same one they're fighting every day in the streets. If I win, they win. I lose, they lose. Anybody black who thinks Frazier can whup me is an Uncle Tom. Everybody who's black wants me to keep winning."

Frazier hated Ali for that. The last of thirteen children of Dolly and Rubin Frazier, a one-armed vegetable farmer on the flat lands of coastal South Carolina, Frazier had risen from desperate beginnings, first as his father's "left-hand man" and later stripping sides of beef in a Philadel-phia slaughterhouse for $105 a week. Next to Frazier's life, Ali's had been the idyll of a golden child. When Ali said, "I'm gonna give Joe Fra-zier a ghetto whuppin'," the man up from nothing snapped, "What he *know* about the ghetto?" Frazier could not match Ali's verbal dexterity and did not reply in kind to the character assassination. "I'm no god-damned Uncle Tom," he said. "I'm blacker than him. Next time I see him, I'm gonna ask him to show me one black spot on his brown body."

On fight night, along Seventh Avenue between Thirty-first Street and Thirty-third, at the entrance to Madison Square Garden, a caravan of long, sleek, black limousines delivered their ladies and gentlemen in for-mal evening dress, gowns and tuxedos, hot pants and mink-trimmed jumpsuits, peacocks all, movie stars and astronauts, senators and singers, Joe Namath with a goatee, Hugh Hefner with a Playmate in see-through chiffon, not the Atlanta show only because in New York the sen-sational was de rigueur. More than twenty thousand people gathered for The Fight, the promoters claiming that closed-circuit television to thirty-five countries would reach three hundred million people from London to Hong Kong to Christchurch, New Zealand. The glitterati included Cosell on a busman's holiday, passed over for the closed-circuit broadcast by the fight's promoter, Jerry Perenchio, who had found himself shouting dur-ing the Ali-Bonavena telecast, "Howard, will you shut up!"

All to see "just a couple of men jumpin' around in a ring together," Ali said. It was nine o'clock, an hour before fight time, when Ali woke from a nap in a room high above the Garden floor. He took an elevator down three levels to his dressing room, there to be rubbed by Sarria, to have his hands taped by the old trainer, Chickie Ferrara. When it was time to dress, Ali pulled from a bag a pair of red velvet trunks with a white stripe down each side. Everyone in his corner would wear red sweaters that night.

Ferdie Pacheco thought, "Red?" He had told his wife that Ali never wore anything but white. And the shoes. White shoes. At the top of each shoe, red tassels.

"What the fuck is that?" Pacheco said.

"So the judges can see me dancin'," Ali said.

"Yeah, and what if they see you knocked on your ass and those tassels are dancin' in the air?"

Only the least emotionally involved or the most experienced fight-watcher sees both men in the ring. Neither description fit me on March 8, 1971. I was Ali's Louisville reporter. I had known him four years. He had held my son in his arms. The loudmouth stuff, the Nation of Islam and its mothership, Malcolm X, refusing the draft, putting his career and millions of dollars at stake on a principle, the contemptible slurs against opponents—all that was entertaining, inspiring, disturbing, confusing. I knew one thing for sure. He was the greatest athlete I would ever see in a lifetime of sportswriting. When he was in the ring, I saw *him*. Always, the other guy had been a blurred figure, a pale shadow, nothing really.

But not this time. This time even I saw Joe Frazier.

Ali played to the twenty thousand people in the building. He wore the tassels so they could see him dance. He stood in his corner between early rounds so they could see his disdain for the other guy. Frazier did not see the twenty thousand, nor did he care about them. Nothing existed except the man in front of him. I had seen Frazier fight twice. The first was a mismatch in a small arena with a small crowd. My seat was first-row ringside. I heard Frazier's exhalations, *chuh-chuh-CHUH,* as he marched forward, head drawn down between his shoulders, lip curled, nostrils flared, feet spread wide, gloved fists turned in to his chest, coming to hurt the kid in there with him. A Frazier hook splattered the kid's blood on my notebook. One round was all he needed. Later, I saw Frazier beat Jimmy Ellis in four rounds, knocking him down twice in the last thirty seconds. Ellis remembered only the first knockdown.

Now Frazier came for Ali.

Early, Ali moved easily. He shouted to Frazier, "Don't you know I'm God?" Frazier seemed clumsy, taking jabs and crosses as punishment for his gracelessness. Ali separated his words with punches: "Don't . . . you . . . know . . . I'm . . . God?" Three rounds, four rounds, five, Ali did what Ali always did—what Frazier's strategist, Eddie Futch, knew he would do. Go to the ropes and wait. Ali might con the innocents with his minute dancing and two resting. Even as he leaned back to keep his head out of Frazier's reach, he looked down into the first press row at ringside, popping open his eyes. He bellowed, "No contest! NOOOO contest!"

A fight master long removed from innocence, Eddie Futch considered Ali's charade an invitation. He told Frazier, "When he goes to the ropes, you go to his body with both hands." Frazier thundered against Ali's ribs, waistline, hips. Six rounds, eight rounds, Ali playing when he needed to fight, Ali putting a glove against Frazier's forehead, as if holding off a child, Ali against the ropes and pitty-pattying taps against the aggressor's noggin, Ali allowing Frazier in. "Come on, man," he said. "Is that the best you got?" After the eighth, Ali's trainer Angelo Dundee scolded him: "Stop playing. Do you want to blow this fight? Do you want to blow everything?"

After ten rounds, Frazier's face had become a grotesquerie of hematomas bulging from his jawline, cheekbones, and brow, squeezing his eyes to slits, his swollen lips pulled back from a mouthpiece once white and now red. Ali no longer danced even the minute of earlier rounds; now he moved on the same plane as Frazier. Whatever notes I made were hieroglyphics of anxiety, unreadable. All along I had felt something shameful at being thrilled by these bloody pieces of commercial brutality, but I rationalized it and justified it as part of the human condition. Will Durant's *The Life of Greece* reported prizefighting fifteen centuries before Christ on the island of Crete where "heavyweights, coddled with helmets, cheekpieces, and long padded gloves, fight till one falls exhausted to the ground and the other stands above him in the conscious grandeur of victory."

Thirty-four centuries later, not on vases but five feet from me, Ali stood in with Frazier, the beauty of it terrible.

Now, the eleventh round. The farmer's left-hand man had thrown Ali's insults into the roaring furnace of his belly and had come to do work until the work was done. That work was Ali. Frazier had become concentration incarnate. Even as Ali reconfigured his face, Frazier kept coming. He was willing to run into punches as long as the movement put him nearer Ali. His world was small now, closing down as the eye's pupil closes against light. Just him and Ali at arm's length. In the eleventh, Ali sought to rest against the ropes. But that was not enough for this most vainglorious of men; with his right hand, Ali waved Frazier in, inviting him to throw more punches, mocking him, really, for who ever *asked* to be hit by Joe Frazier?

What Ali didn't expect was that Frazier would reach him with his most powerful shot, a left hook to the side of the head. It was the ninth round three months earlier when Bonavena put Ali into that electric zzzzz daze with a series of punches in the ninth round. Late in the eleventh round this time, Frazier did it with the single hook. Ali reeled on a drunk's legs into ring center, there teetering, a wire-walker in a high wind. But wait.

He straightened up. He put his feet together and wiggled his hips in exaggeration of a fighter in trouble. Was he hurt or was he faking it? Before Frazier could find out, the round ended—and Ali now had one minute to recover.

Referee Arthur Mercante came to Ali's corner for the necessary look at the fighter's condition. When last Ali had left his corner in danger, seven years earlier, blinded by an oil of some kind, he danced away from Sonny Liston. But that was the fifth round and he had seldom been hit. This would be the twelfth against a man beating him senseless. Angelo Dundee slapped Ali's thighs and shouted in his ear. He had never seen Ali in worse shape. A wonder, he thought, that his guy had survived the eleventh.

Ali did not invite Frazier to hit him again. To get through the next three rounds, Ali used the guile gained in seventeen years in the ring, in thousands of rounds, in hours of watching films. He moved near Frazier to smother his punches. He clutched at him, leaned on him, put his arms behind the smaller man's head and pushed him down. It became apparent that Ali believed he needed a knockout. He started the last round, the fifteenth, with two left-right combinations. He wanted then to throw a right uppercut. A fighter who drops his right hand to start an uppercut has no defense against a left hook. At that moment, Frazier's hook thundered against Ali's head. He went down.

Ali had been knocked down twice in his professional career, both times by left hooks early in fights by lesser men who couldn't reach him again. This was Frazier, his peer, in the fifteenth round. He had been hurt in the eleventh and now he fell backward onto the canvas. Ali's legs rose above his head toward the ring lights, and those red tassels danced in the air, and Luisita Pacheco stood below Ali's corner, seeing in real time what she had already seen in dream time. Her husband shouted, "Oh, God! Oh, God!"

The brain is a fragile organ, a gelatinous mass of nerve tissue floating in the cranium. It is damaged when shaken so violently that it collides with the skull. At great enough force, that collision of brain and bone ruptures the brain's blood veins. Permanent damage follows if brain tissue is scarred or dies. Best-case scenario: A left hook rattles your brain. Worse: The trauma causes an electrical short-circuit, the brain going dark, a knockout. Worst: A hemorrhage kills you.

A testament to his will and his body, both extraordinary, Ali was back on his feet quickly. Such was the force of Frazier's blow that the right side of Ali's face immediately puffed up, so quickly that some people at ringside insisted they could see it growing even as Ali fell, as if the cheeck were pumped up by hydraulics, outward evidence of what might have happened inside his skull. Though up and moving, Ali had nothing left but his refusal to go down again. Frazier was spent as well, yet throwing punches, both fighters enveloped by the waterfall's roar of twenty thousand celebrants giving witness to sports history.

And then the referee Mercante put himself between Ali and Frazier. The fight was over.

I had heard no bell because the crowd's roar was so loud I could barely move, let alone hear, and then the only sound that mattered was the voice of ring announcer Johnny Addie. He said, "Referee Arthur Mercante scores eight rounds for Frazier, six rounds for Ali, one round even . . . Judge Artie Aidala scores nine rounds for Frazier, six rounds for Ali . . ."

Bedlam in the ring. Dolly and Rubin Frazier's thirteenth child leaped into the arms of his long-time trainer, Yank Durham, who shouted, "You done it, Joe, you done it."

Immediately after the fight, Ali went to a hospital. Frazier met the press. A handler pressed an ice pack against the champion's left cheekbone. "You've got to give him credit," Frazier said. "He takes one good punch. That shot I hit him in the fifteenth round, I went 'way back to the country to throw. He's got a good punch and he's a good man. God, he can take it. . . . Now let me go and straighten out my face. I ain't quite this ugly."

In his dressing room, someone loaded ice into a sink. Frazier dropped his face into the ice and held it there until he needed to breathe. He did it four times, last surfacing to mumble, "You whipped him." He saw himself in a mirror and said in mumbling mimicry of Ali: "You flat-footed. You dumb. You ugly." He might have smiled only a smile hurt too much. "Hah," he said, "we saw about that." Then he remembered another of Ali's insults. "Yank! Hey, Yank, go get Clay. Go tell him to come in here and start crawlin' on his hands and knees like he said he would."

Ali went to Flower Fifth Avenue Hospital, uptown from Madison Square Garden, a seventy-block limousine ride that Dr. Pacheco insisted he make for an examination of the swollen jaw. X-rays showed nothing broken, but doctors recommended that Ali stay overnight. He said softly he didn't want to do that. "Make it look like Joe Frazier put me in the hospital, and that's not true. Take me back to the hotel." Pacheco and Dundee helped him off the table and supported him walking through a crowd of interns and nurses. He entered an elevator, and as its doors closed he announced, "The Greatest is gone."

The morning after, more human in defeat than in victory, Ali sat in his room at the New Yorker Hotel, across from the Garden. "Next time would be different," he said. "Myself would make it different. When you get as big as I got in this game, you get intoxicated with so-called greatness. You think you just have to run three miles a day. That's all I did for this fight. And I didn't rest properly, didn't train hard as I used to. You convince yourself you'll get by on natural talent, that it will all just explode in there on the night. But it don't."

It had been nine years since that icy February day in Albany when A. J. Liebling first encountered the boyish poetics of Cassius Clay and noticed "a faint odor of *hubris*, like Lilac Végétal." Now Ali's failure to train properly and his misguided comedics against Frazier suggested that the aroma had reached a full and terrible richness.

Still, on this morning after, the good grace of common sense fell into Ali's oratory. "I've never thought about losing," he said, "but now that it's happened, the only thing is to do it right. That's my obligation to all the people who believe in me. We all have to take defeats in life. We lose loved ones, or a man loses his property or his job. All kinds of things set us back, but life goes on. If so-called great people can take these defeats, whatever they are, without cracking, the others are encouraged. They feel strong.

"You don't shoot yourself. Soon this will be old news. People got lives to lead, bills to pay, mouths to feed. Maybe a plane will go down with ninety persons in it. Or a great man will be assassinated. That will be more important than Ali losing. I never wanted to lose, never thought I would, but the thing that matters is how you lose. I'm not crying. My friends should not cry."

Someone interrupted. "Champ . . ."

"Don't call me the champ," Ali said. "Joe's the champ now."

Bob Lipsyte reminded him of 1964. "Remember before the first Liston fight when you said that if you lost, you'd be on the street the next day hollering, "No man ever beat me twice'?"

Ali's face was swollen and scratched, but he could smile. "I remember.

And you know what I say now? Get me Frazier. No man ever beat me twice." His voice rising. "I'll get by Joe this time. I'll straighten this out. Joe, you hear me?" Now shouting. "Joe, if you beat me this time, you'll *really* be the greatest."

Ali might go to prison before there could be a second fight. He stood convicted in the draft-refusal case, later identified by Supreme Court scholar David O'Brien as "a symbol of the troubled 1960s." Ali's chances of winning a reversal from the high court were small. Certainly, the justices were not eager to establish a precedent that would allow all Nation of Islam members to avoid service by filing as conscientious objectors. As they had done in 1969, the justices in January 1971 voted privately not to hear the case. Again, Ali was at the jailhouse door.

This time Justice Brennan intervened. He asked that his colleagues reconsider. A liberal on a court that tilted, if only slightly, to a conservative ideology, Brennan didn't expect a reversal. But he did persuade them to hear the case again. His rationale: Imprisoning a high-profile war dissenter without according him the full protection of the legal process could be seen as proof that the government prosecuted the case on a political basis.

So, on April 19, 1971, the Ali case came before eight justices. (Thurgood Marshall recused himself because he had been solicitor general at the time of Ali's conviction.) Four days later, they voted five to three to affirm the conviction. For the sixth time, Ali had lost in court. On May 3, Chief Justice Warren Burger assigned Justice John M. Harlan to write the Court's majority opinion.

How odd, in the year 1971, that Justice Harlan would hear a case titled *United States of America* v. *Cassius Marsellus Clay*. (On his original Selective Service papers, Ali had misspelled his own name.) Odd because the justice's grandfather, the first Justice John M. Harlan, had been a friend of the original Cassius Marcellus Clay in their Kentucky days. But oddity, Pacheco's idea of "Ali's luck," or even mysticism seemed an inadequate explanation for what Justice Harlan did next.

He changed his mind.

He did that after consultation with his clerks, those young lawyers who did their boss's legal research and wrote opinion drafts that he would finish up. They may not have had an idea of Muhammad Ali's stature as a fighter, but they understood the issue before the court. Thirty-two years later, I spoke with a Harlan clerk named Thomas Krattenmaker. He said, "I suspect that every one of us, consciously or unconsciously, had a sense that we could just as easily have been in uniform as to have this wonderful opportunity to spend a year in the Court. By the grace of God, or by luck, we were not sent to Vietnam. In 1970 the average twenty-six-year-old white male law-school graduate was not part of a group that vigorously supported the draft and thought it was a good idea to tell people who didn't want to go fight in Vietnam that they should do it anyway."

Krattenmaker had been an antiwar protester himself while a student at Columbia University's law school. "Nothing radical there," he said. "I did petitions and marches, just a law-abiding citizen exercising my First Amendment rights along with hundreds of thousands of others in New York City." He knew Ali had said, "I ain't got no quarrel with them Viet Cong," and admired the way a man without a fancy education reached the argument's central point in "a very commonsense way that explained what was wrong with forcible conscription for people to fight that conflict."

As Justice Harlan began the work necessary to write the majority opinion that would send Ali to prison, Krattenmaker spoke up. More than that, he became, in his words, "a bit of a pest." He believed there was precedent for ruling in Ali's favor, stemming not from his own antiwar views but from solid legal reasoning.

His reading of *The Autobiography of Malcolm X* persuaded Krattenmaker that Nation of Islam beliefs were similar to those held during the Korean War by Anthony Sicurella. A member of the Jehovah's Witnesses, Sicurella had claimed exemption as a conscientious objector on grounds that his religious beliefs permitted him to fight only "in the interests of defending Kingdom interests, our preaching work, our meetings, our fellow brethren and sisters, and our property against attack." Ali's willingness to fight was even more limited; he was on record as saying Muslims "do not go to war unless they are declared by Allah himself." Krattenmaker believed that such a war was "a purely philosophical speculation . . . that wasn't really going to happen."

In *Sicurella* v. *United States,* the Court had ruled for Sicurella for exactly that reason. Krattenmaker said to Harlan, "I bet you're going to find that Ali is a Sicurella CO." He did just that. On June 9, he announced that he would vote to overturn. His memo to the chief justice cited the Nation of

Islam's religious doctrine opposing war as found in Elijah Muhammad's book, *Message to the Blackman in America*. But Harlan could not persuade another justice to join him, and a four-four deadlock meant the conviction would stand. Ali had lost again, for the seventh time.

Or had he?

Now, the justices faced what the scholar O'Brien described as "the unhappy prospect of Ali's case going down as an affirmance by an equally-divided Court." Especially troubled was Justice Potter Stewart, who had been in the original minority voting for Ali. A clerk, Tom Rowe, told me that Stewart was "steamed because he thought the Court was going to let Ali go to jail wrongly without those voting to affirm having to write anything." Stewart asked his clerks to find precedent that demanded publishing an opinion when there was an equally divided affirmance. "He wanted to try to smoke people out," Rowe said. "He suspected the justices favoring affirmance of succumbing to the temptation to let the conviction stand as long as they didn't have to try to justify that in writing."

In the meantime, Stewart suggested a compromise. To qualify as a conscientious objector, Ali had to show, one, that he was opposed to all wars, two, that his objection was based on religious beliefs, and three, that he was sincere in that objection. In oral argument to the Court, the government conceded that Ali met the last two requirements while arguing that his willingness to fight in a Muslim war meant he had simply chosen not to fight this particular war. But the draft appeal board that rejected Ali's original claim had not identified any basis for its finding. That was the opening Stewart needed.

He argued to his fellow justices that the appeal board decision could have been based on grounds that the government now conceded were wrong. Besides, the Justice Department's own special-hearing officer, the Louisville judge Lawrence Grauman, had found Ali sincere in his religious beliefs almost five years earlier, only to be ignored. Stewart's compromise would work at several levels. If accepted, it kept Ali out of prison and so avoided further inflaming the controversy around him; it did not set a precedent, and it freed justices from explaining in writing why an equally divided court put the nation's most famous draft resister in prison. The other justices bought it. Stewart's suspicion that his brethren simply wanted nothing to do with explaining themselves was confirmed by how quickly the five-three vote to affirm become eight-nothing to overturn.

On June 28, nineteen days after Harlan's memo, the Court's decision was announced. The opinion written by Justice Stewart did not read as an endorsement of Ali's religious beliefs, nor did it decry a governmental vendetta against Ali. The decision was based on a technicality so slight that Justice Harlan referred to it as "a pee-wee," meaning a decision with no precedental force. "When you turn it sideways," Thomas Krattenmaker said, "it doesn't cast a shadow." The justices could disguise their intent in legal jargon; still, there was little doubt they believed it was time that someone did right by Ali. To this point, in all of America, only one legal officer had ruled in Ali's favor. That man was Lawrence Grauman. The judge sat in Ali's hometown, a city that had spiritually abandoned the fighter it once adored. There he decided that the most sincere person in the arguments was Ali.

Ali seven times had been one step from jail only to be reprieved. The eighth time, he was on a morning drive through the South Side of Chicago. He stopped at a neighborhood store for a glass of orange juice. As he left the store, a small, black man ran to catch up. "I just heard on the radio," the man said, "the Supreme Court said you're free, an eight-to-nothing vote." Ali went back into the store and bought orange juice for the half-dozen people there. An hour later, a reporter asked if he would sue the government for damages. "No," Ali said. "They only did what they thought was right at the time. I did what I thought was right. That was all."

No celebrity ever talked to more reporters in more odd places than Muhammad Ali did, and now he sat in a Travelodge motel lobby talking softly, saying he didn't want to fight much longer. "I just want to sit one day and be an ordinary citizen, don't talk to nobody, no more lectures. Just rest." He did not really want that, or he would not have added the next story. "But a man told me the other day, he said, 'You're marked.' He said, 'You'll never be free, young man. From here on out, you'll be called for something.'"

CHAPTER TWELVE

"I'm the Only One Who Can Tell It"

FRANK GIFFORD MOVED WITH the easy grace of the great athlete and the self-assurance that came with knowing that women adored him and men wanted to be him. Because Cosell well knew those attributes were beyond his reach (not that he would admit as much), he staked out for himself the undoubted position of intellectual and professional superior. Gifford had a certain boyish charm as a broadcaster for CBS television. But Cosell considered him mediocre at best, the very prototype of the jock-in-the-box that he scorned at every opportunity.

So, in the winter of 1971, Cosell knew that Arledge had a personnel move in mind when he asked, "How would you feel about working with Frank Gifford?"

Arledge knew the answer to *that*; it was his way of serving notice that Gifford would be added to the *MNF* package. Cosell and Meredith were national celebrities by then, leaving vulnerable the play-by-play man, Keith Jackson, a veteran broadcaster with skills Gifford could never match.

"Are you kidding?" Cosell said.

"No," his boss said.

"On what grounds? Keith did a hell of a job."

Unlike Gifford, Jackson was not Arledge's close friend and golfing buddy. From the start Arledge had wanted Gifford as the Monday night color man and settled on Meredith only when Gifford could not leave CBS. Arledge believed Gifford had prime-time star power and avowed to Cosell, of all people, that research showed Gifford to be "the most popular sportscaster in New York."

Cosell said, "I don't think that's true." He also doubted Gifford could do the complex work of fitting play-by-play into the lulls between Cosell and Meredith flights of fancy. Years later, in one of his memoirs, Cosell allowed only that Gifford came with a certain appeal. "First, the looks," wrote the man with the Bela Lugosi–like face. Then, the man whose major athletic achievement had been finishing second in the New York City Public School Athletic League's standing broad-jump event added of Gifford, "Second, the fact that he *played the game.*" Cosell always put a twist to those last three words, for he had made public his distaste for those men whose athletic glamour opened doors closed to more qualified broadcasters. That distaste was exacerbated by Meredith's winning an Emmy the first time out for Best Performance in Sports Programming, an achievement, Arledge said, that "made Howard absolutely nuts." Now came Gifford, yet another athlete lifted to the big leagues of broadcasting without once having strapped a Magnemite tape recorder to his back.

The new man, Gifford, went to dinner with Meredith and Cosell the night before the 1971 season opener in Detroit. After a few drinks while waiting for a table, Cosell came to feel *very* Cosellian. He made it his work to introduce Gifford to every woman in the bar. "Look at him standing there," Cosell declared. "A veritable Greek god. America's most famous football hero. The dream of the American working girl. The single most sexually dynamic man in the chronicle of the male sex. He's in room nine fourteen at the Ponchartrain."

Had Gifford been less secure, he might have been so offended by Cosell's fulsome praise as to physically assault him. At the least, a man less genteel would have advised Cosell to shut up. Gifford only smiled. "If I were one-hundredth the man Howard is making me out to be, I'd be the greatest man alive," he said. At dinner's end, Gifford left for his hotel. "I am going to barricade my door and get ready for the game."

Cosell called Gifford "Faultless Frank" and Meredith "Dandy Don." In turn, as Lombardi did, they called Cosell "Coach." All the nicknames came with a serving of irony that became apparent in the 1971 season's third game. Cosell had elicited a comment from Meredith, who directed his response to Gifford. Bringing Gifford in was Meredith's way of easing the anxiety of a rookie play-by-play man, perhaps even a thank-you to Gifford for having recommended him for the job in the first place.

But Cosell saw the world through a mirror, darkly. He believed the exchange was evidence that the two good-looking, charming jocks intended to rob him of air time. That night, at 1:30 A.M., Cosell made another of his all-hours telephone calls done on the theory that if he were awake, everyone should be. He reached his attorney, Robert Schulman. Though he had never used an agent in fifteen years, Cosell told Schulman that in light of the conspiracy against him he now needed representation in all dealings with the network.

The next week's game matched Meredith's and Gifford's old teams. The Cowboys and Giants were so dreadful that they threatened the league's record for fumbles and gave Cosell a chance to throw a barb at the football heroes alongside him. He said, "Gentlemen, neither of your respective teams is showing me very much this evening." Meredith answered in kind. "Well, Ha'hrd, at least we do have respective teams."

Aware of the tension under lines that came off as in-joke comedy on the air, the director Forte helped out his buddy, Cosell. From the control truck outside the stadium, Forte keyed his mike to Cosell's earpiece. He reported a factoid about Meredith and said he would turn a camera on him. "Yes, indeed, the very man at whom you are looking," Cosell intoned, "held the all-time NFL record for individual futility. It hardly comes as news to any of you that Don Meredith fumbled more times in one game than any other man in the history of the National Football League."

Meredith took the shot with a smile. "Aw, I didn't do that, did I, Ha'hrd?"

Cosell had passed through sports journalism. Those elements once thought to be disqualifying liabilities—his vulpine countenance, that Klaxon voice, his penchant for melodramatic bloviation—catapulted him from the simple stardom of a prime-time network television show into the rare air of show-business celebrity.

He showed off a note from Woody Allen, received shortly after doing his scene in *Bananas*: "Enclosed is your jacket and handsome ABC felt medallion which enables you to free admission at sporting events and one hot meal per month. Let me tell you again what a pleasure it was to work with you and now that you have gone, the entire film company walks around talking in your voice. I am glad your wife enjoyed herself and she confirms my racial theories that Gentiles have better proto-plasms."

Cosell played himself in an *Odd Couple* sitcom episode (after which the show's star, Tony Randall, chuckled and said, "He believed he knew how to act!"). He made the talk-show rounds of Johnny Carson, Dick Cavett, Mike Douglas, and David Frost. He traded repartee on variety shows with Bob Hope, Dinah Shore ("Of course, I know I am great!"), Flip Wilson, Dean Martin, and Danny Thomas. Shortly after Burt Reynolds posed nude with his hand as a fig leaf for *Cosmopolitan* magazine, the actor appeared at a benefit dinner in Cosell's honor and said that in the next issue, "Howard Cosell will be the centerfold with his vital organ covered—his mouth."

Increasingly, he chafed at the limitations of sports. He thanked Allen for the "chance to show that I'm a whole human being, something more than a long-term denizen of the dugout." As a substitute host for Cavett, Frost, and Douglas, Cosell did interviews with authors of books on the Vietnam War as well as with his fellow NYU alum Stanley Kramer, by then a distinguished moviemaker. Nothing he had done in broadcasting matched those moments, he said, "simply because the horizons far transcended sports."

Until, or unless, he could arrange an escape from sports, what could be better than to squire the vice president of the United States around the Baltimore Colts' locker room? An hour before a midseason Monday night game, Cosell walked uninvited into the room where the Colts, facing a big game against the Rams, sat in meditative silence—until Cosell tripped over offensive back Tom Matte's foot and covered the stumble with bluster: "There he is, Tom Matte, number forty-one. Does nothing well, but somehow everything well enough to win. And thus typifies this curiously unspectacular but nonetheless championship Colt team."

The self-parody induced laughter all around, even from the great hard-case quarterback Johnny Unitas, who offered color commentary: "You're talking through your asshole, Howard." Cosell had only begun. Vice President Spiro Agnew, once the governor of Maryland and always a Colt fan, stood with the team owner, Carroll Rosenbloom, who knew trouble when he saw it in a canary-yellow blazer bearing the ABC Sports logo. Rosenbloom said to Agnew, "Do you know this man?"

"Howard and I have worked the banquet circuit together," Agnew said.

"Absolutely true, Mr. Vice President," Cosell said, "but presently irrelevant. Tell me, sir, what is your position on Jewish ownership?" Rosenbloom flinched.

Agnew played along. "There is no statute that bars them, Howard."

It would be nice, Cosell told America's second-in-command, to go around the room and wish each player luck. Shortly, they rounded a corner to a niche occupied by four black players, John Mackey, Willie Richardson, Ray May, and Roy Hilton. There Cosell intoned for the operative so often dispatched by Richard Nixon to beleaguer political liberals, "Then your conclusion, Mr. Vice President, is that this team is saddled with too many blacks?"

"I didn't put it *that* way," Agnew said. "What I said was that an intelligent reexamination of the quota is in order."

Accepting an invitation to open the show that night, Agnew rode in an elevator to the press box with Cosell and his wife, Emmy. "You know, Howard doesn't need me," Agnew said to Emmy, "He's just giving me a break."

Cosell said, "Mr. Vice President, you're telling it like it is."

He had every reason to be happy. The lonely child of an unhappy marriage, Cosell adored his wife and daughters. He had traded the ennui of law for the obscurity of weekend local radio reports paying twenty-five dollars a show and now enjoyed the celebrity and wealth of a national television persona. He had come of age in low-rent apartments, but lived in a leafy suburb and in a luxury Manhattan apartment. (From the apartment's twenty-seventh-floor terrace, he once surveyed the skyline and the people scattered below and said to the old Dodger, Bobby Bragan, "Take a look out there, Bobby. I own 'em all.") As Ali was the first athlete in the television age to announce his own greatness, Cosell was the first broadcaster. Ali's extravagant performances had taught Cosell the value of unbridled egotism, and no one played the role of Howard Cosell, unbridled egotist, with more delight than Howard Cosell.

Yet, there ran through his work a discontent. His belief that Meredith and Gifford conspired against him caused a chill throughout the 1971 season. In interviews with his dread newspaper enemies, he declared SportsWorld beneath a man of his intelligence, achievement, and distinction. What Ed Murrow did, what Cronkite, Huntley, and Brinkley did— *that* was broadcast journalism.

Only the occasional piece of work engaged him. The first week of April 1972, Cosell did an emotional interview with Jackie Robinson. For twenty years he had admired Jack Roosevelt Robinson, to use the old Dodger's full name, as Cosell invariably did. He knew Robinson first as a player, then as a man of principle fighting for black Americans' civil rights, and in the end as a friend and neighbor. At age fifty-three a year younger than Cosell, Robinson had diabetes and high blood pressure; he had survived two heart attacks, was blind in one eye, could see only blurred shapes with the other, and had endured the hellish trials of his son's drug addiction and his death in a car accident after recovery.

They did the interview sharing a limousine ride back to the city after the funeral of another Dodger, Gil Hodges. Robinson's hair had gone white, his face puffy. Cosell led Robinson through a conversation that became the eloquent farewell of an American hero. "Oh, we've had a great life," Robinson said. He included his wife, Rachel. "We've accomplished so much. There's so much more to be done I guess we'll not have the chance to do it. Oh, what a great life we've had."

If intimations of mortality first came in whispers to Cosell, in the fall of the year they came as shoutings. In Munich, Germany, at seven o'clock on the morning of September 5, 1972, he opened his hotel room door to admit Harris Curtis, an ABC radio engineer assigned to tape Cosell's shows during the Olympic Games. Curtis asked, "Did you hear the news?"

"No, what?"

"Arab commandos got into the Village, took over the Israeli building, shot some of them dead, and are holding the rest hostage."

In Germany, Jews dying again.

Even as Roone Arledge left the Olympic Broadcast Center at four-twenty that morning, eight men walked outside the fence surrounding the nearby Olympic Village. In duffel bags hidden under athletic gear, the men carried Kalashnikov machine guns and hand grenades. Athletes from all countries had made a habit of pulling themselves over the chain-link fence around the Village rather than walking to a guarded entrance. On this morning, the eight men joined Americans returning from a night out. As everyone scaled the fence, the Americans gave the strangers a hand hefting their bags over the top. Once inside, the eight moved through the darkness to the Village's main street, Connollystrasse. On that street, in Building 31, lived athletes and officials from Israel.

One Israeli, Yossef Gutfreund, came awake at the sound of scratching at the apartment's ground-floor door. As he reached the door, it opened. Gutfreund saw gun barrels and shouted, *"Have tistalku!" Take cover!* At 4:47 A.M., a cleaning woman reported hearing gunfire. Within minutes, two Israelis had been murdered and nine taken hostage. A body was rolled into the street outside the apartment.

At 5:08 A.M., two sheets of paper floated down from the balcony at 31 Connollystrasse. They settled into the hands of a German policeman. They carried the demands of Black September, a violent faction of Yasser Arafat's Palestinian Liberation Organization. The demands included the release of 234 Palestinian prisoners and Andreas Baader and Ulrike Meinhof, leaders of Germany's infamous urban guerrillas, the Baader-Meinhof Gang. Failing their release by 9:00 A.M., the Black September leader, Luttif Afif, known as "Issa," told the police, one hostage would be shot every hour thereafter.

By eight-thirty, Cosell gained entry to the Village by persuading a guard that he was a Puma shoe salesmen. Immediately, Cosell felt a dissonance. As on any morning, athletes moved casually along Village walks, carefree, laughing, hard rock music rattling the air, all of it at odds with reality. From ABC's European correspondent, Peter Jennings, Cosell learned details. Then he put himself across the street from Building 31, near an underpass that became a meeting place for police. By walkie-talkie, he told Arledge in ABC's headquarters, "More cars pulling up beneath the underpass . . . police getting out . . . submachine guns and pistols plainly visible."

The American newspapermen Shirley Povich of the *Washington Post* and Jim Murray of the *Los Angeles Times,* once at the gate with Cosell and using his debate with the guard as diversion, had found another way into the Village. Povich saw terrorists with guns patrolling balconies. He believed doctors arriving by ambulance were policemen with weapons under their white smocks.

Cosell saw uniformed police vanish into buildings adjacent to the Israelis' place. He saw snipers on rooftops. At dusk, in a scene Cosell described as "the eeriest I have ever seen," he did a report on hundreds of athletes gathered behind police ropes. They watched in silence, perhaps out of respect, perhaps waiting for the hellfire of a gun battle. On a rubbing table in the Village, one athlete thought first of himself. He was the American decathlon star Bruce Jenner. If the invasion and killings caused Olympic leaders to stop the Games, Jenner's event might not be finished. Even as Jenner watched a Black September killer patrolling on a balcony, he expressed his annoyance. "It's all a bunch of shit," he told Murray. "Why do we have to cancel a day? We can walk around the building on the way to the track, can't we? We don't have to go through it." It may have been unfair of Murray to consider Jenner's self-absorption extraordinary, for here was Povich's take on the ambience in the Village that day: "As a group, it was quite jolly. If anybody was in trouble and about to get killed, so what?"

By afternoon, as the terrorists held off more killings, the West German government had offered to meet any demand it could. But the Israelis reiterated their long-held refusal to negotiate with terrorists. Day turned to night. Still at his vigil position, Cosell realized an epiphany of pain. "I had never felt so intensely Jewish," he said. All his life he had put distance between himself and Jewishness. He had no relationship with organized religion, and he had abandoned his parents' culture. Now, more than ever, he felt the hatred bred by anti-Semitism. To be in Munich, twenty-two miles from Dachau's brick ovens, to know that Jews had died on this day in this place and more likely would die, was to understand more profoundly the agonies that moved his grandparents to flee the pogroms of Alexander III.

Shortly after nine o'clock, as police roped off a plaza, Cosell asked a police official, "What goes on here?"

"A deal," he said. "The helicopters will be here. In moments they come." They came in an hour, far from that plaza, and carried the terrorists and their hostages to a suburban airport where they were promised a flight out of Germany to Egypt. When Cosell heard from Arledge that he could take a break, he returned to ABC's compound where an advertisers' party was under way. Gifford and Meredith skipped such parties before Monday night games. Cosell, the loyal company man, believed it was his duty to show up. He also loved the attention, and rarely more so than on this night when he could bear witness to tragic history. He also needed a drink.

At eleven-thirty, the Reuters news service transmitted a stop-press/flash bulletin: "ALL ISRAELI HOSTAGES HAVE BEEN FREED." Almost immediately, that report was cast into doubt by an Associated Press report of a gun battle at the airport. Four terrorists and a police officer were dead. What had happened to the hostages was unknown. On the air, ABC's sports anchor Jim McKay said, "The word we get from the airport is that, quote, 'All hell has broken loose out there,' that there is still shooting going on. There was a report of a burning helicopter. But it all seems to be confusion. Nothing is nailed down."

Then came a phone call saying the Germans would have a press conference at Olympic headquarters. Arledge hadn't decided what to do about the Reuters report yet, as it was in conflict with the AP's. In walked Cosell, fresh from the advertisers' party, shouting to Arledge, "I want to go on. Got to be part of this story. Put me on, Arledge. I'm the only one who can tell it." Cosell leaned into his boss's face. Arledge thought, *Four silver bullets minimum. Maybe five.*

"Dirty bastards," Cosell said. "They already killed six million of us. What's a few more?"

"No, Howard," Arledge said. "We're in the middle of it. There's no place for you."

"C'mon! Put me on the air! Gotta get on!"

"*No*, Howard." Arledge moved him toward a door. "Trust me. You'll be the first one to thank me in the morning."

At two-eighteen in the morning, ABC's logistics chief, Marvin Bader, called Arledge with an off-the-record report from an assistant to the chief Olympics spokesman. The hostages were dead, all of them. But Arledge could not afford to be wrong on that report. He waited and told McKay through his earpiece, "Looks very dark for hostages. Announcement soon. Don't get their hopes up."

At three-seventeen, the Reuters news machine again rang the five bells of a stop-press report: "FLASH! ALL ISRAELI HOSTAGES SEIZED BY ARAB GUERILLAS KILLED." Arledge again, whispering to McKay: "Official. All hostages dead." Snipers had started the gunfight at twelve-thirty; the Arabs shot the bound Israelis inside the helicopters and set one machine afire with a grenade. Six terrorists were killed, two captured.

To Arledge, it was the first time in that long and terrible day that McKay looked tired. He had been rushed from the hotel swimming pool at eight-thirty the morning before; sixteen hours later, still with his swim trunks on under his clothes, McKay sat in ABC's studio. At Arledge's cue, McKay looked into Camera Two and reported: "They've now said there were eleven hostages. Two were killed in their room this—ah, yesterday morning. Nine were killed at the airport tonight."

The slightest pause, and . . .
"They're all gone."

Seven weeks later, October 24, 1972, Jackie Robinson died. From ABC News studios in Washington, D.C., Cosell did two radio shows on the man he treasured as a friend and respected as a leader of social change. He remembered a day in 1969 in the nation's capital. There for baseball's All-Star Game, Cosell heard an angry exchange between Robinson and Bob Feller, a Hall of Fame pitcher. Feller suggested that blacks who criticized racism in baseball did a disservice to democracy and the game; they should, in effect, be grateful for what baseball had done for them. Here Robinson confronted Feller. "Suddenly," Cosell said, "the room was like 1947 all over again."

Cosell had an idea of what baseball had done for Robinson: "It tortured him, tormented him. What he had to live with was the greatest debasement of a proud human being in my lifetime. But he gave baseball the appearance of being a democratic business—that's what he did for baseball—and he gave it a place in American history by his mere presence."

The night of Robinson's death, Cosell made a dinner speech in Washington. He told the story of Jack Roosevelt Robinson, who in 1947 became the first black player in twentieth-century major league baseball. The day of Gil Hodges's funeral, on legs once quick and now dying, Robinson came around a corner toward the church. He walked haltingly on the arm of an old friend. A youngster whispered, "There's Jackie Robinson," and the whisper spread until it became cheers of "Hey, Jackie." The church sidewalk became Ebbets Field. Cosell saw Robinson, the number 42 on his snow-white Dodgers uniform, "swinging around first in that wide turn, tantalizing the outfielder: Does he throw to second or does he dare throw behind Robinson to try to pick him off? No, he daren't, because surely Jackie would take second. But is he going to take second anyway? Is he going to try and make it with the unexpected burst of speed and that evasive, sweeping slide?"

For a moment, Cosell was again a kid, fresh out of the army, a husband and father, a young lawyer and Dodgers fan in "an age when baseball mattered as a sport in this country and, more importantly, when it symbolized to all the world that America could cope with its most terrible of

all problems—the problem of race. This was what Jackie Robinson symbolized. He helped inspire the image that this nation was capable of
racial amity instead of racial anguish, and that was the best thing that
ever happened to baseball."

The shine of celebrity that came with *Monday Night Football* dazzled
Cosell. Show business, not journalism, now owned his attention. For Jack
Roosevelt Robinson, though, Cosell felt the passion that had made his
work important. To the dinner audience in Washington, he said, "There is
only one word to describe Jackie Robinson and that is 'unconquerable.'"

Then he left for New York to do the work necessary to create in only
two days a half-hour documentary on his friend. With the twenty-five-
year-old producer Don Ohlmeyer, Cosell lined up interviews, arranged
coverage of the funeral, and interviewed Robinson's closest friend, a doctor who said that diabetes would have required amputation of Robinson's legs within the year.

It was a documentary done virtually live. With no time to review film,
pieces were chosen from memory. There was no time to put the show on
tape as a completed package; it was only half-done when Cosell was asked
to do voice-overs on the tape setting up and coming out of each piece. He
sat in a darkened booth watching videotape that he was seeing for the first
time. There was no script because he never wrote anything and never
asked anyone to write for him on the air. He would say to producers, "Tell
me when to go." Now, near the show's end, Ohlmeyer had time for a
coda. He said into Cosell's earpiece, "Howard, we need you to fill."

"How much?"

"Forty-five seconds."

"Tell me when to go."

Ohlmeyer had seen the Coach do it a hundred times. Still, Cosell's
mastery of the broadcasting arts thrilled the young producer. As re-
quested, Cosell did forty-five seconds to wrap up the show. Not forty-six
seconds, not forty-four. He did it live and to the second, and once more
he rendered Jack Roosevelt Robinson human, proud, unconquerable.

Ohlmeyer went into the booth. "Howard, that was incredible."

Cosell couldn't speak. Tears were moving down his cheeks.

In that winter of 1972, three years into *Monday Night Football*, Cosell said
to an interviewer, "Do you think that I, at fifty-two years of age, and at

the peak of my intellectual prowess, am going to spend the rest of my days worrying whether Roger Staubach's shoulder will heal in time for the Washington game?"

He filled the skies of New York with trial balloons suggesting he would leave sports to serve in the United States Senate as the Democratic senator from New York. The idea fit with the image Cosell had cultivated of the genius surrounded by sports' mental midgets. But it apparently appealed to no one except Cosell. His wife and daughters, considering a future of political reporters hounding their man, begged him to forget it. Political operatives with auditory nerves so acute they could hear a lobbyist fold a hundred-dollar bill on the other side of town reported not a whisper of enthusiasm for a Cosell candidacy.

Cosell did bring to SportsWorld an uncommon intelligence that was neither wasted nor inconsequential. His extraordinary career across fifteen years in radio, television, and print for *SPORT* proved that sports reporting and commentary could be as rewarding as any job in journalism. It was also true that Cosell's complaints about a life in sports rang hollow. He could have left at any time, just as he had left the law for broadcasting. In David Remnick's youth as a sportswriter, years before he became editor of *The New Yorker*, Cosell upbraided him for wasting a Princeton University education. "But, Howard," Remnick said, "you have a law degree and you're doing sports." To which Cosell said, "Yes, but I have made *fucking* millions." The longer Cosell stayed, the richer, more famous, and more celebrated he became. Staying even as he complained about staying allowed critics to call the complaints the aggrandizing rhetoric of a man who hated himself.

Though in Munich he had said, *I'm the only one who can tell it,* Cosell couldn't have believed that. He was no fool. But on the scene of the biggest news story in the world, he had worked as little more than a legman for Jim McKay. He felt shut out, ignored, second-rate, insecure, and unhappy. Not that he could say any of that out loud. Nor could he say that his self-absorption and superciliousness were his enemies, not Gifford and Meredith. Instead, loudly and often, he declared his magnificence. Don Ohlmeyer understood the noise and forgave Cosell for it. "Howard's bravado," the producer said, "was a classic cover for his insecurities. He was not a lovable guy, and there are very few people that I will say I loved in my life, but I loved Howard."

"Take a gander at these limbs," Cosell said. In Kingston, Jamaica, on January 22, 1973, he sat with Emmy for drinks on the terrace of the Stony Hill Hotel, high on a ridge over the city, at dusk, lights coming on in the valley. Cosell was at ease in Bermuda shorts when he invited George Plimpton's inspection of the legs thereby revealed. "At the Public School Athletic League championship held in 1931 at the 168th Street Armory in Manhattan, these legs carried me to a second-place finish in the standing broad jump. My wife wears the silver medal on her charm bracelet. Don't you, Emmy?" She confirmed possession of the precious medal.

Discovering that Plimpton was staying in a downtown hotel, Cosell said, "What sort of slob thing is that to do?" He preferred Stony Hill's tropical opulence. "How inelegant and pedestrian to be staying elsewhere. Emmy and I are living in the Errol Flynn suite where, I have been told by the proprietor of this hostelry, Flynn watched Beverly Aadland dance in the nude. We have a pet lizard that comes in from time to time. I have named him Roscoe."

Plimpton said, "Why 'Roscoe'?"

Cosell said, "Because he *is* Roscoe. What other name is possible?"

The occasion for Cosell's presence in Jamaica was Joe Frazier's defense of the heavyweight championship against George Foreman. Few observers gave the kid a chance against a man who had beaten Ali. But Cosell said, "I have been with George since the 1968 Olympics in Mexico City when he took out the Russian, Ionis Chepulis, on a TKO in the second round. Tomorrow night there are going to be some shocked people in the world."

The next night, at his ringside microphone, in the second round, Cosell began shouting, "Down goes Frazier!" Now screaming. "Down goes Frazier! DOWN GOES FRAZIER!"

All for one knockdown. "The heavyweight champion is taking the mandatory eight-count, and Foreman looks as poised as can be. . . . He has Frazier in a corner! Frazier's knee buckles!" Cosell's voice was at a shriek's high pitch. "He is down for the fourth time in the fight!" Cosell's body quivered and his hands trembled alongside his mike. "It's target practice for George Foreman! It is target practice!" At that moment, it was as if the man Cosell had disappeared and only the voice, his essence, remained. "It is over! George Foreman is the heavyweight champion of the world!"

Then, in the ring, waiting to speak to the new champ, Cosell looked into a television documentary maker's camera, cool and smug. "Did I tell you?" he said. "Did I tell you Foreman would do it?"

The obvious big-money fight for Foreman was with Ali, but he was in no rush to put the championship at that risk. He fought only once in the twenty months after Frazier, knocking out Jose Roman in the first round. His reluctance to work stood in contrast to Ali's manic schedule. In the twenty-three months since losing to Frazier, Ali won ten times on five countries on three continents. He fought 101 rounds against a motley crew that included a former sparring partner, a grossly obese mediocrity, and three aged men he was beating up for the second time. But as another shot at the heavyweight championship seemed inevitable, Ali lost to a fighter, Ken Norton, whose most recent fight had drawn three hundred spectators and paid him seven hundred dollars.

On March 31, 1973, Ali suffered a broken jaw in the second round and lost a twelve-round decision to the strong, unorthodox Norton, one of those heavyweights good enough that most contenders avoided him but not so good as to move with the big boys.

It took Ali six months to recover. Back in the ring, he beat Norton by stealing the last round on all cards. Next came a slow-dance victory over Rudi Lubbers. Then, measuring by the thrill of the unexpected, Ali's best performance in a year came in Cosell's ABC studios. It was a star turn that spoke of his Gorgeous George influence.

When Joe Frazier came to the studios on January 24, 1974, he'd had it with Ali. The week after their fight in 1971, Ali began a campaign to persuade everyone that he, not Frazier, had won the fight, that he had put Frazier in the hospital for two weeks, that, in effect, Frazier had been unworthy of the heavyweight championship. Ali also ratcheted up the tension by repeating his slurs that Frazier was "too ugly" and "too dumb" to be the champ. He did that on the *Dick Cavett Show* before sitting alongside Frazier and Cosell for a *Wide World of Sports* segment. They were there to promote their second fight, coming up in four days, and to review film of the '71 classic. When Frazier saw Ali's jaw swell again, as it had that night three years before, he said with pride and satisfaction, "That's what he went to the hospital for."

They had agreed not to talk about hospitals. Ali had X-rays on his jaw and refused a doctor's recommendation to stay overnight. Frazier had attended an all-night victory party instead of resting and was admitted to a hospital two days later, dehydrated and exhausted. Now Frazier had said the H-word. Unamused, half-watching the fight film, Ali tilted his head toward Frazier. "I went to the hospital for ten minutes," he said. "You went for a month."

Frazier tried a wisecrack. "I was resting."

"That shows how dumb you are," Ali said. "People don't go to a hospital to rest. See how ignorant you are?"

Cosell's producer, Dennis Lewin, had made the decision to seat Ali and Frazier side by side instead of separating them with Cosell. He thought it would make for better pictures. There was no need to worry about that. Had Frazier been in a separate room it would not have changed his behavior on again hearing Ali disparage his intelligence. Frazier stood and turned his back to the camera. He looked down at Ali, still seated. "I'm tired of you calling me ignorant all the time. I'm not ignorant. Stand up, man!"

Now Ali's face lit up with mischief, as if to say, *You serious?*

Frazier leaned over Ali. "Stand up!"

"Sit down, Joe," Ali said dismissively.

Ali's brother, Rahaman Ali, had come onto the stage. Frazier said, "You want to get in this, too?"

Ali half-rose from his seat, still with that mischievous smile. In a flash he wrapped his right arm around the back of Frazier's neck and tugged at him, saying, "Sit down, quick, Joe." Ali seemed to be playing, as if saying, *Now we'll have some fun.*

Frazier had boiled over. He bulled into Ali's midsection and the men went rolling onto the studio floor trying to find a grip on each other. A dozen men from both fighters' camps rushed from the wings to break up the scuffle. Cosell, still seated, told his television audience, "Well, we are having a scene. . . . It's hard to tell if it's clowning or if it's real between the fighters."

The scuffle lasted a few seconds, after which Frazier walked off-camera and out of the studio. "A bad and ugly scene," Cosell said. As Frazier disappeared, Ali straightened his suit coat, returned to his seat alongside Cosell, and endured with sullen irritation a paternalistic scolding by ABC's master scold.

Four days later, Ali defeated Frazier in a fight as dull as the first had been brilliant. He was thirty-two years old, making fights that were somber marches toward twilight. He fought four times in 1973, each fight going the full distance of twelve rounds. Now he had gone twelve rounds with Frazier, and if his performance suggested the shadows of time gathering, he cared only that he had won the fight. It earned him one more shot at the heavyweight championship, and there now seemed an urgency to it. Time was no longer on Ali's side.

Foreman was twenty-five years old, as tall as Ali, bigger in the upper body, undefeated in forty fights, winning thirty-seven by knockout, the last twenty-four knockouts in succession. He had shoulders the size and consistency of cannon balls. He had batted Frazier around in ways that Ali never did. Then, in March 1974, with Ali and Cosell at ringside in Caracas, Venezuela, Foreman needed only two rounds to knock out Ken Norton.

As their plane from Venezuela began its descent to New York, Ali went into the cockpit to talk with the pilots. Joe Louis, in a wry mood, turned to Howard and Emmy Cosell and asked, "Didn't a plane hit the Empire State Building."

"Yes," Emmy said.

"Didn't something else happen over New York?"

"Two planes crashed head-on over Brooklyn," she said. "Why?"

"Because with Muhammad in the cockpit, something like that is sure to happen to us."

Before taking his seat for landing, Ali asked Louis, "Joe, did you ever chop wood when you were in training?"

"All the time."

"Why'd you do it?"

"Because they told me to."

"I think I'll chop some wood in Africa before the Foreman fight," Ali said.

Louis said, "Better chop a lot of it."

In the face of the doomsaying, Ali, his best athletic years behind him, professed no concern.

"George Foreman is relying on one thing," Ali said. "He's relying on his power, but I'm relying on a lot of things. I've got speed of hand, I'm fast on my feet, I can take a punch, and I've got experience. I've gone fifteen rounds a number of times, and he's only been ten rounds twice. I can go the route. If someone knocks me down, I get up again. My jaw gets broke, and I keep on fighting. We don't know how George will be after five rounds with a man who's sticking and moving. We don't know what happens to George when he finds hisself taking a whuppin'. I never seen George tired yet, huffing and puffing, get winded and have to take a few punches. And when George gets tired, I'll still be dancing. I'll be picking my shots, beating him at will. If George Foreman don't get me in seven, I'm telling you now, his parachute won't open."

Nor was Angelo Dundee worried. Ali's trainer said, "Sure, Foreman is a killer if you stand still and let him beat you to death. But who is crazy enough to think Muhammad will do that? Muhammad has the equipment to beat this guy, he knows how to handle that job."

The Scottish sportswriter Hugh McIlvanney had long marched under Ali's banner. But Foreman, what a man. All those knockouts. Ali's best days gone. McIlvanney went to his typewriter and tapped out a sentence of foreboding: "I, too, know a way to beat George Foreman, but it involves shelling him for three days and then sending in the infantry."

CHAPTER THIRTEEN

"I Ain't Gonna Wind Up Like Malcolm X"

AFTER HIS ROADWORK THE MORNING of July 8, 1974, Ali drove Gene Kilroy's white Cadillac from his Pennsylvania mountaintop training complex to a boys' camp in a nearby forest. These were boys serving tough-love punishments after minor scrapes with the law. They cleared brush, and brought down dead trees. Kilroy, the Ali camp's business manager, had dropped two pairs of boxing gloves into the car. Ali liked to stage mock sparring sessions with fans. He got knocked down every time.

The day was already warm, the temperature soon to reach ninety degrees. Perspiration stained Ali's long-sleeved blue silk shirt. He wore loose-fitting khaki work pants and the heavy, black leather boots he carried around the world for roadwork. As Ali drove, he talked to me in the front seat. In the back was my friend Gary Tuell, once a sportswriter at the *Courier-Journal*. He said nothing, rendered mute by fright as Ali pushed the lumbering boat of a car to eighty-five miles per hour on a dirt logging road scarred with ruts.

At that speed several thoughts occurred to me: *Here's the most famous man on Earth, everything going for him, good looks, money, women, a five-million-dollar payday in two months, and he's driving like a bat out of hell on a crazy logging road.* Trees passed the Cadillac's door handles in a blur. I also thought: *Please, God, don't let a truck be coming the other way.*

I asked, "Muhammad, you afraid of dying?"

"You don't ever want to die," he said.

"Glad to hear that."

"But the man who built this road is dead now. The man who built that farmhouse over there is dead. There are guys I fought, Sonny Liston, Zora Folley, Eddie Machen, Alejandro Lavorante, dead. Liston rottin' in his grave, nobody cares. We ain't nothin'. We're nobody. We don't own nothin' on this Earth. We just borrow things. When you die, another man comes along and your daughter calls him Daddy. Death is the tax the soul has to pay for having a name and a form."

This was Ali in his prime, one hand on the wheel rockin' 'n' rollin' through a forest, cool, calm, talking with hometown sportswriters. On the plane trip east, I asked Tuell, a newlywed fresh off his honeymoon, "The truth—which is more exciting, getting married or this?" He had grown up in Louisville, done some amateur boxing, papered his bedroom walls with Ali photographs. He leaned to me, as if his bride might hear us from thirty thousand feet five hundred miles away. "Don't ever tell her," he said.

Now, in the car . . .

"This Cadillac, I used to think it was important to have a new Cadillac, a gold watch, rings, and things. First car I bought was a brand-new Cadillac, 1962, ten thousand dollars. Today, it's in some junkyard. Now I just ride around lookin' at the landscape. I don't need anything but this. I've had seven Rolls-Royces, but I bought them before I realized that you can't buy the true valuable things in life. Only God can make the valuable things, like trees, grass, mountains, lakes."

One hand on the wheel. The Cadillac bouncing. Ali asking, "You writin' this down? Better write this down. Very few people get supreme wisdom. When I talk to you, you get it—for free. You're gettin' a helluva story, my man from Louisville. No way possible I'd give this story to all those other people. You writin' this down? Free wisdom."

"Tuell's taking notes," I said. "You always drive like this?"

"I don't like to go slow."

The bosses at the tough-love camp hoped Ali might inspire a young man to straighten up. He brought along two pairs of boxing gloves, and when a skinny little kid flailed at him, the Greatest of All Time fell to the ground, dust rising from the collapse. Back in the Cadillac now, leaving the boys' camp, Ali said, "This is my last fight," meaning the five-million-dollar fight coming up against Foreman.

"Last fight, win or lose?"

"Yup. But I ain't gonna lose. I'm gonna be stickin' and movin' and he gonna be puffin' and bleedin'. What's gonna win this fight is condition. He can't go past five, six rounds, and he knows it. Most people I fight are surprised I'm so fast. They don't realize it until the fifth round or sixth round—when they get tired and, POP-POP-POP, I'm still comin'. In this fight I will move just a step ahead of him. If Foreman moves two miles per hour, I'll move two and a half miles per hour. None of that jumpin' around, like with Liston, that was when I was a kid. I must conserve my energy."

"He's awful strong," I said. "Howard Cosell says he fears for your safety."

"How-word Co-sell, here's what I think about How-word Co-sell: Political jokes during election years are to be expected, but political jokes like How-word Co-sell sometimes get elected. Cool, huh? Howard says I'm not the same fighter I was ten years ago. I'm gonna ask his wife is he the same man in bed he was ten years ago."

"But Foreman is something."

"Foreman's nothin'. I tell myself, I'm fightin' for my people's freedom. I got all the rednecks and all the Uncle Toms pullin' for me to lose. I can't lose. I gotta win. Not for money, not so I can have a blonde hangin' on each arm. So I can spread pride to the black people, preach to the black people. It takes faith to move mountains. Now I got the faith to move George Foreman. I'll be tellin' Foreman, 'You represent white redneck Americans and Uncle Tom Americans. You think I'm easy, so shoot it, sucker, SHOOT IT! Try takin' me out, chump.'"

All this was said with one hand on the wheel, except for those extra-thrilling moments when Ali turned sideways, balled up both fists, and pop-pop-popped punches at me.

"Oh, man," he said, "please bet your money on me. I got too much ridin' to lose. The whole world gonna be shook up that night. I predict a miracle. We gonna rumble in the jungle."

In Kilroy's Cadillac, flying back to Ali's camp, talking about the five-million-dollar rumble with Foreman, I told Ali, "Tuell's a fighter, too."

Ali looked in the rearview mirror. "You?"

"He's been in with Golden Gloves champions," I said. "He knows what he's doing."

Ali to Tuell: "What time you wanna box?"

Tuell: "Er, uh . . ."

"Two o'clock, when we've got a crowd."

The rest of the drive, Ali occasionally caught Tuell's eye in the mirror and shook his head slowly side to side, as if to express regret in advance for the damage to be done. At the appointed hour in Ali's gym atop a mountain outside Deer Lake, Pennsylvania, Tuell came into view wearing a white terry cloth boxer's robe with MUHAMMAD ALI in black lettering across the back. I told Tuell how good he looked. Really good. I also said, "We'll bury you in the robe."

"Ladies and gentlemen," Ali shouted to spectators, "this little white man running around in my robe is 'The White Muhammad Ali'! Yes! Yes, he is fast like me, can talk like me. He can do everything but box like me." When Tuell disrobed, revealing an expanse of abdomen seldom seen in a heavyweight contender's camp, Ali called across the ring, "You look like a plucked chicken, all pink and fat. You serious?"

"Gonna knock you out," Tuell said.

"You're makin' history. I'm only doin' this because you're from Louisville. I wouldn't do this with no Chicago writer. Ladies and gentlemen, you're seein' history. The Greatest of Allllll Time, will fight the Great Fat Hope."

In the ring, Tuell on his toes, moving, suddenly aware of Ali's size, "how enormous he really is," the wooden floor under the ring canvas trembling under Ali's dance, Ali with that Michelangelo body, all silk and all steel.

"Keep your hands up," Larry Holmes had told Tuell. Holmes was a kid, Ali's three-hundred-dollar-a-week sparring partner. "You hear me? Hands up. And watch his left. He throws it soooo fast. Just don't drop your hands. Keep away from him. If he does hurt you, fall down. He won't hit you if you're down, you hear me?"

Tuell aimed his best right at Ali, certain Ali would flinch when hit. Only, as Sonny Liston learned, as they all learned, it was one thing to throw a punch at Ali, it was another to hit him. Tuell's punch missed. In a clinch, Ali shouted, "Hit me, hit me!"

He did, a right on Ali's jaw, which caused Ali to say, "C'mon, hit me! Hit me!"

"I just did," Tuell said.

"Hit me again."

Another right, and down went Ali, Tuell dancing beside him, reciting Ali's own words over Liston in Lewiston, Maine, nine years earlier, "Get up, sucker, get up, chump," only when Ali rose, it wasn't to quit as Liston

did, it was to shout at Tuell, "You called me nigger. You called me NIG-
GER! I heard what you said."

"Not me, champ . . ."

Ali, laughing: "Hit a fat man in the stomach, hit a fat man in the stomach." Three or four lefts and the vast white expanse of Tuell's stomach
became a vast expanse of red welts. When Tuell tried another weak
punch, Ali threw up his hands in mock fear and ran out of the ring.

Ali's camp sat far above the northeastern Pennsylvania village of Deer
Lake. There were giant boulders on the grounds painted with names of
past champions ("Jack Johnson" was a mammoth chunk of coal). The
camp was a compound of log cabins: the gym, two bunkhouses, two
guest houses, Ali's house, and, the heart of the place, Aunt Coretta's
Kitchen. At home in this place he loved, Ali was talking . . .

"Foreman, he dance like a mule, no flash, not like me, I look like a
champion. He's got them big arms, like logs, like Sonny Liston, all mus-
cle-y, but he can't throw no hooks, he throws straight-ahead punches,
hits hard, but hittin' hard don't mean nothin' if there ain't nothin' to hit,
and he ain't gonna hit me like that.

"He knocked out the two people, Frazier and Norton, who gave me
hell, so they figure he'll give me hell. But you can't give the devil hell, and
I'm hell in the ring. I can't let Foreman win. This man represents Christianity, the American flag. He's a bad image for the youth. He represents
pork chops, he runs with Jim Brown and them who do them exploitation
Negro films. I believe God just weakened Frazier and Norton to build up
this man Foreman for me. Frazier is better than that, you know it, Norton is better, you know it. God has set him up for me.

"God knows the world wants me to win. You ever been to Egypt?
Egypt's somethin'. No white people over there. Imagine, a whole country
with no white people. Now ain't that strange? And me, a little black boy
from Louisville, Kentucky, who was named Cassius Clay, who couldn't
eat with no white people, and here he is ridin' through Egypt on a camel
with a prince, and women bowing down at my feet, people shouting,
'Muhammad Ali, Muhammad Ali!' Kings of countries worship me,
women so happy to see me they cry when I touch them. ME! A little Negro boy from Louisville. I'm the black Henry Kissinger!"

On July 8, 1974, in Aunt Coretta's Kitchen, Ali explained that he wanted to quit fighting because "people die, and people bet and lose their houses on me when I fight and lose. It's a fact that people die of heart attacks every time I fight. It's not right. Too serious. No fun. Whole countries, sad. The women in Egypt cry. Me, the greatest fighter of all time, losing, how could I lose? Me losing, the king of Egypt said it was the second-worst thing ever happened to them. I don't want that. I'm gonna have to turn down five million dollars, ten million. But I got to quit. One more fight, my friend, and I'll get out. It's a miracle I got through fightin' like I did. I'll retire with money, land, good health, and wise investments. No reason to hang around. All I can do is go downhill."

One day that summer, a somber Cosell sat with Ali on a bench in New York's Central Park. As if the circle were about to be closed, he asked Ali to tell "how it all started for you."

"Somebody stole my bicycle and I wanted to learn to fight so I could beat up the boy who stole it," Ali said softly.

Then, brightening, "And I'm going to pretend George is the one who stole my bike." *I'm gonna dance! George won't find me. By the third round, all that dancing, George be panting. No contest, Cosell.*

After Ali left the bench, Cosell did a stand-up commentary for a single camera. In a monotone near funereal, he said: "The time may have come to say good-bye to Muhammad Ali because, very honestly, I don't think he can beat George Foreman. It's hard for me as a reporter to be totally objective in this case because Muhammad Ali has been a significant factor in my own career. I thought, before he was idled for three and a half years, he was the best fighter I've ever seen. I still think he's a remarkable athlete and one can never put anything beyond him. Maybe he can pull off a miracle. But against George Foreman, so young, so strong, so fearless? Against George Foreman, who does away with his opponents one after another in less than three rounds? It's hard for me to conjure with that."

Zaire was once Congo, despoiled by colonizing Europeans. In 1974 it was a nation of forty million people living in poverty under the rule of Mobutu Sese Seko, a dictator infamous for the killings of tens of thousands as well as the looting of his nation's copper and cobalt treasure. "A bank vault in a leopard-skin hat," the French called him. Not that Ali or

Foreman cared how Mobutu came to power and remained in power. They just wanted their cut of the dictator's money. They left that dirty work to promoter Don King, who slithered within reach of the Mobutu bank vault and came away with ten million dollars for the fighters, five each. The deal gave Mobutu cause to post signs along roads:

A FIGHT BETWEEN TWO BLACKS IN A BLACK NATION ORGANIZED BY BLACKS AND SEEN BY THE WHOLE WORLD: THIS IS THE VICTORY OF MOBUTUISM.

THE COUNTRY OF ZAIRE WHICH HAS BEEN BLED BECAUSE OF PILLAGE AND SYSTEMATIC EXPLOITATION MUST BECOME A FORTRESS AGAINST IMPERIALISM AND A SPEARHEAD FOR THE LIBERATION OF THE AFRICAN CONTINENT.

THE FOREMAN-ALI FIGHT IS NOT A WAR BETWEEN TWO ENEMIES BUT A SPORT BETWEEN TWO BROTHERS.

Ali, cocky after a day's training in Zaire, walked with his amen-choir of hangers-on, each shouting huzzahs to the master when someone told him that Cosell, back in New York, again had predicted Foreman would win the fight. Ali looked into a camera and sent a message to his old buddy: "Cosell, you're a phony, and that thing on your head came from the tail of a pony!"

Turned on his heel, laughing, and disappeared.

One night, for the fun of it, Ali ran his finger down a yellow piece of paper that listed predictions by American sportswriters. When he came to "Foreman in 1," he crooked a finger at Tom Callahan, of the *Cincinnati Enquirer*. Callahan had seen Foreman bounce Frazier like a basketball. Foreman reminded him of Sonny Liston, only more so. Callahan followed Ali into the moonlight and they stood by the river Zaire. Mysterious shadows moved on the water. Soft music came from birds nearby and, in the distance, the bass notes of unknown animals. "I'm going to tell you something," Ali said to Callahan, "and I don't want you ever to forget it. Are you ready? Are you listening to me?"

Callahan listened.

"Black men scare white men more than black men scare black men."

An hour before the fight, Ali walked to his dressing room, his arms hanging loosely, a swagger in his movement. Unsmiling. A black shirt, black slacks, those heavy work shoes. Dave Anderson of the *New York Times* was there in the catacombs of Mobutu's Twentieth of May Stadium, watching Ali in the hallway gloom, thinking that he looked huge, bigger than ever. *As big as Foreman.*

A half-hour before the fight, a dozen people gathered in Ali's dressing room, all silent. In came Ali, blinking against the glare of light reflected by the room's morgue-white walls. Ceiling fans turned slowly. Ali felt the mood and said, "What's wrong around here? Everybody scared?"

Before going to sleep the night before, he'd watched a horror movie, *Baron of Blood,* and *that* scared him. But not this. Not George Foreman, not the second Liston. "No, sir!" he said, and everyone waited for an explanation of that impossibility, which was, "This ain't nothin' but another day in the dramatic life of Muhammad Ali."

He had never said anything in one skinny sentence that could be made into a fat paragraph. Now was no time to change. "I am used to dramatic things, but when I think of our leader—for forty-two years predicting the doom of America and the weight of this on his shoulders—why it makes *this*"—gesturing toward the ring—"look like a child's kindergarten. When I walk out, it's easy. I am fighting for a man who is the Messenger of the Lord. *Scared?* A little thing like this? Nothing much scares me. Horror films. They scare me. Mummies scare me. I also fear Allah, thunderstorms, and bad plane rides. But this is like another day in the gym."

As Dundee taped his hands, Ali talked to Doc Broadus, sent over by Foreman's camp to watch the procedure. "Tell your man to be ready to dance," Ali said.

Broadus muttered, "He can't dance."

Ali asked Bundini Brown, "What's he say?"

"George Foreman's man says he can't dance."

"He can't *dance!* He can't dance! But what we goin' to *do* if he can't dance?"

When word came to Ali that Foreman's dressing room was silent, the champion at rest, his face covered by towels, only his eyes showing, Ali announced, "He's getting warmed up for the Big Dance. Are we goin' to dance with him?"

"All night long," Bundini said.

Round one, Ali danced. He hustled to center ring to bop Foreman with the fight's first punch, then retreated and moved for almost three minutes. Only near the round's end did Foreman catch Ali on the ropes. There he threw a long hook of the dynamite kind that on landing had made him feared—but this one missed. Ali had leaned back against ropes that had gone limp in a long day's tropical heat. Foreman's hook crossed in front of Ali's face. A second hook followed the same airy path. Those hooks with Ali on the ropes prompted Bundini Brown to leap to the ring apron between rounds with intent to tighten the ropes and give them the tautness that would help his man spring away from any Foreman trap. But Ali saw Brown and shouted, "No, don't. Leave 'em alone."

Ali also looked over Tom Callahan's shoulder at ringside to catch Herbert Muhammad's eye. He told his manager, "Leave him to me." Callahan turned to Vic Ziegel of the *New York Daily News,* and said, "Wrong again, Vic."

Round two, Ali did not dance. He did not go to Foreman. He went to the ropes, spread his feet wide, and lay back. He put his hands alongside his head and invited Foreman in. *Come on, hit me.* For the entire round, given time to throw any punch any way he wanted, Foreman whaled away. George Plimpton shouted to Norman Mailer, "Oh, Christ, it's a fix." Ali's cornermen were apoplectic. "Get off the ropes," Walter Youngblood said. Bundini Brown: "Dance, Champ, dance!" Between rounds, Dundee told Ali, "Get back on your toes. Move! Don't let Foreman tee off on you like that."

"I know what I'm doing," Ali said. He had told Tuell and me in Deer Lake that he would let Foreman hit him. He would conserve his energy. Foreman would tire out. Conditioning would win this fight, Ali had said. All that talk about dancing was to mess with Foreman's mind. No more dancing, none in round three when he occasionally interrupted Foreman's work with a quick jab of his own. After round four, on his corner stool, Ali told Dundee, "He's got nothin' left. Now he's mine. Now I can knock him out."

"Do it," Dundee said. "Do it *now.*"

"Not yet. He's had his turn. Now I'm going to play with him."

Foreman had delivered his best stuff and for the first time found it was not good enough. He saw Ali cringe under a killing body shot and saw in Ali's eyes a look that said *I'm not gonna let you hurt me.* Ali was talking: "Is that the best you can do? . . . Show me something, George. That don't hurt. . . . That's a sissy punch!" He was at such ease that he tied up Foreman with one hand and with the free hand led cheers from the crowd of sixty thousand joined in the Zairean chant that had become Ali's mantra for weeks: "Ali, *bomaye!*" Ali, *kill him*.

Round five, round six. As Foreman's strength disappeared, Ali rattled counterpunches off his face. "Give it *back* to me! It's mine! Now it's my turn!"

Round seven. Ali looked down at Archie Moore, the great old fighter once his mentor and now in Foreman's corner. Hands grasping the low strand of the ring ropes, the seventy-year-old Moore shouted instructions to Foreman. Ali caught Moore's eye and said, "Be quiet, old man. It's all over." Foreman rose unsteadily from his stool for round eight, as if buffeted by the crowd's exultations. Ali had called Foreman "the Mummy" and did a mime's caricature of the champion as a dead-eyed hulk lumbering forward with its arms flailing at what it couldn't see. Now, the mummified Foreman lumbered after an Ali who could choose the time and means of the knockout.

He chose a moment near round's end. He chose a left-right combination. Then another combination and another, and Foreman staggered forward, a man falling down stairs, Bundini Brown screaming, "Oh my Lawdy, he on Queer Street!" Last, a hard right directly into Foreman's eyes. Foreman reeled away from Ali in an off-balance pirouette that spun him to the canvas, knocked out.

Ferdie Pacheco left the Twentieth of May Stadium in a convoy of limousines and buses returning to Ali's quarters forty miles away. By then, after a thunderclap announced nature's intention, high winds delivered a rainstorm of flash-flood proportions. There were no lights along the road through the jungle, and Pacheco's car windows were beaded with the rain. As the doctor looked through the watery blur into the jungle's darkness, he asked a passenger, "Damn, do those trees look like they're moving to you?" With the first dim light of dawn, Pacheco saw the movement had not been trees. He now saw phantasmal figures walking out of the jungle. He saw they were natives moving to the edge of the road to hold their babies up so they could see Ali go by. The people held palm fronds over their babies' heads against the rain. Pacheco said to the man next to him, "When we left, Ali belonged to America. Now he belongs to the world."

Jerry Izenberg saw in the rainstorm a metaphor. That morning, October 30, 1974, standing with Ali by the river Zaire, the air sweet with the aroma of flowers, the columnist felt that the hatred and ugliness of Ali's life had been washed away. Ali looked out over the river and said, "You'll never know how long I waited for this. You'll never know what this means to me."

Foreman didn't frighten Ali.

But the Nation's muscle did.

Malcolm X and Leon 4X Ameer were not the only men who turned up dead after being declared *persona non grata* by the Nation of Islam's leaders. Pacheco once told me, "Thirteen people around Ali were, shall we say, disappeared." The more you knew, the darker it became. The doctor said a man once sold Ali and the Nation a block of downtown Detroit. When the property turned out to be a multimillion-dollar liability, the man was murdered. On January 18, 1973, in Washington, D.C., a killing squadron of at least nine Nation of Islam men massacred a family of seven, shooting all except a nine-day-old baby that was held under water in a bathtub until air bubbles stopped rising to the surface. The family's megalomaniacal patriarch, Hamaas Abdul Khaalis, that afternoon gone from the home purchased for him by basketball star Kareem Abdul-Jabbar, doubted the validity of the religion created by W. D. Fard and sustained by Elijah Muhammad. He said as much in letters to Muhammad, NOI ministers, and the media. After the massacre, Khaalis called the Black Muslims "executioners of babies" and "back-shooters of women." At Muhammad's next public appearance, a two-hour speech on Savior's Day, 1973, he condoned what his biographer Karl Evanzz would call "the demonic transgressions of his misguided acolytes." I once broached the subject with Ali by way of an indirect question about Abdul-Jabbar's connection to Khaalis. His reply: "Don't know nothin'."

Pacheco also knew a drug runner called Live Wire, who sold Herbert Muhammad a customized limousine loaded with cocaine in secret compartments. Live Wire died in a prison-yard murder six weeks after sentencing. Another grifter, Reggie, was cunning at mathematics until one too many cunning maneuvers resulted in his disappearance, perhaps in the Okefenokee swamp. It was the frightened Ameer who had suggested at the last press conference of his short life that the Nation would kill him as a warning that Ali should remain loyal to Elijah Muhammad. In fact, Ali often spoke warily of the Messenger. In 1964 he told George Plimpton and Alex Haley in separate interviews that it was not a good idea to buck Muhammad. In 1967 he asked Sugar Ray Robinson to come to his hotel and there he said, *But I'm afraid, Ray, I'm real afraid.* That same year, sitting with Bob Lipsyte in a Chicago coffee shop, he said, *They're not going to make no Malcolm X out of me.*

Now he sat with Tuell and me. A month after Zaire, it was "Muhammad Ali Day" in the new heavyweight champion's hometown. For three hours we talked in the presidential suite at Louisville's Galt House hotel. We heard the basic Ali performance: "I want Frazier! And Foreman! The same night! Ten million dollars for me! It will be history!" But his attitude and tone changed when two stern-faced men with the look of Fruit of Islam warriors appeared from another room in the suite. They told Ali he had an appointment pending.

"No, leave us alone," Ali said. "These are my people. These are my reporters. I don't spend this time with reporters from other cities, but these are my Louisville men. They can stay as long as they want. Don't bother us again." The two men returned to the room from which they had come. Ali told us they were bodyguards doing their job. He also said he didn't like it, that he couldn't be alone with the people he chose. He said, "They always got somebody watching."

I asked, "Who are 'they'?"

"I would have gotten out of this a long time ago," he said. "But you saw what they did to Malcolm X. I ain't gonna end up like Malcolm X."

Ali whispered, as if to be certain his voice would not carry to the men in the other room.

I asked, "You afraid?"

"I can't leave the Muslims," he said. "They'd shoot me, too."

His voice ran low and fearful. I looked at Tuell. We knew now.

We knew that Ali must have believed what Ameer had said, that crossing the Nation anytime in the previous ten years would have put his life in danger. He had seen enough men go on the fatal adventure of bucking Mr. Muhammad. So he refused the draft, as the Messenger had suggested. And he continued to fight under the Herbert Muhammad management even as men around Ali believed the Nation siphoned away most of his fortune. "Sad thing was," Harold Conrad said, "Ali thought Herbert was Jesus Christ. He'd do anything Herbert told him." As to why the sweetheart son of a Baptist church lady had so long adhered to the tenets of a religious sect teaching race-based hate, now Tuell and I knew.

The fear was gone four months later. The Nation of Islam became a kinder, gentler place when, on February 14, 1975, Elijah Muhammad died. Leadership passed to his seventh son, Wallace Dean Muhammad. The succession was accepted by Ali as Elijah's wish and was one more example of what Pacheco called "Ali's luck." Wallace Dean Muhammad quickly acted to renounce his father's religious distortions and turn to orthodox Islam.

Now freed of Elijah's theology, Ali no longer spoke of the mothership and blue-eyed white devils. In the spring of 1975, Ali talked to Lipsyte about the Nation. "We're in a new phase, a resurrection," he said. "Elijah taught us to be independent, to clean ourselves up, to be proud and healthy. He stressed the bad things the white man did to us so we could get free and strong. Now, his son Wallace is showing us there are good and bad regardless of color, that the devil is in the mind and heart, not the skin."

The Messenger's death set Ali on a journey to moderation in race, religion, and politics. As he would demonstrate that fall while preparing to fight Frazier in Manila, it was not a moderation repeated in his personal life. His wife, Belinda, had tolerated his adultery for years, even befriending the mother of one of his illegitimate children. She knew about the latest mistress in the Ali traveling party and allowed her husband to pass off the beautiful woman as a secretary and baby-sitter. She said, "I thought she was just another one of the bunch." But then Ali flaunted the infidelity.

At home in Chicago, Belinda read in the newspapers about Ali and his *wife* meeting Ferdinand and Imelda Marcos in Manila's presidential palace. There were pictures of the happy couple, Ali and Veronica Porsche, one more gorgeous than the other. Questioned about the woman, Ali told reporters, "I know celebrities don't have privacy. But at least they should be able to sleep with who they want to. The only person I answer to is Belinda Ali and I don't worry about her."

That answer did not please Belinda Ali. A twenty-hour plane trip put her in Ali's suite on the twenty-first floor of the Manila Hilton. There she stopped a television interview by shouting to Ali, "We've got to talk." The six-foot-tall former karate student took Ali into a bedroom where she threw curses, chairs, and, in the direction of Ali's procurer, Lloyd Wells, her championship ring. The last sentences of her tirade were a message for Veronica Porsche: "You tell that bitch, if I see her I'm gonna break her back. If I see her anywhere, I'm gonna break her back."

After his workout that day, Ali assured reporters that Belinda's arrival meant nothing. "She don't worry about publicity, she knows I love her and she's my wife." But at four o'clock that afternoon, as Dave Anderson waited in a corridor chair for an interview session with Ali, he saw a bell-boy pushing a cart with six suitcases away from Belinda Ali's suite. She followed, tall and striking in a white suit, white turban, and gold earrings.

"Why are you leaving?" Anderson asked.

"I'm not wanted here," she said. "Muhammad Ali doesn't want me here. Nobody wants me here. I'm not going to force myself here. I don't like an impostor coming in and taking over my family after eight years and destroying my life."

An Ali bodyguard said, "Belinda, the elevator's here."

"I don't like one woman wiping me and my whole family out—"

"Belinda," the bodyguard said softly.

"—because she wants to show off." The woman scorned was gone to the airport. And on the twenty-first floor, Anderson was told, "The champ ain't talkin'."

She was seventeen when they were married and he called her "my little Indian girl" because he first had seen her with a single braid of hair down her back. They had four children together. She had sustained him emotionally during the exile, and often traveled with him to college speeches, sometimes writing them for him. Dry now were the streams of forgiveness from which she had drawn for strength to pray with Ali before his fight in Zaire. On the night her husband would fight Frazier a third time, October 1, 1975, she sat on a couch in Wallace Dean Muhammad's basement to watch the closed-circuit telecast from Manila. She wanted Frazier to win and to inflict upon Ali a measure of the pain Ali had caused her.

She watched until she thought Ali might win. Then she went upstairs with Muhammad's wife, Shirley, and a family friend, Robyne Robinson, fifteen years old. Rage and sadness cast their reds and shadows over her face. She wanted him punished. Too many times she had seen his indifference to morality. She had suffered his cruelty delivered by public humiliation. She had heard him too many times explaining why he could do anything he damn well pleased.

"Oh, no, if he wins," she cried out, "he'll really think he's God."

———

The greater Ali's anxiety, the greater his slurs. Not since Liston the first time had Ali feared any fighter more than he feared Joe Frazier. His behavior became damnable. Again, he insulted Frazier's intelligence and his looks. This time, unspeakably, he suggested Frazier was subhuman. He did it laughing, as if his calumnies were the stuff of high comedy rather than the lowest of insults. In Manila, Ali sing-songed:

> It will be a killer
> And a chiller
> And a thrilla
> When I get the gorilla
> In Manila.

The heavyweight champion of the world pulled from his pocket a black rubber toy in the shape of a gorilla. He said, "This here is Joe Frazier's conscience. I keep it everywhere I go. This is the way he looks when you hit him." Holding the toy by its legs, Ali punched its head over and over. "All night long, this is what you'll see. Come on, gorilla, we're in Manila. Come on, gorilla, this is a thrilla."

The campaign to denigrate Frazier was a mistake. It not only was reprehensible human behavior, it brought fury to Frazier and made him a better fighter when that was the last thing Ali needed. Frazier's trainer, the clever Eddie Futch, believed the Ali who won in Zaire was vulnerable. He thought Ali fought off the ropes against Foreman because it now was the only way he could fight. He was no longer the dancing wraith of 1966 who surrounded and mystified poor Cleveland Williams. Nine years had passed, and this was a lesser Ali, still good, maybe great, but this was Ali, not Clay.

Since his return from exile, Ali had trained seriously only for Foreman. "He didn't want to pay the price after Foreman," Futch said. A superhuman (as Belinda Ali must have heard more than once) need not worry about mere mortals. A slothful Ali could win fights. But he could not be the greatest of all times. By his arrogance, Ali diminished the physical gifts of reflexes, hand-eye coordination, grace in movement, strength, and stamina that had made him the best ever. As Cassius Clay, young, you could not hit him. As Muhammad Ali, old, you could not miss him. He had become a different fighter and a lesser one. Arrogance at the threshold of hubris had cost him his wife's love, not that he cared much about that. But now it cost him what he had always loved most. Himself. He became a Muhammad Ali hologram, pretty and illusory.

The difference was terrible. He had ignored Fred Stoner's lessons, and Joe Martin's, and Angelo Dundee learned the futility of trying to teach him. Ali never learned to fight defensively. He relied instead on astonishing reflexes to pull away from danger, or, if need be, he simply ran. Cus D'Amato said, "The only time you touched Ali was when you touched gloves before the fight." Now, the legs gone, the reflexes going, he had no defense at all. He was reluctant to attack because that brought him near danger and no one feared his punching power. Atop all that, rich and famous, the guest of kings and presidents, Ali lost his taste for training. Perhaps that's to be expected, as the jockey Eddie Arcaro once noted: "It's hard to get up in the mornings when you're sleeping in silk pajamas."

Against this Ali, Eddie Futch wanted his man to wage a war of attrition. If Frazier could beat on Ali's arms and bring them down, that pretty face would be there for the taking. But only a man in whom hatred ran deep and ran hot could have the patience to bang away at the granite of Ali's body until it yielded. Foreman couldn't do it. But Ali's insults guaranteed that Frazier would be such a man.

The first three rounds, Ali set himself in ring center in the misguided hope that he could knock out Frazier early, as Foreman had done in Jamaica. But Ali was not Foreman, and this Frazier was not going down. Ali's heaviest punches stopped Frazier's advance for only a heartbeat or two, and in the fifth round Ali heard an unfamiliar sound. From the crowd of about twenty-five thousand people came the chant, "Frazier . . . Fra-zier." The man on the march had made the fight his. "Lord, that man can punch," Ali said on his stool. Sixth round, two evil left hooks to Ali's head. Both were greater than the hook that had set Ali's tassels upside down four years earlier. But this time Ali stayed up. Frazier, relentless. Ali, backing to the ropes, hearing Dundee, "The center of the ring!"

Easier said than done when Joe Frazier is swinging sledgehammers at your hip joints. Through another four rounds, another twelve minutes, another lifetime, Ali was under siege, protected only by idiosyncratic right leads and that gyroscope whirling in his brain that somehow kept him standing upright. At the end of the eleventh, Ali wanted no more. He didn't so much sit down on his corner stool as use it to interrupt his collapse. Dundee noticed his man's weakness and said, "Muhammad, now we're going to separate the men from the boys." He pulled Ali's trunks away from his waist and poured in ice water. "You've got to suck it up."

Anyone who saw that twelfth round had to believe that no fighter had ever done what Ali did. He teetered at exhaustion. Frazier was always there. The tin-roofed arena was an oven under Manila's midday sun. Then, from some dark and scary place, Ali borrowed against his future. He decided there was only one way to settle this, and that was at arm's length, trading punches. Through the twelfth and into the thirteenth, Ali brought it all. Frazier had bled from the mouth most of the night, and now his face began to swell at those places where veins had been crushed to bursting and blood was on the run and looked for somewhere to go and could find no way out. The gathering, clotting, lumping blood pushed tissue toward Frazier's left eye and soon he looked through a slit. In the thirteenth, he didn't see the Ali right that ripped his mouthpiece out and sent it over the ropes into ringside seats, its bloody saliva a comet's tail.

Came the fourteenth and Ali sent nine straight rights to Frazier's unseeing face, maybe thirty by round's end, and Eddie Futch, from his stool at eye level with the ring floor, saw his man defenseless and brave. It was terrible and he had seen it before. He had seen a fighter named Jimmy Doyle on a stretcher, eyes open, empty, the fighter soon dead. He had seen Talmadge Bussey, saved by the bell, dragged to his corner, sent out by his brothers for the next round in which one more punch left him dead. Davey Moore talked boxing for hours with Futch, Davey Moore a world featherweight champion, and Futch had seen Moore go down, a freaky thing, his neck whiplashed against the bottom rope, the man dead. Bob Dylan wrote a song asking, "Who killed Davey Moore, why, what's the reason for?"

Now, after forty-one rounds with Frazier, after the fourteenth and most savage round on this night, Ali said, "Cut 'em off." He wanted the gloves off. He had said those words before. His eyes on fire against Liston, he said, *Cut 'em off.* That night eleven years before, Dundee sprayed water into his fighter's eyes and told him to run. This time he ignored Ali. He knew he wouldn't quit. Across the ring, with his man in against a great finisher, Eddie Futch crouched in front of Frazier and asked, "What's with his right hand?"

"I can't see it," Frazier said. "I can see the left, but when I move away, I get hit with the right."

"I'm going to stop it, Joe, the fight's over," Futch said.

"Don't do that," Frazier said, jumping to his feet. "I can finish."

"Sit down. The fight's over. This is the best thing to do."

Futch turned to referee Carlos Padilla and said, "That's all."

In Ali's corner, Gene Kilroy saw it happening and shouted, "It's over! It's over!"

Ali told the press, "What you saw tonight was next to death," and Frazier said he didn't want to quit but wouldn't argue with Futch. Later that night, one of Frazier's cornermen, George Benton, walked to the edge of the fighter's bed and heard his man's heavy breathing. "Who is it?" Frazier said. "I can't see. Turn the lights on." Lights were on. Another was turned on. *Sports Illustrated*'s Mark Kram wrote: "The scene cannot be forgotten; this good and gallant man lying there, embodying the remains of a will that had carried him so far—and now surely too far. His eyes were only slits, his face looked as if it had been painted by Goya. 'Man, I hit him with punches that'd bring down the walls of a city,' said Frazier. 'Lawdy, Lawdy, he's a great champion.'"

That night Ali went to a party. He did not bring Veronica. Ali sat with Imelda Marcos, the president's wife, and signed her guest book, "To Mrs. Marcos—Muhammad Ali—death is so near and time for friendly action is so limited. Love and peace always." On his return to the United States, Ali exchanged Belinda for Veronica, though their marriage didn't take place for another year and a half, delayed by Herbert Muhammad's demands for a prenuptial agreement. Veronica finally accepted the deal. She soon asked her husband to tear it up. He did.

After hard fights, even winners don't want to fight again. Ali told reporters, "You may have seen the last of Ali. I want to get out of it. I'm tired and on top." At the Marcos party, he said it again, only in phrases suggesting peril: "This'll kill you. I'm a superhuman. So when I'm that tired, it's dangerous."

Ali said the words. He also ignored them. Fighters, especially the best of them, cannot be talked into quitting, not even by themselves. Theirs is an addiction. They need the adrenaline rush of athletic competition and the narcissistic pleasures of celebrity. Only multiple examples of irrefutable defeat can get them off the stuff. Gene Kilroy had wanted Ali to retire after Zaire. There, by courage, skill, and the will necessary to accept extraordinary punishment, Ali had won back what had been stolen from him. It was the moment for a cinematic exit in triumph. But Ali could not leave then nor after suffering the hells of Manila. Kilroy saw only darkness ahead and told Ali, "You can beat everybody, but you can't beat Father Time."

Nor could he leave millions of dollars on the table. Herbert Muhammad saw to it that no dollar anywhere missed its chance to leap into his pocket, there to be divvied up among himself, the Nation, and Ali. Within a year of being "next to death" in Manila, Ali defended his championship four times. He was indifferent against anonymities Jean-Pierre Coopman, Jimmy Young, and Richard Dunn. Then came a third fight with Ken Norton, a fight he could not have wanted except for its six million dollars.

Norton always had perplexed Ali. Strong, quick, and moving from a crouch in a lurching, splay-footed gait, Norton won the night he broke Ali's jaw and lost the rematch in twelve rounds on an arguable decision. For this one at Yankee Stadium on September 28, 1976, Ali worked himself into the best shape a wastrel's habits allowed. He brought conditioning and guile, but little else. Ali's jab, once a snake-lick weapon, was now an ineffectual pawing activated by ancient memory. Without it, he could mount no sustained offensive. Even winning four of the previous five rounds, Ali came to the fifteenth with his championship in doubt.

Dundee told Ali, "You've got three more minutes. Fight like hell. We need this round." Across the ring, Norton's manager, Bob Biron, told his man he had it won. For two and a half minutes, then, Norton was passive. That was a mistake, for no fighter ever closed a show more persuasively than Ali did, with both flair and substance. Ali won the fight by the margin of that round.

The pattern of Ali's fights had become clear and disturbing. Every decent fighter put him under siege. Defenseless, he now survived because he had discovered a truth that should have terrified him. He could take a man's best punch and not go down. He went forty-one rounds with Frazier, thirty-seven with Norton—seventy-eight rounds with men who hadn't lasted six rounds total with George Foreman. No fighter, no matter how brave, no matter how willing to take punishment, no matter how zealous in the belief that his mission is divinely inspired—no fighter can fight siege wars for long. Ferdie Pacheco saw the evidence. After the Yankee Stadium fight, the doctor went to Norton's dressing room. "If it's any consolation to you," he told the fighter, "you just retired Ali. He's pissing blood." What Pacheco couldn't know, but suspected, was that Ali's brain bled as well.

With Elijah Muhammad dead, the only person who could have ordered Ali to stop fighting was Herbert Muhammad. His influence flowed directly from his father and had been reinforced by years on the road with Ali in brotherly pursuit of cash and women. But Herbert would not make that order because he knew Ali was in no financial position to retire. Corporations did not seek out one of America's most controversial figures from the 1960s to endorse their products. (Ali did one television commercial, a demeaning pitch for a roach spray.) Despite fifteen years in the ring for purses of forty million dollars, Ali lived from paycheck to paycheck. It all went somewhere: taxes, the Nation, Herbert's one-third cut, Dundee's fees, salaries to his entourage, handouts to assorted hangers-on, divorce settlements, agreements with women claiming to be mothers of illegitimate children. (Dundee once pointed to an electrical outlet and said, "If he stuck his dick in there, that light socket would get pregnant.")

Herbert Muhammad also understood that Ali's need for money ran a distant second to his need for attention. Only fighting guaranteed both. If Herbert did his manager's job well, he would, at that perilous time in Ali's career, find the least dangerous opponent for the most possible money. He accomplished half of that equation on May 16, 1977, when Ali made his first start since Norton. Yet Ali went fifteen rounds for a decision over a Spanish neophyte, Alfredo Evangelista.

Four months later, Herbert put Ali in with Earnie Shavers, in a fight that should not have been made for any reason except for money in the Frazier/Norton neighborhood. It was for much less, maybe one million dollars. Shavers was a feared, head-hunting journeyman who had won fifty-four of fifty-nine fights, fifty-two by knockouts, twenty of those in the first round. Only Russian roulette would have been a much more dangerous game for Ali, who seemed to sense it.

In his room at the Hotel Statler near Madison Square Garden, Ali told Jerry Izenberg, the *Newark Stark-Ledger* columnist, "Do you know how many years I've been fighting? Do you know how tired I am? Do you have idea how hard that man is going to beat on my head tomorrow night?"

Izenberg said, "So why do it?"

It was money, glory, what people wanted. Ali said something like that.

"Do yourself a favor," the newspaperman said. "Sit down and play back that roach-spray commercial you just made, because I listened to it ten times before I was able to make out the word 'fog.' I couldn't understand what you were saying. And then take any of the tapes you made over the years, and listen to your voice the way it used to be."

He told Ali of a neurological study done in 1928 by Dr. H. S. Martland, who found that a boxer's brain continues to disintegrate for two years after his last fight. "That's something you should think about after Shavers," Izenberg said. "It'd be a horrible tragedy, you punch-drunk."

Izenberg's concern was not shared by Ali. His reaction was less than a yawn but no more than, "Uh-huh."

In the second round, Shavers dropped an overhand right on Ali's head. Only Frazier ever hit Ali harder, but he didn't go down. Once, if you reached to touch him, he had fluttered away. But the time for pretty metaphors was gone. Instinct that once removed him from danger now told him to cover up. *Playing possum,* Earnie Shavers thought when he saw Ali wobble, saw him wobble more, as if to draw Shavers into a trap. Once a butterfly, now a possum. Once a comic poet, now a roach-spray shill.

How desperately must a man need what comes with boxing to put up with that, and with Earnie Shavers beating on his head in the thirteenth and fourteenth rounds when, again, Ali did not go down. He won the last round, big, and won the decision, big, but no one who saw the fight believed that winning meant he should continue to fight. Ali was on his way to a press conference the next morning when the Garden's matchmaker, Teddy Brenner, stopped him.

"Champ, why don't you announce your retirement?" Brenner said.

"What for?" said the man four months shy of thirty-six years old who had gone fifteen rounds three times in a year.

"Because sooner or later," the matchmaker said, "some kid that couldn't carry your bucket is going to beat you. You're going to be beaten by guys that have no business being in the ring with you. It's just a matter of time. If you take a big piece of iron and put it down on the center of the floor and let a drop of water hit it every ten seconds, eventually you'll get a hole in the center of that piece of iron, and that's what happening to you. You're getting hit, you're gonna get hurt. You've proven everything that a great champion can possibly prove. You don't need this. Get out."

For a man's brain is not iron, and gloved fists are not water.

Brenner announced that Madison Square Garden would never bid on another Ali fight. "I don't want him to come over to me some day and say, 'What's your name?'" Ferdie Pacheco already was in trouble with Herbert Muhammad after being quoted on Ali's womanizing. "A pelvic missionary," the doctor called Ali, an exponent of "the horizontal rhumba." Then Pacheco heard from the New York State Athletic Commission's doctor that Ali's kidneys were disintegrating. Pissing blood again. Believing that Ali should retire, Pacheco wrote letters to Ali, Veronica, Herbert Muhammad, and Angelo Dundee. He attached a written report from the commission doctor. When no one responded, Pacheco resigned.

What Ali needed was a truly easy fight. Then he saw the man he needed. Leon Spinks was an Olympic champion, as Floyd Patterson, Joe Frazier, and George Foreman had been. Ali liked the promotional value of beating yet another gold medalist. He had seen Spinks on television stumbling to a draw against the palooka Scott LeDoux. Even rawer than Alfredo Evangelista, Spinks had had seven pro fights. That, Ali really liked. Here was a kid who couldn't carry his spit bucket.

And on February 15, 1978, in Las Vegas, Spinks won a fifteen-round decision convincingly. Ali's work was pathetic. He did nothing in training because he didn't want to, and did nothing in the ring because he couldn't. At his typewriter that night, Dave Anderson wrote of Ali, "His face, that wonderful face which once was hardly ever marked in a fight, suddenly had seemed stretched and aged as he plodded out for the final round. And now, up close, there were purple bruises above and below his right eye and over the bridge of his nose. His forehead was swollen near his left eye. Blood from his cut lower lip spotted his white satin trunks and his white terry-cloth robe."

After a night in a bathtub full of ice, Ali arranged himself carefully in an easy chair to talk to sportswriters, most of us his fellow travelers on a journey so exotic—Zaire, Manila, Kuala Lumpur—that he worked at dreaming up new venues. "I'm sorry, men," he said from behind dark glasses. "We never made it to Tibet."

"Champ," said Ed Schuyler of the Associated Press, "with this guy, we'll be lucky to get to Scranton, Pennsylvania."

"I messed up," Ali said. "I was lousy. But I don't want to take anything away from Spinks. He fought a good fight and never quit. He made fools of everybody, even me." He also said he would fight again. "Yeah. I'll win it for the third time. I'll be the first one to get it for the third time. I'll get in better shape."

The rematch was made for September—not in Scranton but in New Orleans. Eight days before that fight, before dawn, Hugh McIlvanney found Ali stretched naked under the stars. Always enthralled by Ali, the London journalist often conducted eccentric academic inquiries into the fighter's habits and spontaneous combustions. This time Ali had finished a thirty-minute run through the heavy darkness of a Louisiana night. He rested on a quilt spread over a rubbing table in the backyard of a suburban New Orleans house. A towel covered Ali's midsection as his masseur, the silent Cuban named Luis Sarria, rubbed oil over his body and massaged his feet. Phantasmagoria ensued, with McIlvanney there to record Ali's words . . .

"So I'm out there with him in the Superdome, and the world is amazed. This ain't the fat man that took him casual in Las Vegas last February, that didn't train or eat good, that listened to all the talk about how easy he would be, saw him as just a kid out of the amateurs with seven nothin' pro fights to his name, a novice who didn't belong in the ring with the best heavyweight of all times. No, this is the real Ali, lookin' beautiful and movin' fast, hurtin', pop, pop, with the jab, then the right hand, the hooks, the combinations, pressure he can't take. It's a mismatch, by seven or eight it can't go on, the referee is jumpin' in to stop it. It's all over. Muhammad ALLEE is champion of the world for the third time. This is a miracle . . . and I go and pick up my briefcase, get in my Lear jet, and fly off to see some president of a country somewhere."

Fun as always, McIlvanney decided, and indeed Ali had done the serious training he had so long and successfully avoided. Still, he was four months short of age thirty-seven. McIlvanney posed for his readers the salient question: "Can all the systematic honing of his physique restore the swiftness of reflex, the judgment of distance and sharpness of timing that once made other heavyweights look as if they had sludge in their veins?"

CHAPTER FOURTEEN

"A Twentieth-Century Torture Device"

BECAUSE COSELL'S MNF PRODUCER, Don Ohlmeyer, had asked coaches what they would do in certain situations, he knew that on first-and-goal between the five- and ten-yard lines the Redskins would throw in the end zone to tight end Jackie Smith. So he hit the microphone key to Cosell in the booth. "Next play, Howard," he said, "will be a pass to Smith."

Gifford mumbled, Meredith muttered, and Cosell, armed with the intelligence received from Ohlmeyer through his earpiece, said, "Well, Danderoo, you must never forget the angular one, the tight end Jackie Smith."

As if the ensuing Smith touchdown weren't enough, Cosell reprised his all-knowing performance when the Redskins lined up at the thirty-eight-yard line for a field goal attempt by Mark Moseley. Ohlmeyer to Cosell again: "Too far for Moseley. The holder, Theismann, will run it."

Gifford mumbled, Meredith muttered, and Cosell said, "Well, Danderoo, this distance may be too much for Moseley. Keep an eye on the holder, little Joey Theismann, the fresh recruit from the Canadian Football League."

Theismann's dash for a touchdown off the fake field goal pleased Cosell so much that he left Ohlmeyer waiting in the ABC limousine a half-hour after the game. They were to leave immediately for a private plane returning to New York. Ohlmeyer thought he knew the reason for the delay. His suspicion that Cosell couldn't leave the stadium that night in the winter of 1974 without taking bows at every stop was confirmed when the broadcaster stepped into the limo, sat beside the man who'd whispered in his ear, and asked, "Don, did you hear me tonight? Prescient as always, calling the plays before they happened, calling them while the baboons are talking about buffoonery. Did you hear me, Don? 'Coming next, a touchdown pass to the angular one!' Then the call of the fake field goal! What other announcer could have done such brilliant work? None!"

Cosell lifted a cigar to those lips which had given flight to his prescience only to hear Ohlmeyer said, "Howard, cut the bullshit. This is me you're talking to. Or do you think that thing in your ear is your brain talking to you? That bullshit won't work on me."

At which point, Cosell said, "Right, kid," and the ride to the airport assumed a great silence.

However audacious Cosell could be, his five most outrageous words may have been, "Ricky, get me the Beatles!" John, Paul, Ringo and George— reunited. At his request, the most famous singing group in music history would end the dissolution that each Liverpudlian had said was irrevocable. He would cause this miracle of popular culture to happen for the premier of his variety show broadcast from the Ed Sullivan Theater in Midtown New York. What the Beatles themselves had put asunder, he would put together on *Saturday Night Live with Howard Cosell*.

With Arledge as his producer, Cosell intended to use their talents, influence, access, cash, and satellite television technology to bring the universe of entertainment into American homes. At last he would be where he deserved to be. Enough of sports. A man of his intellect educated at constitutional law should not suffer for all eternity by proximity to jocks with rocks in their head. The variety show had been conceived by Fred Pierce, the ABC network president, who saw in its development the means to satisfy Cosell and Arledge, both restless in sports. Already, they had teamed up with Frank Sinatra on a concert called The Main Event with Cosell as the master of ceremonies at Madison Square Garden. When that show was a ratings hit, Pierce said to Arledge, "Hey, maybe Cosell could become the next Ed Sullivan."

As the Beatles had made their American debut with Ed Sullivan in 1964, now, in 1975, five years after their breakup, Cosell wanted them to perform on his first show. His pursuit of the boys began with that order to Rick Sklar, his old New York radio boss who had made WABC the first station in the United States featuring Beatles music.

Without market tests, but with absolute faith in the Beatles' virtuosity, Skylar ordered disc jockeys to play every Beatles record the day it arrived and to identify the station as "W-A-Beatles-C." In the years since, he had become good friends with John Lennon, who then lived in the city.

When Cosell asked for the Beatles, Sklar blanched. He loved the antic Cosell. He knew Cosell's endless loop of sports reporting through the 1960s had helped make WABC, in Cosellian understatement, "the most listened-to radio station in the history of broadcast." But the Beatles had rebuffed all talk of playing together again, and Sklar knew private details, through Lennon, that made a reunion impossible. Cosell, however, believed Lennon was his pal. They had met two years earlier in San Francisco when Lennon and Governor Ronald Reagan made halftime bows in the *MNF* booth. "You take the governor," Cosell told Gifford, "I'll take the Beatle."

First question that night, Cosell to Lennon: "Will the Beatles ever reunite?"

"You never know, you never know," Lennon said. "I mean, it's always in the wind. If it looked like this"—he looked around the sold-out stadium—"it might be worth doing, right?"

"You did just spend a weekend with Ringo."

"Yeah, and I promised him I would mention his album out now, and I wouldn't mention my own, which is out now, too. Forget it."

In the summer of 1975, when Cosell dropped Lennon's name in a newspaper interview promoting the upcoming variety show, there came a note.

> Dear Howard:
>   Someone told me that you mentioned me in a newspaper in regard to your new show. For personal reasons I must decline any commitments until next year. I might add that equally weird and wonderful monsieur Ringo Starr might well be available for your variety show! (and perhaps more suited.)
>   I wish you all the best,
>   I'm sure it's going to be a big hit!
>   love and dressed fishes,

yer old pal,
what's his name?

John L.

More than enough there to persuade Cosell that Lennon was his buddy for life. He told Sklar, "On opening night, Ricky, we're going to recreate the night that the Beatles first appeared on American television. And we're going to do it from the same theater, on the same stage." Sklar finally gave in and invited Lennon to the 21 Club. The Beatle may have been 21's only lunch guest ever who arrived wearing a black velvet jacket decorated by a large silver pin set with diamonds spelling out *Elvis*. There Cosell made fuss and flattery over Lennon as the quintessential *MNF* guest, a giant who raised the level of the night's entertainment. Lennon enjoyed it until Cosell came back to the question he had asked in San Francisco.

"John," he said, "I want you guys on my show."

Lennon said, "What do you mean 'you guys'?"

"You, George, Paul, Ringo."

"I don't know. I don't know. After what's gone down, I don't know . . . I thought you wanted *me*."

"Of course, I want you," Cosell said. "But let's be realistic. This is bigger than both of us."

It was time to speak practically. Lennon said any Beatles reunion would not happen on free home television. It would be in a stadium with closed-circuit television around the world. There would be a motion picture and an album. But even with that promised, a reunion was as unlikely as ever.

Cosell persisted. "Think of it, John. Imagine restaging the most electrifying moment in American television."

Lennon finally said a flat no. Before leaving the table, however, he did shake Cosell's hand and say he would be pleased to be a *MNF* guest again.

So the first *Saturday Night Live with Howard Cosell* featured a Scottish boy-band called the Bay City Rollers and introduced by Cosell as "the next Beatles." As if that were not insult enough to the American public that he long had insisted deserved the full glory of his intelligence, Cosell allowed tone-deaf tennis star Jimmy Connors to sing with Paul Anka and pronounced the resulting squawk "a great magical moment in musical history." Sinatra, doing a cameo to thank Cosell for emceeing his Garden comeback, floated a too-true wisecrack: "This show will be a millstone on American TV." Not for long, though. Ed Sullivan's show lasted twenty-four years. Cosell's debuted September 20, 1975, and its cancellation was announced eight weeks later. The dispirited Arledge walked away from the wreckage making a joke about the show's time slot. At eight o'clock on a Saturday night, he said, "You could have Elizabeth Taylor doing a striptease and it wouldn't get a fifteen share." The most curious explanation of failure involved Cosell. The man who invented vitriol on television had been too nice. Rather than seek out controversy, Cosell ran from it. Once, ordered by Arledge to tell the audience that Patti La-Belle had refused to sing, Cosell balked on grounds he would be sued. On stage with real, live show-business performers, Cosell was starstruck. He loved everyone. Everyone was brilliant. Never had there been an entertainer on stage anywhere at any time as incandescent as the next to stand alongside Cosell. At no time did he cast his penetrating vision upon the actors and declare them incompetent, unprofessional, and unfit to be seen on ABC's air—not even when they walked out on him, as LaBelle had. He had crossed over. He had become the obsequious poseur he had forever scorned.

He even asked for cue cards. In every broadcast of his career, he had ad-libbed every word. Cosell talked. *Copy? I need no copy! I am a fucking genius!* Now he wanted a script to read. For all the insecurity revealed by his years of kvetching, there had never been more persuasive evidence of that insecurity than his use of cue cards at his moment of greatest hope. That was not Cosell. Every nerve ending in the real Howard Cosell was on fire when he screamed, "Down goes Frazier! Down goes Frazier! DOWN GOES FRAZIER!" That Cosell, you had to hear. This Cosell, America decided, was eminently missable.

For Cosell, the failure was profound. This was no cheap shot from a know-nothing columnist in the hinterlands. This was national television in prime time. The debacle affirmed for critics their view that sports could do well without Cosell but that Cosell without the games was an earache. It also brought to an end Cosell's insistence that he belonged alongside Sinatra, Woody Allen, and Bob Hope. He once said, "I always felt most comfortable in Hollywood where I was taken for granted as a superstar and paid homage to by the greatest stars in show business." More significantly, because Cosell and Arledge still had to work together at ABC Sports, the show added to Cosell's grievances against his boss. Arledge already had burdened him with the jocks on Monday nights, refused to rescue him from that punishment, and denied him prominence on the Munich broadcasts. This time Arledge had abandoned him by producing the *Saturday Night* shows carelessly. Cosell could be outraged by even slight affronts. This time his sorrow left no room for anger. He acknowledged Arledge's bewilderment in the face of unexpected defeat and added, "It wasn't easy for me, either, and sometimes I wondered how I could go on."

Arledge believed that Cosell, for all his protestations about the integrity of his work, would announce a children's game of Pick-Up Sticks if promised it would be on national television. Shortly after *Saturday Night*'s failure, he tested that theory by creating a one-shot show called *Battle of the Network Stars* with Cosell as its host. Of course, Cosell embraced the concept. He had already done hyperbolic play-by-play of the 1973 Billie Jean King–Bobby Riggs tennis match. The next year Cosell and his canary-yellow blazer certified the legitimacy of an Evel Knievel motorcycle jump over Mack trucks. In the winter of 1976, the integrity of his work could be damaged only slightly by reporting the thrill of victory and agony of defeat as rendered in a footrace between comic Gabe Kaplan and actor Robert Conrad.

The *Battle* concept was simple. Personalities from the three networks made fools of themselves in quasi-athletic events reported by the matinee idol sportscaster from *Bananas*. Kaplan captained ABC's stars, Conrad NBC's, and Telly Savalas the CBS contingent. There were tugs-of-war, obstacle-course races, roller skating, table tennis, monkey-bar gymnastics, and assorted water events designed to maximize the male demographic's pleasure in viewing wet T-shirts worn by jiggly starlets.

The show aired during a network sweeps week when ratings determined the next season's advertising rates. It was the broadcast equivalent of a circus shill inviting hayseeds into the tent to leer at girls. Cosell justified his presence by declaring *Battle* to be the most honest show he had ever done, "pure entertainment." Some viewers not under contract to ABC called it "trash sports."

Monday Night Football had made Cosell ubiquitous. He sat with Johnny Carson five times in a year, did three Dean Martin celebrity roasts, and twice played himself in *Odd Couple* episodes. The self-parodies made him an easy target. In the Woody Allen film *Sleeper,* a health food store owner was awakened in the year 2173. He saw TV file footage of a prattling gasbag Cosell. When asked if that was a "a twentieth-century torture device," the store owner replied, "That's exactly what that was." The comic Buddy Hackett said there were differences of opinion on Cosell. "Some people hate him like poison," Hackett said. "Other people just hate him regular."

Seeing Cosell's apparent willingness, even eagerness, to be involved in projects outside traditional parameters, ABC vice president Irwin Weiner went to him with a program idea. He would spin off *Monday Night Football* into a Saturday morning cartoon. It would feature animations of Cosell, Gifford, and Meredith, with the men doing their own voices in humorous sketches of Monday night life. Cosell was aghast. "Young man," he announced, "do you know whom you're speaking to? I am the biggest name in show business today. And you want to make a cartoon character of me!"

As if he hadn't already done it.

Winston Churchill wrote of playwright George Bernard Shaw, "The world has long watched with tolerance and amusement the nimble antics and gyrations of this unique and double-headed chameleon, while all the time the creature was eager to be taken seriously." Only Cosell took himself so seriously as to believe he could be the next Walter Cronkite, a proposal he made in May 1977.

Arledge had used the leverage of his success with ABC Sports to gain control of the network's moribund news division. Early rumors had Arledge dumping the *Evening News* coanchors Harry Reasoner and Barbara Walters. Unsolicited, Cosell told Arledge, "Put me and 'The Midget' together."

The allusion was to Jim McKay, a small man but not that small. The idea was ludicrous. Because he disliked confrontation, especially with the relentless Cosell, Arledge hedged: "Don't think I haven't thought of that. I'm not through with that idea yet." Cosell closed with a pitch that quoted Walter Winchell, the legendary radio newscaster: "Winchell said, 'Other people report the news. I make it public.' I do the same thing." Arledge respected Cosell's craftsmanship, performance skills, and appeal to a broad spectrum of viewers. But he considered Cosell—and Winchell before him—a broadcast version of the highly stylized newspaper columnist who delivered sensational news and opinions. There would be no place on the *Evening News* for a melodramatic pundit and failed variety-show host who most recently had done breathless commentary on starlets in wet T-shirts.

With *MNF,* Cosell was the perfect broadcaster. He was as opinionated as the next guy at the bar; his thunderous bombast matched the game's, and his feel for a storyline added richness to the drama of human competition that Arledge had long ago identified as the heart of ABC Sports coverage. Only Cosell could do what he did. If he had a sense of humor about himself as well as belief in the value of his work and a smidgeon of humility, he could have said, "Walter Cronkite is good, very good. Walter Cronkite is credible. I cannot do Walter Cronkite. But I can do Cronkite better than he can do Cosell. You think not? Let's hear Walter Cronkite ad-lib two minutes and fifteen thrilling seconds of halftime highlights never having previewed the video. I rest my case."

Instead of disarming Arledge with such a speech, Cosell added the brushoff to his lengthening list of slights real and imagined.

CHAPTER FIFTEEN

"You Know You Need Me More Than I Need You"

BOMBASTIC ON MONDAY NIGHTS, Cosell was subdued when performing with Ali. Ten years into the act, Cosell knew its real star. On a *Wide World* segment after Ali had regained the heavyweight championship, the partners did a journalistic examination of the fight's strategy and then moved to the repartee. Cosell had heard that Ali wanted to fight Frazier and Foreman on the same night. "What's this nonsense . . ."

"Oh, you call it nonsense," Ali said. "American, European boxing authorities may say it's illegal. But I think I can do things other fighters can't do. And I want to fight Joe Frazier and George Foreman the same night. Hank Aaron's record was broken. Floyd Patterson was the first to retire . . ."

Cosell offered a straight line: "Babe Ruth's record was broken."

"Babe Ruth, right. And people out to set records. I want to set a record that will never be broken, that fits the image I have of being the greatest fighter that ever lived, of all time. And if I fight Frazier first and then Foreman jump in right behind him . . . I think we'll have to take it to a Communist country, Russia or Red China. We're already in contact with Russia. Both fighters will be paid five million dollars apiece for fighting myself."

Cosell wrapped it up. "It sounds as unreal to me as your once-projected fight against Wilt Chamberlain. I want to thank you so much for coming by. You've become a towering figure on the international scene by virtue of your victory."

"And thank you for following me around"—Ali, slyly—"and getting praise also."

"And thank me for having picked George Foreman to beat you, for which I again apologize. Good luck to you, you are the greatest."

Immediately, Ali slid down in his chair and exhaled melodramatically. "Whewwww," he said, "I won Cosell." There was an air of mock triumph, as if after a long struggle he could rest, his place in history certified by Howard William Cosell.

"Now let's go back to Jim McKay," the broadcaster said, and from the next chair there came another sigh, the fighter again saying, "I won Cosell."

Cosell claimed an "intimacy of knowledgeability" about Ali and often mentioned "private" conversations by way of establishing a question's authenticity. If viewers were left with the impression that he and Ali were friends of a special kind, so much the better. But Ali once defined friendship with words that specifically excluded Cosell. Trapped on a late-night flight with Ali, Bob Lipsyte heard him ask, "You ever hear my lecture on friendship? It's not so heavy as my lecture on the heart of man, but it's real good," Ali said. From an attaché case on his lap, he produced a stack of frayed-edge index cards. They were his cheat sheets written in black script. Lipsyte thought to read a card, but Ali pulled it away. "I'll say it slow so you can write it down."

"I've got a tape recorder with me," Lipsyte said.

"That's good. You can concentrate on listening."

For a half-hour, Lipsyte listened. As if he had a choice. As if people at the back of the plane had a choice. Lipsyte reckoned Ali's volume at concert hall force.

" 'Whenever the thought of self-interest creeps in,'" Ali said, reading, " 'that means a destruction of friendship. Every little thought of profiting by it means destruction.' This is what I'm doing, things I'm doing today. It can never develop into a real friendship, it can only develop in a business relationship. It will last as long as the business relationship lasts. Like me and Cosell. I lose, he goes to somebody else."

Ali was not reluctant to remind Cosell which man had top billing. He delivered the message clearly on a *Wide World* early in 1977. Ali had defended his championship eight times in eighteen months and done it across ninety-five rounds. He was recently divorced and planning a third marriage. The question was, would he fight again?

"The truth is," Cosell said, "you have told me repeatedly, privately . . . that deep in your heart, you don't want to ever fight again. The reason you'll fight again is because of the marital entanglement and your present need for money. Let's put it on the table, isn't that true?"

Ali's answer, delivered rapidly with a smile and a rising voice: "No, sir, that is not true. As far as money is concerned, we never got enough money. Rockefeller still lookin' for money, J. Paul Getty still looking for it, Howard Hughes's firm still lookin' for it—and I'm still lookin' for it—and *you* are still lookin' for it. *You* called me yesterday and you got this thing up. You know you need me more than I need you. That's why I come in to do this show. Keep that in your mind with all your smart questions." Eyes twinkling now. *You need me more than I need you.*

Cosell at a loss. "Well, that's entirely . . ." Pause, then a grudging syllable at a time, "prob . . . a . . . ble." Hoping to regain lost ground, he added, "Though it's a matter to conjure with." Recovering, he said, "And if I do, you've got a scoop, buster."

But when Cosell said Ali wanted to fight Duane Bobick before a Foreman rematch, Ali again delighted himself by saying, "I don't have to answer to you. I told you, you need *me* more than I need *you*. I don't need you."

What to do when faced with a truth that cut so near the bone? Cosell laughed out loud, and the laughter came with a bit too much heartiness.

"You're laughing, but it's true," Ali said. "I don't need you. I never see you again, never do an interview with you, I'm still going to be a world figure. You're just an American figure. I'm a world figure. Look, I am the lord of the ring, Howard. It all comes around me. I know my value. I know who I am."

Ali, the world figure, returned from Moscow in June 1978 to tape a *Wide World* interview with Cosell. He had finished a twelve-day tour of Russia that included a Kremlin meeting with Soviet leader Leonid Brezhnev. For a fee reported to be fifty thousand dollars, Ali and his entourage had brought back film.

"Brezhnev didn't talk about small things such as fights," Ali told reporters before leaving Moscow. "He talked about peace and love for humanity. He told me he'd like me to do all I can to better relations between our countries, and he made me an unofficial ambassador for peace to the

United States, so don't be surprised if you see me in the White House soon. It felt good to be a little black boy from Louisville, Kentucky, who couldn't hardly meet the mayor of that place a few years ago. Now I'm sitting in Russia, talking to the most powerful man in the world."

It was hard to imagine greater naïveté than Ali's. Even as he marveled at Brezhnev's talk of peace and love, the Soviet Union was engaged in, or had recently concluded, bloody military adventures in Czechoslovakia, Vietnam, Cambodia, Laos, and great regions of Africa. At age thirty-six walking in Red Square, Ali was as gullible as he was at nineteen meeting a Nation of Islam captain in Miami. Naive—and expedient: In Zaire he took millions from a dictator who had looted his nation's treasury and massacred thousands of its people. After Zaire, Ali agreed to a fight in South Africa even though Nelson Mandela wasted in prison and every black person in the country lived under apartheid terror. (The fight was canceled when Ali's fee was not guaranteed.)

Now, back from the Kremlin, Ali arrived in Cosell's studios an hour late for the taping and greeted his second banana by announcing to his entourage, "I made this hangaround famous. He'd be nobody if it wasn't for me. Before I came along, he was nothing but a football announcer."

"These goddamn niggers," Cosell said. He raised his arms and balled his long and slender hands into fists. "See these lethal weapons?" he said. Woody Allen had said Cosell was more Cosellian off the air than on, that at dinner he broadcast the meal. Fists raised, Cosell did play-by-play: "A mute Ali watches in awe, wishing he could perform with the spontaneity of the greatest performer in the history of television."

As they watched film of the trip, Ali rehearsed his commentary: "There I am eating apple turnover." He was bored and listless until Brezhnev came on the screen. "Supposed to be the world's baddest man, giving me a kiss. I can't tell you what he said to me. Do you realize that nobody else in America but [President] Carter can get to see that cat?" He declared, "I'm sharp today, boy. After fifteen years, I'm still number one and getting bigger. Only way I can get any bigger is to be the first spook on the moon."

"Shut up," Cosell said, "and look at the camera. Show them your succulent lower lip and malleable upper one."

"You'll be surprised, honey," Ali said, pursing those lips. "I'm gonna tell the world about *us*."

"I'm glad you've finally come to grips with yourself," Cosell said. "We've always known this about you."

"I'm a *world* man now," Ali said. "I'm doin' you a favor to come on this show. I'm bigger than Kissinger and Andy Young. I've *outgrown* the likes of Howard Cosell. They're startin' to believe me after all these years when I tell them how I'm the greatest, bigger than Cosell. When I'm on TV with *you*, we're the greatest combination in the world."

"You *used* to be the greatest," Cosell said, "when you could fight."

"Yassuh, boss," said Ali, who four months earlier had lost his title to the raw kid Leon Spinks. The film showed a bloated Ali fighting exhibition rounds against Russian heavyweights. Cosell was offended by the sight of Ali at 254 rounds, even more by the lack of discipline that produced the pillowy belly. "You look misshapen," Cosell said. "As a matter of pride, how can you let yourself be seen in such shape as that?"

"I never did like to train," Ali said, but his vanity sidetracked that train of thought into a sudden poem.

> *Howard Cosell*
> *If I had a lower IQ*
> *I would enjoy*
> *This interview.*

"Ain't it somethin', Coach," Ali said, "that I'm still here?"

"Yeah, but you used to be so great."

Ali countered, "And you used to have hair."

For all of the unscripted dialogue that occurred, it was not true that the Ali-Cosell act was always an improvisation. Here Cosell had served as the segment's narrator, producer, director, and cheerleader. ("Now, Muhammad, I don't want you to look bad, and I'm not going to let you look bad. You sound down, and I want you to look interested, and be enthusiastic, and up.") The first run-through of commentary on the film served as a foundation for what would be said on the air. Several lines were reprised in the actual taping, others were reshaped, and some edited on second thought.

One of those edited dealt with money. As they did the run-through, Cosell framed a question about Ali's financial circumstances. Ali's answer included the information that "if I sold everything I had, tomorrow, I'd be worth three and a half million dollars." That might have opened Ali to another question, about how a man whose fight purses over eighteen years amounted to more than forty million dollars could be worth no more than 10 percent of that. Instead, as taped, the question and answer became this:

"It has been written and written that you're dead broke, you have no money. Is that true?"

"No money?" A quizzical look. "That don't make no sense."

"You do have some?"

"Do you have money?"

"Yes."

"Well, if you got it, you know I got it. I've made ten times more money than you."

"That's true. Then you're not broke?"

"Broke? Whatcha talkin' about?"

End of conversation.

Done with the taping and displeased by the money talk, Ali walked quickly toward a studio exit, his entourage in tow. Cosell called after him, "I love ya, Muhammad, you know that." Ali moved on, saying nothing, and Cosell was left asking of no one in particular, "Anybody want my job?"

Ali's victory over Spinks by decision on September 15, 1978, was the product of guile and will. Across fifteen rounds—Ali's fifth straight fifteen-round fight in twenty-three months—the sixty-three thousand witnesses in New Orleans' Superdome saw Ali use every old fighter's trick, a heel of his glove in an eye, a forearm scraped across a nose, the bigger man clutching, holding, leaning so heavily on the champion as to double him over. Only occasionally did Ali throw a blurred combination of the kind he once threw in multiples of five.

Yet emotion charged Cosell's broadcast. At age thirty-six, Ali again had done what seemed unlikely, and for a moment or two in each round he did what only he ever could do. Cosell was sixty years old himself, no longer a phenomenon but still the best in his profession as Ali was the best in his, though fading and glorious. They had come a great distance together to stand in the twilight. Even as the fighters threw punches in the final minute, Cosell did what only he could ever do. His voice tremulous, he paid tribute to Ali by quoting Bob Dylan lyrics:

> *May your hands always be busy,*
> *May your feet always be swift,*

May you have a strong foundation
When the winds of changes shift.
May your heart always be joyful,
May your song always be sung,
May you stay forever young.

The next morning, when Cosell asked him about retirement, Ali said, "The title is too hard to get. I'm not goin' to give it up without thinking. I'm going to sit down for six or eight months and think about it. Then I'll decide whether to fight again. I would never want to go out a loser. I've always wanted to be the first black man to retire undefeated, and to do it now after being champion three times would be somethin' no one could ever equal."

But nine months later, having not fought since Spinks, Ali announced that he was done. Never did he look more pitiable with Cosell. His face was puffy, his eyes lost, his voice an airy gurgle. He didn't seem able to smile. Though the retirement was anticipated—"Everybody gets old," Ali said—Cosell asked if it were true that promoter Bob Arum had paid Herbert Muhammad three hundred thousand dollars for Ali to give up the title.

"If that's true," Ali said, "I know nothing about it." He acknowledged getting "a great sum of money" for a retirement party in Los Angeles. "But can't nobody pay me to retire." Meanwhile, Herbert Muhammad told reporters he had no recollection of any three hundred thousand dollars.

Cosell asked Ali, "Are you glad it's over?"

"Yes, sir, Howard. So glad that it's all over. I'm glad that I'm still intelligent enough to speak. I'm glad that I'm three-time champion. I'm glad I got to know you. And thank you for all the backing. I remember when the Vietnam crisis was going, you'd go on television and say, 'If you don't believe Muhammad Ali is champion, then get in the ring with him.' I want to say that helped me during my exile."

"You are the greatest, aren't you?"

"I try to be." He managed a tight smile. "Maybe it's just you thinking."

"Good luck to you. And it's not good-bye, it's *au revoir*, my friend."

Not good-bye, not yet. They met again in Las Vegas fifteen months later when Ali came out of retirement to fight the new champion, his old sparring partner and protégé, Larry Holmes. "Question one, Muhammad," Cosell began. "A year ago on a farewell show on *Wide World of Sports,* you said then, flatly, 'I'm finished, this is it, I'm not going to go out the way Joe Louis and some others have done. I'm going out on top.' Why come back now? What's the inner reason?"

"At the time I told you, Howard, that I wasn't going to come back, I was serious at that moment," Ali said.

Cosell might have laughed out loud. But the second banana's job is to make the boss look good, not silly. He listened as Ali explained that a man can change his mind, that he can promise to love until death do us part and still get divorced, as he had twice. What Ali didn't explain—couldn't?—was that he simply wanted to be Ali again, the spotlight fixed on his pretty face, everyone's eyes turned to him. He also wanted the payday, at eight million dollars the largest of his career.

"I promise you," Ali said, "I will deee-stroy Larry Holmes."

Cosell let pass without examination Ali's talk of winning a fight when even the most zealous admirer hoped for no more than Ali's escape without injury. The fight was about money and notice, nothing else. This was Cosell at his most unbecoming, as shill, engaged with Ali in a shadow play that had become parody. Both men now pretended to be what they once were. But only one of them would put his brain in harm's way.

PART FOUR

Falling

SIXTEEN

"You Feelin' Any Pain, Joe, Feelin' Any Pain?"

IN TELLING COSELL THAT HE had always wanted to be "the first black man to retire undefeated," Ali ignored the truth that he had been beaten three times. Nor could he have been the first black man to retire as champion: Joe Louis had done it in 1949. But great fighters are seduced by the devil's bargain of cash and celebrity offered in place of retirement's inconsequentiality. Joe Louis had come back in sixteen months.

Ali was only seven months into retirement when he learned that he could be ignored even as President Jimmy Carter's envoy. In February 1980, the president asked Ali to gain African support for a boycott of that summer's Olympic Games in Moscow. After the Soviet Union invaded Afghanistan, Congress and the U.S. Olympic Committee voted not to send Americans to the Games. Carter believed Ali's fame in Africa would be helpful as he explained America's commitment to freedom and human rights. At last, it seemed to Ali, he had become the diplomat he had described to Hugh McIlvanney, picking up his briefcase and flying off to talk to some president in some country somewhere.

How odd, this mission: If anyone had reason to distrust the American government, it was Ali; politicians had stolen his championship, and the federal government had wanted to imprison him. Surely, someone in the State Department must also have known that Ali was a diplomatic cipher, uninformed and naïve.

Nevertheless, Ali was flattered. In India, where State Department officials briefed him, the USSR ambassador also whispered in his ear. Ali told reporters: "It made me feel real big. It made me feel real powerful. It made me, a little boy from Kentucky who couldn't meet the mayor of Kentucky a few years ago—all of a sudden now, I've got two superpowers telling me to say this and say that and go here and go there. Makes me feel real big."

The mission was even more curious in execution. At Ali's first stop, Tanzania, the nation's president refused to see him and let it be known that he considered it an insult that an athlete/entertainer had been dispatched to him. Then Ali was flummoxed by questions of state. A reporter said, "Mr. Ali, the Soviet Union has been providing very important support to African liberation movements while the U.S. has not provided any material support. Yet you are here asking that African countries support a U.S. boycott of the Olympics against the Soviet Union. Do you feel that African states should take this stand and perhaps jeopardize their good relations with the Soviet Union?"

Ali had no clue. "I know nothing about the Soviet doing so much for Africa. Could you give me a couple of examples and educate me on what they have done? I don't know." The idea of a liberation movement was news to him. He seemed to believe that if the Soviets were enemies of the United States, they must be everyone's enemies. "I can't answer the question of what America did or didn't do or what Africa did because I don't know," he said. "But I can box. I can tell you about boxing."

Next question: "But do you think President Carter was correct then in sending you, a boxer, here rather than a diplomat to discuss this very sensitive issue?"

"I know a lot about issues in the world, especially when it comes to Islamic nations. But not about this particular issue you've just asked about."

"Since you are not very much fluently aware of the current situation in the world, how do you expect to succeed in your mission?"

For that question he had no answers, as he had none for questions on how the United States could ask African nations to boycott Moscow when the United States had refused to join twenty-nine African nations in a boycott of South Africa's presence in the 1976 Olympics. He could only insist that he was there to do good for his black African brothers. Repeatedly, in Tanzania and Kenya, Ali said he undertook the mission to prevent nuclear war. Perhaps the State Department had told him war was a possibility, or perhaps Ali made the leap himself. But when cornered by questions on America's moral authority, he said the Soviet Union had invaded Afghanistan as the first step toward taking Iran to gain a fresh-water port, dominate the world's oil supply, spread its atheistic ideology, and threaten peace everywhere.

Ali believed a boycott of the Olympics would tell the Soviets they should stop with all that. If they continued, he said, there was an alternative: "We can push a few buttons and shoot a few missiles and rockets and start a nuclear war. I don't think that will be good for you all or anyone. Bombs will be flying over here that can destroy the world." Perhaps only Muhammad Ali, in a breath or two, could have escalated an Olympic boycott into a nuclear Armageddon. Ending a press conference in Kenya, Ali wanted to add one thing. "This," he said, "is much tougher than Joe Frazier."

From Tanzania and Kenya, Ali went to Nigeria, Liberia, and Senegal. Only Kenya joined the boycott, and it had been on America's side before Ali arrived in Nairobi.

A month after the African debacle, Ali created another. He ended his retirement to fight Larry Holmes for the heavyweight championship on October 2, 1980, in Las Vegas. Those who cared for Ali knew it was madness. Ali's old friend, the rock 'n' roll legend Lloyd Price, told him it was time to hang it up. He did it with a story.

Price told Ali he went on tour in 1963 and agreed to help out a friend new to the recording business by letting one of his groups open for him. But when he noticed the group getting more applause than he did, he replaced them. Ali asked the group's name.

"Some guys I'd never heard of before," Price said. "Smokey Robinson and the Miracles."

His friend sent him a new opening group, and this time it was worse for Price, who heard such raucous applause that he ordered a ten-minute break to calm down the audience before he went out there. "Who were they?" Ali asked.

"Three black chicks called the Supremes."

So Price called his friend, whose name was Berry Gordy and whose record label was Motown, and asked him to please not send another group but to send one singer and one only. Here came Marvin Gaye.

"And that was it," Price told Ali. "I said to myself, 'I don't know what these folks have, but whatever it is, I don't have it.'" Price left the road, bought a club in New York, and signed a fifteen-year deal to promote Mo-town concerts. "I heard the bell," he told Ali.

It was no surprise that Ali would not hear Lloyd Price's bell. Imagine being Muhammad Ali, one-two with the pope as the most famous men on Earth. Imagine the silence of retirement for him. Before one fight, Ali moved into Harold Conrad's New York apartment to get away from his hotel's crowd. When Conrad told Ali he had to go out for the evening, Ali asked, "You gonna leave me here all alone?" He did not enjoy silence. Diplomacy, movies, the stage, commercials—none was forthcoming. He could earn eight million dollars fighting Holmes. Only in the ring did he matter. There he was *Ali*.

But Ali was now thirty-eight years old. I saw him in June 1980 when he was paid five thousand dollars to shill for a fight in Montreal. His face was puffy, his eyes streaked by blood lines and coated with a veil of tear water, that viscous and lifeless look seen on men who sleep on street grates. His voice was a gritty whisper, words indecipherable, as if his vo-cal cords leaked air. He stuttered and at one point he said, "I have sur-passed storps," then adding a repair to the sentence, "er, sports."

"See how good I look?" Ali said. In fact, he was a rheumy-eyed whale graying at the temples and behind the right ear. His shirt was unbuttoned at the throat under a tie loose and pulled askew. The way he looked, the way he moved, slowly and unsteadily, I would have taken him for a weary sales rep who had had one too many. I noticed the index and middle fin-gers of his right hand. They had a fine tremor to them. The trainer Ray Arcel, a master for half a century, later said, "All those fights after the Manila fight destroyed Muhammad Ali."

When I arrived in Las Vegas in October, three days before he would fight Holmes, I was astonished to see Ali looking good. "Montreal, that was my thyroid glands actin' up," he said. "I took two pills a day for a month and it's all cleared up now." He had lost thirty pounds. His eyes were bright, his voice again in full cry, the gray hair gone ("a little black hair rinse"). In ten minutes at a press conference, he dropped names of buddies and fellow stars: Brezhnev, Qaddafi, Khomeini, Carter, Billy Gra-ham, Oral Roberts, Jesus Christ, and Ben Vereen.

Then he saw Joe Louis.

Slumped in a wheelchair.

Joe Louis. The first fighter's name he ever heard. His father talked about Joe Louis, how his boy was a little Joe Louis. Gene Kilroy once took

Ali to a nursing home where a toothless old man in diapers looked up and said, "That's Joe Louis." Ali said, "That's right," and signed an autograph, *Joe Louis*. Afterward, Ali said to Kilroy, "His whole life, he wanted to meet Joe Louis. We all look alike, so let him think he met Joe."

God only knows why, but now someone rolled Joe Louis into Ali's press conference. The great old champion was lifeless. He was sixty-six years old. He had a bad heart. He had endured three strokes. He lived under paranoid delusions exacerbated by cocaine. He believed the Mafia tried to kill him with poison gases introduced into his bedroom through air vents and under doors. His skin was yellow-gray, the color of old newspaper clippings.

"Joe," Ali shouted, "I'm gonna put a whuppin' on him." This was for the television cameras, and Ali came to the wheelchair. "You gonna be there, Joe?" No answer. Louis wore a Stetson hat and cowboy boots. "Joe, I watched films of you the other night, Joe, you and Schmeling. Your combinations were somethin' else, Joe. That one-two you hit Schmeling with in the first round, that's what I'm gonna hit Holmes with. One round, Joe, I might do it in one round. So don't be late, Joe, you might miss it."

Joe Louis sat there. The hands that had hit Schmeling lay dead in his lap. Cassius Marcellus Clay, Jr., had touched a telephone pole touched by Joe Louis. Now Ali touched the great old champion's knee and bent down to whisper to him. I heard what he said, meant for Joe and not the television cameras. "You feelin' any pain, Joe, feelin' any pain?" Louis grunted and moved his head an inch, yes.

"You eatin' good, Joe, you eatin' good?"

Another grunt, this one a no.

To the television cameras then, Ali said, "Thanks for comin' by, Joe, it's gonna be a great fight." And in a whisper, his mouth next to Joe Louis's ear, Ali said, "I'll try to come see you, Joe, before I leave. I'll come to your house."

Ali that day was an illusion. As good as he looked and sounded, he had shown nothing in the gym, and it was a nothing different from those days when he allowed sparring partners to hit him. Now he couldn't stop them. He gave Larry Holmes reason to say, "Ali was a great fighter once, and I was proud to be his sparring partner. But now he's just a tired, old fighter trying to take my title away. You been seeing him work out? A little old middleweight is hitting him. If he can hit him, I damn sure'll hit him. I'm going to hurt him bad."

Holmes touched his temple. "I'm going to make Ali drunk up here." He stabbed his ribs with his fingertips. "And I'm going to mug him down here."

Two or three days before the fight, Howard Cosell walked into the Caesars Palace parking lot where the ring would stand. With him was his boxing producer, Alex Wallau. Theirs was an uneasy working relationship. Unlike most of Cosell's associates, Wallau did not stand in awe of the broadcaster. He believed Cosell's self-aggrandizing behavior was evidence not of great ego but of an emptiness. To Cosell's pronouncements, then, Wallau often disagreed, as in the Caesars parking lot when Cosell said, "You know, Holmes is vulnerable to the right hand, and Ali has always been able to land the straight right. I think the old master is going to do it one more time."

Wallau said, "Howard, not only is Ali not going to win the fight; not only is he not going to win a round; he's not going to win ten seconds of any round."

By then, commerce had overwhelmed common sense. As if it cared, the Nevada boxing commission ordered Ali to undergo a medical examination. The Mayo Clinic in Rochester, Minnesota, declared him healthy, though neither the clinic nor the commission made the report immediately public. All week, Ali had felt strange. When Gene Kilroy tried to pump up his confidence by saying, "I'm gonna bet everything on you," Ali said, "No, don't. Something's wrong." Before dawn the day of the fight, unable to rest, Ali went out to run in hopes the work would make him feel better. He ran less than a mile, stopped, and was taken to a hospital where he was given fluids in treatment of severe dehydration.

Yet Ali came to the fight full of bluster. At the end of the second round, he shouted across the ring to Holmes, "You about ready? You ready?" A round later: "You're through." Ali hadn't landed a punch, hadn't stopped one. Late in the fourth round, the twenty-five thousand spectators were silent. They had been silent for Ruffhouse Walker, a preliminary fighter, a pug no one cared about, and now they were silent for Ali.

By the sixth round, the silence had been replaced by boos. Holmes had won every round so easily that he once stepped back from Ali and invited the referee's intervention. None came. The eighth round, Angelo Dundee said, "I'm gonna stop it," and Ali said, "No, don't do that."

I sat below Ali's corner, next to Herbert Muhammad, who for fifteen years had controlled every aspect of Ali's professional life. During the fight, silent, he kept his head down. He said he prayed during Ali's fights rather than watch, but I thought he just didn't want to see the train wreck that he had arranged.

In the ninth round, Holmes sent Ali to the ropes with an uppercut and followed with a mugging to the body that, as promised, hurt him bad. Jerry Izenberg, a pro's pro in a lifetime of journalism, did what no reporter should ever do. He stood at his ringside seat and screamed to referee Richard Greene, "Stop it, Richard! Stop the fight, Richard!" The grizzled Cuban masseur, Luis Sarria, looked at Dundee, and the trainer said, "Don't worry, Sarria, the next round."

Tenth round, enough. Ali's bodyguard, Pat Patterson, shouted to Herbert Muhammad, "What do you want done?" Herbert Muhammad nodded yes. As Dundee stopped it, Ali sagged on his stool, a portrait in misery, head dangling like a broken doll's, his face a swollen mess of purple bruises.

Two hours later, Holmes sat on the edge of Ali's bed in suite 301-2 in Caesars Palace.

"Man, you're bad," Ali said.

"Look at the teacher I had," Holmes said. "Hey, you ain't gonna fight again, are you?"

"Oh, yeah. I'm comin' back for Holmes. . . . Holmes! . . . I want Holmes."

"You wanna go a few more rounds now?"

Quickly, "No, I'm tired."

Hugh McIlvanney wrote it down, and his column on the fight began, "The ring activities of Muhammad Ali now have all the grace and sporting appeal of Russian roulette played with a pump-action shotgun. If he seriously considers inflicting on himself and his admirers across the world another experience like Thursday night's disaster in Las Vegas, there may be a case for taking him into protective custody." The man once untouchable was now unmissable. In Manila, Joe Frazier hit Ali 440 times; Leon Spinks, in the first fight with Ali, landed 482 punches, and Holmes hit the old man 320 times with 125 of those punches coming in the last two rounds.

Eleven years later, a biographer was given the unreleased Mayo Clinic report of Ali's neurological examination before the Holmes fight. It was then obvious why secrecy shrouded the report at fight time. It said that Ali "seems to have a mild ataxic dysarthria (difficulty in coordinating the muscles used in speaking). He does not quite hop with the agility that one might anticipate, and on finger to nose testing there is a slight degree of missing the target." A man so impaired should not have been fighting anyone, let alone the undefeated heavyweight champion of the world.

In Ali's defeat, Cosell recognized his own melancholy: "I couldn't shake the gut-wrenching anguish of watching Ali in his twilight as one comeback after another stripped him of his dignity and stature." The morning after the Holmes fight, Cosell went on camera alone and said, "It was no fight at all. From the very beginning, the laws of physiology destroyed Muhammad Ali. He had no fight in him, no punch in him. Holmes dominated in every round. There remained only the one remarkable Ali trait, the ability to take a punch as well as any man ever had.

"But he had nothing within him. He had ballooned to 260 pounds, dropped fifty pounds and more within the previous six months. There was no strength left. The skills were gone, the reflexes were gone, there was only the beating to be taken. It was a sad sight."

Though Cosell was in Las Vegas, Ali did not come down from his suite for an interview. Instead, they talked by telephone, Cosell's hand trembling against the phone as he asked, "Muhammad, how are you feeling? Feel okay?"

"Yes, sir, Howard."

Because Ali had told the press he wanted to fight again, Cosell asked, "Do you really want to entertain that thought?"

"Yes, sir. I'll tell you something, Howard. I don't know what was wrong. Something wasn't right . . . it don't make no sense." He wanted another chance. "I never give up," Ali said, and then, ending the conversation abruptly, he said, "Okay. Thank you, Howard."

"Okay. Thank you. Bye-bye."

Cosell was weary, dark circles under his eyes. The old broadcaster put down the phone. He closed with a commentary delivered in lifeless tones: "It is impossible for me to believe he should fight again and that he will fight again because, as I said earlier, the laws of physiology are inexorable. Legends die hard. But if this fight proved anything, it proved that, like all of us, Muhammad Ali is mortal."

For twice the eight million dollars, the fight should not have happened. But the next week, determined that it wasn't over yet, Ali went into a hospital to find out why he had been so lethargic against Holmes. The blame fell to a thyroid medicine, Thyrolar, that he had taken on the advice of Herbert Muhammad's personal physician. Thyrolar speeds up the body's systems, changing the heart rate and metabolism so dramatically that the body can dehydrate and muscle tissue can be destroyed. No wonder Ali found himself in a hospital before dawn the day of that fight. Ferdie Pacheco believed that treating Ali with Thyrolar was the equivalent of "burning the tires off a race car, and then telling the driver to race without wheels." Death in the ring by stroke or heart attack had been possible.

The thyroid excuse was enough for Ali to do what McIlvanney feared. A year and two months after Holmes, Ali fought a mediocrity named Trevor Berbick. This time the madness ended, and not with a bang or a whimper but with a cowbell's pot-metal clunk. The fight promoters put up a ring behind second base on a kids' baseball field. When they discovered they had no ring bell, they went to a pickup truck and took a cowbell off the front seat. At the end of rounds, somebody hit it with a hammer. This was not Quarry in Atlanta, Frazier in the Garden, Foreman in Zaire, Spinks in the Superdome. This was a nobody on an island in the ocean, and for the first time since that night seventeen years before when he had said, "Let go of the mike, Cassius," Howard Cosell had nothing to do with an Ali fight. No shilling, no interviews, no analysis. Nothing.

The scorecards said Berbick won nine of ten rounds. Ali knew better. He had lost not to Berbick but to the opponent that is undefeated. "Father Time got me," he said, and he told Gene Kilroy, "When I held him, his body was hard, and my body was soft." Old men notice such things. The next morning, maybe a dozen sportswriters sat in a small room of his hotel for a half-hour listening to Ali's graceful valedictory. "I didn't show," he said, "and now I know." He said it could have been worse, a knockout, an injury, a cut that would disturb the beauty of his face. "I'm happy because I'm still nice looking. Look at me. I came out good for an old man."

Then, brightening, he said, "I shall return . . ." Smiling. " . . . to Los Angeles."

CHAPTER SEVENTEEN

"I Know Who I Am"

HER HUSBAND'S BALANCE WHEEL, the voice of common sense, Emmy Cosell was the only person who gained sweet silence by saying, "Oh, Howard, we've heard enough from you." Once, asked what it was like to go to bed with Howard Cosell, she said it was no big deal: "He comes in in his pajamas smelling like milk and Mallomars cookies." She suffered no fools, not even Roone Arledge. "Roone," she said during a late-stage Arledge-Cosell confrontation, "the jury is still out on you." She became so much her husband's safe harbor that Cosell was uneasy without her nearby. They often traveled together during the *Monday Night Football* days, once spending the night in the Dallas home of an old WABC colleague, Murphy Martin. The next morning, Cosell came downstairs for coffee in a short night robe, no toupee, his sprigs of forsaken hair sprouting in all directions, a cigar in his mouth. He announced to Martin that he felt bad and was worried about the Monday night assignment, Washington against Dallas.

"What's wrong?" Martin asked.

"An inner ear infection," said Cosell, the son of a hypochondriacal mother and himself a practitioner of medicinal anxiety. Emmy and Martin's wife, Joyce, joined the men and heard Howard say, "I don't know if I'll be able to work tonight."

Emmy said, "Howard, neither Murphy nor Joyce nor I have ever heard of anyone dying from an inner ear infection. You'll work." That, he did.

Every Monday night now seemed more burden than joy. Arledge said Gifford and Meredith resented a Cosell "completely out of control." The boss believed "the antipathy that they all feel for each other is so palpable it's obvious on the air." He called a cease-and-desist meeting before the first game of the 1980s, the beginning of *MNF*'s tenth season. Arledge ordered the boys to end the petty bickering. Otherwise, "You're going to destroy this thing."

ABC did a tenth anniversary *MNF* special. On camera, Cosell, Meredith, and Gifford laughed about the good times and set the record straight. "I've heard people say we don't get along," Gifford said. "Don's fighting with Howard. Howard's fighting with me. Howard's fighting with all of us." Oh so sincerely, he added, "That's simply not true." Sitting next to Faultless Frank, Cosell did not rise to tell it like it is.

The night of December 8, 1980, a young man on a motorcycle collided with a taxicab in New York's Central Park. The rider was Alan Weiss, a news producer for WABC-TV. Because his left leg was injured, Weiss was taken to the emergency room at Roosevelt Hospital. He was lying on a table waiting to be treated when he heard a commotion in the ER. Police had rushed in. Weiss heard voices, one with startling news. John Lennon had been shot. The singer was being brought to that hospital.

Weiss limped to a telephone to call WABC. Within minutes, the news reached Roone Arledge. He could have the network news division interrupt the night's programming with a bulletin from the newsroom. That's how it was usually done. But the moment's programming was *Monday Night Football*. Arledge considered news a commodity, not a sacrament, and to him the most profitable use of this news was to make it part of the network's most-watched show. He called Cosell in the booth at Miami's Orange Bowl, late in a Dolphins-Patriots game. "Howard, I know you can handle this," Arledge said to the man he didn't trust to handle Munich eight years before. "The country doesn't even know. They just shot John Lennon."

Cosell broke into the game with that news, and soon followed with worse: "ABC News has confirmed that John Lennon, a member of the famed Beatles, maybe the best-known member, was shot twice in the back outside of his apartment building on the West Side of New York tonight. Rushed to the Roosevelt Hospital. Dead on arrival. An unspeakable tragedy."

Then he did a quintessential Cosellian turn. He delivered an instant eulogy of Lennon the man and the icon whose music reflected a generation's social consciousness. At a time like this, he said, can a football game be enjoyed? He closed by quoting the first line of John Keats's "Ode to a Nightingale," " 'My heart aches, and a drowsy numbness pains my sense . . ."

Cosell first read the Keats poem as an English literature major at New York University. The ode presented the world as Cosell saw it, a quivering balance of light and darkness, joy at the edge of pain, life becoming death. He called it "the most beautiful poem ever written. Keats understood that beauty is but transitory, as is life. Marvelously sensual, phrases like 'winding, mossy ways.' You had a sense of smell with Keats, taste, of being, of being enveloped by everything around you."

In the summer of 1981, Cosell was sixty-three years old. He worried about his health, but he did not change habits that brought him pleasure. He remained a world champion consumer of martinis. He favored Monte Cristo cigars the size of riot sticks. He had lived the last ten years at a frenzied pace on a working schedule that allowed virtually no time off, not that he wanted it then or now. His work was his life. Being Howard Cosell was a full-time job done in radio and television studios, in stadium broadcast booths, airports, hotels, limousines, boxing arenas, baseball parks, and bars. To do that work, he pushed himself to the verge of breakdown. "The brass ring only comes around once," he said. He knew the nightingale's song had an end.

> Fade far away, dissolve, and quite forget
> What thou among the leaves hast never known,
> The weariness, the fever, and the fret
> Here, where men sit and hear each other groan;
> Where palsy shakes a few, sad, last gray hairs,
> Where youth grows pale, and spectre-thin, and dies.

Until then, by damn, he would be Howard Cosell, or, failing that, he would be the best Cosell impersonator there ever was. In the summer of 1981, he was in Kansas City, Missouri, for a Monday night baseball game.

"Whatcha doin', Alfalfa?" Cosell said to his young broadcast partner, Al Michaels. "Let's go to dinner." They went to the Savoy Restaurant in a white stretch limousine driven by ABC's customary chauffeur in Kansas City, a woman named Peggy. The men done with dinner and drinks, returning to the hotel about nine-thirty, Peggy steered the big white limo through a dark streetscape at the edge of town.

At a stop light, Cosell saw two young black men fighting. A serious fight. Five or six other young men dancing around the fighters. Then Michaels and Peggy heard Cosell's door open. They saw him headed for the fight. *Oh, my God,* Michaels thought. He shouted, "Howard! Howard!" *They attack him, what are we supposed to do?* Peggy said, "Mr. Cosell!" The door left open, the slump-shouldered old man strode to the scene, cigar aglow. Michaels heard that voice.

"Okay, okay, listen up," Cosell said. The young men turned to see Gramps in his rich man's suit and tie, a cigar in his face. "okay," Cosell went on. "It is quite apparent to this observer that the young southpaw does not have the jab requisite to the continuation of this fray."

The young men struck an attitude. *The fuck's this shit?*

"And, furthermore, his opponent is clearly a man of inferior and diminishing skills."

Shut the fuck up, old man.

"This confrontation is halted posthaste," Cosell said.

Everyone stopped. Michaels saw mouths go agape and eyes open wide. *Now, what? Do they kill him?* A combatant bellowed, "How-word Co-sell!" They gathered around him and from somewhere came a pen and from somewhere came a scrap of paper and there in the night on the street Howard Cosell signed autographs.

Back in the limousine, Michaels breathless, Peggy silent, Cosell smug, they came to a stop two blocks down the street. Peggy turned and said, "I don't want to bother you, Mr. Cosell. But I must tell you. I have been driving for twenty-five years. I thought I had seen everything. I have never seen anything like that."

Cosell leaned back, took a long drag on the cigar, raised it in triumph, and said, "Peg-a-roo, just remember one thing. I *know* who I am."

There was in his declaration an echo of Ali, who four years earlier had defined himself for Cosell as a world figure and said, *I know who I am.* Did Ali know, really? Did Cosell know, really? What they knew, without doubt, were the roles they had chosen to play in their mad worlds.

That summer of 1981, CBS Sports decided that journalism mattered. It promised real reporting on SportsWorld. At ABC, the man who invented sports journalism in broadcasting could not let the challenge pass. Cosell obtained from Arledge a commitment to a monthly half-hour show called *SportsBeat.*

Cosell would do reporting and offer opinion, as, in his mind, he always had. His earliest influences had been a dozen idiosyncratic Brooklyn and New York newspapers. For him, the printed word carried authority. During his mad rush to celebrity in the 1970s, he had pulled free of those journalistic moorings. He had subjected his credibility to self-parody and compounded the crime by a failure to recognize his own disregard of principle. He had sold out to Woody Allen and jiggly starlets. He did a television commercial in which he stretched over a cliff's edge to interview an apple—maybe it was a pear—for Fruit of the Loom underwear.

But now, with CBS in the game, Cosell came to air with *SportsBeat* on August 30, 1981. Cosell and his staff of hustling young reporters and producers did a news-breaking feature on tennis star John McEnroe (who turned down a one-million-dollar offer to play in apartheid-divided South Africa). A piece on NFL players suggested a 1982 strike (it happened), and Cosell closed with thunder-dunking Darryl Dawkins trying to shatter the NBA's new backboard (he failed).

The NFL strike cut the *MNF* schedule to twelve games, and Cosell resented even those. He had never liked football, never understood its nuances. For most of a decade he had inveighed publicly against the purblind incompetents alongside him in the booth. Yet he knew that the game and the men he held in contempt had helped deliver him to stardom. Cosell accepted that conflict for a reason familiar to every intelligent, talented, self-absorbed, frightened, insecure person. Like Ali, he needed attention.

He was on the downside of fame. To cover the fear and pain of the descent, he made a fetish of his disdain for football. In hotel lobbies, he did sing-song verse:

> *You isolate the setback*
> *On the linebacker;*
> *He dodged a bullet,*
> *And came to play.*
> *Just ask the jocks,*
> *It's holy war.*

Boxing was worse. He heard Ali's speech becoming more slurred, often a mumble. They were last on the air together, on-camera, before the Larry Holmes fight in 1980. Their last broadcast conversation was the brief telephone call the morning after. They next met at a banquet in Los Angeles following the Berbick fight. Cosell saw Ali, still a young man, forty years old, moving deliberately, his face puffy, his speech a pastiche of whispers. "Too many blows to the brain," Cosell told a friend, "had transformed him into somebody I no longer knew."

That night, Ali put his arm around Cosell and whispered, "I'm gone, and you're still on top."

Cosell said, "Don't ever say that to me again, Muhammad. You're part of American history. You'll never be gone."

For Cosell, boxing died November 26, 1982. He was at ringside in Houston's Astrodome for ABC's coverage of a Holmes defense against Randall (Tex) Cobb. It seemed a mismatch. The undefeated Holmes was the equal of any heavyweight champion since Joe Louis, with the exception of Ali in his prime. Cobb could catch punches with his face and keep smiling. He caught hundreds on this night. After five rounds, during which Cobb may have hit Holmes once, Cosell, at ringside, criticized referee Steve Crosson for allowing the fight to go on.

In the ninth round, Cosell called the fight "an assault on the sense of any civilized human being. Twenty-six unanswered blows." Cobb's face, no prize to start with, looked "like hamburger meat." Still, the fight continued, as did Cosell's assault on the referee: "Doesn't he know that he is constructing an advertisement for the abolition of boxing?"

Across fifteen rounds, Cobb may have landed three punches. Had Cosell said nothing for the last ten rounds, his silence at the microphone would have been eloquent, but it would not have been Cosellian. He denounced Crosson relentlessly. At fight's end, when director Chet Forte told Cosell that New York wanted him to interview the referee, Cosell refused. On the air he said, "I will not dignify this fight with any interviews. I think what you have seen tonight speaks for itself." Of course, he had spoken thousands of words.

At the *Washington Post* the next morning, sports editor George Solomon said, "You hear Howard last night?"

"Didn't *everybody?*" I said.

"What'd you think?"

"A little much, but that's Howard."

"Too much, I thought. Why don't you give him a call?" Cosell told me he would never work another professional fight. He had done heavyweight championship fights for twenty-three years. There was in Cosell's voice the weariness and melancholy of a man who had passed from love to anger to resignation. In testimony before various legislative bodies, including the United States Congress, Cosell had long demanded protection for fighters against injury and exploitation. He had seen the beauty of Floyd Patterson's life, the art of Ali's movement. But in Holmes-Cobb, he saw boxing's fundamental brutality. This was not sport. This was savagery licensed for profit.

We talked for a half-hour. "I have a deep feeling for the men who fight," Cosell said. "The other day, Ken Norton walked into my office. My God, he's as thick-tongued now as Ali. Somewhere along the road, Tex Cobb will pay for the punishment he was allowed to take."

This was familiar ground for us. Cosell had heard my argument against boxing: It is the only sport in which the stated goal is to injure an opponent's brain. That's what a knockout is, an injury to the brain. It makes boxing the only sport in which the more often and more effectively you injure someone's brain, the more handsomely you are rewarded. Cosell blamed boxing's sickness on three groups. "First, the networks who make possible the continued existence of organizations such as the WBA and WBC, which exist only for the purpose of creating championships that in turn create fights that the networks, including ABC-TV, can sell for top dollar. Second to blame are the ruthless, sleazy promoters. And third is the vast majority of the print-media members who are apologists for boxing." He proposed that the networks declare a moratorium on boxing until legislation mandated safety rules and medical examinations, created an honest system of ratings and records, and established a federal commission to administer boxing. Cosell said, "Either that, or abolish the quote-sport-unquote."

My column was stripped across the top of the sports section's front page under the headline: FIGHTING MAD, COSELL WALKS AWAY FROM SPORT TURNED SPECTACLE. The story was a big deal for a week, though discounted by many Cosell critics. They believed that with Ali retired, Cosell wanted out because he no longer would be a star himself. They saw his righteous indignation as a hypocritical charade from a man who had made a reputation and a fortune at ringside. I saw it as real. I saw it in keeping with his public testimony on the need to reform boxing. ABC itself had carried Cosell's interviews in which, face to face, he scolded Ali for cruelty inflicted on Patterson and Terrell. At the same time, I saw it as a sign of Cosell's ennui. He was trapped and exhausted by the celebrity he had sought. A dozen years of football games, maybe two hundred of them. Fights, baseball, *SportsBeat*, *Battle* twice a year, speeches, sponsors' parties, Olympics—no one ever worked harder at sports broadcasting.

The arc of Cosell's career reminded the critic Ron Powers of a media celebrity from the nineteenth century. Cosell now *belonged* with the monied and powerful. At the same time, thanks in large part to *Sports-Beat*, he remained an outsider afflicting the comfortable. Powers thought of Mark Twain, who spent his most productive years "torn by the conflicting wishes to lampoon the mannered pretensions of the Gilded Age and to be a leading light of that age." As Twain managed that balancing act, so did Cosell—only Cosell did it before unblinking cameras revealing even that which a man might think to hide. "No sportscaster," Powers said, "ever left a larger residue of his personality on the medium than Howard Cosell."

When Ali said, "I'm gone, and you're still on top," he could not know the distance he would travel in the next twenty years. Nor did he know of Cosell's disenchantment with all that once enchanted him. In January 1983, Cosell stepped into an elevator in a Minneapolis hotel. Already in the elevator was a young ABC production assistant, Tony Tortorici, thrilled to see the man himself for the first time. Tortorici said, "Howard, what do you think of the game tonight?"

"Young man," Cosell said, his tone withering, "the Russians have shot down a Korean jetliner, taking hundreds of lives. Fighting is raging in the streets of Beirut. Death squads are terrorizing the innocent in El Salvador. The world is gripped by political crises. And you ask me about a *football* game. What does a football game mean against all of that?"

The young man watched as the doors opened and the old man walked away.

CHAPTER EIGHTEEN

"Mother Cosell, Saving Us All from Prostitution"

FOR COSELL, THE 1983 SEASON of *Monday Night Football* had been a forced march. After thirteen years, he despised it all. No longer could he abide what he called the immorality of the National Football League's owners and executives addicted to greed and political machination. He was bored by games that replicated every other game ever played. In the booth it was worse. If he never again heard the Giffer call Dennis Thurman "Thurman Munson," if he could pass a week without hearing the Danderoo sing or wonder what in the hell language O. J. Simpson spoke, he would be pleased. Besides, Emmy wanted him out. One night in a Las Vegas hotel room, she heard her man mention *Monday Night Football*.

"Booo," she said. "I don't like it. The hassles. The crowds. I go with Howard to every one of them. I can't stand it. The crowds, the people clawing at Howard."

The Monday nights across America had long since lost their glamour as she saw her husband made miserable by the travel, speeches, appearances, sponsors' lunches and dinners, press criticism, and crude insults from fans. Because his back seemed to become increasingly stooped and his hands trembled so much—more than Ali's at this point—I asked if he had Parkinson's disease. He attributed the tremors to genetics and fatigue. Others blamed some of it on vodka.

Across the years, he had threatened dozens of times to quit *MNF*. Arledge usually managed the current crisis by assuring Cosell he was the indispensable man. The necessary stroking of the star's ego had the added virtue of being true. Cosell made *MNF* unique, second only to *60*

Minutes as television's longest-running prime-time program. With Cosell on the air hundreds of hours each year, ABC Sports kept the network viable. But this time Cosell's threat coincided with Arledge's eagerness to be done with him. The chief believed the show's ratings were down at least partly because viewers sensed that the vein of fun in the Cosell–Dandy Don dialogues had become so thin as to reveal animosity. Cosell's unwillingness to acknowledge the complexities of football strategy, tactics, and techniques came across as contempt for the sport. Arledge told friends that Pete Rozelle, once Cosell's champion, wanted him off the broadcasts. The drinking, temper tantrums, charges that "the jocks" conspired against him—Arledge had had enough.

The decision to let Cosell go had its roots in an unlikely controversy. He was accused of a racial slur. Were it not so inflammatory a charge, it would have been laughed off because Cosell's record on race was unimpeachable. He stood alongside Muhammad Ali, lionized and befriended Jackie Robinson and Floyd Patterson, gave Tommie Smith and John Carlos their say, praised outfielder Curt Flood's refusal to be a slave to baseball's owners, and campaigned for black managers in baseball and black coaches in football. He introduced Grambling College to white America.

The trouble began in the first *MNF* telecast of 1983 when Cosell called a Washington Redskins receiver "that little monkey." Alvin Garrett was a black man five feet, seven inches tall, once with the Giants before being signed by Washington coach Joe Gibbs. Taking a pass from Joe Theismann, Garrett skittered for good yardage. "Gibbs wanted to get this kid," Cosell said over an instant replay, "and that little monkey gets loose, doesn't he?"

At home in New York, Arledge sensed trouble and called Washington to ask producer Bobby Goodrich, "What's the reaction?"

Goodrich said, "The press guys are going apeshit."

On Arledge's order, Cosell addressed the issue on air. "According to the reporters," he said, "they were told I called Alvin Garrett a 'little monkey.' Nothing of the sort, and you fellows know it. No man respects Alvin Garrett more than I do. I talked about the man's ability to be so elusive despite the smallness of his size." What he meant to deny was that the phrase carried any suggestions of race. But the denial was done so imprecisely as to compound the problem by seeming to deny words recorded on tape.

Before game's end, the Reverend Joseph Lowery of the Southern

Christian Leadership Conference told Leonard Shapiro of the *Washington Post*, "While he may not have meant it as disparaging, it is offensive to many people." The suggestion of Cosell as racist was so far off-base that many prominent blacks defended him, among them Arthur Ashe, Bill Cosby, Jesse Jackson, John Thompson, Harry Edwards, and Rachel Robinson, Jackie's widow. When Garrett himself thanked Cosell for the notice, the issued died as national news within a week.

But for Cosell, it touched too many hot-button anxieties to go away quickly. To hear himself called a racist was to doubt the lasting significance of the work that had given him the greatest satisfaction. To see the Lowery charges in newspaper headlines was to feel helpless against blood enemies who bought ink by the barrel. He was sixty-five years old, miserable, and it was the season's first game. By the last game, ratings were down 20 percent. Cosell wanted out. He had made *Monday Night Football*, and he had wanted to love it, and somehow it had become a thing he hated.

One year to the day after the Alvin Garrett episode, I stood with Cosell on the steps of the ABC building in New York. He raised his face to the sun and closed his eyes. When he opened them, he said, "Free at last, free at last." He and Arledge had decided: No more Monday nights for Cosell. I asked, "Any sadness at all?"

"An absolute exhilaration," he said.

"Really?"

"It's a mix of sadness and exhilaration only in this sense. It has been your life. You miss every place you've been and everything you've done because it has been your life. But if you do anything long enough, if you have a brain in your head, it becomes a terrible bore. How many times can you look at those games?" We walked somewhere for lunch, not so much for lunch as for the revivifying effects a walk on the streets of New York produced in Cosell. A woman in a red skirt passed into his line of sight, and he said loudly enough that she would hear, "A man could fall in love on a day like this." She said, "Hi, Howard."

The sun was soft and warm. "Look at me, David. Have you ever seen me this way? So at ease. Completely content." A push-cart vendor shouted, "How-word, baby." Cosell loved it. We bought sandwiches to take to his office. "Let's walk a while," he said, "lest we deprive the people of their adulation." Back at ABC, he said, "What a day. I'm tempted to go to the airport and get a charter to the Hamptons to be with Emmy. A fifteen-minute plane ride. I miss her." He had not retired; he would do baseball for ABC, continue *SportsBeat,* and work the occasional Kentucky Derby. But no more Monday nights, which was his wife's wish. "No more fights, no more football, and I left one million dollars on the table for that. But Emmy wanted me to stop."

In his office now, I asked, " 'Free at last,' is that good?"

"It's good if you're sixty-six and your father died alone at sixty-five in a Charlotte hospital." Cosell long since had resolved to not repeat the unhappiness of his parents' marriage. His mother had stayed home while his father worked on the road. For much of Cosell's travels, Emmy was at his side. He mentioned his father in a voice so soft I was not sure I had heard him correctly. I asked if he thought about death and he said, "Sure."

His hands trembled so much that he had trouble holding his sandwich. "There is a whole generation who think I was born rich. A whole generation thinks I always had it made. There's a misconception that I made it because of extreme intelligence. I do have total recall. But that's no talent, David. That's something you're born with. The only talent involved in recall is the relevant use of that recall. That, I can do. But the true reason for my success is, nobody ever worked harder and longer hours than I did." He said he was working when news came of his father's death. "Emmy was out in Maplewood, New Jersey, at her parents' home with our two girls, and I was with Dick Groat and Don Hoak, trying to make a name for myself, interviewing them for radio." He said he still felt guilty about not being at the hospital with his father. He began a sentence, "That's why I am so determined . . ."

He stopped.

"When I made up my mind if . . ."

No pompous bore here, no showman, no journalist. Here he was a man, a husband, a father, Emmy Cosell's sweetheart.

Softly, "If, God forbid, Emmy should go first, I want to be there with her. And if I go first, which is more likely, I want to know that Emmy's there. And we're agreed on that."

The melancholy mood lasted only a moment because we were in Cosell's twelfth-floor office by his *SportsBeat* mavericks, four floors down from ABC Sports. There he was happy. Years later, Mike Marley said,

"Howard loved it, like we were the French Foreign Legion." Marley's journalistic life first intersected with Cosell's in 1964 when he was the thirteen-year-old editor of the International Cassius Clay Fan Club newsletter riding with a pimp and his prostitutes to the second Clay-Liston fight. Grown up, he became the *New York Post*'s boxing writer. On *SportsBeat*, then, Marley was connective tissue between Ali and Cosell.

Cosell loved *SportsBeat*. The sports editor of the Alexander Hamilton High School *Ledger* now had his own version of a newspaper, the first television show devoted to sports journalism. Away from the jocks for whom he had no intellectual respect, comfortable with his chosen band of bright young journalists, Cosell became father, friend, confidant, teacher, coach, reporter, commentator, star, and provocateur-in-chief. Jimmy Roberts, an associate director and producer, thought of ABC Sports as the center of the sports television universe with Cosell the sun around which all revolved: "He always talked about the 'three Cs of television: Cronkite, Carson, and Cosell.' Outrageous as he was, he walked the walk."

One of Cosell's reporters was Peter Mehlman, who in the 1990s would write for *Seinfeld*. He had grown up in Queens and timed his arrival at Knicks games so he could hear Cosell's WABC radio show, *Speaking of Sports*. In the office one Monday evening, Mehlman took a phone call from the boss, working at Yankee Stadium. "Peter," Cosell said, "I forgot my ABC blazer. It's hanging behind my door in my office. Get it! Get in a taxicab, and bring it up to me. You can put in for it. You can come up and watch the game from the booth."

In the booth with Cosell and his director, Chet Forte, Mehlman mostly watched a beautiful young blonde with a fabulous body. Her job was unclear. Whatever it was, its obligations were less apparent than her qualifications. Mehlman chatted her up, and in a limousine returning downtown, Cosell said to him, "So you like that girl?"

"Yeah, she's really something."

"You really ought to fuck her."

Mehlman went, "Uhhh."

"Because it will be the last thing you do on this earth," Cosell said.

"What?"

"That's Forte's bimbo. The Boomer. You'll be in the East River."

Mehlman now went, "Whoa."

Two days later, at 6:00 A.M., the ringing telephone awakened Mehlman. "Hullumph," he said.

"Peter, it's Howard," Cosell said. "Put on the Boomer, I know she's with you. Put her on the phone." They both knew the Boomer had better places to be, and it was near 7:00 A.M. when Mehlman finished laughing.

SportsBeat ran five seasons, 1981 through 1985. Cosell called it "honest, probative, enlightening journalism" about a multibillion-dollar industry that involved "the media, the courts, the Congress, medicine, educations, the arts, you name it. And, as such, the obligation exists to throw a searchlight on the owners, coaches, players, officials, and agents, much as the network news departments and newspapers probe politicians, businessmen, lawyers, and doctors."

Under Cosell's guidance, *SportsBeat* broke news stories on Herschel Walker's first pro football contract and Olympic champion Sugar Ray Seales fighting professionally despite detached retinas that in a civilized sport would have disqualified him. There were single-issue shows on the Colts' skulking off to Indianapolis, Oakland's eminent-domain suit against the Raiders, a point-shaving scandal at Tulane University, and Cosell's talk with Roger Maris after the old Yankee learned he had cancer.

Beginning in the 1930s, "Murrow's Boys" reshaped CBS radio news with their mentor, Edward R. Murrow. "Cosell's Boys" did it for the Coach at ABC. He called them "people of energy, imagination, and a keen awareness and appreciation of sociopolitical issues." Cosell most often found them working in print, or, in Mike Marley's case, suspended from working in print. As Marley described it, he had had "a little problem" with his sports editor at the *Post*, after which "I think I threatened to go in and strangle the guy." A man after Cosell's own heart. Then the phone rang at Marley's desk.

"This is Howard Cosell. Is Marley there? I hear he got suspended."

"This is Marley. Who's this?"

"This is Howard Cosell."

"Yeah, right. Who is this?"

"Howard Cosell. Are you Marley?"

Marley said, "Yeah, what're we doing here, Abbott and Costello 'Who's on first'?"

The way Cosell explained the job, Marley would do investigative reporting for a show that would be the *60 Minutes* of sports. Not only did he offer fun, Cosell would be doing Marley a favor. "I'm taking you off the street," Cosell said, "and making an honest man out of you."

Most times he came into the office, Marley heard the Coach announce,

"Marley the In-de-fat-i-ga-ble, the bulldog reporter, never had a sick day in his life." Cosell's crew worked six days every week except on seven-day weeks, always with Cosell there. By 1984 Marley had decided Cosell was "the greatest boss in history." He called him "Mother Cosell, saving us all from prostitution. I loved the guy."

Jimmy Roberts said, "Howard was a three-ring circus 24/7, insuffer-able and at the same time incredibly lovable. Go figure." Because Roberts was five foot six inches tall, Jewish, and cultivating a mustache, Cosell once answered Roberts's phone with a performance that began, "So you want to talk to the tiny, mustachioed Hebrew?"

In endearing contrast to the *MNF* Cosell, the *SportsBeat* Cosell laughed at himself. One morning Cosell walked down the office hallway without his toupee in place. He stopped by offices, apparently to make small talk. The unprecedented sight of Cosell's undressed pate left the journalists in a quandary. To say or not to say?

Soon enough, everyone gathered by reporter Peter Bonventre's desk, someone asking, "So where's the toop?"

Then came Cosell striding into the hallway. "Okay, everybody out," he said. "Everybody out here." Then, "What is wrong with you people? I don't have the toop on, and nobody says *anything?*"

"We thought maybe you forgot," someone said.

"Nah, I screwed up. I got the toop at the cleaners."

The extent of Cosell's misery on football Mondays became clear to Mehlman, who measured it against the Coach's joy in the office. Cosell once canvassed his boys, asking, "What's in a mezuzah?" Rabbis know the scroll known as a mezuzah contains the first words of the Shema. Mehlman said, "I believe it's a list of the AP top 20." For weeks, any time Cosell passed within earshot of Mehlman, he said, "Huh! The AP top 20!"

Cosell one day sat with Harry Edwards, a black sports activist six feet eight inches tall, powerfully built, instrumental in the Smith-Carlos demonstration at the 1968 Olympics. As Mehlman dropped off a note, Cosell said, "And, Peter, what do *you* think of black coaches in the NFL?" Mehlman said, "You know, Howard, there are so many black players. Does there need to be coaches, too?" Cosell blinked. Then he roared, and the big, black guy joined the raucous laughter, and Mehlman's heart re-sumed normal activity.

Mehlman saw evidence of the Coach's attachment to Ali. At a Mid-town Manhattan law school, a Cosell lecture on sports' distorted role in

American society became a diatribe on the injustices suffered by Ali during the 1960s. Mehlman was astonished, not only by the power of Cosell's arguments but by his ability to deliver them while weeping.

"Minutes after Ali chose to refuse the step forward for drafting into the United States Army," Cosell told the law students, "a political hack in New York, his name Edwin Dooley, the state's boxing commissioner, stripped Ali of the world heavyweight championship and of his license to fight in New York State. In other words, a political hack of no integrity and no guts deprived Muhammad Ali of the property he had earned and of his right to make a living."

Tears came down Cosell's face. "At the time of Dooley's announcement, there had been no arraignment, no grand-jury hearing, no indictment, and no trial, let alone a conviction with every person's right of appeal to a higher court." He kept talking. "This was an historical constitutional law case involving a defendant with the will and the means to pursue justice to the court of last resort, the United States Supreme Court. But due process had not even been initiated, let alone exhausted, before Edwin Dooley slammed shut the door on justice."

Students sat in silence. "The Fourteenth Amendment to the Constitution is a guarantee that no citizen may be deprived of life, liberty, or property without due process of law. Yet in lockstep with the New York State Athletic Commission's actions against Muhammad Ali, every other state that sanctions professional boxing followed in the fool Dooley's footsteps. Now here was Ali: unable to fight anywhere in America, then stripped of his passport and the right to leave the country, thereby unable to fight anywhere in the world."

Mehlman thought, *Unbelievable.* "And while Muhammad Ali was robbed of every American's right to constitutional protections for no reasons beyond political vengeance and racial prejudice, an overwhelming majority of the press and public gloated." It was a performance, as all of Cosell's public life was a performance. But Mehlman saw more. He saw Cosell as a man whose emotional commitment to Ali reached beyond principle to a real human connection. He thought, *Those aren't a performer's tears. They're real. There's passion for Ali. And for his own life going by.*

Bonventre, a writer and magazine editor before trying television, wrote Cosell's third memoir, *I Never Played the Game.* Through almost daily contact for two years, he gathered thoughts for the book, to be published in 1985. As he finished a chapter, it went to Cosell for approval of content, tone, and language. Better than anyone, Bonventre knew the Coach's positions on issues and had heard them expressed so often, on the air, in the office, over lunch and dinner, that his writing was as true to Cosell's voice as a ghost memoirist could achieve.

Cosell was pleased, save for a chapter titled "Monday Night Blues." On a last reading of the manuscript before delivering it to his publisher, Cosell had concerns about withering criticisms of *MNF*. He portrayed Arledge as a power-obsessed, lying, Machiavellian character. Gifford was incompetent, Meredith cruel, O. J. Simpson inarticulate. Cosell wrote that if he watched the show at all in 1984, he rarely made it through the halftime highlights before falling asleep.

He called the telecasts "dreadful." His analysis was acerbic: "There was never a story line, only discussions of play upon play upon play. No perspective. No reportage beyond the game. No humanization of the players. Only feeble attempts at humor, trying to be funny and prove they could prosper without me. There wasn't a skilled performer among them. . . . Meredith was lost. . . . Unlike Meredith, at least the Juice had points to make, but he was ultimately miscast. He couldn't articulate spontaneously. . . . As for Gifford, I got embarrassed listening to him make mistake after mistake. . . . And he came across like a male mannequin, his voice still too weak and undramatic to have any impact."

On a Sunday before the manuscript was due at the publisher the next morning, Cosell called Bonventre. "Peter, can we talk about the book one more time before we hand it in? Come on over to my apartment and have a drink with me and Emmy." Bonventre thought, *He wants to get rid of the Monday Night chapter.*

"Pete, I'm having second thoughts," Cosell said. "I know your name's on it, too. But I know these people. I'm the one who's going to take all the shit. I don't know if I want to bear that or live through it. What do you think?"

"Howard, this is your book, not mine," Bonventre said. "And you say some pretty rough stuff, and you're right, you're going to create a shit-storm. Now, we have to hand in a chapter on *Monday Night Football*. You cannot just ignore it. It's the biggest part of your career. You have to talk about it. So what in hell are you going to write? If you don't say what you said already, everybody that you're close to—from Donald Trump and George Steinbrenner to the lowest producer at ABC, all of whom have heard you say these things about these people countless times—what are they going to think when this book comes out and there's a chapter on *Monday Night Football* in which none of these things are said, and it's all sweetness and light? What are they going to think of you? You're the man who tells it like it is. What are they going to think of you?"

Cosell asked his wife, "Emmy, what do you think?"

She said, "Pete's right."

"So you think, dear, I should go with it?"

"You know what I think, Howard."

Cosell said, "Okay, we're going for it. We're going to hand it in."

The book was not yet published when Al Michaels worked a baseball game with Cosell in the last week of the 1985 season. Michaels had reason to wonder what Cosell might have written about their relationship. But he did not ask. He just wanted to get through the day and move on. They were in Minneapolis for an insignificant Kansas City–Minnesota game broadcast to maybe half the nation; it drew a one-point-three rating. That day Michaels saw Cosell as sullen, surly, sarcastic, and unhappy.

The year before, they had engaged in an argument that began with vodka and escalated through a a snippy on-air exchange. Late in an eleven-inning American League Championship Series game, Cosell suggested strategy that made no baseball sense. The third man in the booth, Hall of Fame pitcher Jim Palmer, gently dismissed the Cosell suggestion. Cosell tried to sell Michaels. But Michaels agreed with Palmer. Cosell must have seen the Giffer and Dandy Don teaming up against him again. Only now their names were Palmer and Michaels. After the game, Cosell confronted Michaels and told him he would never be a good broadcaster until he learned to take a stand.

That did it for Michaels. "Okay, Howard, here's my stand," he said. "You're drunk. You're drinking in the booth. This is bullshit. You're ruining the fucking telecast. You ever come in like that again, I'm not gonna work with you, okay? You do it on your own. That's my stand. Is that all right for you?"

In the ensuing silence, Michaels decided *he* needed a drink. He handed a paper cup to the press lounge bartender. "Can you fill that with vodka, please?" he said. As he reached for the cup, it was a quarter full. "A little more, please," Michaels said, only to hear, "Mr. Michaels, I'm so sorry. Your colleague, Mr. Cosell, drank the rest." He had drained a bottle of vodka during the game on top of what he had drunk at the hotel that afternoon.

They had worked nearly a hundred baseball games together. In contract talks with Arledge that winter, Michaels insisted that Cosell be ordered not to drink if they were to share a booth again. The ultimatum might have had an effect because through a dozen baseball games in 1985, Michaels believed Cosell did not drink.

Next for them, after Minnesota and Kansas City, would be the World Series in two weeks. The men shared a ride to the Minneapolis airport. As they separated to walk to their planes, Michaels saw Cosell walking alone down a concourse, in silence. It had been a nothing game watched by nobody. Cosell was sixty-seven years old, a stooped, forlorn figure, far from home. He might have been Willy Loman.

Arledge was infuriated by *I Never Played the Game.* Cosell was taken off the World Series. *SportsBeat* was canceled. With both sides enraged, lawyers arranged a buyout of Cosell's contract. That baseball game in Minnesota became his last appearance on ABC, though not his last television show. Early in 1988, Don Ohlmeyer created a television version of *Speaking of Everything.* It lasted three months before Ohlmeyer said, "Howard, I love you. But life's too short. You don't want to hear what I say about the show, and for the first time in my life I don't want to hear what you have to say. I can't do this anymore."

Cosell was back where he started thirty-five years before, doing radio only, now doing it from his apartment, 27-M, at 150 East Sixty-ninth Street. My wife and I, in the city to see a show, dropped by to say hello. His daily sports commentary was due in eleven minutes. It was 4:19 P.M., June 13, 1988. He was on the telephone to his ABC Radio assistant, Michelle. "Son of a BITCH! Cut OFF!" At his kitchen table, he dialed again. Michelle's phone was ringing, but it was not ringing fast enough for Cosell. Then it was not ringing at all. "What the *FUCK?*" Then, Michelle was there, and Cosell's voice slipped from shouted obscenity to whispered flirtation as he said, "The sports news, Michelle, what has happened today in *SportsWorld?*" His friend, the *Times* man Bob Lipsyte, had written a book, *SportsWorld: An American Dreamland,* to describe a sweaty Oz in which sports, once a source of inspiration, was co-opted and cheapened and no longer could be trusted to ennoble. Cosell always put a sardonic twist on it, *SportsWorld,* as if speaking of a pretentious theme park for silly little fools.

"Larry Brown," he said into the phone. "How much money? Three-point-five. For how many years? Five. Anything else?" Michelle gave him the name Don Chaney, the new Houston Rockets coach. "Anything else?" Wimbledon men's seedings, the American favorite John McEnroe eighth.

Three minutes to air, and Cosell left the kitchen table. "Follow me," he said. He was barefoot. Otherwise, he was dressed for dinner, slacks, shirt, a tie tossed around his neck. The barefoot boy broadcaster went to his study at the back of the apartment, sat in an easy chair (on a pillow bearing the words, *O Lord, Give Me a Bastard with Talent,* a gift from George Steinbrenner), and pulled on a headset.

"Michelle," he said into a microphone wired to ABC Radio. "Michelle! Mi-*CHELLE!* Is this up? Michelle, are we up? Let's do it, MICHELLE! IS ANYBODY THERE? Son of a *BITCH!* Is any-THING WORKING?" He handed me the microphone. "Here, talk into this mike while I go try to raise them by telephone." I put on the headset. I was Cosell, a scary thought. "Mi-*CHELLE!*" I said. A tiny voice came into my ears. "Who's there?"

"Hold on, I'll get Howard."

It was four-twenty-nine, one minute to air, and now Cosell had the headset on, and there was a transformation, the heartbeat turned up a notch, and I heard a different voice, *that* voice, a voice which was to voices what the Grand Canyon is to ditches. That voice said, "Hello again, everybody, this is Howard Cosell speaking of sports. Everyone in sports is a role model. We know that . . ."

Cosell wrapped Brown, Chaney, and McEnroe into a two-minute news/commentary package on role models. Brown was a glorified winner who in truth was a hypocrite if not a liar for pledging loyalty to Kansas University while using that spring's national basketball championship to get a better deal in the NBA. Chaney had paid his dues as an NBA player and long-time assistant coach who deserved a chance to make it big. The maligned McEnroe was a man of integrity who turned down an offer of one million dollars to play an exhibition in South Africa. In five minutes, Cosell had scratched down three names, divined a connecting thread, and ad-libbed two minutes of meditation on role models.

"Good job," I said.

"Not a bad notion, was it? *SportsWorld,* an American dreamland."

Again, that twist. Why, if he cared so little, do the radio shows?

"Nobody else will tell the truth. Somebody has to do it." A smile. "Besides, they pay me . . ." Here a pause for long division. "They pay me seventy-five hundred a week. Not bad. I don't need the money, but I want to provide for my family, our girls and the grandchildren."

While Cosell did his radio broadcast, Emmy talked with my wife, Cheryl. For Emmy it had been a frightening year. In the spring, diagnosed with lung cancer, she underwent surgery that might have killed her. "If Emmy doesn't make it," Cosell said then, "I don't know that I want to be around." Now the four of us sat in the Cosells' living room. "It has been a miracle," Emmy said. "Now I can even say the words. 'Lung cancer.' Before, I couldn't say it. But now I'm going to be okay." Cheryl later told me that Emmy, in case she did not survive the surgery, had written farewell letters to her daughters with advice about Howard. My wife called Emmy "just the sweetest woman."

If Red Smith's grace with the language was one ideal for a sports columnist, Cosell's hard-edged reasoning was another. But when we met at his beach house in the Hamptons to talk about a collaboration on his fourth memoir, I didn't like what he thought. He wanted to do another monologue in which Cosell portrayed Cosell as the lone virtuous man in SportsWorld.

"When it came time for the United States against Muhammad Ali," he said, "95 to 98 percent of the sportswriters in America regaled what happened to 'the traitor.' Some openly recommended deportation. None ever heard of the Fifth and Fourteenth amendments of due process and equal protection. But one man fought publicly on the strongest medium in this country, television. And one man was right, because he had the mentality, because he had majored in constitutional law, because he had edited the New York University law quarterly review, because he had done law notes on the Constitution, on whether there should be an amendment against lynching. In this country twenty years earlier, Ali would have been lynched. That one man, me."

He remembered a 1950s conversation with the great sportswriter W. C. (Bill) Heinz. "Bill had talent, he had integrity, and he once said to me, 'Howard, don't ever do play-by-play. That's for parrots. You be the overseer of this industry. Only you have that capacity.' I said, 'Bill, you're right. I'm going to try to live by that.'" He declared that this fourth Cosell book would say Pete Rozelle did not retire, "he was fired." It would call Mike Tyson "barbaric," Donald Trump "a lot of shit," and Pete Rose "that cheap, little thug, vermin."

His distaste for Rose was made profound by his respect for Bart Giamatti, president of Yale University when Cosell taught a sports-in-culture class there. As Major League Baseball's commissioner, Giamatti banned Rose from the game permanently after a contentious investigation into Rose's gambling habits. "Bart is the best thing that ever happened to sports in America," Cosell said. "A terrific man, a dead-honest man, an extraordinarily brilliant man who showed unbelievable patience in the Rose case."

I didn't want to do the book Cosell described. Better, I said, if he could identify problems while offering solutions. Cosell ignored me to talk about the marketing that would follow the book's publication: "Every city in America will want me on the book tour. Jesus Christ, what a thing." Now I understood. He *was* Willy Loman. His time had passed, he knew it in his soul, and he denied it to everyone, especially himself. I saw now that the ideas in the book were less important to him than the book tour. "Nobody," he said, "can sell a book like I can."

I was afraid that if we did that book—butting heads even on the concept—we would wind up not speaking to each other. Unlike Al Michaels, Roone Arledge, Faultless Frank, and Dandy Don, I had no contractual obligation to put our relationship at risk. Before I could say as much, though, he took a telephone call that was bad news.

Bart Giamatti had suffered a heart attack. Now on the phone to his office, with Emmy joining us on the deck, Cosell said, "What does that mean, 'cardiac arrest'? . . . The heart has stopped? . . . He's been under a doctor's care, you know that, with this Pete Rose thing. God damn Pete Rose. . . . A coronary, fifty-one years old. . . . So you don't know the extent of it except that the heart has stopped? . . . Can you recover from that? . . . You can? . . . If it's caught at the beginning? . . . I didn't have cardiac arrest, no, they called it a 'silent' heart attack . . . okay. Jesus. Oh, God. He's one of the great people I've ever known. . . . What time did it happen? . . . Oh, shit. What a mess. . . . Keep me informed."

He told Emmy, "Bart Giamatti is in full cardiac arrest. Pete Rose has killed him."

Emmy said, "Oh, no. But, Howard. There has to be more to it than Rose."

"A year of it, Emmy. A year of stress. And Bart's a smoker. A year of Pete Rose. Fucking thug ballplayer."

At five-twenty-four that afternoon came confirmation of Giamatti's death, and after dinner that evening, about eight o'clock, Cosell rose from the table, saying nothing. He had begun the day with a golden morning's walk to the beach. Now he moved toward his bedroom. We heard his voice, smaller than ever. He said, "I'm tired."

CHAPTER NINETEEN

"I'd Rather Be Punished Here Than in the Hereafter"

BACK IN LOS ANGELES three weeks after the Berbick fight, Ali showed up in a courtroom. It was a matter of $21.3 million. He had not stolen it, but a thief had shared a small part of it with him. Common sense would tell you to stay away from thieves, especially thieves of $21 million. But Ali came to the courtroom. Someone probably paid him to come downtown from his Fremont Place mansion and be seen, though the appearance might have been an act of loyalty. He liked that day's defendant, Harold Smith, the way he always liked the rogues, mavericks, and con men who handed him money, no explanations given, no questions asked.

Ali took a seat in the gallery as Smith's lawyer, Howard Moore, made his closing argument. He wanted the jury to believe that Smith had not stolen $21.3 million, but had been deceived by an associate who had stolen the money without his knowledge. The lawyer's summation was modeled after Martin Luther King, Jr.'s, *I Have a Dream* speech. Moore argued that his client, too, had pursued a great American dream, just wanting to help young athletes.

The government had charged Smith and two other men with embezzling the millions from Wells Fargo banks to finance boxing promotions under the name of Muhammad Ali Professional Sports. For appearances and the use of his name across three years, Ali may have been enriched by the scheme to the extent of five hundred thousand dollars. But from the start, prosecutors had no taste for pursuing Ali. The assistant U.S. attorney heading the case, Dean Allison, had been an amateur boxer and was an Ali fan. He didn't believe that Ali knew how Smith came up with the cash for him. *The Champ had made far too much money to be tied up in anything crooked,* Allison thought, *and had plenty of professional advisers to safeguard his investments.*

Ali had insisted he knew nothing about nothing. In February 1981, at a press conference at his home, he had overwhelmed suspicion with charm. Seldom had journalists worked in more opulent surroundings than Ali's seven-bedroom mansion with its Tiffany stained glass, Persian and Oriental rugs, Renaissance art, standing urns, billiard parlor, and conservatory. Lest anyone be so bold as to consider sitting on her gilded chairs, the glamorous Veronica Ali, strung velvet ropes between the armrests.

Dozens of reporters crowded into Ali's den where he sat in a high-back chair behind a small desk. He wore a pin-striped suit and a pastel tie loosened at the neck. Thick electrical cords and portable lights transformed the den into a television studio with Ali setting the scene: "The FBI is calling me. The CIA is guarding the house. Everything's on me. I got to be protected by Allah. If I didn't believe in God—Allah—I probably would have cracked up long ago."

The phone rang. Ali answered, "City morgue. Is he dead?"

The phone rang again "Yeah, the White House? You calling from the White House? Hey, Ronald, how are you doing? Glad you called."

Ali's voice was hoarse, his speech slurred and slow, his attention span short. He was out of place in his own home, imperfect in the midst of its perfection. A reporter asked, "Champ, can you tell us the extent of your financial arrangements with Harold Smith?"

Ali did not like the reporter's tone. "What are you trying to say? You asking did I steal it? If I needed money, I wouldn't rob no bank. If I was a bank robber, they'd rate me bigger than Jesse James."

In fact, $21 million was Jesse James squared. The prosecutor, Allison, determined that Ali had received "several payments" between ten and fifteen thousand dollars as well as two payments of "several hundred thousand dollars." One payment came to $223,000. Of that money, Allison said $100,000 went to Veronica to decorate the mansion, with the rest set aside to pay taxes. The prosecutor also decided that Ali's name had been used without his knowledge in Smith's scheme.

Asked if he would meet Smith, Ali said, "I'd tell Harold to meet with the FBI. I wouldn't meet with him alone. They'd say I stole the money and helped him."

Someone asked, "Did you ever wonder where he got all his money?"

"I saw him with all those beautiful girls, planes, boats. I used to say, 'You sure everything's okay, Harold?' He always said everything was fine. I believed him."

"Are you mad at Smith?"

"I'm not mad at all. I'm sorry for his family, his nice little boy and wife. I trusted him. He was a heavyweight, mentally. You see, being Muhammad Ali, *everybody* wants to use my name."

This time, twenty-one million dollars worth. Ali could laugh. "Ain't many names," he said, "that can steal that much."

It was January 4, 1982, when Ali sat in that Los Angeles courtroom. The lawyer Moore told the jury, "I want to talk to you about the dream, a dream of Harold Smith, my client, a dream that is now deferred. I believe that Harold's dream . . ." By then, jury members had their attention drawn elsewhere. As Moore droned on, jurors watched Ali play with a small girl seated near him. Eight days later, Harold Smith was found guilty. He was sentenced to ten years in prison, fined thirty thousand dollars, and ordered to do three thousand hours of community service.

For fifteen years, I had seen Ali four or five times a year, maybe a week each time. This time, in May 1983, I had not seen him for seventeen months. I was in Las Vegas for a Holmes fight and was walking up the steps to the Caesars Palace hotel when Ali stepped out of a long, black limousine. "Ali, you look good," I said. Such a lie. He was huge, maybe two sixty. "What're you up to?"

"Come on," he said. He moved slowly through the casino's cigar haze, his body a burden. A man held out a blue crayon and a keno slip to Ali and said, "Champ, you got a nine-year-old fan in Cleveland. Make it 'To Ian.' He'll treasure this his whole life." Ali stopped behind a woman and clicked his fingers beside her ear, moving away before she could identify the noise but, as she turned, Ali looked back and winked. The imp.

We stopped in a coffee shop. "I am dedicating myself to promoting world peace," he said. His voice was a mumble, as if coming from an attic where the words were covered by the dusts of time. I did not expect him to sparkle. I knew better. I had been there for Holmes, for Berbick. I had seen it. But I did not expect this. Word was he came to Vegas to shill for the fight because promoter Don King paid him hang-around money. Twelve hundred dollars.

Ali showed me a paper with a crude drawing of an airplane over the words, "Children's Journey for Peace." He said fifty children from fifty countries would meet with the world's presidents, kings, and sheiks. "Sheiks of Arabia will donate money, certain people will donate the airplane. It's going to be something, man. Beautiful. Powerful. Boxing was Allah's way of getting me fame to do something bigger. This is ten times bigger than boxing. Powerful."

"Sounds good," I said, knowing better. I had heard about great mosques he would build, and apartment buildings for the needy. They never happened.

Larry Holmes walked by. He smiled at Ali and shouted, so everyone could enjoy it, "I hear you're being ugly about me. You want to do it, Champ? Let's make a comeback."

Ali raised his voice. "I wannnnnnnttttt Hoooooolmmmmes."

"Ali's making a comeback," Holmes announced.

"This nigger's craaaaazzy," Ali said.

Holmes bent down to Ali's ear to whisper, as Ali once had bent down to Joe Louis. "One champ to another champ," Holmes said, "you'll always be the greatest, I'm just the latest."

We moved up to Ali's hotel suite where he said, "You heard my lecture, 'The Meaning of Life'? Islamic evangelist, that's what I want to do." He had pictures of himself with Billy Graham, Pope John Paul II, Reagan, Ford, Carter, and Brezhnev. "The world listens to me." The lecture was on tape. He put the player on the floor so eight people there could hear it. His left arm, resting on his chair, trembled. His left thumb twitched. His voice on the tape was lifeless and stumbling, a schoolboy reading a difficult book. Ali's voice said we can never repay Allah except by being good.

Marilyn Monroe walked in. "This is the Marilyn Monroe look-alike," said a man who delivered her. Ali did not look at the blonde. "This lecture," he said, "is one of forty-seven I've done. We're having one hundred thousand copies made."

As I left the room, I heard Ali's voice, a sad drone. "This next lecture . . ."

Boxing had robbed him of middle age. He was an old man at forty-one. He couldn't sleep at night and might fall asleep in the day sitting up. Walking, he was not sure where his feet would come down next. His face, that pretty face, accomplice to his mischief—now puffy, stiff, more a mask than a face. Holmes had heard a change in Ali's voice. I read his quotation in Dave Anderson's column that week. "Ali's always talked low to me. His voice is lower than it was in 1971, 1973, 1975. It's more slow and softer. He's hard to understand." But Holmes wanted the sports-writer to understand the important part. He loved Ali. He was happy to see him in any condition. "I don't look for him to stumble when he walks and stutter when he talks."

Anderson asked, "Do you see that as a warning to yourself?"

"Life is a warning," Holmes said.

Ali's trips to hospitals once had been emergencies. In his sudden old age, he went to hospitals out of worry. He wanted to know why he couldn't talk. Why he was tired. Why the tremors. Why his face didn't do what he wanted. For answers, a friend suggested he go to New York's Columbia-Presbyterian Medical Center and see Dr. Stanley Fahn.

"I came in here on my own because I wanted to find out what was wrong with me," he told reporters. "I'm not dying, but when the media gets on something like this it sounds like you're about to die." Not to worry, he said. "But my family and friends are scared to death."

After eight days of tests, Dr. Fahn issued a statement. It said Ali did not have Parkinson's disease; his symptoms could be reversed with med-ication; he was not punch-drunk, and he "should be fully able to effec-tively carry out personal appearances and other business activities indefinitely." The doctor's statement pleased Larry Kolb, who had a deal pending with a Saudi needing reassurance that Ali was not a dead man walking. Kolb also spoke to the press: "Look, Muhammad's upstairs do-ing just fine. He's not hurting, not suffering, not out of it, not in danger." Kolb passed along a story. That morning he and Ali had looked down from his hospital window and saw the gathering crowd. Ali raised an imaginary microphone to his lips and went into a mock news-reporter voice: "Is Muhammad Ali alive? Is he dead? No word yet. Tune in tomor-row."

The afternoon of September 20, 1984, he came to the window of his hospital room. On the street below were a hundred people, television cameras, reporters. All there for Ali, who now came down from his room with the Reverend Jesse Jackson, the presidential candidate who knew a photo op when he saw it.

"I hear people saying I'm up there dying," Ali said, "that I can't talk any more, that I'm through, that it's all over for me." His voice was hoarse, the words slightly slurred. "So I decided to come down here and show you all that I'm still pretty, I'm still very pretty, and I'm still the greatest . . ." Now he raised his chin and bellowed, " . . . of . . . allllll . . . tiiiiimmmmme."

There was no shortage of Harold Smith types proposing to use Ali's name. There was a shoe polish. A candy bar. A string of hamburger joints. His new lawyer from Virginia had big ideas. Ali did not remember how he met the lawyer, Richard M. Hirschfeld, and did not know what branch of law he practiced. Ali knew only the most important thing, which was that Hirschfeld produced cash. If he needed ten thousand dollars, Richie gave it to him.

Hirschfeld was an energetic, imaginative entrepreneur. He created Champion Sports Management in partnership with Herbert Muhammad and Ali to raise almost two million dollars to train and manage fighters at Ali's Deer Lake camp and another in Virginia. There was to be an Ali-branded car built in Brazil. The three men were partners in a luxury hotel in Virginia Beach, in the marketing of a West German herpes vaccine, and in the closing of an $800-million oil refinery deal in Sudan.

Trouble followed Hirschfeld. As early as 1974, at age twenty-seven, he created the Hirschfeld Bank of Commerce. It went bust when the Securities and Exchange Commission charged its namesake with fraud in stock sales. In 1984, a year into Champion Sports Management, the SEC shut down that business, again charging Hirschfeld with stock fraud. Had Ali and Herbert Muhammad cared, they could have checked public records and learned that Hirschfeld had never sustained a money-making deal. His modus operandi was a scam artist's. Make big promises, attract investors' money, and move to a new deal when the old one falls apart. Hirschfeld was the scion of a prominent family from Virginia's Tidewater region, a small, trim man, good looking, well dressed, charming, eager, and cunning in his use of Ali.

This cunning: In 1985, with Ali as the key opening all doors, Hirschfeld gained entry to influence peddlers in the White House, State Department, Central Intelligence Agency, and Middle East—all in the guise of Ali volunteering to go to Beirut hoping to persuade Muslim extremists to release five hostages, four of them Americans. It was a scheme fraught with danger. Two years earlier, sixty-three people were killed by a truck bomb at the U.S. Embassy; six months after that, another truck bomb killed 241 U.S. Marines in their barracks. The city was a killing zone, sixty thousand people dead in nine years of civil war.

But Vice President George H. W. Bush briefed the Ali group that included Hirschfeld, Herbert Muhammad, Larry Kolb, and advisers Robert Sensi and Abuwi Mahdi. They had no promise of making contact with anyone connected to the hostages. No one even knew what terrorist organization had done the kidnappings. Advice from the vice president, who had been the CIA chief: Be cautious.

It might have been the strangest "secret" mission ever. With Ali, the group attracted such attention in Beirut that a *Newsweek* reporter defined its strategy as "pure rope-a-dope: to wait until the unknown hostage-takers, attracted by Ali's fame, came to him." One morning, waiting, Ali and Herbert Muhammad sat in their suite at the beachfront Summerland Hotel. Over a breakfast of fruit and yogurt, Herbert discoursed on the Lebanon civil war's etiquette: No shooting until noon, when women are home from shopping. Also: "They can tell the difference between the way an incoming shell whistles from the way an outgoing one whistles. So when they hear a shell, they listen and they know to hit the floor, or they've got time to get in a basement, or just to go on eating."

"Just like me, I can tell," Ali said. "And I'm gonna keep eatin'."

Larry Kolb was the son of a senior American intelligence officer. Asked by the CIA to be a spy himself, Kolb said no, he had other plans. Now with Ali in Beirut, Kolb met a formidable soldier of fortune, an American expatriate named Issa Abdul Ali. He came with a proposal to guide Ali to Ibrahim Amin, a leader of the Hezbollah, a violently anti-American organization committed to the destruction of Israel.

"Okay, we'll go," Ali said.

Kolb thought, *Holy shit.*

Two cars delivered Ali and his crew to two more cars, those armed with machine gunners at the windows and careering through Beirut to a three-story house, once a rich man's villa, now smelling of mildew, and dark with blackout curtains. Herbert Muhammad spoke to Amin. "Ali wants you to arrange the release of another American now . . ." One hostage had been freed, or escaped, the day before Ali's group arrived in Beirut ". . . as a symbol of Allah's boundless mercy and compassion, and as a sign that you are the man we were directed here to meet." There was no answer from Amin, only a smile meaning, *I'm sorry, it's out of my hands.* Here Issa said, "Well, we should go now." They did.

Two days later, the adventurers went to the Beirut airport, its walls pockmarked by bullets. Sensi told a ticket agent, "We'll take the next flight to anywhere." They did.

How strange, all of it. The Ali who had stumbled across Africa in 1980 now had gone into a war zone thinking he could persuade international terrorists to give up hostages. It made no more sense for Ali to follow the scheming Richard Hirschfeld than it had to take money from Harold Smith. Naive, foolish, bored—Ali was all that. Now there were also suggestions of desperation.

His third marriage was headed for divorce. The beautiful Veronica Porsche had married a man who moved on the world stage and could buy a mansion in a gated Los Angeles community of the ultrarich. Ali in descent was not that man. Harold Conrad found him sleeping in a small room, barely the size of a closet, in the twenty-two-room mansion. "Quiet," Ali said that morning shortly before noon, "my wife's asleep upstairs. Can't wake her." Ali's daughter Maryum told a biographer, "And I knew that when my father stopped fighting and the bright lights and money disappeared, Veronica would be gone. . . . She was like a stage wife. She didn't cook. They had somebody else take care of the kids, while she was off being a star."

The trembling in Ali's left arm and hand, the mumbled words, and the indifference to his physical condition were worse. In Louisville, if not in Los Angeles, someone cared. Her name was Yolanda Williams. Her mother was Odessa Clay's best friend, next-door neighbor, and traveling companion during Ali's fighting career. Yolanda—"Lonnie"—first sat on Cassius Clay's knee at age seven when he came home from beating Sonny Liston. By seventeen she had decided that her purpose in life was to marry Muhammad Ali. She graduated from Vanderbilt University and was twenty-five years old in 1982 when she went to Louisville's Hyatt Regency Hotel to meet the man she'd had a crush on forever.

But this was not the Ali she had known. "He was stumbling," she said. Stumbling off the elevator, across the lobby carpet, on the street. "He was despondent." Gene Dibble, a business adviser and Ali's friend, told Lonnie, "Muhammad isn't well. And if somebody doesn't do something to help him, I think he's going to die."

She moved to Los Angeles and was there when the Alis divorced in July 1986. As part of the divorce agreement, the Fremont Place mansion was sold. Either Ali ignored the proceedings or he had not been notified, and one summer day Veronica told him to come to the house, that they had twenty-four hours to divvy up its contents. Ali came to the mansion with a friend, Victor Solano, once a boxer himself, a heavyweight whose only distinction was that as a teenager he had sparred with the great Muhammad Ali. After that, Solano made himself available for whatever the champion needed done in Los Angeles.

Across a decade, while he worked as a process server and raised his own family, Solano became Ali's confidant. Now, they stood on the street outside 55 Fremont Place putting Ali's stuff into a U-Haul trailer, as if he were a deadbeat evicted from a fleabag motel. There wasn't much Ali wanted. His Bibles, a Qur'an, a prayer mat. A picture of himself at one year old. Trophies. A chandelier, a table. As Veronica's brother and father moved gilded furniture, rugs, and art, Ali wandered through the empty spaces. Solano heard him say softly, "Memories, so many." He looked at the pool, the guest house, the garages, the kitchen. In the den, Ali said, "Can you believe all the people, big and small, rich and poor, the important and the not important, legends, actors, bums, hoboes—everyone—I had my doors open to all of them, didn't I?"

Solano had never seen Ali so sad. It wasn't losing the house that mattered. He had lived there only seven years. The divorce had been inevitable for two years. Ali had lost more before and come back. He knew it was different this time. He had come back in other years because he was Muhammad Ali. Whatever happened outside the ring could be fixed inside. Money, attention, and influence flowed to him when he entered a ring to do his extraordinary work. All that was gone. On the street, Solano put his arm around Ali's broad shoulders. "This day, it will only make you stronger," he said. He wanted to believe it.

"You know what would make me the happiest man on Earth?" Ali said. "Just live out of my motor home. Pack it up with my Islamic papers, get enough clothes, some money, and go from city to city preaching. That's what would make me happy, not all this shit." Then he said, "Let's get out of here." They went from the mansion on Fremont Place, where he was unwanted, to a little house on Holloway Drive. There he would be welcome. Lonnie Williams lived there.

For the first time in his life, Ali was adrift. A thousand times, maybe more, Bundini Brown had crowed, "Float like a butterfly . . . "If once the perfect metaphor for the young Ali, all grace and beauty, the words now seemed haunting. Butterflies float into our sight, carried on the whims of air, gone as quickly as they came.

Ali rented an office on Wilshire Boulevard. An empty office. Fifth floor. A telephone, nothing else. On the office door in gold lettering: *TRIPLE CROWN, Inc.* He did no work. He drove his brown Rolls-Royce to that empty office. He stood at the window. He lay on the floor. Sometimes he fell asleep. Sometimes he sat in the Rolls, alone. He told Solano he wondered if the world knew where he was. Solano tried to get Ali in the gym where he had always been happiest. But the man who had won the heavyweight championship three times did not want to work out. He did not want to be seen fat, slow, and clumsy.

On November 19, 1986, Ali married Lonnie, his fourth wife.

Solano so often preached Christianity that Ali came to call him "Jimmy Swaggart" after the evangelist from Louisiana. One night, before Ali's divorce from Veronica, Solano heard Ali talking about religion and forgiveness. He said, "Muhammad, what if I could get Jimmy Swaggart to come by the house? Would you pray with him?"

Swaggart had carried his fire and brimstone to the Los Angeles Sports Arena where he invited doubters, unbelievers, and sinners to give themselves to Jesus Christ and be saved by His grace for all eternity. It was an odd idea, America's most famous Muslim communing with the silver-tongued Christian. But Ali was a Baptist at the start, Odessa Clay's child, the son of a man who painted murals on Baptist church altar walls. Solano thought Ali was a Christian at heart, a Muslim by choice. He knew Ali read the Bible more than the Qur'an. He thought Ali protested too much in arguing the old Islamic theory that "contradictions" in the Bible "prove" it is not the infallible word of God as Christians claim and so must be false in its teachings.

"Jimmy Swaggart's too big to come here," Ali said. "I ain't nobody no more."

"I'm just asking, if he says he'd do it, would you let me bring him here?"

"Yeah, but he ain't coming. I ain't nobody no more."

Two hours later, Solano's old green Datsun stopped at 55 Fremont Place. Behind it was a black limousine from which Jimmy Swaggart appeared and said to Solano, "Let's see what the mighty hand of God can do." Swaggart and Ali talked about Malcolm X and Martin Luther King, Jr., the Bible and the Qur'an. For every "contradiction" in the Bible that was brought up by Ali, Swaggart had an explanation. Finally, Ali said, "Man, Brother Swaggart, at scripture you're too good. I need to get you in the ring."

Swaggart said, "Muhammad, would you mind if I laid hands on you? And would you repeat the Sinner's Prayer with me?"

Ali came to Swaggart, his head bowed. With his hands on Ali's shoulders, Swaggart acknowledged to God the life and resurrection of Jesus Christ and promised to repent of his sins and accept Jesus as his savior. Crazier things had happened in Muhammad Ali's life. But not many. After Swaggart left, Ali laughed and said to Solano, "What do you think would happen if I went on national TV and said, 'I, Muhammad Ali, was wrong'?"

"Wrong, about what?" Solano said.

"Islam. I would shock the world!"

Solano wasn't sure why Ali agreed to meet Swaggart. Maybe at some level he was still Odessa's Gee Gee going to Mount Zion Baptist church every Sunday morning. Or maybe an empty life in a mansion behind closed gates left Ali wondering if anyone remembered him. *I ain't nobody no more.* In either case, Solano never believed Ali would renounce Islam. His religious sincerity, no one doubted; as faithfully as he had heeded Elijah Muhammad's theology, Ali embraced Islam in the decade after the messenger's death.

Solano was just happy to hear his man laughing.

Later, Ali stood at the hospital bedside of his court jester. Drew (Bundini) Brown, Jr., was fifty-seven years old. A diabetic hooked on alcohol and who knew what other drugs, sick and not able to get himself to doctors, poor Bundini stayed in a ratty downtown Los Angeles motel a step up from homelessness. Ali paid for the room. Bundini had passed out, or stumbled, and fallen down stairs. Neck and head injuries paralyzed him. A doctor at Good Samaritan warned Ali and Solano that Brown lay in a Stryker critical care bed, his head positioned inside a steel ring. The bed moved in four directions, first laterally, then in a tipping motion from side to side. The idea was to keep Brown's body fluids moving.

Ali and Bundini had worked together twenty years. He was a mystic conduit to places Ali's imagination wanted to go. Sugar Ray Robinson had sent Bundini to the young Clay, not because Bundini knew boxing but because he was a street-smart hustler who could help the Kentucky kid in the big city. In that happy way that Ali's luck ran, his connection with Bundini produced a thrilling life spark. Bundini—loud, profane, vexatious, endearing, loyal Bundini—was fired a dozen times and welcomed back each time. However he made a dollar off Ali, whatever he stole and pawned, however intoxicated on life and voodoo spirits Bundini became, Ali wanted him beside him, needed him there.

Now Ali stood beside Bundini's shining silver terrible bed. Bundini moved his eyes toward the big man and mumbled. "I'm . . . so . . . sorry . . . champ."

"Quiet, Drew."

Bundini held Ali's hand. Ali asked for a towel and said to Brown, "My turn to wipe your sweat off." Both men began to cry. "Man, just think," Ali said, "you're gonna be up there in heaven with Jesus and Shorty and Joe Louis, Jack Johnson, and all the great ones, and someday me, too. And you're going to be walking up there on streets of gold and diamonds and rubies, like the Bible says."

Brown tried to talk and could not. Ali talked for him. "We'll see you up there someday, I promise." And he said, "Hey, Bundini. 'Float like a butterfly, sting like a bee. Rumble, young man, rumble.'" They had done the bit a thousand times, always a thousand times louder than Ali did it now. Softly, he finished with an open-mouth, "Aaaahhhh." Bundini, trying to smile, opened his mouth to make the sound he could, and Ali laid his hand alongside his friend's cheek and kissed him on the forehead.

As Ali left the room, a doctor asked if he might see a young boy down the hall. He was dying, his skin falling off at a touch. The boy turned his back to the unannounced visitors, and Ali said, loudly, "Where's this boy wants to box me? They say he looks just like Joe Frazier!"

The boy laughed, and Ali said, "Why, you're better lookin' than Joe Frazier. I am *in trouble!* C'mon, boy." He raised his fists and gnawed at his lower lip as if itching for a fight. "C'mon, you're next!"

Ali kissed the boy on the cheek, and he left the hospital, and within a week Bundini and the boy were gone.

They saw Sugar Ray, too, but the great old fighter recognized only Solano, who as a twelve-year-old child had fetched him water and orange juice from a liquor store and delivered it to the Main Street gym. Now it was 1987 and Robinson had Alzheimer's disease, reduced to a shuffling, silent shell. His wife, Millie, said, "Ray, look who came with Victor. Look at who's sitting over there. Who's that?" Robinson stared at Ali, a steady stare. Finally, he said, "Champ."

Ali said, "Ray, you've been my main man all my life." It had been twenty-seven years since the kid Cassius Clay sought out Sugar Ray in Harlem, to meet the great fighter, maybe to ask him to be his manager, maybe get an autograph. As Ali had been solicitous of Joe Louis in his wheelchair in 1980, now he spoke softly to Ray Robinson. "God taking good care of you, Ray?" he said. Robinson said nothing.

He said nothing more at all, and it was time to leave, and Solano saw Ali look into Robinson's trophy case with its glitter of silver and gold, six championship belts, the symbols of a lifetime's work that ended in a man's silence. There were tears in Ali's eyes. Solano said, "Don't worry about Ray, he's okay, God's taking care of him, Muhammad." Ali said, "I'm going to be like that someday. I know it. Just like that. I'm going to die just like that. I'm not going to know anybody. Just like that."

As Ali became weaker and his tremors more obvious, he told his oldest daughter, Maryum, he wanted no one's sympathy.

"But, Daddy . . ."

"I see them, I hear them. They go, 'Oh, look at him.'"

"Daddy, Daddy."

"May May, they shouldn't feel sorry for me."

He had come to an uneasy peace. "I did a lot of wrong in my life," he told her, "and I'm trying to repent and go to heaven. I'd rather God punish me now than in the hereafter. Maybe this is my punishment. I'm okay with it."

Sugar Ray Robinson died April 12, 1989, eight years to the day after Joe Louis.

For the first time since he was a twelve-year-old misbehaving in Fred Stoner's church-basement gym, Ali was offstage. He had come to every extraordinary athlete's purgatory, those empty moments when the life-giving electricity of applause is gone. He was all but mute, the gloriously expressive face of his youth now an unmoving mask, his movements those he had parodied in lesser men stiff, slow, shuffling. "The Mummy,"

he had said of George Foreman. Once the world champ at vanity and nar-
cissism, Ali himself was now the mummy.

Maybe no man in such condition can blame himself for it. Certainly,
Ali would not. From Los Angeles, he had moved to an eighty-acre estate
in Berrien Springs, Michigan, across Lake Michigan from Chicago. There,
early in 1988, he told journalist Peter Tauber, writing for *New York Times
Magazine*, that if he had it all to do over again, he would do it the same
way again. He said it was worth it because it made him so famous that
people would listen to his preaching and, in fact, whatever small infirmities he had were actually assets.

"I've got Parkinson's syndrome," he said. "I'm in no pain. A slight
slurring of my speech, a little tremor. Nothing critical. If I was in perfect
health—if I won my last two fights—if I had no problem, people would
be afraid of me. Now they feel sorry for me. They thought I was Super-
man. Now they can go, 'He's human, like us. He has problems.'"

Tauber was a novelist and screenwriter who came of age in the 1960s
as an antiwar activist. He saw in Ali everything he wished he could see in
himself. Big deal if Ali could not explain his opposition to Vietnam. Who
expects a boxer to be Hans Morgenthau? Tauber saw Ali as a symbol of a
culture protesting against authoritarians who would impose their values
on young people. He believed that Ali's refusal to accept a privileged
army tour of duty and his willingness to pay the price for that refusal—
the bankrupting of his celebrity status—was an astonishing act of brav-
ery. Tauber didn't care if the legal grounds for the refusal were suspect,
didn't care if Ali did it on Elijah Muhammad's orders, and certainly didn't
care if Ali could not find Vietnam on the globe. Bottom line was, Ali did
it. No other superstar of the 1960s did it. No one else gave up so much
and risked so much more.

Tauber was a friendly interviewer with a knack for delivering a barb
with a smile. "You're old, you're fat, you're slow," he said to Ali. They
played in Ali's living room, the journalist pretending to fight Ali. Tauber
also broadcast the event using his best replication of the Howard Cosell
voice and style.

"They say the next time you get in the ring, if you win, it'll be the
biggest dive since Jacques Cousteau went down in the Mariana Trench,"
Tauber/Cosell said, flicking a jab toward Ali, who had yet to decide how
crazy this white man was. "Look at you, a shell of the former self who
beat Foreman and Liston and Joe Frazier twice! And on some good days

even could handle Kenny Norton. Now, look. You can't even touch a slow, white, short, Jewish guy with glasses."

Ali smiled.

"And if you do touch me, you'll wind up on *Nightline*. Accused of racism." At which point, Ali became Ali, rolling his shoulders, gliding left, snapping off a half-dozen jabs, each from a new angle, bare knuckles stopping just short of Tauber's nose—except for one past the writer's ear that led to Ali pulling him into a hug, both men laughing.

Tauber's story was so kind and respectful that Lonnie Ali read the original draft to her husband. It included a sentence that editors had cut out. The sentence followed Ali's declaration that he would live his way the same way again despite his physical condition. Tauber's sentence said: "Not a curse to him—just to his fans—to him, his ailment is a perverse gift. Not a tragic turn, it is an answered prayer."

Tauber argued that the brain damage relieved Ali of the expectation that legendary figures find onerous. Everyone wants the hero to do the same tricks again. But instead of the brash, impolitic Ali of a decade earlier, Tauber portrayed the infirm Ali as serene, meditative, spiritual. Where others had seen tragedy in Ali's weakness, he saw strength.

As Lonnie read Tauber's story aloud, Ali had tears in his eyes.

"He understands," Ali said.

Tauber later wrote me a note on Ali: "I saw him not as a Superman/Superstar-gone-to-seed, but as a Universal Teacher, using the loss of all his powers (how very Islamic! Total prostrateness!) to teach us all how to walk with dignity down that road of aging and infirmity all must go. If you take a Champion and strip him even more naked than when he was in the ring, and, devoid of all the skills and trappings, he *still* instructs by using his Charisma to light a path—well, I think that's a very powerful position."

CHAPTER TWENTY

"Your Unconquerable Soul"

ALMOST THIRTY YEARS AFTER his father's death, Cosell said he still felt guilty about not being at the hospital with him. He vowed that he would not let that happen with Emmy. So when she survived the lung cancer and told him to go do what he needed to do, Cosell boarded an airplane for a charity appearance in Kansas City. It was November 18, 1990. That day Emmy Cosell died at home of a heart attack. A week later, her husband brought himself to an ABC Radio microphone. Sorrow lay heavy on his voice. He said: "This is the most difficult broadcast I have ever had to do in my whole life. A man's grief should be a private thing, but sometimes there has to be public notice taken.

"I have lost the treasure of my life. My wife and I had forty-six and a half marvelous years together. Moments never to be forgotten, people never to be forgotten.

"And everybody who ever touched Emmy Cosell knew that she was special, that she was warm, compassionate, that she was not fragile. She was valiant. Everybody who ever knew her knew that she was indeed the better half of my life. It will be difficult to go on without her, but go on I must, with our two daughters, with our five grandchildren. Life has been so good to us, sometimes almost unbearably so.

"And she knew my favorite poem. She knew that the most beautiful poem ever written was John Keats's 'Ode to a Nightingale.' 'My heart aches, and a drowsy numbness pains my sense, as though of hemlock I had drunk, or tasted of Flora or some sweet Provencal song.'

"And then the poem went on because John Keats was just a boy, even though a genius. And death was waiting for him. And he understood that life is but transitory, and so is beauty. He understood all of it. Everything.

He said to himself, 'Forlorn! the very word is like a bell to toll me back from thee to my sole self.' He knew that he was dying. But he also knew that he had tasted the beauties of life. And he wrote the most sensitive words ever written.

"And so I say in memory of my glorious wife, my heart aches, and a drowsy numbness pains my sense, and I thank whatever gods may be, Emmy, for your unconquerable soul."

In failing health himself, Cosell found little to sustain enthusiasm for life. "Eighty-five percent of him died right there," Justin Cosell said. Cosell rarely left the Sixty-ninth Street apartment. There he felt the presence of the woman he had adored since first seeing her in an army major's office nearly fifty years before. "So many memories of her," he said. In the summer of 1991 doctors had removed a cancerous lump from his chest. Emmy's farewell letters to Hilary and Jill had told them their father had never paid a bill in his life, wouldn't know how to do it, and would wind up on the street if they didn't take care of him. What she could not provide for, though, was the emptiness. He missed her voice. The sight of her. A touch. The assurance that came with knowing she loved him.

Shortly after Cosell's cancer surgery, Bob Lipsyte asked how he felt. Cosell said, "Leave me alone. I just want to die." Because Lipsyte loved the old man, he called again the next day. "I told you, leave me alone," Cosell said. A third day, Lipsyte told Cosell that ABC's new bosses refused to release videotape of Cosell's work for a television documentary. This time Lipsyte heard the Cosellian roar. "That man," Cosell said of the offending executive, "is *DEAD!*"

Lipsyte called me that night with the story. "Just wanted you to know that I brought Howard back to life today."

"Well, he needs enemies, and you provided another," I said.

"That man floats on a river of bile." He said it with a certain warmth, as a nephew might talk about his crazy favorite uncle. "He is terrible."

I had spoken to Cosell often since Emmy's death because, like Lipsyte, I believed he was worth the aggravation. I knew, too, how much he missed his wife. Now, in the summer of his loneliness and illness, he told me he still relied on Emmy's strength. "One more surgery for me," Cosell said, "and then, in the immortal words of George Foreman, 'Good Lord willin' and the creek don't rise,' I'll be fine."

"Did I hear Howard Cosell quoting George Foreman?" I said. "What's this world come to?"

"Clearly, my boy, it is time," Cosell said, alive again, "for you to pray for me."

Radio was Cosell's first love in broadcasting and he stayed faithful to it. For thirty-nine years, he did a daily five-minute show, *Speaking of Sports*. For thirty-five years, he did a weekly half-hour, *Speaking of Everything*. When he retired from radio on January 31, 1992, it was unlikely that any broadcaster anywhere had more air time than Howard William Cosell. The man himself told an audience at the Museum of Television & Radio that he saw no heir who could cover his range of topics with equal intelligence or morality.

Lipsyte loved that remark. "The first time I met Howard Cosell," he wrote in the *Times*, "he hit me with a tape recorder. It was no accident. I was in his way. This was in 1962, at the New York Mets' first spring training. Cosell, desperately swinging his thirty-pound Nagra, whaled his way through a pack of reporters surrounding Manager Casey Stengel. Cosell whacked me on the left flank. He would not have cared if it were my head.

"The welt eventually faded, as did my anger, replaced first by disdain for this storky, nasal, pushy radio hack, and later by admiration for his humor and intelligent doggedness in pursuit of a story, and finally by an enormous appreciation for the most important sports journalist of this century, and one of the most influential electronic voices of our time."

Cosell that week asked the *Chicago Tribune* sports columnist Bob Verdi, "So, Verdi, what are you doing with your life? Are you still writing those little columns nobody reads about those little games that don't matter? Is that what you're doing? Follow that little bouncing ball to eternity?"

"But, Howard," the poor man said, "it's my job."

"Young man," Cosell said, "you know and I know there are jobs, and then there are jobs." As if Cosell himself had not spent a lifetime inviting people into the SportsWorld tent (only to berate them for wasting their time at such foolish entertainments).

"College sports? Boxing? Who cares? I've got too many other things to think about." In six weeks he would be seventy-four years old. He wanted to lecture, teach, write. "I've got to speak to our nation's youth, about education, about what really matters." Still Cosell, still raging, he told Verdi he might also speak "about the inherent perils of sports writing."

Damned if Howard Cosell would go gentle into that good night. "Old age," the poet Dylan Thomas wrote, "should burn and rave at close of day; rage, rage against the dying of the light." The last week of his broadcasting career, Cosell demanded that baseball ban Pete Rose forever, called for a federal investigation of the National Football League, and advocated the abolition of boxing.

Sometime early in 1992, at age seventy-three, weak and tired, Cosell agreed to videotape a birthday message to Ali. Their lives again had moved to parallel tracks, Ali no longer a newsmaker, Cosell no longer a nationally broadcast television star. They met only by happenstance in 1990 when both were invited to a Radio City Music Hall television production, *Night of 100 Stars*. They enjoyed the reunion, Cosell greeting Ali with a hug and hearing the imp whisper in his ear, "Let's go on tour, Cosell. They still love us."

Now Cosell sat in his apartment before a camera for the taping. He had not been seen on television in four years. His voice, once so distinctive, carried faint echoes of its familiar rhythms. The tape would be played March 1, 1992, on the ABC broadcast of "A 50th Birthday Tribute to Muhammad Ali." He said into the camera, to Ali: "It's hard to believe, all the years, everything that's passed between us. It's so hard to believe and so memorable. And now it's time to say to you, Muhammad, God bless you, and happy birthday to you. Fifty years old! I never thought *that* could happen, not to you. But it has, and you are something."

Cosell pressed his lips tight against their tremblings. "You are exactly who you said you are. You never wavered." There was a tear in his voice, and there was a tear in Ali's eye. "You are free to be who you want to be. I love you. Happy birthday."

CHAPTER TWENTY-ONE

"The World's Waiting for Me"

WHATEVER WAS WRONG WITH ALI physically was only part of the darkness that gathered around him in the 1980s. No longer relevant in social and political debates, gone from the sports pages, he had become a relic left over from another age. "Broke on his ass," Harold Conrad said, "and I blame Herbert Muhammad for that." Now people paid him to show up, the way they once hired Joe Louis. It was 1988 when he came to a Mike Tyson fight in Atlantic City, Tyson against Larry Holmes, who came for the cash, a grandfather who thought three million dollars was enough to take a beating from Cus D'Amato's new creation, a kid champ whose game plan was the same every time out: "I want to drive his nose-bone into his brain," said Tyson. They threw Ali a forty-sixth birthday party, even gave him a cake.

The next morning, I was with Ali in his hotel room when he said to writer Budd Schulberg, "Levitate it. You watchin'?" Ali lifted a perfume bottle off a chest of drawers in demonstration of its intended flight path. "Levitate now. You watch." He wiggled the fingers of his right hand at the bottle. Schulberg watched. I watched. It would not be the first miracle we had seen Ali perform. When the bottle stayed put, Ali laughed out loud. "April fool," he said.

Tyson's quick knockout of Holmes didn't impress Ali, who said, "Larry the time he beat me would have beat Tyson."

I said, "You in the seventies, not even at your best, would've beaten Tyson."

Ali asked, "You think Tyson's as good as Joe Louis in his prime?"

"No."

"Rocky Marciano?"

"No."

Ali, more loudly: "Jack Johnson?"

"No."

Louder yet: "And they're saying I'm better than all of them. At last, they're saying I was the greatest of alllll time." He raised high his right arm in triumph.

Four months later, on June 9, 1988, a front-page headline in the *Washington Post* declared: "Ali Still Has a Way With Words." The story began: "At first the pronouncements seem odd coming from Muhammad Ali . . ." Then the writer reminded readers that Ali's speech of recent years had been slurred and slow. "Now he's talking like a machine gun, floating and stinging, jabbing and stabbing, like the Ali of old and about everything that pops into his head from Jesse L. Jackson to Mikhail Gorbachev. . . . The thoughts, the words tumble out faster than a reporter can note them down."

I had no doubt that the *Post* reporter, Nancy Lewis, was the victim of a hoax. She quoted Ali on Jackson: "I like Jesse, but I think his timing's off." On Gorbachev: "If it's all a show, he's a better actor than Ronald Reagan." On himself: "God gave me this physical impairment to remind me that I am not the greatest. He is."

Lewis wrote, "During a rare telephone interview, the champ was in his old form, and he was clearly pleased with himself. 'I bet you're surprised I'm talking this good,' Ali quipped. 'See, I'm not stupid. I'm not brain-damaged. The mind is good. I just sometimes have trouble articulating.'" Ali offered opinions on Virginia's governor and senator, the evolving nature of Strom Thurmond's politics, and the current troubles of Attorney General Edwin Meese III. He called Utah senator Orrin Hatch "a very trustworthy person" and noted that Ted Kennedy "seems real concerned about abuses in the judicial system." As for Meese, he "might have made some errors in judgment. But that doesn't make him a crook. . . . If he's right, I'm in his corner. If he's wrong, he'll have to pay the piper."

Not only had I never heard anything remotely like that from Ali, I had never read anything like that from him. He was neither a political creature nor an introspective thinker. Two elements in the story confirmed my suspicions of deception. Lewis noted the "astonishing contrast" between Ali on the telephone and the Ali she had heard at a congressional ceremony the week before. Second, this paragraph deep in the story rose off the printed page: "Mostly these days, Ali said, he spends his time reading and riding horses with his 'best friend' and lawyer, Richard Hirschfeld."

I soon figured out that someone imitated Ali in hundreds of phone calls to at least fifty-one politicians, Capitol Hill staffers, and journalists—including me. I left a message at Hirschfeld's law office saying I had read the *Post* story. With the Democratic National Convention coming up, I would like to speak to Ali about politics. The next night, "Ali" called me. In twenty-one years, I had mostly listened to Ali monologues. With "Ali," I had a pleasant back-and-forth conversation that lasted forty minutes.

It was a nice imitation, complete with Ali's rhythm, Ali's language, his breathing patterns, all done by someone who knew the minutiae of his life. It was someone doing Ali as that person wanted Ali to be: the voice gone airy and soft but the mind retaining the young Ali's wit and charm. The hoaxer's mistake was in going too far. He was too easy using "fallacious" and "dispossessed," too clever with "a poem" about his political leanings: "I don't wear any particular label/I'll support any man who's honest and able." Near the end of our talk, "Ali" said, "You know the movie *Mr. Smith Goes to Washington?* This is *Mr. Ali Goes to Washington.*"

The real Ali visited seven U.S. senators: Hatch, Thurmond, Kennedy, John Warner, Arlen Specter, Joseph Biden, and Sam Nunn. The visits had two things in common: Ali stood mute, and Richard Hirschfeld did the talking. It turned out that Hirschfeld had two personal issues on the line. He pushed a friend and legal associate for an assistant attorney general's job. He also wanted the senators to press the Justice Department for an investigation of a federal prosecutor in Norfolk, Virginia. Her transgression? She was investigating Hirschfeld on a fraud charge.

But the major objective in *Mr. Ali Goes to Washington* became money. When the Supreme Court overturned Ali's draft case conviction in June 1971, reporters asked if he would file suit for damages. His answer then: *No. They only did what they thought was right at the time.* But in 1984, he did sue for fifty million dollars. Had Ali won the case, his lawyer likely would have been in for 33 percent of all monies. The lawyer was Richard M. Hirschfeld. On September 6, 1988, a federal judge dismissed that lawsuit. The statute of limitations for such filing had passed ten years earlier.

Immediately following the dismissal, Senator Hatch went to work for

Ali and Hirschfeld. He proposed legislation that he called a "concession of error remedy." It would allow a person whose conviction had been overturned by the Supreme Court to seek damages if the government admitted error in the original conviction. In effect, it would be Ali's second chance at the $50-million jackpot. Because Hatch attached the proposal to a drug bill designed for unanimous consent by the Senate, even one senator's objection would kill it. When Hirschfeld learned that Senator Nunn was opposed, he brought Ali to Capitol Hill and met with the senator in a corridor outside his office.

"Tell us what your objections to the bill are," Hirschfeld said.

The senator said, "I really haven't made up my mind yet."

That night, Hirschfeld called Peter Tauber. After Tauber's magazine story, Hirschfeld had discussed with him several literary projects involving Ali. "Peter, do me a favor," Hirschfeld said. "Call Sam Nunn and tell him you're from the *New York Times* doing a story on the Hatch proposal and would he spell out his objections to it."

Tauber became angry. "Richard, what are you talking about? I can't do that. I'd never work in this town again. Goddamn, Richard. That shit gets lawyers disbarred."

Though I did reporting on the "Ali voice" story every day, I could not write anything because I had found no one who could confirm that Ali had not made the telephone calls. Hirschfeld insisted it was Ali. I sat with Ali at a dinner on September 8 and said, "I think Richie's been imitating your voice all year in phone calls to politicians and reporters."

"How's Richie gonna talk like me?" Ali said. "Sounds crazy. Sounds crazy, don't it?" He looked at me and said, "I smell trouble. I'm through talking about it."

I asked if he called the *Washington Post*. He snapped an answer: "As soon as I made the call, they printed it." That was interesting. It showed he knew about the stories. He then began a stream of consciousness ramble by saying he wanted to run for president. "The world needs a president who is sincere and will fulfill his promises. All you need is people to vote for you. People know I won't lie. I fear God too much to lie."

I interrupted him. "Just one political question. Why did you favor the Fair Housing Act and what arguments did you use to change Orrin Hatch's mind?"

Ali had no answer. Instead, he said, "I'm calling somebody else tomorrow about the drug bill and I'm calling somebody on the bums problems in the streets." It was interesting, too, that he intended to call someone about the drug bill, which was the legislation to which Hatch hoped to attach his Ali rider. But on September 21, the Utah senator acknowledged that his Ali rider was "probably dead right now." Four drug bill sponsors opposed it. Sam Nunn called it unfair to people whose convictions were overturned below the Supreme Court. Some senators simply did not like the appearance of a celebrity lobbying for a bill that would enrich him directly and maybe exclusively.

Still, the story could not be written. The story wasn't the bill. The story was the con game. I tracked down Ali. In Las Vegas on November 7, he sat at ringside for a Sugar Ray Leonard fight. I bent down to him and said, "Ali, I've gotta talk to you about politics again."

A twinkle in his eye, he whispered, "You're gonna get your ass sued."

"What?"

"You're gonna get your *ass* sued."

"I just want to get the story right, Ali."

"That little Jewish lawyer's gonna sue your ass."

"Okay. But I gotta ask you again. Did you make those political phone calls?"

"I didn't call 'em. Why would a Black Muslim fuck with politicians? I don't care."

"Did you know the calls were being made?"

He shook his head no.

"No idea?"

Shook his head again.

"Who made the calls?"

He indicated he did not know, and I said, "What about Richie? People have told me he sounds like you."

"Naw. He's white. How could he sound like me?"

"But people have told me . . ."

"I can't see Richie doing it."

I said, "Why did you go to Capitol Hill with him?"

"The senators, Richie said they wanted to see me."

With confirmation from Ali that he had not made the calls, I wrote a story that began, "In an act of political deception . . ." The newspaper's editors, no doubt in compliance with legal advice on the libel laws, would not allow me to identify Hirschfeld as the "Ali voice." I wrote that the evidence pointed to him.

In the Harold Smith scam, Ali seemed to have been guilty only of taking a half-million dollars from a crook without asking questions, without demanding explanations. In contrast, whatever Hirschfeld's game might have been, Ali knew about the calls, knew about the drug bill, and did his bit by accompanying the lawyer to Capitol Hill. He had skated free from the Smith embezzlement scheme, perhaps due to a prosecutor's hero worship. Similarly, he had not been tainted by Hirschfeld's troubles in their earlier business adventures.

But this. Running a con game on the U.S. Senate?

"So you think I'm bad for Muhammad," Hirschfeld said to me.

I said, "Damn right."

Ali was an innocent easily manipulated by the likes of Richard Hirschfeld. Ferdie Pacheco said, "What the fuck does Ali know about politics? You hand him 'policy' to read, he couldn't read it." The fight doctor considered Ali a beloved figure whose charisma and charm had properly earned him universal affection. He also said, "The brutal thing is, he's a simple man who did not develop past a certain point. Ali never talked, as we think of talk. They were monologues. Ali sent, he never received. Nothing but b.s., this deep thought attributed to him. He was an instinctual animal. 'I'm hungry, I'll eat.' He lived on a primary level, like, 'Today is a good day. I'm going to have an ice cream soda. I'm going to get laid. I'm going to drive my Rolls.' As such, he was always vulnerable to unscrupulous people."

Cosell laughed out loud at the idea of Ali discussing legislation. "You know how much I loved Muhammad," he said. "But in the best of times, Ali's attention span was brief. We both know that these are not good times for him."

My stories in the *Atlanta Journal-Constitution* pointed to Hirschfeld as the practitioner of a bold and bizarre hoax. A day after the series concluded, Ali called a press conference on the steps of the U.S. Capitol. He gave to reporters a hand-written statement that included this fabulous sentence: "Richard Hirschfeld, my lawyer, said I should not have this press conference because I will make this Dave Kindred famous, like I did Howard Cosell."

Cosell roared. "Save it for the memoirs," he said.

Hirschfeld was not the only unusual person in Ali's wobbling orbit that year. A newspaper item reported that Ali underwent medical treatment at Hilton Head, South Carolina. Ali's search for cures for his physical impairments had led him to Rajko Medenica, a Yugoslavian expatriate. The doctor told me that Ali "absolutely does not have brain damage," nor did he have Parkinson's disease. "He is having a metabolic, immunological, neurological disorder from the pesticides, which we will treat. Ali will improve very well. He's very active now, he doesn't have any problems except tiredness and slurred speech. I think he will be recovering completely." Medenica said he was certain of his diagnosis of pesticide poisoning because he had reviewed films of sixteen Ali fights and came away with this finding: "Ali seldom was blow in the head."

"With all due respect, sir," I said, "Muhammad took terrible beatings."

"This I never see," said Medenica.

In any case, he added, the brain is remarkably resistant to injury.

Oh, my.

The doctor ordered a procedure called plasmapheresis in which a patient's blood is removed and cleansed before it is returned. Ali said three technicians attended him for the treatment, which he described to me: "Doctor cleansed my blood. Five hours. Took it through a machine. Took it out of one arm into the machine. Cleans dirt out of it, and it comes back around in the other arm. Clean now. They found pesticides. They got five sacks of dirty blood. I had a tendency of staying tired. That don't happen no more."

As Ali spoke, he lay in a hotel bed and raised his arms. "Don't have Parkinson's," he said. "If I got Parkinson's, can't do this." He held his arms steady. "Shake if I got Parkinson's."

I said, "It must be encouraging now. The doctor says you'll be completely recovered."

Ali's eyes were closed. "What they all say."

Shortly after my trip to Hilton Head, I asked Floyd Patterson what he thought of Dr. Medenica's diagnosis.

"No brain damage? Pesticides?" said Patterson, Ali's old rival, then the chairman of the New York State Athletic Commission. "Next you'll be hearing he was bit by a cockroach. I wasn't born yesterday. Of all the heavyweights ever, he was the best at taking a punch. And he took shots for a long time. When he lost his legs, he lost his defense. He's been hit in the ring for twenty years, my God. The brain slaps up against the skull and it causes scar tissue. That scar tissue makes your brain not work. Common sense tells you it's obvious what's wrong."

While Peter Tauber came to his *New York Times* story intending to reshape perception of Ali, I had no such ambition with my Hirschfeld story. If it chased away the little lawyer, good. Similarly, if the Medenica story caused the Alis to rethink medical treatment, good. But for all I knew there were a hundred Hirschfelds and Medenicas whispering in Ali's ear. At the same time, Lonnie Ali inserted herself into the financial mess of her husband's life. In October 1988, she moved against Herbert Muhammad. She created a book proposal in competition with a Herbert/Hirschfeld plan. She asked the William Morris Agency in New York to find an author for a definitive biography of Ali.

The agency represented a writer of Ali's generation who had done distinguished books on boxing, politics, and race relations. The writer had also been a Wall Street lawyer. His name was Thomas Hauser.

Not that Ali should remember, but in 1967, just before the Zora Folley fight, the same Hauser had interviewed him for the Columbia University radio station.

Now, in 1988, Hauser proposed that he write an oral history with Ali's cooperation in providing access to interview subjects, medical records, and legal documents. Before committing to the project, however, Hauser wanted to satisfy himself that Ali was healthy enough to make a contribution. A meeting with Ali settled that issue as well as a more personal one. He wasn't certain he could be in Ali's presence and do the work well. "Other than John F. Kennedy, who was my boyhood hero," Hauser later wrote, "I don't think there's a person on the planet who would have affected me in that manner."

On the second morning of a visit to the Michigan farm, Hauser saw Ali at the breakfast table finishing cereal and toast. Ali looked up and asked, "Do you want cornflakes or granola?" Not an icon. Just another man having breakfast. At that moment, Hauser decided to do the book.

Lonnie Ali used Tauber's piece to encourage her husband to be a public figure. Mine gave her reason to reconsider Ali's ties to Hirschfeld and the con man's angel, Herbert Muhammad. Hauser's book, *Muhammad Ali: His Life and Times*, appeared on best-seller lists in 1991 and put Ali in the national news for the first time in a decade. Like Tauber, Hauser presented a moving, human portrait of Ali. Despite his "physical difficulties," Hauser wrote, Ali "is healthier, happier, more alert, and more content than most people realize. He enjoys his life; he believes he's doing God's work, and he's as satisfied with each day as anybody I know."

The book told Ali's story in reportage never before done. It presented the simple truths that Ali's autobiography of 1975 evaded and that most Ali books ignored in favor of literary imaginings. As a partner in the oral-history project, Ali spoke to Hauser and asked friends, business associates, and doctors to speak freely. Hauser tracked down men presumed dead and from them extracted keys to understanding both Ali the myth and the man.

Cosell's opinion of Ali's physical and mental conditions was so extreme that he first refused to do an interview with Hauser, who then wrote a second request dated January 18, 1989:

> Dear Mr. Cosell,
> Muhammad Ali suffers from a cavum septum pellucidum and scarring of the basal ganglia. As a result of this condition, he has difficulty speaking. He is not, as you put it, "a vegetable." If you took the time to sit and talk with him at length, as I have over the past few months, you'd find that he thinks clearly and has the same emotions as other people. Instead of hiding, he's struggling to overcome his impediment, and he deserves the same respect as anyone also battling the effects of a physical handicap.
> Muhammad has been horribly exploited by countless people. I am not one of them. I'm a responsible author trying to write what I consider to be an important book. Because of the role you played in Muhammad's life, and because over the years you've embodied the best in broadcast journalism, I'd like very much to include your views in the oral history I'm writing."

The "best in broadcast journalism" could not allow himself to be left out of Ali's story, and there followed an interview session with Hauser the likes of which the author had never experienced. Early one afternoon in his apartment, Cosell sat on a sofa. He placed Hauser on a nearby chair and began talking, only to fall asleep, rouse himself, fall asleep again, and wake to announce he would take a short nap.

"Here, read this," Cosell said, stretching out on the sofa and handling Hauser a small book written by former New York mayor Ed Koch. Hauser appraised his position at the head of the couch and thought, *Psychiatrist and patient!* Twenty-five minutes later, Cosell came awake talking. "I love that kid." He meant Ali. "I used to dream about him all the time. And I still do." Then he began singing, low and soft, the lyrics to "A Foggy Day in London Town." Somehow, the man on the sofa transported himself on a stream of consciousness trip to August 1966, to England, for Ali's fight against British contender Brian London. "Flying up to Blackpool. London. Not there. At his training camp. Going to London's home. We flew out of Gatwick in the ABC News plane. His wife, a big-titted woman with a great body. 'Where's Brian?' 'He's playing squash.'" Cosell, eyes closed, laughed.

"Off we go to Whitney Air Force Base. Off we go. This is the base where they shot *Twelve O'Clock High*. Remember that movie? One of the great motion pictures of World War II. Gregory Peck. Gary Merrill. The son of a bitch was playing squash. And he was a better squash player than he was a fighter. I'll tell you that. Believe me.

"So they bring London over, and I say to him, 'Everybody says you don't have a chance, that you're no fighter at all.' He says, 'I'm gonna kill you.' I say, 'It's not me saying it, it's the goddamn newspaper people.' He says, 'I'll kill those sons of bitches.'"

At last, Cosell left London to deliver an oration on the injustice of Ali's title being taken from him by the dictate of a political hack who ignored the Fourteenth Amendment to the Constitution of the United States. Then he returned to his nap.

When Hauser finished the manuscript, which came to more than one thousand pages, he read it aloud to Ali, Lonnie, and Howard Bingham, a longtime friend of Ali's. Eight hours a day. Witness after witness to Ali's life. Voices from his past explaining his past. Voices as disparate as those of presidents and movie stars, con men and sportswriters. Hauser read it all to Ali. At the end, the writer thought, *Now he has a feel for his place in history. He understands that he didn't just reflect the times in which he lived, he helped shape them.*

In June 1991, promoting the book, Ali accompanied a busload of sportswriters to his old Deer Lake training camp. Two hours out of New York City on Pennsylvania's State Route 61, we heard Bingham call from the front of the bus. Bingham was a newspaper photographer when he met Ali on an assignment thirty years earlier. He became Ali's confidant and traveling companion, his camera the repository of Ali's history. He had been on this Deer Lake road a hundred times. "Ali," he said, "we're going up the hill."

Up the hill.

A half-mile up Sculpshill Road.

How many times had Ali finished the morning's roadwork up that hill?

Ali turned to look out a window and almost smiled, as if in memory of the roadwork done as Ali Triumphant. Later, the pear-shaped Michael Katz of the *New York Daily News* huffed and puffed to the crest of the hill and told Ali, "That hill has gotten a lot bigger since '78."

Ali said, "So have you."

An old opponent came along. In retirement, Earnie Shavers had become a minister. He said he had always loved Ali. "Now your heart has to go out to him. He's a shell of the man he used to be. I feel sorry for him. You almost ask, 'Why Ali? Why not somebody who deserved it?' Not that anybody is deserving of it. But Ali doesn't resent it or regret anything. He says if it's Allah's will, so be it."

In the camp kitchen where he ate before the fights against Foreman and Frazier and Norton and Holmes, Ali said boxing had been a way to get famous. Now the real work would begin. He wanted to raise one hundred million dollars for charity. He would build a mosque on the mountaintop. He would become a preacher preaching to more people than all the other preachers put together.

"Muhammad Ali's just getting started," he said. "The world's waiting for me."

CHAPTER TWENTY-TWO

"You Stood Up and Told the Truth"

IN THE DAYS AFTER Emmy's death, I often spoke to Cosell by phone. But it had been four years since he hectored dear Michelle for the day's sports news. I wanted to see him at home again, maybe, I thought, for a last time. "I'm still battling," he said. He sounded weak, defeated. He told someone, "Dave Kindred, an old friend, is in town. Wants to come up. Wants to know if anything's on." Another voice said, "No, Mr. C, nothing's doing."

When I arrived, an Irish woman named Cecilia Bonner, Cosell's twenty-four-hour nurse, asked me to come to the telephone. Cosell's younger daughter, Hilary, said, "I'm uncomfortable talking to you, because of what I have to say. Howard, you may know, has had several strokes affecting his left side and is not good at conversation. For a man with a photographic memory now not to be able to remember things is terrible."

I assured her I was there only to pay my respects. She asked that I not stay too long. "Howard gets tired easily," she said. The apartment was as I remembered it. Neat and well appointed, with four paintings: of pastel flowers, a snowy New York street scene, a Westhampton movie house, and three lemons on a butcher block. On a table were photographs of Emmy and the extended Cosell family. Frail, moving slowly, Howard wore a brown cardigan sweater over a white shirt and a tie painted with the names of his five grandchildren. His left hand trembled as he drank an orange soda. He smoked a cigar. Occasionally he broke into song.

It was December 14, 1992. He sang, "It's beginning to look a lot like Christmas," to which the Irish nurse said, "Mr. C, he would like to be Frank Sinatra." For no apparent reason, he once interrupted my conversation with the nurse by exclaiming, "What are we all about?" Repeatedly, he said, "Oh, dear God," removed his glasses and rubbed his face. Though he must have asked me five times, he asked again, "What did Hilary say to you?" Each time I said she had only wanted to say hello.

"I don't go out anymore, except to the doctor's," he said. "Hilary and Jill want me to stay here." I left after a half-hour. At the door, telling me good-bye, Cosell said, "I'm not sure if I'll leave this apartment alive." He had suffered a series of small strokes, the damage no doubt exacerbated by years of drinking. He had been diagnosed with multi-infarct dementia. "Holes in his brain," as Jill put it. No one could know when the dementia first presented itself in Cosell's life, but doctors told Jill that it might have affected his judgment for ten years. It might have accounted for the bitterness and vitriol that colored his later life. A psychiatrist had prescribed anger-control medication. At age seventy-four he "had trouble finding words," Jill said. "And this was a man never at a loss for words. Try that one on for size." As Ali and Cosell had climbed to greatness together, now they were together in decline. Ali's movement spoke of beauty no longer, and Cosell's ideas no longer shaped his world.

The television broadcaster Bryant Gumbel often came by. Before moving to the morning news-and-talk shows, Gumbel had been a sports broadcaster whose style and philosophy were influenced by Cosell's. Whatever money had come to Gumbel, whatever celebrity accrued to his work and that of sports broadcasters everywhere, he insisted that three-quarters of it belonged to Cosell. The old man and his protégé played chess in the quiet apartment. The young Howard Cohen, as his yearbook noted, had been a member of the Chess Club at Brooklyn's Alexander Hamilton High School. With Gumbel, the chess board served mostly as a gathering spot for small talk of the smallest kind.

Gumbel thought, *This is a man waiting to die.* Cosell would dismiss attempts at real conversation. *If I ask about Ali, he'd be offended, like, "That's all I'm about? All I am is Ali? Why do you look at me and see Ali, ask about Ali?"* Gumbel visited as an act of kindness to a man he admired. *I don't want to say anything that sets off huge fireworks.*

Sports Illustrated's Frank Deford sought to take Cosell out, an invitation that thrilled the old man. "Frank Deford's here, and he wants to go to lunch with me," Cosell said to Hilary on the phone. Then, disappointed, he told Deford, "We're going to stay here." Deford realized the daughter's instincts were correct, that her father could not function in public.

Cosell greeted Deford with affection and delight, then placed himself in front of a television set. He popped olives into his mouth, now and then averting his gaze from *I Dream of Jeannie* to say, "I have to put up with this crap all day." Deford thought, *My grandfather.* His grandfather had been a banker, a brilliant man who suffered a stroke, and Deford remembered his mother saying, "Oh, God, if he'd only died."

Now all the fun that had made Cosell tolerable, the idea that there was humor at play in everything Cosell said—that was gone from him. Deford decided it made no sense to visit again. He did see a moment of sweetness when Cosell shuffled to a bookshelf and with his long, frail fingers picked up a piece of statuary. Deford thought the piece might be African. He knew only that Cosell handled it with extraordinary affection and said, "Muhammad Ali gave me this, Frank." And said it again, "Muhammad Ali gave me this himself. Isn't that magnificent?" For a moment, Deford saw a glimmer of the old glory in Cosell.

On Cosell's seventy-fifth birthday, March 20, 1993, Lipsyte came by the apartment in time to hear the phone ring and Cosell answer, "Hello. . . . I don't know you. . . . No. Thank you. . . . Good-bye."

"Who was that?" Lipsyte asked.

"A guy who wanted a favor."

"What kind of favor?"

"Be on his air."

Cecilia Bonner chimed in. "Someone wanted you on his radio show, and you were rude, Mr. C." Mr. C grinned and closed his eyes.

When he opened them, he saw the painting of three lemons on a butcher block. "I love to look at it, my favorite painting," he said. "Reggie called me."

Reggie Jackson had invited Cosell to a party. Lipsyte judged the curl of Cosell's lips to be a sneer, the judgment confirmed by a trace of once-familiar disdain in the voice. "He's giving a party in honor of himself."

"Are you going?"

"I'm a prisoner here."

Cancer, congestive heart failure, kidney disease, diabetes, those little strokes that added up so big—he was in decline, and he looked past Lipsyte to the three lemons and said, "Sooner or later, sooner or later."

"C'mon, you're only seventy-five," Lipsyte said. "People run marathons at seventy-five. You'll be back on the air driving people nuts again."

Cosell laughed. "Frankly, I don't give a damn." He coughed and said, "That's what seventy-five is." He pointed to the painting.

"Seventy-five is lemons?"

Mr. C nodded and closed his eyes.

Lipsyte had brought Cosell a teddy bear in a baseball uniform. Leaving now, he gave the old man the toy and, in case he never saw him again, a kiss on the cheek.

In that winter of his seventy-fifth year, Cosell achieved the ultimate honor in his business. He became the first sports broadcaster elected to the Academy of Television Arts & Sciences Hall of Fame. He joined the medium's greatest talents, among them Lucille Ball, Milton Berle, Bob Hope, Jack Benny, Johnny Carson, and, more important to him, the newsmen Walter Cronkite, Edward R. Murrow, Eric Sevareid, John Chancellor, Chet Huntley, David Brinkley, and his old boss Roone Arledge. There they were, as Jimmy Roberts had heard so often: *The three C's of television: Cronkite, Carson, and Cosell.*

It was a bittersweet moment for Jill Cosell. The awards ceremony honored her father when he was unable to leave his apartment. She thought, *Why couldn't you have done this when my parents were both here?* She sat at a table with Ali, there to receive the Hall of Fame trophy for his old friend, and Jill found no pleasure in Ali's company, either. His words were unintelligible. Jill's daughter wept as she cut his food for him, and Ali could not rise to accept the trophy.

It was the spring of 1995. A fall in his apartment, a broken hip, and surgery to replace the hip put Cosell in the Hospital for Joint Diseases. He was frail and weak, a skeletal figure at one hundred twenty pounds. He moved in and out of consciousness. There were moments when he recognized friends and family, moments when he spoke to them. One night, feeling stronger, he sat up in bed. He watched a Rangers hockey game with his grandsons, Justin and Colin, who loved the old man they called "Poppa." When the boys said they were leaving for pizza, he said, "Guys, take me with you."

Andy Robustelli prayed over him. The great old football star was Cosell's dearest friend, a neighbor in Connecticut who had known him for forty years and more, first in Robustelli's days as a Giants player and later as the team's general manager. Jill Cosell wept when she saw the big man lean over her father's bed and say, "Don't try to talk, Howard. I'm here. I'll do the praying."

Robustelli asked Cosell if he wanted Cardinal John O'Connor to come to him. Howard had done so many eulogies at St. Patrick's Cathedral that he and the cardinal became friends. Howard and Emmy had visited the cardinal's quarters for dinner. It was indicative of Howard's life-long ambivalence about religion that the Jewish man nodded yes to Robustelli. That night the Catholic priest prayed with Cosell.

Cosell died there April 23, 1995. He was seventy-seven years old. Later, Justin Cosell said, "I was twenty-one when Gam died, and twenty-five when Poppa died. My parents were divorced when I was eleven, and the 'children of divorce' are said to have a hard time. My brother, Jared, and I looked at each other and I said, 'Did you ever feel that?' Neither of us did. Look, I worshiped Poppa and Gam. I talked to them every day. They were unbelievable, and my life has never been the same. The whole world looks a hue darker. It's so hard to imagine life without Poppa the king, without Gam in her chair with a book and a cigarette."

Though Jewish theology does not permit cremation, Cosell's will ordered it. The ashes were buried in Westhampton Beach Cemetery alongside the remains of his wife. On their shared gravestone was engraved an echo of Cosell's eulogy on the death of Emmy: "We thank whatever gods may be for your unconquerable souls." Obituaries, appreciations, and tributes portrayed Cosell as a brilliant journalist and television performer. Frank Deford, in a National Public Radio commentary, called him "the most significant sports journalist of this century." "He's a seminal figure not only in sports, but in all of television," said Dick Ebersol, the NBC Sports president who as a young man did legwork for Cosell. Roone Arledge said, "His greatest contribution was elevating sports reporting out of daily play-by-play and placing it in the larger context of society."

The coincidence of Cosell's death in the same week as that of the movies' glamorous dance queen Ginger Rogers led CBS television broadcaster Charles Osgood to report, "They both were dancers, in a way. Cosell, the sportscaster, danced around convention. His staccato, polysyllabic, deadpan New Yorkese was the opposite of what we had been taught to expect. Not the ordinary sportscaster's boyish rah-rah, but deep analysis, grave and considered, with maybe more than a little mockery thrown in of his subjects and of himself. He enjoyed being the man so many people would love to hate because he'd 'tell it like it is.'"

The Providence, Rhode Island, *Journal-Bulletin*'s editorial page editor, Robert Whitcomb, knew Cosell through a friendship with Hilary Cosell. Charmed by the broadcaster's "capacious memory, courtly manner, social insecurities, and desire to be completely honest," Whitcomb wrote that Cosell "was a throwback. He had a fierce, if sometimes obnoxious, respect for truth (at least as he saw it) and a quaint sense of honor. And, paradoxically, his oft-parodied use of windy words was generally directed against cant. Even the pomposity was something of a parody of pomposity (he well knew how pompous he could appear) that recalled W. C. Fields. In his personal life, Mr. Cosell was, of all things, something of a Victorian—intolerant of sleazy behavior, true to his word, immensely loyal and generous to family, friends and good causes, intensely hardworking, learned and public-spirited. (Of course, also arrogant and boorish on occasion) . . . I always saw him as a larger-than-life character out of an Anthony Trollope novel; and he was one of the few people in his trade that I could imagine reading that Victorian's works."

Muhammad Ali, Joe Frazier, and Floyd Patterson came to a memorial service for Cosell at Manhattan's Church of St. Paul and St. Andrew. Also in the pews were New York mayors Rudolph Giuliani, Ed Koch, and David Dinkins beside the network news anchors Peter Jennings, Tom Brokaw, and Dan Rather. The service was led by a rabbi and by a priest representing Cardinal O'Connor. Jackie Robinson's widow, Rachel, spoke of Cosell's "grace disguised by bluster." Grandchildren remembered "Poppa" and his fondness for Mallomars. Another maverick from Brooklyn, the pro football team owner Al Davis, told of Cosell visiting his wife in a hospital: "He walked into the room as if he had been sent as a messenger from God to deliver her a miracle. He turned around to three doctors and a neurologist and said, 'I hope you are doing everything possible to get this girl well. The whole world is watching.'" Immediately, the doctors "snapped to attention," Davis said, and soon enough his wife recovered. A smile here. "But don't think Howard didn't take credit."

In her eulogy, Jill Cosell said her father was "complex, but not complicated," a beloved father, husband, and grandfather who believed "in all the clichés: in God, country, family, fidelity, and very hard work. In truth and justice. In honesty and integrity. And he was rewarded for those beliefs beyond hope or expectation. His code was simple: tell the truth, people will listen. Tell the truth, you can effect change. Tell the truth, you can make the world a more decent and just place.

"No, he wasn't very complicated, and not one of us, not Emmy nor Jill, nor Hilary, and not Dad himself, ever understood what all the damned fuss was about. It was simple. You stood up and told the truth. You stood up and you were counted. And you remembered always that what is popular is not always right, and what is right is not always popular."

She asked her father's friends in the church to remember a song he loved, Bob Dylan's lyrics that he had delivered with passion at a moment of Ali's transcendence, and she recited it one more time for her Daddy . . .

> *May your hands always be busy,*
> *May your feet always be swift,*
> *May you have a strong foundation*
> *When the winds of changes shift.*
> *May your heart always be joyful,*
> *May your song always be sung,*
> *May you stay forever young,*
> *Forever young, forever young,*
> *May you stay forever young.*

She took a seat next to Ali. He touched a finger to his face to tell Jill he had cried. He patted her hand and in that airy voice of his declining years said, "That was good."

PART FIVE

Rising

TWENTY-THREE

"He's America's Only Living Saint"

BY THE SUMMER OF HIS fifty-fourth year, Ali had lived a dozen men's lives. A world champion at twenty-two . . . back from political exile . . . rescued from prison by the Supreme Court . . . his not-a-quarrel with the Viet Cong transformed by time from petulant whine to principled act of defiance . . . a Muslim who gained forgiveness for his Nation of Islam racist ravings . . . the greatest athlete of the twentieth century, three times the heavyweight champion . . . survivor of three marriages . . . adjudged an innocent in assorted money-grubbing adventures alongside bad guys . . . lost in a black hole of depression in the 1980s . . . and still one of Earth's most famous people when they asked him, in that summer of 1996, to light the flame opening the Olympic Games in Atlanta, Georgia.

No, he said.

"Parkinson's," he said.

Once he was all silk and all steel. Now he lived in a reduced state of being. Once he demanded to be seen. Now he sought shadow.

"Ali, this is a big, big thing," said his friend, Howard Bingham, the man trusted to make the request. "It's a big honor."

"Parkinson's."

Bingham knew his man did not want to be seen with his arms trembling, his feet shuffling. He said, "This is the thing where the world is saying, 'Thank you for all that you've done over your life.'"

"Big?" Ali said.

"*Big,*" Bingham said.

As old married folks use code words to shorten conversations, Ali and Bingham did not need Cosellian polysyllabic superlatives to define moments. To declare a moment *big* was to declare it a must-do.

Bingham closed the deal. "There will be three billion people watching," he said.

"Billion?" Ali said.

"BIG."

Ali's agreement was the conclusion of a secret, aggressive campaign by Dick Ebersol, the president of NBC Sports, whose network in 1995 paid $3.55 billion to the International Olympic Committee for rights to every Olympics, summer and winter, through 2008. Without Ebersol's insistence, the Atlanta Committee for the Olympic Games would have had nothing to do with Ali. ACOG chairman Billy Payne's conviction was long-standing: "As a nineteen-year-old freshman at the University of Georgia who considered himself a patriot, I had considered Ali a draft-dodger." Payne liked Henry Aaron, the Atlanta baseball legend, and fighter Evander Holyfield, a hometown hero and Olympic bronze medalist who became heavyweight champion. The chairman preferred either one to a man whose baggage included but was not limited to a claim that he threw his 1960 Olympic gold medal into the Ohio River in protest against a Louisville restaurant's refusal to serve him. (The collaborator on his autobiography invented the fiction to dramatize Louisville racism. If the medal went missing, chances are it went missing in Bundini's pocket.)

Ebersol's choice of Ali had its beginning in his own passion for the Games, beginning with his work for Roone Arledge on the 1968 Mexico City Olympics. He also had come of age professionally in the early days of the Ali and Cosell act. For Ebersol, the choice of Ali was obvious. It worked in every way from history to theater to NBC's financial stake in driving up ratings for the Games. He just had to give Payne reason to change his mind. Ebersol chose the velvet glove/iron fist approach. He sent to Atlanta a package of tapes, books, and readings. The material identified Ali as an Olympic champion, the twentieth century's greatest athlete, an international diplomat without portfolio, and the most recognizable person on Earth. Unsaid but hardly unnoticed, the package also reminded the ACOG chairman that NBC expected the deference due to Atlanta's indispensable financial angel.

When Payne reluctantly agreed that Ali was the man, the question remained: Could Ali, weakened by his injuries, physically hold the torch that would light the Olympic flame? Under secrecy so secure that not even Lonnie Ali was told of the decision, Bingham flew to Atlanta for a walk-through of what Ali would be asked to do. He decided, "Piece of cake." However, when Ali came to Atlanta for a rehearsal, his tremors were such that he dropped the torch. Payne created a backup plan. The swimmer Janet Evans would be the last runner, handing the torch to Ali; if she saw Ali having trouble, she was to help him.

Came the night of July 19, 1996. Nearly eighty thousand people gathered in Atlanta's Olympic Stadium. Hundreds of millions watched on television. Evans ran up a long flight of stairs carrying a torch that she would touch to another held by . . .

There was no one there . . . until . . .

A spectral figure, wearing the torchbearers' whites, came into view.

Ali.

On a platform near the stadium's rim Evans touched her torch to Ali's, and he moved slowly, stiffly, raising his burning torch high. There arose in the stadium, from the assembled thousands, a waterfall's roar of delight. In Las Vegas, Ali's daughter May May thought, *This is so cool! Don't drop it, please don't drop that torch!* In New York, Jack Newfield wept. Tom Callahan: "For a horrible second, I thought he might light himself." Budd Schulberg: "I couldn't help thinking of the quick-moving, marvelous athlete that he was, and to see him like that . . ." Ed Schuyler: "The saddest thing I ever saw. Those pricks from TV made him into a dancing bear. Jesus." Edwin Pope: "His arm, it was just ratcheting. I was overcome by sadness that in what should have been a moment of exaltation for Ali and the world, instead we saw the deterioration of a man who once was a great symbol of hope for an entire race." George Plimpton: "My God! That white shimmering figure. The hand trembling. Ali, again! It was just wonderful." In that Atlanta night, with fire in his hand, Ali became more than a relic of the 1960s. David Israel, a sportswriter who had moved into television production, said, "He's America's only living saint."

Ali lowered his torch to ignite an apparatus that, once on fire, would slide up a cable to light the flame in the giant Olympic caldron. But the thing refused to light. Flames danced back over Ali's wrist. For twenty seconds, maybe thirty, Ali held his torch down with no result. Clearly, something wasn't working. But, finally, the device caught fire and whooshed up the cable and the Olympic flame burst out of the caldron. Ali turned to the crowd, holding high his torch.

The symbolism was exquisite, Ali's resurrection in a city risen from the ashes of the Civil War, home to Martin Luther King, Jr. That night in the Olympic stadium the multitude saw a videotape of King's "I Have a Dream" speech and heard the Baptist preacher's rolling thunder of a voice demand, "From every mountainside, let freedom ring." He cried out for a world in which the content of a person's character mattered more than the color of his skin. When King's voice fell quiet, there against the night sky stood Muhammad Ali, tragic and triumphant. An hour later, Ali was taken to a private meeting place under the stadium because the president of the United States had asked to see him. Bill Clinton put his hands on Ali's shoulders and said, "They didn't tell me who would light the flame. But when I saw it was you, I cried."

Standing before the world weakened, he became beloved. There was a feeling that somehow we, the American public, angered by his long-ago affiliation with the Black Muslims and his denunciations against white devils, had been the cause of his affliction. We punished him for opposing a war that we all came to see as a needless waste of life. We asked him to entertain us the only way he could, by fighting, a bestial sport with appalling consequences there to be seen at the rim of the Olympic stadium. Naturally, and perhaps especially with Ali, we could not react to our guilt with anything resembling moderation, and so we poured the holy waters of sainthood over the fallen warrior. As a result, there came the fear, expressed by the scholar Gerald Early, that Ali "may become absolutely overesteemed by the society in which he lives. This would put him in danger not only of having his considerable significance misunderstood, but also, ironically, of being diminished as both a public figure and a black man of some illustrious complexity." Not a saint, not a martyr, not a thinker—Early saw none of that in Ali—but an extraordinary combination of "talent, showmanship, and a genius conceit of himself." Like all great heroes, Early wrote, Ali "showed us the enormous possibility of the true meaning, the incendiary poetics, of actual self-determination."

Jerry Izenberg, Bingham, and I joined Ali in his hotel room the next morning. Ali's torch leaned against a wall. Sleepless and exhausted, Ali lay flat on a bed, a pillow under his head. To hear his mumbled, slurred answers, I sat on the bed. Ali's body trembled from his shoulders to his feet. My corner of the bed shuddered like a boat on rippling water.

"It wouldn't catch," Ali said of the device to be ignited. "I looked around." But no one could help. "Then I puffed on it." He pantomimed an exhalation. "The whole world is watching." Now laughing, his eyes a scamp's. "Three billion people, and I look like a fool." He felt the fire's heat against his wrist until, finally, it caught. *"Whoosh."*

Those answers came in the course of an hour, elicited with the help of Bingham, who translated Ali's mumblings. Meanwhile, Ali engaged Izenberg and me in his theological exercise of "contradictions." He gave us each a Bible. Then he brought out a yellow legal pad with columns of Bible verses noted in his penciled printing. He held the pad toward me and pointed to a verse, then to my Bible. Bingham said, "He wants you to read that verse."

I read, " 'And Joab gave up the sum of the number of the people unto the king: and there were in Israel eight hundred thousand valiant men that drew the sword; and the men of Judah five hundred thousand men.'"

"Now, you, Jerry," Bingham said. Izenberg read his verse: " 'And Joab gave the sum of the number of the people unto David. And all Israel were a thousand thousand and an hundred thousand men that drew sword; and Judah four hundred three score and ten thousand men that drew sword.'"

"See," Bingham said. "Ali says there are thirty thousand contradictions in the Bible. He says how can it be the word of God if there are contradictions?" When Ali asked for another verse, I read, " 'Jehoiachin was eighteen years old when he began to reign . . .'"

He turned to Izenberg. "You."

" 'Jehoiachin was eight years old when he began to reign . . .'"

"Powerful," Ali said.

Ali's literal reading of the Bible and Qur'an led him to that moment's curious tableau. His vision of hell always had been vivid. He once told his friend and agent Larry Kolb that an angel watches each of us every day and if the angel gives us more good marks than bad, we go to Paradise. "If we've got more bad marks," Ali said, "we go to Hell." He described hell for Kolb: "Mash your hand down in a fryin pan. Feel your skin sizzlin' and burning'. Now hold your hand there and multiply that times a thousand, and that's Hell. For eternity! Can you imagine that? I've done a lotta bad things. Worldly things. Gotta keep doing good now. I wanna go to Paradise."

Thomas Hauser found Ali "very fearful when it comes to religion" and said Ali so often did Herbert Muhammad's exploitative biddings "because Herbert threatens him with going to hell if he does something that violates the tenets of Islam." When I asked Hauser what the Qur'an said about hell, he reached for the book and read aloud: " 'Hell is a burning fire. Those who reject our signs, we shall cast unto the fire. As often as their skins are roasted through, we shall change them for fresh skins, that they may taste the penalty, for God is exalted and power wise.' "

The next year, Ali spoke of hell with an ESPN television reporter who asked what his faith meant to him. "Islam is like the Christian faith," Ali said. "We're going to die one day and wake up for resurrection. God will judge us by our actions. So what I do is I carry a box of matches with me, and if I see a pretty girl or something that I'll do wrong, or whatever it is that's against God, I take the match, and, oooooh . . ." He gestured as if burning a finger. "Hell's like this. Hell's hotter, hell's hotter. It reminds me that I'm judged one day, so I carry fire with me and when I think something's wrong, I stick fire to myself and that makes me straighten up."

Jimmy Swaggart might have argued to Ali that Christian scholars believe the Bible is not the direct word of God but the divinely inspired work of forty authors over fifteen hundred years with inevitable variations in copying, translation, and cultures. Biblical scholars also remind Muslims that the Qur'an—accepted by Islam as the literal message dictated by Allah—cites the Bible as a historical source. As for God's judgment, another preacher might have argued that redemption is a matter of His unconditional grace, not a man's acts.

I just wanted a quotation for my column. So, another torch question. "What did the night mean to you?"

"An honor," Ali said.

"In what way?"

"Mankind coming together. Martin Luther King's home. Muslims seeing me with the torch."

My hero Red Smith always closed his notebook when he had enough grist for the day's typing. He would say, "I'm rich." Once again, Ali had left me rich and bewildered.

At a formal dinner in July 2003, Ali wore a tuxedo and that trimmed mustache which he believed lent a certain elegance to his famous face. I whispered, "Hello, Dark Gable." It was his line, thirty years old, and he looked up with a smile to see what fool remembered it in the twenty-first century. The occasion was an American Civil Liberties Union banquet an-

nouncing the first Muhammad Ali Champion of Liberty prize. To entertain folks at his table, Ali did his disappearing-handkerchief trick. While
he showed how the trick was done—the mechanics involved a fake
thumb from a child's magician kit—I asked Lonnie if I could come visit
them in Michigan.

"Sure, what's up?" she said.

"I just need to talk about how Muhammad has become this saint
figure."

Lonnie laughed. "A saint? No, no. We know better than *that*, don't
we?" But, yes, come to the farm. "Share the humidity." She laughed
again. "But sainthood? I don't think so."

In August, I was in Ali's office when I heard his voice behind me. "My
man," he said. He looked good in blue jeans and a pink golf shirt, both
loose-fitting. The famous face was still decorated with the Dark Gable
mustache. Ordered off sweets and onto new medicines, he had lost forty-
six pounds, down to 222.

"Your fightin' weight," I said.

"I'm coming back," he said. "I want Lennox Lewis."

I came to talk about Cosell and a hundred things, but understood that
we probably would not. It had been fifteen years since Ali had done sub-
stantive interviews, those for Thomas Hauser's oral history. When I
mentioned my work on a dual biography pairing him with Cosell, he
said, "Howard, my buddy." Nothing more. He moved behind his desk
and, with a Sharpie in hand, he slid a two-foot square of clear plastic onto
the desktop. He drew a boxing ring and two stick figures, one labeled
FRAZIER, the other ALI. He tapped the Sharpie against the plastic. Tap,
tap, tap. Dozens of black dots grew into hundreds. He kept tapping. I
asked about the dots.

"People," he said. "Watchin'."

Tap, tap, tap, tap.

The office secretary, Kim Vidt, told me that charities auctioned off
Ali's tappings, some for hundreds of dollars.

Tap, tap, tap.

"Ask his wife," Ali said.

It took me a second to understand that those words were part of a familiar Ali-Cosell routine, Howard saying, "Muhammad, you're not the
man you used to be," and Ali responding, "Howard, I'm going to ask your
wife if you're the man you used to be."

Tap, tap.

He next brought out a sheet of drawing paper and from a box of colored pencils chose an orange to draw two steep lines converging at the center.

Kim noticed. "Good, Muhammad. The cliffs and boat."

For most of an hour, head down, never speaking, Ali made a drawing that showed a boat on deep blue water passing between two high cliffs, one with an orange lighthouse on top. He drew a plane in the sky. A long time before, in a Houston courtroom on the day of his conviction for refusing the draft, he had doodled on a yellow legal pad. That day he drew a plane crashing into a mountain. This time the plane passed through the air space beneath clouds and a sliver of yellow moon.

Finished with that drawing, he started another on a small piece of paper. He made a pair of curving lines and added five or six curves inside those lines. A dot here, a dot there, and it became a sketch of a woman, nude. Ali followed that with an outsized penis directed toward the woman. At which point Kim wandered by. "Oh, Muhammad," she said. Ali ducked his head, a boy caught in mischief, and scrunched up the drawing.

"Maybe we should watch some videotape now," I said.

I brought a tape of an Ali-Cosell interview in hopes it would prompt conversation. At the beginning of the tape, Cosell says, "I made you, Muhammad, and you know it, you know that without me you are nothing." Hana Ali, standing behind her father, started chanting, "Dad-dy, Dad-dy." She was delighted to see him young, fresh and brash, eyes twinkling in that glorious face, declaring, "Howard, you know you need me more than I need you . . ."

I looked at Ali on a couch facing the TV. Even as the videotape played, he had gone to sleep, chin on his chest. Thirty minutes later, he was still asleep.

Until the Atlanta Olympics, Ali had little commercial value. He could not speak well enough to be a corporate endorser. His name, his only asset, was often misused by incompetent schemers. I figured he avoided scandal only because no prosecutor wanted to be famous for having nailed Muhammad Ali. Or, as he whispered into my ear when asked how he avoided the troubles that dogged Mike Tyson: "Never got caught." Lonnie Ali's business empire positioned her husband as an icon of goodwill whose appearances helped charities raise millions of dollars. The movie *Ali* preceded a Benedikt Taschen megabook that in a special edition sold for ten thousand dollars. Along the way, Ali and Lonnie let go of family and long-time friends and partners. Rahaman Ali, who lived in Louisville on Muhammad Ali Boulevard, complained that he had been cut off from contact with his brother. Ali's thirty-year business and personal relationship with Herbert Muhammad ended. Thomas Hauser moved in Ali's inner circle for nine years. But he had served his purpose in helping to bring Ali back into the public spotlight. And when Hauser questioned the direction of the Ali revival, he was pushed away. *Sports Illustrated*'s Mark Kram saw Ali as El Cid and said, "None of what's happening is anything Ali would do on his own."

In the summer of 2005, Gene Kilroy told me he got his old boss on the phone and said, "For a guy who was 'free to be me,' you're the un-free-est guy I know."

"Yeah," Ali said.

"I'm gonna come kidnap you."

"When?"

Lonnie knew, from twenty years of seeing it done, that Ali, left on his own, would give away time and money to anyone who asked. Nor could he be counted on to take care of himself medically. Her mission when leaving Louisville for Los Angeles was, in essence, to save Ali from himself. That she did, and that she intended to keep doing. "It's no more than any wife would do for her husband," she said. While Ali slept in the next room, undisturbed by the young Ali rapping with Cosell, his wife sat behind her office desk, casual, confident, in charge. "It's what Nancy Reagan does for President Reagan."

That image chilled me, for in his last years Ronald Reagan suffered from Alzheimer's disease and no longer remembered having been president. Great fighters had descended into Alzheimer's, hurried to that terrible darkness by their brutal sport. But Lonnie insisted that Ali's condition was the result of Parkinson's disease, not of injuries incurred in the ring.

"Hauser's book says it's brain damage," I said. The book quotes Columbia-Presbyterian's Dr. Stanley Fahn, whose 1984 examination of Ali led to a diagnosis of "post-traumatic Parkinsonism due to injuries from fighting." Fahn added, "Muhammad himself told me he thinks that most

of the damage came from the third Frazier fight, the one in Manila.
. . . My assumption is that his physical condition resulted from repeated
blows to the head over time."

"Tom is so very, very wrong," Lonnie Ali said. "Now, I'm not going to
say that boxing didn't have some kind of physical effect on Muhammad.
Yes, it did. But did it cause his Parkinson's? No, it did not."

She allowed that Ali once had Parkinsonism, meaning the symptoms
of the disease without the disease itself. "Now it's worse, though. He has
idiopathic Parkinson's, run-of-the-mill Parkinson's." Lonnie proposed
pesticide poisoning as a cause. Her authority was the Yugoslavian doctor,
Rajko Medenica, who ordered plasmapheresis to remove toxins from
Ali's blood. However, Dr. Dennis Cope of the UCLA Medical Center, who
monitored Ali's care at the time, ran tests on September 14, 1988, to de-
termine the presence of chlorinated pesticides in Ali's blood and told
Hauser, "There was no evidence of them whatsoever."

Lonnie defended Medenica. "I don't care what anybody says about
Medenica, that man was a brain. To me, he's the one who kept Muhammad's Parkinson's from progressing for so long. He's the one who told
me Muhammad had pesticide poisoning. And all Muhammad ever said
was, 'Ah, that's bull. That's not true.' Well, doctors have found out that
you can get Parkinson's from toxins in the blood. And when you think
about the camp at Deer Lake, all those cabins and spraying for bugs, and
God knows what he was susceptible to when he was sweating and training and breathing it in. And that stupid cabin that he slept in, built out of
creosote-soaked railroad ties, that was poisonous by itself. So you don't
know what caused it. It could have been any of that."

Another doctor, Abraham Lieberman, the founder of the Lieberman
Parkinson Clinic of North Bay Village, Florida, has examined Ali and diagnosed the presence of Parkinson's disease. "Muhammad's Parkinson's
disease began unilaterally," Lieberman wrote to me by e-mail in the summer of 2005, "has progressed relatively slowly and his mind is intact. He
resembles idiopathic Parkinson's disease more than dementia pugilistica.
Whether this is what his brain would show on post-mortem is a guess.
Remember, the diagnosis of idiopathic is a clinical one with a fifteen percent error rate."

In layman's terms, dementia pugilistica is "punch drunk." It signifies
injury to a boxer's brain that results in diminished cognitive ability and
can lead to psychiatric changes. Neither of the diagnostic possibilities for

Ali was a happy one, but dementia pugilistica was among his sport's most appalling consequences. Joe Louis drifted in cocaine-addled madness. Nurses put Sugar Ray Robinson in a diaper. Floyd Patterson could not remember his wife's name even as she cared for him. Ingemar Johansson lived in a special-care home. Jerry Quarry died at age fifty-three. Maybe the greater the fighter, the greater the brain damage because his career put him against the best competition for the longest time. There was no greater fighter than Muhammad Ali.

A saint.

Or was he?

Mark Kram asked me, "How can people consider Ali a historic figure from the 1960s? He wasn't for civil rights; he was for separation of the races. He wasn't for women's rights; he treated them like second-class call girls. He was never really against the war; he was told not to go by Elijah Muhammad because it would be a PR disaster for the Muslims. These were the hot issues of the sixties, and he was on the wrong side of history in all of them. Yet people today somehow think Ali belongs right next to Martin Luther King. Why isn't it enough for people that Ali was the greatest fighter ever?"

A saint? Gerald Early spoke of him as a black man of "illustrious complexity." Most often, I thought we layered complexity onto a simple man. I thought of that icy day in 1962 when he lectured New York lawmakers on the subject of time. *The trees get leaves, you see people walking the dogs, time changes their mind. They don't want that chili but popsicles and ice cream— the mind changes into light clothes.* I thought of Ali as Chance the gardener, the Peter Sellers character in the 1979 movie *Being There.* A light's on, but nobody's home in sweet Chance's head. The gardener learns speech and gestures from television. Through twists of fate, his immaterial words are taken as great truths and he becomes a possible presidential candidate. It's not that Chance is being deceptive. He simply mirrors the needs of everyone around him. At movie's end, he walks on water because he doesn't know it's not possible. So, too, Ali did whatever he felt like doing and left it to others to figure out how and why he did it.

Out of the ring, through the 1960s and 1970s, Ali danced on a high wire in the wind with no net. He not only courted danger, he was danger. *That* Ali was a black man who walked to the edge of the racial divide in the United States of America and shouted across it, *I don't have to be what you want me to be. I'm free to be who I want.* He demanded his rights when such a demand could put steel in the spines of lesser men. "To many," Hauser wrote, "he was the ultimate symbol of black pride and black resistance to an unjust social order." *That* Ali was a wonder, a rogue and rebel espousing a dozen themes, most of them contradictory, all wrapped in razor wire.

Since Ali's last fight, in December 1981, he had been a phantom. There were glimpses of him: Ali on a rescue mission in Beirut, Ali in a courtroom, Ali at Richard Hirschfeld's side on Capitol Hill. But he was inconsequential. Then came Hauser's book talking aloud, and the Olympics came shouting: Ali was back and there was no reason to be angry at him. Vietnam was over. He had renounced the Nation of Islam in favor of true Islam. No longer a clamorous egotist—still full of himself, but muted—he became a silent, sweet, stoic Buddha gliding among us, carrying one message: peace.

He visited the Vietnam Memorial. Photographer Neil Leifer proposed the morning trip. They arrived early, virtually alone. If Ali recognized the irony of his presence at the memorial for more than fifty thousand dead American service men and women, he did not express it. He looked at the wall of black granite so polished he could see his face reflected. He said, "All those names." Within minutes, Ali stood in a crowd of admirers, everyone smiling, laughing, happy to see him.

After Atlanta, Ali became the living logo of GOAT, Greatest of All Time, Inc. We were asked to admire him and respect him because—well, because he was the sainted Ali. He became a commodity for sale to television, movies, charities, philanthropists, car companies, and watchmakers. He was sanitized by revisionists who preferred the sainted Ali to the dangerous Ali on the grounds that it's best to offend as few customers as possible. When the twentieth century turned to the twenty-first, Lonnie and Ali stood in New York's Times Square in freezing cold beside the city's mayor, Rudolph Giuliani, with hundreds of thousands of revelers. There had been a time, in 1968, in a New York hotel room, doing a radio interview, that Ali imagined the distant future with people talking about him in wonder: *Where is he at? There he is, over there sittin' on the garbage can with the wine heads. He don't have to be over there. There he is talking to the prostitute. There he is pickin' up the brother out of the alley, taking him to the Muslim temple. There he is selling the prostitute a Muslim newspaper. Ain't that something. He really don't have to do it.* Instead, he waited for a glitterball to descend at midnight. The old rock 'n' roll singer Lloyd Price, who once gave Cassius Clay advice on girls, saw Ali with Giuliani. He called Las Vegas and said to Gene Kilroy, "Are you watching that shit?" Ali was numb with the cold, trembling, all but oblivious to the moment. Price wept for his friend.

When Hauser was invited to write for the Ali retrospective produced by the German publisher Taschen, he wrote an essay titled, "The Lost Legacy of Muhammad Ali." Its thesis: Ali's life story had been rewritten for commercial purposes. The most egregious example came in the 2001 movie *Ali*. It never showed Ali as the fire-breathing preacher of the Nation of Islam's ideology during the ten years after he won the heavyweight championship in 1964. Hauser wrote that such distortion did a disservice to both history and Ali, for unless a life's journey is told fully and honestly, the true measure of that life cannot be made. But Hauser's essay did not appear in Taschen's book. Lonnie killed it.

The Ali of the Olympics was a sweetheart, and I liked him, but I liked the original Ali more. I missed the Ali voice—both the physical voice, because it was always fresh and fun, and the voice he gave to ideas, the content and hard edge and the challenge that was always there. He forced us to think about race and religion and politics and the conditions of life in black and white America. But that Ali was disappeared, with the result that a generation of Americans knows only the sanitized Ali who refused to answer a question about Al Qaeda seven months after 9/11. "I dodge those questions," he told the television interviewer David Frost. "I've opened up businesses across the country, selling products, and I don't want to say nothing and, not knowing what I'm doing, not qualified, say the wrong thing and hurt my businesses and things I'm doing." The original Ali might have said, "What's our quarrel with them Iraqis?"

Even in Atlanta, Ali did business with another schemer who gave him money. Yank Barry, a Canadian, hired Ali in 1994 to attract worldwide investors for a dehydrated food product called VitaPro. Barry and Ali promised in the summer of 1996 to feed a half-million refugees displaced by civil war in Liberia. That nation's honorary American consul, Walter Young, said, "This mission proves, once again, that Muhammad Ali is one of the great goodwill ambassadors of the world." But when Ali and Barry flew to Africa a year later, they delivered food and medical supplies at a refugee center housing not a half-million Liberians but 477.

By then, VitaPro's $33.7-million deal with the Texas prison system was under investigation. Barry was a felon and admitted drug addict who in 1982 under his original name of Gerald Barry Falovitch had served ten months of a six-year sentence for extortion. In January 1998, Barry was charged with bribing the Texas prison boss. On August 17, 2001, jurors hearing the Barry case returned from an afternoon break to a surprise in the courtroom. The *Houston Chronicle* reported: "Jurors were agape. 'The Greatest' was standing in the gallery. Some gasped, many craned their necks, some openly gawked." Ali had come to sit with Barry's friends and family, invited by the defendant's lawyers to show that Barry did not lie about relationships. One lawyer said, "How better to do that than to have Muhammad Ali step inside the courtroom and sit on our side of the room?" Four days later, evidently no more impressed by Ali than Harold Smith's jury had been, the Houston jury convicted Barry. He faced seventy years in prison and a two-million-dollar fine. (Procedural delays allowed Barry to stay free while awaiting sentencing. His wait ended on September 8, 2005, but not with a trip to jail. His conviction was overturned in U.S. District Court by Judge Lynn Holmes. She ruled that the prosecution's only witness to an alleged bribery was "a felon, a thief, a cheat, and a liar," and therefore not credible. In an interview with the *Montreal Gazette*, Barry painted himself and Ali as victims of malicious prosecution, a "Jewish, white Canadian with a black, Muslim partner" selling a meat substitute in the cattle capital of the world. A government appeal of the decision was possible.)

As the well-compensated endorser of a convicted felon, most men would have found their reputations diminished. American media mostly ignored the story, and Ali accepted it with a nonchalance born of experience with partners who operated at the edges of the law. Lord only knows how many such men used his name around the world. (Most audaciously, Richard Hirschfeld. Convicted of tax fraud in 1991 in a case not involving Ali, he served four years in federal prison; later, indicted on charges that included threatening a judge, he fled to the Canary Islands and Cuba; in 2005, arrested in his Fort Lauderdale mansion and ordered to trial, he committed suicide by hanging himself in a Miami jail's laundry room.) Gene Kilroy had long since stopped counting the scam artists. "Anybody with a 'deal' became Ali's 'agent,'" he said. "There must've been nine thousand of 'em."

Ali simply walked away. Just another of his lives.

At Berrien Springs in the summer of 2003, awake again, Ali looked at a photograph. It showed the young Ali warming up before an exhibition in Louisville. The year was 1967. I was the young reporter in the picture, notebook in hand. "You?" he said, smiling. I pointed to the handsome young fighter in the white robe and said, "You?"

To a new Cosell question, this one about the last time he had seen Cosell, his answer was a mumble, "Wutfrm." He repeated, "Wutfrm." Someone said, "He's asking, what did Cosell die from?" Eight years before, Cosell had died of congestive heart failure. "I think he had just used up his body," I said. "There was some of everything going bad at the end."

Ali's head fell back, his mouth open. His eyes were open wide, unblinking. His arms fell to his side. He sat there, dead still. Still. Ten, fifteen seconds. Dead.

I had seen this act before.

"Come on, Muhammad," I said, laughing. "Show me the gym."

Outside of his office building, he stopped and turned his face to the sun. "No traffic," he said. "No people." He raised his arms. "Quiet." Nine years earlier, on the steps of the ABC building in New York, Cosell had turned his face to the sun, happy to be alive.

I took a couple of steps toward the gym and stopped when I realized Ali hadn't moved. I looked back and there he was, stuck. I had seen the same thing with my father-in-law, who had Parkinson's disease for twenty years until he died at age sixty-one. There were times he could not lift his feet to walk. His knees quivered as he tried to move his feet, and he would lean his upper body forward. The heel of a foot would come up first, only making the step more difficult because now his body's weight was centered over the foot. Only when he lifted the entire foot could he take a step. With his body already falling forward, he had to take quick little steps to keep his feet under him. I had seen that in my poor father-in-law. Now I saw it in the most graceful athlete of my time. Lurching forward, Ali reached out for help. His left hand grabbed my right forearm and held on as we walked sixty feet to the gym. I remembered what Gene Kilroy had said before I made the trip to Michigan: *We gotta pray for him.*

I had been with Ali in the Fifth Street Gym in Miami Beach, Gleason's in New York, and Bud Bruner's second-story hall in Louisville. They were gritty sweatboxes with creaking floors and old fight posters tacked to the walls. Ali's place in Berrien Springs was *Architectural Digest*'s idea of a gym. A red-roped ring with a snow-white canvas stood among shining silver exercise machines. I asked Ali, "How much do you work out?" With his index finger and thumb, he made a zero.

A lifetime ago, in the ring, he had been as near to living flame as man can be. The Reverend Timothy S. Healy, once president of Georgetown University, wrote, "The ancient Greeks knew it was a good thing to watch beauty, especially when that beauty involved movement, suddenness and improvisation. . . . Watching anyone do anything well enlarges the soul." It was Howard Cosell's favorite poet, the young John Keats, who wrote:

> *"Beauty is truth, truth beauty—that is all*
> *Ye know on earth, and all ye need to know."*

On the walls of Ali's gym, as in a museum, were framed photographs of the beauty that was Ali. One showed him in conversation with a man. Ali said, "Malcolm X." Another showed Cosell in a fedora outside a courthouse, holding a microphone up to Ali. "My buddy," he said. Ali stopped at a bench and picked up thin leather gloves. He asked me to fasten them at his wrists. He walked to a spot in front of a heavy bag suspended by a chain. He shoved the bag with his left hand to put it in motion.

In the classic boxer's stance, he threw a light jab at the bag. *Slap.*

Followed by a right, heavier.

And another jab.

The punches came faster now, the sounds gathering force.

He bent lower, asking his body for more. And he threw a hook off a jab and it made a heavy sound. *Whooomp.*

And now the punches came so quickly with such ease and such force that in that moment, that sweet passing moment, the sound was a sound heard in another gym in another time, a sound one young fighter heard as Lash LaRue cracking his whip, a sound that only one kid ever made with his jab, a sound announcing the little kid named Cassius Clay.

EPILOGUE

"The Alpha and the Omega"

REMEMBERING THE STILL of a starry sky, Muhammad Ali whispered, "It's quiet, *shhhh*. Can't hear nothin', nothin', nothin'." It was the winter of 1988 and he remembered a time in the spring of that year. Taken to Utah by his lawyer to campaign for a politician he had never heard of, Ali lay in bed in Room 1723 of the Little America Inn in Salt Lake City, Utah. He remembered waking up that spring in his farmhouse at two-thirty one morning. He showered and prayed and walked into the dark, into the still, chill blackness outside. "Stars and moon," he said. "Nothin' else. Peace in the sky. No phone ringin'."

He walked on a blacktop road for two or three hours. "Close your eyes," he said, and he closed his. Every now and then, he said, there would be a car. His eyes came open. "I'd see the lights comin', a mile away. It's quiet. And then you could hear the car. It would go by. *Whoooosh*. Almost hit you. Don't see you until right on you." His voice was a whisper that moved as if to music only he could hear. He was back on that road in the still of the chilly dark.

"So dark, boy. Hear things." His eyes moved to one side. "A wolf. Wolf out there. Wild dogs. Black out there. Keep walkin', middle of the road, can't see nothin', gotta look down at the road, see the white line. See 'em comin' from a mile. So dark out there." He said he stopped and prayed for his mother and father, did some calisthenics, kept walking. "Man, it was quiet and scary. *Scary*. If I wasn't a believer in God, I'd have been scared. Five miles from home in the dark. Then I turned around. Went home. Sun's comin' up. Birds singin'."

He let his eyes fall closed again, a smile on his lips, and in that story was the story of Ali's past and future. The fight doctor Ferdie Pacheco

323

knew the story of Ali's life. He had seen the darkness. Ali's abandonment of Malcolm X. His connection to Nation of Islam thugs. The wives, the women. The beatings by Frazier, Norton, Shavers, Holmes. Early on, the doctor saw the immediate damage of those fights and later saw the cumulative damage that left Ali shuffling in silence. Still, Pacheco perceived a light greater than any darkness and said, "God took away the main weapon, Ali's mouth. But look at him. The most incredible person I've ever met."

The doctor wept. "He taught me, don't give in."

Pacheco talked through his tears. "Do not give in. Never. Shit, keep on trying. Thing is, not to stop."

"The Alpha and the Omega, the first and the last," Coretta Clay said of her brother's son, Muhammad Ali. Howard Cosell's daughter, Jill, called her father "the one and only." Even allowing for familial hyperbole, the aunt and the daughter had it about right, for these were extraordinary men who shaped their times and times to come.

Jimmy Roberts, a network sportscaster whose rookie job put him in Cosell's company, said, "Ali and Cosell were two very, very smart men who got it." Another broadcaster, Charlie Steiner, said, "It was an absolute perfect marriage because Ali elevated Howard's game and Howard elevated Ali's. They were also politically in tune. Howard was a true political liberal, a walking ACLU, and his standing by Ali made a lot of people uncomfortable." In the whitebread suburbs of Connecticut, a young man watched Ali & Cosell with more than a child's interest. The interviews taught him about sportscasting, his career goal. Almost subliminally, he learned greater lessons. "There was no prejudice in my family," said Keith Olbermann, who became one of television's brightest commentators, "but there was also very little exposure to anybody that didn't look exactly like me. And to see these two men who were obviously intelligent, from different backgrounds, from different kinds of education, and yet sparring in a verbal sense—it was an opportunity for me to see that intelligence didn't belong to just the white guys or just the black guys or just the Jewish guys or just the Gentile guys. That's a pretty big hurdle for a kid to leap just by watching a sports broadcast." Some of the nation's leading sportscasters in the twenty-first century counted Cosell as their point man and benefactor. "The George Washington of TV sports journalism," Roberts called him. Steiner said, "He's our Mount Rush-more, all by himself." For Len Berman, a New York sports anchor, Cosell's performances were magical: "He had a way of reaching through the glass and touching you." "Without Howard Cosell," Olbermann said, "I'd be a sports columnist in Altoona, Pennsylvania."

Cosell and Ali developed a relationship that was unprecedented and would never be repeated in their lifetimes. It was built on their unmis-takable identities as a race man and an overt Jew. Columbia University professor Samuel Freedman, an author on the Jewish-black experience, said, "Cosell and Ali were perfect for the sixties when the melting-pot myth was giving way to cultural pluralism. Ali—loud, audacious, refus-ing to be the credit-to-his-race stereotype. Cosell—abrasive, outspoken, intellectually aggressive, big-nosed. They were avatars of pluralism, ex-pressing in their essences this refusal to melt." They were public partners as few blacks and Jews had been. Jack Benny, a Jew, had allowed himself to be mocked occasionally by his black butler, Rochester. But that was an ensemble comedy on radio. It was 1976 before Hollywood paired a Jew and a black, Gene Wilder and Richard Pryor, as the stars of a major movie, *Silver Streak*. Through the 1960s, Cosell and Ali had performed for a generation of antiauthoritarian Baby Boomers growing up with televi-sion itself. They represented that audience's penchant for rebellion. They did it gracefully. At a time of racial tension, there was Ali—big, strong, handsome, sexy, defiant, demanding, and black—the embodiment of that tension. He stood alongside Cosell, the white Jew, usually laughing with him. "America's white population was very nervous and scared of racial conflicts," said Lawrence J. Epstein, university professor and author of a study on comedy teams, *Mixed Nuts*. "I believe Ali's and Cosell's joking reduced some of the racial friction in society."

Cosell not only created sports broadcast journalism. He showed how it best could be done. Not by shading truths, not by shying away from con-troversy, but by doing the reporting and thinking necessary to form an opinion that could be directly expressed. It was the journalism he had grown up reading in New York newspapers. On an afternoon in Septem-ber 1972, Sam Freedman was a high-school senior in New Jersey. He drove his mother's car back from a print shop after dropping off page proofs for his school paper. On the car radio, he heard that voice. "I have the most indelible memory of Howard Cosell's broadcast," Freedman said. "I can tell you the exact intersection in New Brunswick where I heard him declare it a travesty to have all that blood shed by terrorists and the Olympic Games go on."

Ali's impact on his profession faded quickly. Sugar Ray Leonard, a 1976 Olympic gold medalist and three-division world champion, came to the ring with the swiftness and showmanship of Ali. No one else merited mention in the same paragraph with Ali, let alone the same sentence. For a year or two, Mike Tyson was a terror as the heavyweight champion. But his troubled life reduced him from champion to convict to pitiable facsimile of a prizefighter. The veteran trainer Teddy Atlas, a television fight commentator, ranked Sugar Ray Robinson the greatest fighter ever, with Henry Armstrong second, and Ali third. The only other heavyweights in the Atlas top ten were Gene Tunney, ninth, and Joe Louis tied for tenth.

The sports opinion industry would be fractionalized by radio talk-show hosts, television's shouting heads, writing-at-the-top-of-their-voices newspaper columnists, and legions of bloggers floating across the endless Internet universe. For that blight, Cosell's influence was blamed—as Ali's was blamed for those trash-talking, me-first showboats who demanded immediate attention. It was not their fault. Those columnists, broadcasters, and athletes were coming as times changed. The media grew exponentially. Athletes became national and international celebrities earning millions of dollars. It just happened that the first of them, Cosell and Ali, turned out to be the best of all times.

The Dalai Lama had paid attention. He invited Ali to his dedication of a temple on the grounds of the Tibetan Cultural Center near Bloomington, Indiana. It was near noon on a sunny, warm September day in 2003 when Ali, his gait uncertain, arms trembling, took the Dalai Lama's offer of a hand to walk the hundred feet from a car to his seat.

In his traditional orange robes, the Dalai Lama was a small man, sixty-seven years old, roundish and bald, with a twinkly smile at his lips. Ali rose from a chair to acknowledge an official's welcome that had a please-introduce-him-this-way sound to it: "Muhammad has raised more money for American charities than any other living person." The Dalai Lama slapped him on the back and said to Ali, "May you live very long and continue to serve as an inspiration to people all over the world."

How far past unimaginable was the reality of Ali's life. The kid from Louisville's West End, maverick and scamp, disturber of the peace, reviled and revered, partner to crooks, the best there ever was at beating up people—and he became a back-slapping pal of a Nobel Peace Prize winner, the Dalai Lama.

When Ali put his hands together, fingertips to his chin in approximation of the Dalai Lama's prayer position, His Holiness adopted a stance of his own. He put up his fists and said, "It has been a great pleasure for me to see Muhammad Ali in person. I have seen his boxing matches in the past." Here the Dalai Lama smiled. "In my own case, if I were to step into the ring, I would be knocked down with the first punch."

While Ali shook his head, no, no, someone at the lectern made a fuss about a gift for Ali. A man from the host committee said, "What do you give a three-time world heavyweight champion? What do you give Muhammad Ali?" He held high the gift he had finally chosen. It was a sweatshirt bearing the Indiana University athletic department logo.

Ali, the imp, then said his only words of the great day, "Is this all I get?"

In the summer of 2005, in a living room on Long Island, New York, Howard Cosell's grandson, Colin Cosell, heard that voice and called to his mother, "Poppa's on." Jill Cosell then sat with her son to watch the fun: Howard Cosell in a tuxedo over a blue ruffled-cuff shirt . . . the golden child Muhammad Ali glistening after a fifteenth-round knockout victory over Oscar Bonavena.

On the television, it is December 1970 at Madison Square Garden. Cosell is at center ring reaching for Ali. "Muhammad," the broadcaster says, touching the fighter's shoulder. "Could I get you to just face that camera?" Immediately, Cosell cuts to the chase with a lawyer's leading question: "Muhammad, you know that you're a slower fighter tonight, don't you?"

"Mom, what's with the ruffles?" Colin Cosell said.

"The seventies," said Jill Cosell.

On the television, because Ali doesn't hear the question, Cosell repeats it, only this time it is a statement: "You know you didn't have the old speed tonight."

Transfixed by his tuxedoed grandfather, Colin Cosell said, "An unfortunate fashion statement." Jill Cosell laughed because she saw her father with a telephone pressed to his ear while he interviewed Ali and directed

Ali's attention to a monitor, the broadcaster multitasking in the bedlam of the ring. "Look, Colin," she said. "Now Daddy is telling Muhammad that he's got Joe Frazier on the phone and Joe is saying he's going to go after Ali and put him away even though Bonavena couldn't.'"

On the television, Ali says to Cosell, "Tell him if he do, he's a good one. Look like we don't have to talk no more."

Colin Cosell said, "He's dressed like Prince."

Jill said, "Now he's giving the phone to Muhammad."

On the television, thirty-five years earlier, in the first season of the *Monday Night Football* show that would make him the most distinctive commentator in television history, the Howard/Prince character says, "Hold on a second, Joe. I'm going to put Muhammad on the phone." Maybe other broadcasters worked with producers as creative as Cosell's, but only Cosell could have made this piece of foolish business seem the stuff of journalism. One minute after going into the fifteenth round with a brawler, the sweating, heavily breathing Ali is talking on the phone on television. All because Cosell, in his blue ruffled-cuff shirt, asked him to do it. "Now, Muhammad," Cosell says. "You report what Joe says to you."

Ali speaks to Frazier on the phone. "You're not frightened of me, are you? All I have to say is, if we can't get along, it's time to get it on!"

Cosell blurts out, "What's he saying, Muhammad?"

Ali tells Frazier, "Howard Cosell is agitatin', as usual."

On the television, the agitator smiles broadly. In a Long Island living room, the agitator's daughter and her son laughed out loud.

ACKNOWLEDGMENTS

Because it's the kind of pep talk an agent gives an apprehensive author, David Black said, "It's the book you were born to write." He didn't mean this one. Years ago, we were in a New York coffee shop talking about a biography of Muhammad Ali. When life, work, and dozens of Ali books persuaded me to drop that idea, I told Black, "I could do Cosell." Serendipitously, Doug Pepper, an editor at Crown Publishers, came to ask David, "Do you have anyone who could write a biography of Howard Cosell?"

"Yes, I do," Black said.

Good agent.

Black then said, "How about a dual biography? Cosell and Ali?"

Great agent.

Soon enough, the dual biography became narratives of Ali's life, Cosell's life, and the life of their relationship. I had never heard of a tri-biography, and now I have written one. In the doing, my authorial kvetchings surely tested the limits of friendships. And what a thing. Gary Pomerantz, Jane Leavy, Tom Callahan, John Feinstein, Lesley Hunt, Billy Reed, Juliet Macur, Paul Attner, and Verenda Smith—bless 'em all—they said, "Shut up already. Go write."

It may seem Cosellian bluster to say that only three people could have written this book this way. But here, of all places, I need to tell it like it is. Jerry Izenberg and Bob Lipsyte knew Ali and Cosell in important ways that I never did. I thank them for their vivid reporting, their encouragement to me, and their generosity in sharing what only they knew.

Because Cosell had resisted the intrusions of most journalists, his personal life was a mystery. For guidance I depended on the kindness of his daughter, Jill. Her sons, Justin and Colin, also were helpful, as was Cosell's other daughter, Hilary. The early years in Cosell's professional life were blank pages until filled with the memories of Ray Robinson, Ed

Silverman, Les Keiter, Murphy Martin, and W. C. Heinz. For an understanding of Cosell's place in television history as well as sports' place in the medium, Ron Powers's *SuperTube* was indispensable. Former ABC Sports publicist Bob Wheeler consistently reinforced my opinion that Cosell was a good and decent man.

Ali lived so publicly that a biographer becomes disoriented, even dizzied, by information overload. I trusted two secondary sources above all: Thomas Hauser's *Muhammad Ali: His Life and Times*, and *Black Is Best: The Riddle of Cassius Clay*, by Jack Olsen. George Plimpton's *Shadow Box*, Budd Schulberg's *Loser and Still Champion*, and Hugh McIlvanney's anthology, *McIlvanney on Boxing*, were inspiring as well as instructive. The most brilliant illumination of the Ali phenomenon: Dr. Gerald Early's introduction to *The Muhammad Ali Reader*.

Ali and his wife Lonnie invited me to their office in Berrien Springs, Michigan. Though Ali's infirmities made an interview impossible, he did his damndest all day to entertain me with drawings, magic tricks, and lunch (spooning to me a mountain of butter pecan ice cream). There was also a moment in his gym when he again made thunder music on the heavy bag. Maryum (May May) Ali showed me her father as a man, not a myth. Friends, confidants, and associates answered questions on old times and new. Chief among the witnesses were Gene Kilroy, Victor Solano, Larry Kolb, Peter Tauber, Angelo Dundee, Joe Martin, Jr., Tom Zollinger, and Gordon Davidson.

Gary Tuell, once my sportswriting colleague, accompanied me to Ali's training camp at Deer Lake before the Foreman fight. Happily, the trip remained indelible in his memory and filled the spaces in mine. Thomas G. Krattenmaker, a clerk for Justice John M. Harlan at the U.S. Supreme Court in 1971, walked me through the untold story of how his boss came to make the decision that kept Ali out of prison.

Bob Liter, the managing editor of the *Lincoln* (Illinois) *Evening Courier*, paid me every Friday during the summer of 1959 with thirty-two one-dollar bills, unwrinkled and sharply edged. I didn't care if they were counterfeited in the back shop. I loved the work then and love it still. Newspaper sports editors turned me loose to do the work that brought me to Ali and Cosell. They were Jim Barnhart, Earl Cox, George Solomon, Van McKenzie, and Frank Deford. Columnists were my heroes: Red Smith, Jimmy Cannon, Dave Anderson, Blackie Sherrod, Dan Jenkins, Furman Bisher, Edwin Pope, Jim Murray (who once said, "I want to be Ali for a day. Got a dozen guys I'd like to knock out, a dozen women I'd like to take out"), Jack Murphy, Si Burick, Jimmy Breslin, Murray Kempton, Mike Royko, Anna Quindlen, John Schulian, Roy McHugh, Dick Fenlon, Ira Berkow, Shirley Povich, Barney Nagler.

David Black came to me with the Ali & Cosell idea. My ad hoc board of advisers, Pomerantz, Leavy, and Callahan, helped me figure out how it could be done. Martin Beiser, a senior editor at Free Press, improved the manuscript with every question, suggestion, and scratch of his No. 2 pencil. Beiser's assistant, Kit Frick, surely was surprised to learn that her job description included, "Pull author off window ledge when he can't figure out how to attach a file to an e-mail." At her feet, I spread rose petals.

I married Cheryl Ann Liesman two years and a day before Cassius Clay beat Sonny Liston the first time. Seems like yesterday. I owe her the most.

NOTES

PROLOGUE: THEY CHARMED AND BEDEVILED US

2   *"She took one look"*: *Boston Globe,* November 16, 1965.

4   *"Arrogant, pompous:* Cosell, *Cosell,* 117.

6   *"Cosell, you're a phony"*: Leon Gast movie, *When We Were Kings,* 1996.

6   *"You're being extremely truculent"*: ABC Sports, March 11, 1967.

7   *A night in Baltimore:* Ed Silverman interview, March 27, 2002.

ONE: "BOUND TOGETHER BY A COMMON SYMPATHY"

11   *"In less than an eyeblink"*: Richardson, 101.

12   *"a striking combination"*: Ibid., ix.

12   *"He would fight the wind"*: Smiley, 4.

12   *"For those who obey"*: Richardson, 76.

12   *"I was advised"*: Ibid., 86.

13   *"He is about"*: Robertson, 46.

13   *"the culminating act"*: Richardson, 88.

13   *By then:* Officials at the White Hall State Shrine, Richmond, Kentucky, confirm the story of the name's progress.

13   *Millions of Jews:* Researcher April White reported the immigration records of Cosell's grandparents.

TWO: "AMERICA WAS IN EVERYBODY'S MOUTH"

14   *They spent three weeks:* This account of an immigrant's journey is taken from Howe, 36–40.

15   *"America was in everybody's mouth"*: Ibid., 27.

15   *"a land of sweatshops"*: Abramovitch and Galvin, 6.

16   *"when I watched my mother"*: Ibid., 11.

16   *"No one will ever know"*: Howe, 178.

16   *"Izzie, that's enough"*: Cosell, *Like,* 271.

16   *"I'll tell you"*: Jill Cosell interview, July 24, 2005.

17   *"They put me"*: Cosell, *Like,* 271.

18   *"Show them how"*: Ibid., 284.

18   *"You may be"*: Ibid., 285.

18   *"He'll be a reporter"*: Alexander Hamilton High yearbook, 1936.
18   *"photographic in its preciseness"*: Cosell interview, January 20, 1980.
19   *"as though he were grinding"*: Halberstam, 19.
20   *"this cute, pudgy blonde"*: Cosell, *Cosell*, 120.
20   *"twinkle in her eye"*: Ibid.
20   *"Would you marry"*: Robert Lipsyte interview of Emmy Cosell, 1984.
20   *"undertaken under adverse"*: Cosell, *Cosell*, 119.
20   *"the biggest man"*: Ibid., 121.
20   *"You knew, by God"*: Ibid., 122.
21   *"His whole life"*: Jill Cosell interview, November 19, 2002.
21   *"Later, when I was"*: *Cosmopolitan*, August 1979, 216.
21   *"Emmy, on that first"*: Cosell interview, March 23, 1979.
22   *"Can you loan"*: Joseph Marro, Jr., interview, December 10, 2002.
22   *"I can get up"*: The Sporting News, August 10, 1955, 4.
23   *"Well, I could help"*: Ibid.
23   *"Howard Cosell is not"*: Ibid.
23   *"I'll listen to this"*: Ray Robinson interview, May 15, 2002.
24   *"He'd call and say"*: Bobby Bragan interview, July 15, 2005.
24   *"half the length"*: Silverman interview, December 1, 2003.
25   *"There's a new young"*: Silverman, March 27, 2002.
26   *"For all of Poppa's"*: Justin Cosell interview, July 19, 2005.
26   *"Play-by-play, parrots"*: Silverman, December 1, 2003.
26   *"You're like shit"*: Cosell, *Cosell*, 126.
26   *"some schnorrer"*: George Vecsey interview, June 8, 2003.
27   *"I must have looked like"*: Cosell, *Like*, 125.
28   *"Floyd! Floyd!"*: ABC radio broadcast, June 26, 1959.

THREE: "YOU GOT A LITTLE JOE LOUIS THERE"

30   *"Nurse, this is not"*: Olsen, 61.
30   *"I was always excited"*: Ibid.
31   *"A pretty hard life"*: Hauser, *Ali*, 15.
31   *"Yes, indeed"*: Olsen, 57.
31   *"Cassius is the most"*: Ibid., 61.
31   *"Well, there's another"*: Ibid., 62.
31   *"Gee gee"*: Ibid., 65.
31   *"an aggressive kid"*: Lewis, C., 18.
32   *"You always knew"*: Ibid., 19.
32   *"That was all"*: *Louisville* (Ky.) *Courier-Journal*.
32   *"A sheik"*: Olsen, 95.
32   *"Don't I look"*: Ibid., 93.
32   *"was a troubador"*: Ibid., 95.
32   *"There!"*: Ibid., 108.

33   *"There weren't no"*: Ibid., 57.

33   *"He looked exactly"*: Ibid., 56.

34   *"You got a little"*: Ibid., 62.

34   *Many a black man:* The tale of the stolen bicycle makes sense. I yet believe Fred Stoner was Ali's first trainer. A black man in a black neighborhood would be a more likely teacher for the son of a man who distrusted white people, especially policemen. Ali made Stoner part of 1974's "Muhammad Ali Day" celebration in Louisville. Asked what Stoner had taught him, Ali said, "Everything I know about boxing." In addition, Tom Zollinger knew on first sight of Clay in Martin's gym that the kid was more than a neophyte.

35   *"delightful, well mannered"*: Mike Kallay interview, June 1, 2003.

35   *"All that talkin'"*: Joe Martin, Sr., interview, February 24, 1971.

36   *"either a cutting"*: Olsen, 71.

36   *"Now, look, take him"*: Ibid.

36   *"Mr. Dundee, my name"*: Angelo Dundee interview, February 8, 2005.

37   *"Some nut downstairs"*: Ibid.

37   *"Mr. Price, I'm Cassius"*: Hauser *Ali*, 261. (Clay was seventeen when he first kissed a girl. She was a fellow student at Central High. "I had to teach him how," Areatha Swint told the *Courier-Journal* seventeen years later. "And when I did, he fainted. Finally, when he got up, I said, 'Are you okay?' and he said, 'I'm fine, but nobody will ever believe this.' We had a big laugh about that.")

37   *"Here he comes"*: Schaap, 71.

38   *"See you in a couple"*: Lewis, C., 25.

38   *"I looked him"*: Ibid., 26.

38   *"How'd you know?"*: Schaap, 73.

38   *"his developing"*: Ibid.

38   *"First time I ever"*: Ibid.

39   *"The kid's gonna"*: Pacheco, *A View*, 16.

39   *"Sully's main"*: Pacheco, *Fight*, 14.

40   *"Press"*: Ibid.

40   *"I've got a kid"*: Conrad, 123.

40   *"Hey, Cash"*: Ibid., 124.

40   *"Do Ah"*: Ibid.

40   *"It's policy"*: Flip Schulke interview, January 3, 2002.

41   *"Look at Gorgeous"*: Ibid.

41   *"I want to get"*: Ibid.

42   *"was to the world"*: Pacheco, *View*, 5.

42   *"He was their"*: Ibid.

42   *"The hardest"*: Olsen, 89.

42   *"over and over"*: Olsen, 179.

43   *"I'm Cassius Clay"*: Hauser, *Ali*, 90.

43   *"I knew if I could":* Ibid.
43   *"His aura was too":* Angelou, *Heart,* 197.
44   *"Malcolm was very":* Hauser, *Ali,* 98.

FOUR: "LISTON IS Á TRAMP, I'M THE CHAMP"

45   *"Boxing is at":* Liebling, 213.
46   *"A real fruitcake":* Deford interview, March 5, 2002.
46   *"Which man do you":* Cosell interview, March 23, 1979.
48   *"Watch his brains":* Torres, 29.
48   *"His fist actually":* Sports Illustrated, May 5, 1969, 48.
48   *"If they ever make":* Torres, 130.
48   *"Look at that":* Harold Conrad interview, September 27, 1976.
49   *"I'm over him":* ABC, July 23, 1963.
51   *"Naw . . . I just put that":* SPORT, March 1964, 59.
52   *"A functional illiterate":* Gary Belkin interview, July 12, 2005.
52   *"Clay comes out":* Columbia Records, *I Am The Greatest,* 1963. (Belkin died July 28, 2005. The *New York Times* obituary said George Plimpton and David Remnick "publicly questioned" how many of Ali's poems Belkin wrote. If Ali wrote anything, he wrote two- or four-line doggerel. I have no doubt that Ali, a poor student three years out of high school, was incapable of writing a thirty-two-line poem of intricate comic construction. I believe Belkin's insistence that he wrote every word of the 1963 album on which Ali performed with such delight the "eclipse of the Sonny" poem. First, the album's liner notes gave Belkin credit. Second, Belkin told me he that over the years he had demanded and received payment from media outlets that had used the "eclipse" poem without his permission.)
53   *"I'm gonna":* Cosell, *Cosell,* 173.
53   *"I want you":* Ibid.
54   *"Float like a butterfly":* Hauser, *Ali,* 69.
54   *"I'm ready to rumble":* Ibid.
55   *"emotionally unbalanced":* Ibid., 71.
55   *"Hell, he's close":* Newsweek, March 9, 1964, 50.
55   *"What was all that":* Cosell, *Cosell,* 174.
55   *"Being an old farm boy":* Clegg III, 200.
55   *"If you knew what":* Malcolm X, 303.
55   *"As any official":* Ibid.
56   *"my favorite number":* Ibid., 307.
56   *"This fight is the truth":* Ibid., 306.
56   *"about to meet":* Ibid., 307.
56   *"Clay is moving":* ABC Radio, February 25, 1964.

FIVE: "THE BLACK MAN'S WHITE MAN"

61   *"the Mississippi cemetery":* Irv Brodsky interview, May 14, 2002.

61   *"next to nothing":* Cosell, *Cosell,* 148.

61   *"for being too New York":* Arledge, 91.

61   *"Howard had already accumulated":* Robinson interview, May 15, 2002.

61   *"The ladies took turns":* Heinz interview, June 21, 2002.

61   *"Emmy was a very":* Silverman interview, December 1, 2003.

62   *"My voice is not":* From transcript of an unpublished interview by Jane Leavy, August, 1979.

62   *"Copy? . . . I need no":* Tim Brando interview, April 3, 2005. (When on the road, Cosell went to local radio stations to do his daily five-minute shows. Brando saw one such performance. Like many professional broadcasters, he admired and envied Cosell's mastery of broadcasting's craft. That mastery included a sense of time so precise that he could ad-lib reports to the time allotted. It was said, "He had a Bulova in his brain.")

62   *"Martin, you have":* Murphy Martin interview, July 15, 2005.

63   *"You studied for":* This chapter's Izenberg-Cosell anecdotes come from an Izenberg interview, April 19, 2002.

65   *"But I thought":* Cosell, *Cosell,* 103.

65   *"What Howard didn't:"* Heinz interview, June 21, 2002.

66   *"You're a helluva":* Ibid., 140.

66   *"I don't have any":* Arledge, 18–19.

67   *"I explained to this":* Powers, 113.

67   *"Why the eleven hundred":* Arledge, 21.

67   *"Make it detailed":* Arledge, 30.

67   *"Here to face, television":* Ibid., 30–33.

69   *"Hey, kid come here":* Ibid., 24.

69   *"strange creature":* Ibid., 92.

69   *"So, Howard, do I":* Martin interview, July 15, 2005.

70   *"Roone, we are today":* Arledge, 93.

SIX: "I DON'T HAVE TO BE WHAT YOU WANT ME TO BE"

71   *"That's not the guy":* Mort Sharnik interview, May 19, 2004.

72   *"In America, the Jew":* Lincoln, 177.

72   *"All I have to be":* Lipsyte, *Sports World,* 87.

72   *"a card-carrying member":* Ibid., 88.

72   *"I don't have to be":* Ibid.

72   *"Black Muslim, that's":* I have condensed a series of Ali's contemporaneous quotations from various sources to a single paragraph.

73   *"I'm so glad":* Clegg III, 210.

73   *"It is time":* Evanzz, *Judas,* 171.

73   *"He is the greatest":* Marqusee, 82.

74   *"my companion on my"*: Ibid., 83.

74   *"I tried my hardest"*: Ibid., 84.

74   *"I don't like that"*: Ibid.

74   *"This Clay name"*: Hauser, *Ali*, 102.

75   *"Man, you just don't"*: Evanzz, *Judas*, 216.

75   *"You just don't"*: Malcolm X, 409.

76   *"Cassius?"*: WHAS radio, March 11, 1964.

78   *"He fools them"*: Harper's, April 1964.

78   *"Hey, Herbert"*: New York Times, May 18, 1964, 40.

79   *"During the past eleven"*: Malcolm X, 340.

79   *"Even children knew"*: Ibid., 343.

79   *"Just as the American"*: Ibid., 350–53.

80   *"I saw the birth"*: Hauser, *Ali*, 112.

80   *"Brother Muhammad"*: Angelou, *God's Children*, 144, 146. Marqusee, 128–29.

80   *"Man, did you get"*: New York Times, May 18, 1964, 40.

80   *"Because a billion"*: Ibid.

81   *"Malcolm should have"*: Evanzz, *Messenger*, 300.

81   *"I've learned from"*: Lewis, C. 117.

82   *"I'm not no American"*: Lipsyte, *SportsWorld*, 102.

82   *"Hey, you know what happened"*: Lipsyte, *Free*, 51–52.

83   *"two cents slick"*: Hauser, *Ali*, 114.

83   *"Man, you don't marry"*: Ibid., 116.

83   *"Don't give up"*: Lewis, J., 288.

83   *"The greatest hypocrite"*: Evanzz, *Rise*, 305.

84   *"He must be stopped"*: Ibid.

84   *"beginning to have"*: Marqusee, 136–37.

84   *"Ameer's nothing to me"*: Evanzz, *Judas*, 280.

84   *"Malcolm believed the white"*: Marqusee, 137.

84   *"Ah-meer? Little fellow?"*: Lipsyte, *Sports World*, 98–100.

86   *"You see what you're doing"*: Hauser, *Ali*, 110.

86   *"deserve to be killed"*: Lipsyte, *SportsWorld*, 98.

86   *"It's a time for martyrs"*: Malcolm X, 429.

86   *"And now, without further"*: Ibid., 434–36.

87   *"He criticized"*: Evanzz, *Rise*, 322; Marqusee, 139.

87   *"What people?"*: Hauser, *Ali*, 125.

88   *"Ali, you see about my"*: Edwin Pope interview, April 11, 2002.

88   *"Just think, the whole world"*: Pope, 165.

88   *"You . . . you with glasses"*: Pope interview April 11, 2002.

90   *"This cat had him a car"*: Plimpton, 114.

90   *"Let's stop and eat"*: Plimpton, 117–21, and interview December 16, 2002, and Pope, 54–59, and interview April 11, 2002.

SEVEN: "I AIN'T GOT NOTHING AGAINST THEM VIET CONG"

94 *"Howard Cosell . . . the world's"*: ABC, May 22, 1965.
95 *"People wanted"*: Conrad interview, January 21, 1988.
96 *"look of absolute relief"*: Cosell, *Cosell*, 181.
96 *"the anchor punch"*: ABC, May 29, 1965.
96 *"bedlam, chaos, and confusion"*: Ibid.
96 *"If boxing can survive"*: Cosell, *Cosell*, 182.
96 *"Hello"*: Mike Marley interview, January 7, 2002.
97 *"Come upstairs"*: Hauser, *Ali*, 128, 129.
97 *"You traded heaven"*: Ibid., 129.
97 *"I wasn't going to"*: Ibid., 131.
98 *"Well, if it's not"*: ABC, November 20, 1965.
99 *"Hey, little girl"*: Lipsyte, *SportsWorld*, 112.
100 *"I've got a question"*: Ibid., 115–16, with Lipsyte interview, March 24, 2005. (Lipsyte's story for the *Times* that day did not include the "Viet Cong" quotation; he said he simply didn't use it. Nor did the quotation appear in a story written by Pat Putnam for the *Miami Herald;* Putnam said he did not hear Ali say it. I found no record of the origin of Ali's more famous quotation: "I ain't got no quarrel with them Viet Cong.")
102 *"People can't chase me"*: Hauser, *Ali*, 168.
102 *"Mrs. Clay is a Baptist"*: Lawrence F. Grauman report to Department of Justice, undated (probably August 1966), 5.
102 *"if a year from now"*: Resume of FBI inquiry of witnesses, 7, November 25, 1966.
103 *"Sir, I said earlier"*: Hearing transcript, 110–12.
103 *"After very thorough"*: Grauman report, 10. (Judge Grauman died in late 1969. Thirty-five years later, his son, Phil, said his father was "not a publicity-seeking man" and "never discussed" the Ali case.)
103 *"Muhammad Ali, also known as"*: Cosell, *Cosell*, 178.
104 *"my blood was hot"*: ABC, February 11, 1967.
105 *"I'm always confident"*: ABC, March 11, 1967.
106 *"My God . . . don't do anything"*: Gordon Davidson interview, December 14, 2001.
106 *"What will you"*: Transcript of Hauser-Ali interview, March 1967.
107 *"It's the Army"*: Robinson, *Sugar Ray*, 349, 350.
108 *"I don't want"*: Lipsyte, *SportsWorld*, 122–23.
109 *"What are you"*: Cosell, *Cosell*, 200–201.
110 *"has been so thoroughly"*: Daley, *New York Times*, April 28, 1967, 47.
110 *"Gee Gee"*: Bingham and Wallace, 149.
110 *"Are you going to"*: Cosell, *Cosell*, 201.
111 *"American forces will prevail"*: Associated Press report, *Louisville* (Ky.) *Courier-Journal*, April 28, 1967, 1.

111   *"If ever the tiger"*: Herring, 9.
111   *"Attention . . . you are about"*: Bingham and Wallace, 155–57.
112   *"How bad it hurt"*: Conrad interview, January 21, 1988.
112   *"Look, Muhammad"*: Cosell, *Cosell*, 202–3.
112   *"I strongly object"*: Bingham and Wallace, 158.
113   *"Is there anything"*: Cosell, *Cosell*, 203.
113   *"unanimously decided"*: Bingham and Wallace, 160.
113   *"Mama, I'm all right"*: Ibid.
113   *"left-wing writers, alcoholics"*: Jack Newfield interview, November 18, 2002.
113   *"Injustice on an historical"*: Ibid.
114   *"Forget the war"*: George Plimpton interview, December 16, 2002.
114   *"Ali has been"*: Plimpton, 135–36, and interview. (Plimpton told me that Cosell never complained about the story, but that Emmy "called me up in a great fury and said how dare I have said such a thing, it wasn't true. I said, 'Well, I must have gotten it wrong, forgive me.' And I think I wrote a letter of apology, said I overstated. But I remember very well what happened.")
115   *"absurd, amateurish"*: Newfield interview, November 18, 2002.

EIGHT: "WE DON'T WANT TO LIVE WITH THE WHITE MAN"

120   *"I'd appreciate it"*: Bingham and Wallace, 177.
120   *"This tragedy and the loss"*: Ibid., 178.
121   *"Yes, I accept"*: Hugh McIlvanney interview, April 14, 2002.
121   *"Clay? Is that like"*: Khalilah Ali Camacho interview, November 18, 1988.
122   *"I'm not going to help"*: *Muhammad Ali: The Whole Story*. Turner Home Entertainment, 1996, Tape 3.
122   *"I don't hate nobody"*: Hauser, *Ali*, 189.
123   *"Don't drink, don't smoke"*: Ibid., 187.
123   *"Don't have my wallet"*: Julius Lester interview, December 24, 2003.
123   *"Ali tried to convert me"*: Ibid.
123   *"This is our trouble"*: WBAI broadcast, September 1968.
128   *"It was an evil war"*: Anne Braden interview, April 27, 2004.
128   *"So that's Jack Johnson"*: Bingham and Wallace, 206.
129   *"Come get me"*: Hauser, *Ali*, 198.
129   *"Only one thing"*: Bingham and Wallace, 208.
130   *"When you're the champ"*: Lipsyte, *Free*, 84.
130   *"How is Mr. Clay?"*: *New York Times*, December 3, 1969, 63.
131   *"I feel like a tiger"*: Hauser, *Ali*, 197.
131   *"See my new limousine"*: Bingham and Wallace, 220.
132   *"Just as we had"*: Schulberg, 65.
132   *"it would desecrate the land"*: Bingham and Wallace, 203.
133   *"Yeah, I'd go back"*: Ibid., 209.
133   *"Muhammad Ali is out"*: *Muhammad Speaks*, April 4, 1969.

134 *"I made a fool of myself"*: Bingham and Wallace, 212.

134 *"Can't talk to you no more"*: Cosell, *Cosell*, 206.

135 *"every black man"*: Schulberg, 75, 77–78.

135 *"Oh, God"*: *Courier-Journal*, October 24, 1970, E5.

136 *"Like old times"*: Schulberg, 73.

136 *"He's on his way"*: Ibid.

136 *"Ghost in the house"*: Plimpton, 14.

NINE: "TEL-E-VISION!"

143 *"All I tried to do"*: Unpublished interview by Peter Borrelli, July 12, 1968.

144 *"the warrior saint"*: Edwards, 89–90.

144 *"Do your thing"*: Cosell, *Cosell*, 48.

144 *"Get in there"*: Arledge, 96.

145 *"You'd think I committed"*: Cosell, *Cosell*, 58–59.

145 *"cheering like a damned kid"*: Ibid., 62.

146 *"He makes the world"*: Halberstam, 32.

147 *"Warped mentalities and"*: Arledge, 97.

147 *"some of the best damned television"*: Cosell, *Cosell*, 65.

147 *"genuine celebrity"*: Arledge, 98.

147 *"This is tremendous"*: *Bananas*, 1971.

148 *"What would you think"*: Arledge, 104.

148 *"If it ain't fun"*: Gunther and Carter, 32.

148 *"Get over here"*: Arledge, 109.

149 *"You'll wear the white"*: Ibid., 44.

149 *"With the intelligent viewers"*: Gunther and Carter, 46.

150 *"retching prattle"*: Ibid., 50.

150 *"I listened to that gab"*: Ibid.

150 *"What do you think"*: Ibid., 52.

150 *"More than half of it"*: Cosell, *Cosell*, 287.

150 *"a good case of the blues"*: Cosell, *Cosell*, 294–95.

151 *"one-hundred-and-eighty-dollar-a-week"*: Gunther and Carter, 32. (At least once, Cosell gave the ink-stained wretches a raise. He spoke of "two-hundred-dollar-a-week creeps.")

151 *"Despite my complaints"*: Ibid., 55.

151 *"Let's face it"*: Cosell, *Cosell*, 300.

151 *"You've got"*: Ibid., 299.

151 *"What the hell"*: Gunther and Carter, 61.

152 *"toxic vertigo"*: Cosell, *Cosell*, 307.

152 "Oh, I've seen him drink": Irv Brodsky interview, May 14, 2002.

152 "Monday Night Football": Powers, 185.

152 *"Now, there is an example"*: Gunther and Carter, 56, 58–59.

153 *"to do other things"*: Cosell, *Cosell*, 314.

153 *"They bum-rapped you"*: Ibid., 309.

TEN: "YOU'LL NEVER REALLY KNOW HIM"

154 *"Where is he?":* Cosell, *Cosell,* 212–14.

156 *"But Cosell was not":* Gene Kilroy interview, October 24, 2001.

157 *"Mr. Middle of the Road":* Izenberg interview, May 20, 2005.

157 *"One of the hardest":* Hilary Cosell interview by e-mail, July 11, 2005. (Cosell's daughter wrote a eulogy to William Westmoreland on his death in July 2005. She recounted her opposition to the Vietnam War and told of meeting Westmoreland in 1988 on the show she produced for her father, *Speaking of Everything.* Instead of defending the war, the general shocked Hilary with thoughtful reflection. At one point, Cosell asked the question he himself had been asked many times, "General, are you a bitter man?" "No, Howard," the old soldier said. "Just a tired one." Hilary Cosell called it a moment of "unspoken kinship. The pure understanding of two men whose lives, in completely different spheres, had often been twisted beyond recognition from their original intentions and actions.")

158 *"Hey, Cosell":* Cosell, *Cosell,* 361–62.

ELEVEN: "GOD KNOWS THE WORLD WANTS ME TO WIN"

163 *"Don't bet":* Ferdie Pacheco interview, February 20, 2003. (Pacheco apparently had forgotten Ali's previous fight. In that one, against Oscar Bonavena, Ali first wore the red tassels at the top of his boxing shoes.)

165 *"The only people":* Hauser, *Ali,* 219; Schulberg, 134.

166 *"I'm gonna give":* Pepe, 151.

166 *"Howard, will you shut up!":* Dunphy, 188.

166 *"just a couple of men":* Schulberg, 132.

166 *"Red?":* Pacheco interview, February 20, 2003.

167 *"Don't you know I'm God?":* Cope, 162.

167 *"When he goes to the ropes":* Hauser, *Ali,* 230.

168 *"Come on, man":* Ibid., 229.

168 *"Stop playing":* Pepe, 186.

168 *"heavyweights, coddled with":* Durant, 12.

169 *"Oh, God! Oh, God!":* Pacheco interview, February 20, 2003.

170 *"You've got to":* Pepe, 208, 210.

171 *"Make it look like":* Plimpton, 96–97.

171 *"Next time":* McIlvanney, 47–48.

171 *"Champ":* Lipsyte, *Free,* 90–91.

173 *"I suspect that every one":* Thomas Krattenmaker interview, October 3, 2003.

174 *"steamed because he thought":* Thomas Rowe interview, December 2, 2004.

175 *"I just heard":* Anderson, *Sports,* 201.

TWELVE: "I'M THE ONLY ONE WHO CAN TELL IT"

177   *"First, the looks"*: Ibid., 312.

177   *"made Howard absolutely"*: Arledge, 117.

177   *"Look at him"*: Cosell, *Cosell*, 317.

178   *"Gentlemen, neither"*: Ibid., 321–22.

178   *"Enclosed is your jacket"*: Cosell, *Cosell*, 337.

179   *"He believed he knew"*: HBO documentary, *Howard Cosell: Telling It Like It Is*, November 1, 1999.

179   *"Howard Cosell will be"*: Cosell, *Cosell*, 344.

179   *"chance to show"*: Ibid., 338.

179   *"simply because the"*: Ibid., 341.

179   *"There he is"*: Ibid., 322–323.

180   *"Take a look out there"*: Bragan interview, July 15, 2005.

181   *"Oh, we've had a great life"*: Cosell, *Cosell*, 86.

181   *"Did you hear"*: Ibid., 2. (I was in Munich writing columns for the *Louisville Courier-Journal*. On rising at the home of our German hosts, we were hurried to the television. They spoke only broken English, we spoke no German. The TV screen carried images of men with machine guns, and our hosts' nine-year-old son, Heinz-Karl, said, "We bad people." Earlier, I had been to Dachau and had written of my father's generation's horror. Now, this horror. Thirty years later, Alex Wolff wrote for the *Time* definitive minute-by-minute report of that black day in his story for *Time* magazine, "When the Terror Began."

182   *"Have tistalku"*: Canadian Broadcasting Company, September 5, 1972.

182   *"More cars pulling up"*: Arledge, 133.

182   *"the eeriest I have ever"*: Cosell, *Cosell*, 8.

183   *"It's all a bunch of shit"*: Jim Murray column, *Los Angeles Times*, September 5, 1972.

183   *"As a group"*: *Washington Post*, July 9, 1992.

183   *"I had never felt so intensely"*: Cosell, *Cosell*, 2.

183   *"What goes on here"*: Ibid., 11.

183   *"ALL ISRAELI"*: Arledge, 135.

184   *"The word we get"*: Ibid.

184   *"I want to go on"*: Ibid., 136.

184   *"Looks very dark"*: Ibid., 137.

184   *"FLASH!"*: Ibid., 137–38.

185   *"Suddenly, the room was"*: Cosell, *Cosell*, 73.

185   *"swinging around first"*: Ibid., 84.

185   *"an age when baseball"*: Ibid.

186   *"There is only one"*: Ibid., 74.

186   *"Howard, we need"*: Don Ohlmeyer interview, March 18, 2002.

186   *"Do you think that I"*: Gunther and Carter, 140.

187   *"But, Howard . . . you have"*: David Remnick interview, June 8, 2003.

187   *"Howard's bravado"*: Ohlmeyer interview, March 18, 2002.
188   *"Take a gander"*: Plimpton, 211–12.
188   *"I have been"*: HBO, November 1, 1991.
191   *"Didn't a plane"*: Cosell, *Cosell*, 35–36.
191   *"George Foreman is relying"*: Hauser, *Ali*, 271.
192   *"Sure, Foreman"*: McIlvanney, 54–55.

THIRTEEN: "I AIN'T GONNA WIND UP LIKE MALCOLM X"

(My columns, notes, and memories of Deer Lake in July 1974 were vivid. My friend Gary Tuell remembered those days with photographic precision.)

198   *"how it all"*: ABC, February 3, 1974.
199   *"Cosell, you're a phony"*: When We Were Kings, 1996.
199   *"I'm going to tell you"*: Tom Callahan interview, July 4, 2005.
200   *"What's wrong around here?"*: Plimpton, 319.
200   *"Tell your man"*: Ibid., 322.
201   *"No, don't. Leave 'em"*: Hauser, *Ali*, 276.
201   *"Leave him"*: Callahan interview, July 4, 2005.
201   *"Oh, Christ, it's a fix"*: Plimpton, 324.
201   *"Get off the ropes"*: Hauser, *Ali*, 276.
201   *"I know what"*: Pacheco, *View*, 130–31.
202   *"Oh my Lawdy, he on"*: Plimpton, 326.
202   *"Damn, do"*: Pacheco interview, February 20, 2003. (That was also the night that "Ali mooned the world," as Larry Kolb put it. "He always paraded around naked, and as cameras followed him out of the ring in Zaire—it was the first global satellite transmission—Ali bent over, pulled down his shorts, and inadvertently turned his naked cheeks to the world. I saw it in a theater in Florida.")
203   *"You'll never know"*: Izenberg interview, May 20, 2005.
203   *"executioners of babies"*: Evanzz, *Messenger*, 39.
204   *"Sad thing was"*: Conrad interview, January 21, 1988.
205   *"We're in a new phase"*: Lipsyte, *New York Times Sunday Magazine*, June 29, 1975, 187.
205   *"I thought she was"*: Hauser, *Ali*, 311.
205   *"I know celebrities"*: Dave Anderson interview, February 3, 2005.
206   *"If he wins"*: Robyne Robinson interview, January 4, 2005.
207   *"This here is Joe Frazier's"*: Hauser, *Ali*, 313.
208   *"The only time you touched"*: Cus D'Amato interview, March 5, 1971.
208   *"It's hard to get up"*: Eddie Arcaro interview, May 1, 1976.
208   *"Lord, that man can punch"*: Pacheco, *12 Greatest*, 156.
208   *"The center of the ring"*: Kram, 185.
209   *"Muhammad, now we're"*: Anderson, *Sports*, 55.
209   *"Cut 'em off"*: Hauser, *Ali*, 324.

209   *"What's with"*: Anderson, *Corner,* 247.

210   *"It's over! It's over!"*: Hauser, *Ali,* 324.

210   *"What you saw tonight"*: Anderson, *New York Times,* October 1, 1975, 31.

210   *"Who is it"*: Kram, *Sports Illustrated,* October 13, 1975, 29, 32.

210   *"To Mrs. Marcos"*: Anderson, *New York Times,* October 2, 1975, 49.

210   *"You may have seen the last"*: Anderson, *New York Times,* October 1, 1975, 31.

210   *"This'll kill you"*: Anderson, *New York Times,* October 2, 1975, 49.

211   *"You can beat everybody"*: Kilroy interview, October 24, 2001.

211   *"You've got three more"*: Hauser, *Ali,* 340.

211   *"If it's any consolation"*: Pacheco interview, February 20, 2003.

212   *"If he stuck his dick"*: Larry Kolb interview, February 7, 2005.

212   *"Do you know"*: Izenberg interview, May 20, 2005.

213   *"Playing possum"*: Hauser, *Ali,* 347.

213   *"Champ, why don't"*: Ibid., 348–49.

214   *"A pelvic missionary"*: Pacheco, *View,* 34–35. (At various times, Ali and/or his associates have suggested that sexual activity the night before a fight contributed to Ali's poor performance in the ring. Mark Kram wrote that two nights before the third Norton fight, Ali "seemed to break a record of sorts when he bedded five women to win a bet." In 1974 Ali told Tuell and me that he spent the night before the first Frazier fight with a woman; his wife at that time, Belinda, later told a London newspaper that the woman was "a forty-dollar whore.")

214   *"His face, that wonderful"*: Anderson, *New York Times,* February 16, 1978, A1.

214   *"I'm sorry, men"*: Callahan, 74.

214   *"I messed up"*: Schulian, 14.

214   *"Yeah, I'll win it"*: Anderson, *New York Times,* February 16, 1978, D15.

215   *"So I'm out there"*: McIlvanney, 64.

215   *"Can all the systematic"*: Ibid., 66.

FOURTEEN: "A TWENTIETH-CENTURY TORTURE DEVICE"

216   "Next play, Howard": Ohlmeyer interview, March 18, 2002.

217   *"Ricky . . . get me the Beatles"*: Sklar, 164.

217   *"Hey . . . maybe Cosell could"*: Gunther and Carter, 141.

218   *"Dear Howard"*: Cosell, *Never,* 361.

219   *"On opening night"*: Sklar, 164.

219   *"John . . . I want you"*: Ibid.

220   *"You could have Elizabeth"*: Arledge, 148.

220   *"I always felt most"*:

221   *"It wasn't easy for me"*: Cosell, *Never,* 354.

221   *"pure entertainment"*: Cosell, unpublished interview with Jane Leavy, August 1979

222   *"Some people hate him"*: Arledge, 114. (Cosell claimed in a 1979 interview

with Jane Leavy to have received "fifty death threats" after his criticism of a Dallas Cowboys running back's performance. The FBI's 157-page file on Cosell reported investigations into five threats delivered by mail. One promised a bomb in Buffalo's Rich Stadium, another a bomb in Cosell's car. The file did not suggest the threats were connected to Cosell's relationship with Ali. One letter writer was arrested; an eighteen-year-old in Buffalo was sentenced to a year on probation.)

222   *"Young man . . . do you know"*: Gunther and Carter, 157.
222   *"Put me and 'The Midget'"*: Arledge, 189.
222   *"Don't think I haven't thought"*: Cosell, *Never*, 358.
222   *"Winchell said, 'Other'"*: Arledge, 189.

FIFTEEN: "YOU KNOW YOU NEED ME MORE THAN I NEED YOU"

224   *"What's this nonsense"*: ABC, January 5, 1975.
225   *"You ever hear"*: Lipsyte, *New York Times Sunday Magazine*, June 29, 1975.
226   *"The truth is"*: ABC, January 2, 1977.
226   *"Brezhnev didn't talk"*: Craig Whitney, *New York Times*, June 20, 1978, A4.
227   *"I made this hangaround"*: Jane Howard, *Cosmopolitan*, August, 1979, 215.
230   *"The title is too hard"*: ABC, September 16, 1978.
230   *"Everybody gets old"*: ABC, July 1979.
231   *"Question one"*: ABC, September 28, 1980.

SIXTEEN: "YOU FEELIN' ANY PAIN, JOE, FEELIN' ANY PAIN?"

235   *"It made me feel"*: Transcript of report telegraphed to U.S. Department of State from the American Embassy at Nairobi, Kenya, February 4, 1980, Section 5.
236   *"Mr. Ali, the Soviet Union"*: Report to State from U.S. Embassy at Lagos, Nigeria, February 3, 1980, Section 1.
237   *"We can push a few buttons"*: Ibid.
237   *"Some guys I'd never heard"*: Hauser, *View*, 288.
238   *"You gonna leave me here"*: Lipsyte, *Free*, 111.
238   *"All those fights after the Manila"*: Anderson, *Corner*, 148.
240   *"You know, Holmes"*: Hauser, *Memories*.
240   *"I'm gonna bet everything"*: Kilroy interview, October 24, 2001.
241   *"Stop it, Richard"*: Izenberg interview, May 20, 2005.
241   *"Man, you're bad"*: McIlvanney, 178, 176.
241   *"seems to have a mild ataxic"*: Hauser, *Ali*, 405.
242   *"I couldn't shake"*: Cosell, *Never*, 184.
242   *"It was no fight"*: ABC, October 3, 1980.

243   *"burning the tires off"*: Pacheco interview, August 26, 1988.

243   *"When I held him"*: Kilroy interview, October 24, 2001.

SEVENTEEN: "I *KNOW* WHO I AM"

244   *"He comes in in his"*: Justin Cosell interview, July 19, 2005.

244   *"Roone . . . the jury is still"*: Jill Cosell interview, July 18, 2005.

244   *"What's wrong"*: Murphy Martin interview, July 15, 2005.

244   *"completely out"*: Gunther, Carter, 182.

245   *"ABC News"*: ABC, December 8, 1980.

246   *"the most beautiful poem"*: Cosell interview, April 10, 1989.

246   *"The brass ring"*: Ibid.

246   *"Whatcha doin', Alfalfa?"*: Al Michaels interview, March 20, 2002.

248   *"You isolate the setback"*: O'Neil, 271.

249   *"Too many blows"*: Cosell, *Never*, 185.

249   *"an assault on the sense"*: Ibid., 187.

249   *"I will not dignify"*: ABC, November 26, 1982.

251   *"torn by the conflicting"*: Powers, 197.

251   *"No sportscaster"*: Ibid.

251   *"Howard, what did you"*: Gunther and Carter, 207.

EIGHTEEN: "MOTHER COSELL, SAVING US
ALL FROM PROSTITUTION"

253   *"Gibbs wanted to get"*: ABC, September 5, 1983.

253   *"What's the reaction?"*: Arledge, 286.

256   *"Howard loved it"*: Marley interview, January 7, 2002.

256   *"He always talked"*: Jimmy Roberts interview, April 16, 2005.

256   *"Peter . . . I forgot"*: Peter Mehlman, March 22, 2002.

256   *"honest, probative, enlightening"*: Cosell, *Never*, 308.

256   *"the media, the courts"*: Ibid., 309.

256   *"people of energy"*: Ibid., 317.

256   *"a little problem"*: Marley interview, January 7, 2002.

258   *"Howard was a"*: Roberts interview, April 16, 2005.

258   *"So where's the toop?"*: Mehlman interview, March 22, 2002. (Cosell re-garded the toupee not as a function of vanity but as an appliance neces-sary for his work. As often as not, he hung it on a hat rack. That, or dropped it in his desk drawer.)

260   *"dreadful"*: Cosell, *Never*, 171–72.

260   *"Peter, can we talk"*: Peter Bonventre interview, January 9, 2002.

261   *"Okay, Howard"*: Michaels interview, March 20, 2002.

262   *"Howard, I love you"*: Ohlmeyer interview, March 18, 2002.

NINETEEN: "I'D RATHER BE PUNISHED HERE THAN IN THE HEREAFTER"

268   *"The FBI is calling"*: Allison and Henderson, 64–65.
268   *"several payments"*: Ibid., 65.
268   *"I'd tell Harold"*: Ibid., 66, 67, 68.
269   *"Ain't many names"*: *Parade* magazine, April 5, 1981.
269   *"I want to talk"*: Allison and Henderson, 373.
271   *"Ali's always talked"*: Anderson, *New York Times*, May 20, 1983, A25.
271   *"should be fully"*: Kolb interview, May 30, 2004.
271   *"I hear people"*: John Feinstein, *Washington Post*, September 21, 1984, D1.
273   *"They can tell"*: Kolb, 214–29.
274   *"Quiet"*: Conrad interview, January 21, 1988.
274   *"And I knew"*: Hauser, *Ali*, 432.
274   *"He was stumbling"*: Hauser, *Ali*, 469.
275   *"Memories, so many"*: Solano interview, January 26, 2005.
276   *"Muhammad, what if"*: Solano interview, March 21, 2002.
278   *"I'm . . . so . . . sorry"*: Solano interview, January 12, 2005.
279   *"But, Daddy"*: Maryum Ali interview, March 20, 2002. (At Joe Louis's funeral, Ali put an arm around the great old champion's son, Joe Barrow, Jr., and said, "Your Daddy was really the greatest.")
280   *"I've got Parkinson's"*: Tauber, *New York Times Sunday Magazine*, July 17, 1988, 22.
280   *"You're old, you're fat"*: Tauber interview, December 26, 2001.
281   *"He understands"*: Tauber interview, December 4, 2000.
281   *"I saw him not as"*: Tauber e-mail, December 4, 2000.

TWENTY: "YOUR UNCONQUERABLE SOUL"

283   *"Eighty-five percent"*: Justin Cosell interview, July 19, 2005.
283   *"So many memories"*: Cosell interview, December 14, 1992.
284   *"So, Verdi, what"*: Bob Verdi interview, May 15, 2005.
285   *"Let's go on tour"*: Cosell, *Wrong*, 241.

TWENTY-ONE: "THE WORLD'S WAITING FOR ME"

286   *"Broke on his ass"*: Conrad interview, January 21, 1988.
286   *"I want to drive"*: Mike Tyson interview, November 21, 1986.
289   *"Tell us what your"*: Sam Nunn interview, September 23, 1988.
289   *"Peter, do me"*: Tauber interview, December 27, 2000.
291   *"What the fuck"*: Pacheco interview, August 26, 1988.
291   *"You know how"*: Cosell interview, September 1, 1988.
291   *"Richard Hirschfeld, my lawyer"*: Associated Press report, December 14, 1988.

291   *"Save it for the"*: Cosell interview, December 16, 1988.
293   *"Other than John F. Kennedy"*: Hauser, *Memories,* unnumbered.
295   *"Here, read this"*: Hauser interview, August 30, 2001.

TWENTY-TWO: "YOU STOOD UP AND TOLD THE TRUTH"

298   *"Holes in his brain"*: Jill Cosell interview, November 19, 2002.
298   *"Frank Deford's here"*: Frank Deford interview, March 5, 2002.
299   *"Muhammad Ali gave me"*: Deford interview, March 5, 2002.
299   *"Hello. . . . I don't know you"*: Lipsyte, *New York Times,* March 21, 1993, B7.
300   *"Guys, take me"*: Justin Cosell interview, July 19, 2005.
301   *"Don't try to talk"*: Jill Cosell interview, July 19, 2005. (In a 1981 interview for the William E. Wiener Oral History Library, Cosell was asked, "Have you ever felt a regret that you weren't a bar mitzvah?" He answered, "No. I've never even thought about it. Never even thought about it. I don't have much truck with religious ritual.")
301   *"I was twenty-one"*: Justin Cosell interview, July 19, 2005.
301   *"the most significant"*: Deford, National Public Radio, April 26, 1995.
301   *"crusading moralizer"*: *Jewish Week,* April 28, 1995.
301   *"a champion for human rights"*: *Amsterdam News,* April 29, 1995, 52.
301   *"His greatest contribution"*: *New York Beacon,* May 17, 1995.
301   *"They both were dancers"*: Charles Osgood, *CBS Sunday Morning,* April 30, 1995.
302   *"capacious memory"*: Robert Whitcomb, *Providence* (Rhode Island) *Journal-Bulletin,* May 12, 1995, 14A.
302   *"grace disguised"*: Jill Cosell's videotape of memorial service. (The Cosell memorial service was the third funeral Ali attended in five years. His father, Cassius Marcellus Clay, Sr., died on February 8, 1990, at age 77. His mother, Odessa Clay, died August 21, 1994, also 77 years old.)

TWENTY-THREE: "HE'S AMERICA'S ONLY LIVING SAINT"

307   *"Parkinson's"*: Howard Bingham interview, March 20, 2002.
308   *"As a nineteen-year-old"*: Billy Payne interview, April 11, 2002.
308   *"Piece of cake"*: Bingham interview, March 20, 2002.
309   *"For a horrible"*: Callahan interview, July 4, 2005.
309   *"I couldn't help"*: Schulberg interview, June 25, 2002.
309   *"The saddest thing"*: Schuyler interview, January 19, 2005.
309   *"His arm"*: Pope interview, April 11, 2002.
309   *"My God!"*: Plimpton interview, December 16, 2002.
309   *"He's America's only"*: David Israel interview, March 18, 2002.
310   *"They didn't tell me"*: Bingham interview, March 20, 2002.
310   *"may become absolutely"*: Early, vii.
311   *"If we've got"*: Keller, 133.

311   *"Very fearful when"*: Hauser interview, December 30, 2001.

312   *"Islam is like"*: Transcript of ESPN interview, January 17, 2002.

315   *"None of what's happening"*: Mark Kram interview, June 11, 2001.

315   *"For a guy"*: Kilroy interview, December 14, 2004.

315   *"It's no more"*: Lonnie Ali interview, July 14, 2003.

316   *"There was no evidence"*: Hauser, *Ali*, 443.

316   *"Muhammad's Parkinson's disease"*: Abraham Lieberman e-mail, July 25, 2005.

317   *"How can people"*: Kram interview, June 11, 2001.

318   *"All those names"*: Neil Leifer interview, April 3, 2005.

319   *"Are you watching"*: Kilroy interview, February 24, 2001.

319   *"I dodge those"*: *HBO Real Sports*, June 25, 2002.

319   *"This mission proves"*: News release from PR Newswire Association, July 18, 1996.

320   *"Anybody with a"*: Kilroy interview, July 29, 2005.

EPILOGUE: "THE ALPHA AND THE OMEGA"

324   *"God took away"*: Pacheco interview, February 20, 2003.

324   *"The Alpha and the Omega"*: McIlvanney, 64.

324   *"the one and only"*: Jill Cosell interview, November 19, 2002.

324   *"Ali and Cosell"*: Roberts interview, April 16, 2005.

324   *"There was no prejudice"*: Keith Olbermann interview, October 20, 2002.

324   *"The George Washington"*: Roberts interview, April 16, 2005.

325   *"He's our Mount Rushmore"*: Charlie Steiner interview, October 21, 2002.

325   *"He had a way"*: Len Berman interview, October 28, 2002.

325   *"Without Howard Cosell"*: Olbermann interview, October 25, 2001.

325   *"Cosell and Ali were"*: Sam Freedman interview, January 10, 2002.

325   *"America's white population"*: Lawrence J. Epstein interview, June 15, 2005.

325   *"I have the most indelible"*: Freedman interview, January 10, 2002.

327   *"Poppa's on"*: Colin Cosell interview, July 19, 2005.

327   *"Muhammad"*: ABC, December 7, 1980.

328   *"Look, Colin"*: Jill Cosell interview, July 19, 2005.

BIBLIOGRAPHY

Abramovitch, Ilana, and Galvin, Sean. *Jews of Brooklyn*. Brandeis University Press, 2002.

Adams, Maurianne, and Bracey, John (editors). *Strangers and Neighbors: Relations Between Blacks and Jews in the United States*. University of Massachusetts Press Amherst, 1999.

Allison, Dean, and Henderson, Bruce B. *Empire of Deceit: Inside the Biggest Sports and Bank Scandal in U.S. History*. Doubleday, 1985.

Anderson, Dave. *In the Corner: Great Boxing Trainers Talk About Their Art*. Morrow, 1991.

———. *Sports of Our Times*. Random House, 1979.

Angelou, Maya. *The Heart of a Woman*. Bantam, 1997.

———. *All God's Children Need Traveling Shoes*. Vintage Books, 1986.

Arledge, Roone. *Roone: A Memoir*. HarperCollins, 2003.

Barrow, Jr., Joe Louis, with Barbara Munder. *Joe Louis: 50 Years an American Hero*. McGraw-Hill, 1988.

Bingham, Howard, and Wallace, Max. *Muhammad Ali's Greatest Fight: Cassius Clay vs. The United States of America*. M. Evans and Company, 2000.

Braden, Anne. *The Wall Between*. Monthly Review Press, 1958.

Breitman, George, Porter, Herman, and Smith, Baxter. *The Assassination of Malcolm X*. Pathfinder Press, 1976.

Breitman, George (editor). *Malcolm X Speaks*. Grove Press, 1965.

Brunt, Stephen. *Facing Ali: 15 Stories*. The Lyons Press, 2002.

Callahan, Tom. *The Bases Were Loaded (and So Was I)*. Crown Publishers, 2004.

Campbell, Joseph, with Bill Moyers. *The Power of Myth*. Doubleday, 1988.

Cannon, Jack and Tom (editors). *Nobody Asked Me, But . . . the World of Jimmy Cannon*. Holt, Rinehart and Winston, 1978.

Clegg III, Claude Andrew. *An Original Man: The Life and Times of Elijah Muhammad*. St. Martin's Press, 1997.

Cohen, Rich. *Tough Jews: Fathers, Sons and Gangster Dreams*. Simon & Schuster, 1998.

Conrad, Harold. *Dear Muffo: 35 Years in the Fast Lane*. Rolling Stone Press, 1982.

Cope, Myron. *Double Yoi! A Revealing Memoir by the Broadcaster/Writer*. Sports Publishing, 2002.

———. *Broken Cigars*. Prentice-Hall, 1968.

Cosell, Howard. Transcript of interview by Elli Wohlgelernter, February 12, June 3, 1981. William E. Weiner Oral History Library. New York Public Library.

Cosell, Howard, with Mickey Herskowitz. *Cosell*. Playboy Press, 1973.

Cosell, Howard, with Peter Cohane. *Like It Is*. Playboy Press, 1974.

Cosell, Howard, with Peter Bonventre. *I Never Played the Game*. William Morrow, 1985.

Cosell, Howard, with Shelby Whitfield. *What's Wrong With Sports*. Simon & Schuster, 1991.

Dunphy, Don. *Don Dunphy at Ringside*. Henry Holt & Company, 1998.

Durant, Will. *The Story of Civilization: Part Two: The Life of Greece*. Simon & Schuster, 1966, 12.

Early, Gerald (editor). *The Muhammad Ali Reader*. William Morrow, 1998.

Edwards, Harry. *Revolt of the Black Athlete*. Macmillan, 1969.

Epstein, Lawrence J. *Mixed Nuts: America's Love Affair with Comedy Teams*. Public Affairs, 2004.

———. *The Haunted Smile: The Story of Jewish Comedians in America*. Public Affairs, 2001.

Evanzz, Karl. *The Judas Factor: The Plot to Kill Malcom X*. Thunder's Mouth Press, 1992.

———. *The Messenger: The Rise and Fall of Elijah Muhammad*. Pantheon Books, 1999.

Farr, Finis. *Black Champion: The Explosive Story of Jack Johnson, Who Dared the World to Find The Great White Hope*. Charles Scribner's Sons, 1968.

Gardell, Mattias. *In the Name of Elijah Muhammad: Louis Farrakhan and the Nation of Islam*. Duke University Press, 1996.

Gilbert, Martin. *The Jews of Hope: The Plight of Soviet Jewry Today*. Viking Penguin, 1985.

Gilman, Sander. *The Jew's Body*. Routledge, 1991.

Gorn, Elliott (editor). *Muhammad Ali: The People's Champ*. University of Illinois Press, 1995.

Gunther, Marc, and Carter, Bill. *Monday Night Mayhem: The Inside Story of ABC's Monday Night Football*. Beech Tree Books. 1988.

Halberstam, David J. *Sports on New York Radio: A Play-by-Play History*. Masters Press, 1999.

Hauser, Thomas. *Muhammad Ali: His Life and Times*. Simon & Schuster, 1991.

———. *The View from Ringside*. Sports Media Publishing, 2004.

———. *Black Lights: Inside the World of Professional Boxing*. McGraw-Hill, 1986.

Hauser, Thomas, with Neil Leifer. *Muhammad Ali: Memories*. Rizzoli, 1992.

Herring, George. *America's Longest War: The United States and Vietnam, 1950–1975*. Afred A. Knopf, 1979.

Howe, Irving. *World of Our Fathers: The Journey of the East European Jews to America and the Life They Found and Made*. Simon & Schuster, 1976.

Kazin, Alfred. *A Walker in the City*. Harcourt, Brace & World, 1951.

Keiter, Les. *Fifty Years Behind the Microphone*. University of Hawaii Press, 1991.

King, Florence. *With Charity Toward None: A Fond Look at Misanthropy*. St. Martin's Griffin, 1992.

Kolb, Larry J. *Overworld: The Life and Times of a Reluctant Spy*. Riverhead Books, 2004.

Koppett, Leonard. *The Rise and Fall of the Press Box*. Sports Media Publishing, 2003.

Kosslyn, Stephen M., and Rosenberg, Robin S. *Psychology: The Brain, the Person, the World*. Allyn and Bacon, 2001.

Kram, Mark. *Ghosts of Manila: The Fateful Blood Feud Between Muhammad Ali and Joe Frazier*. HarperCollins, 2001.

Lahr, John (editor). *The Diaries of Kenneth Tynan*. Bloomsbury, 2001.

Levine, Peter. *Ellis Island to Ebbets Field: Sport and the American Jewish Experience*. Oxford University Press, 1992.

Lewis, Claude. *Cassius Clay: A No-Holds-Barred Biography of Boxing's Most Controversial Champion*. Macfadden-Bartell, 1965.

Lewis, John, with Michael D'Orso. *Walking With the Wind*. Simon & Schuster, 1998.

Liebling, A. J. *A Neutral Corner: Boxing Essays*. North Point Press, 1990.

Lincoln, C. Eric. *The Black Muslims in America*. Kayode Publications, 1991.

Lincoln, W. Bruce. *In War's Dark Shadow: The Russians Before the Great War*. Dial Press, 1983.

Lipsyte, Robert. *Free to Be Muhammad Ali*. Harper & Row, 1978.

———. *SportsWorld: An American Dreamland*. Quadrangle, 1975.

MacCambridge, Michael. *The Franchise: A History of Sports Illustrated Magazine*. Hyperion, 1997.

Malcolm X, with Alex Haley. *The Autobiography of Malcolm X*. Grove Press, 1966.

Marqusee, Mike. *Redemption Song: Muhammad Ali and the Spirit of the Sixties*. Verso, 1999.

McIlvanney, Hugh. *McIlvanney on Boxing: An Anthology*. Beaufort, 1983.

Nachman, Gerald. *Seriously Funny: The Rebel Comedians of the 1950s and 1960s*. Pantheon, 2003.

Newfield, Jack. *Somebody's Gotta Tell It: The Upbeat Memoir of a Working-Class Journalist*. St. Martin's Press, 2002.

Olsen, Jack. *Black Is Best: The Riddle of Cassius Clay*. G. P. Putnam's Sons, 1966.

O'Neil, Terry. *The Game Behind the Game: High Stakes, High Pressure in Television Sports*. Harper & Row, 1989.

Pacheco, Ferdie. *Fight Doctor*. Simon & Schuster, 1976.

———. *Muhammad Ali: A View from the Corner*. Carol Publishing Group, 1992.

———. *The 12 Greatest Rounds of Boxing*. Total/Sports Illustrated, 2000.

Pepe, Phil. *Come Out Smokin': Joe Frazier—The Champ Nobody Knew*. Coward, McCann & Geoghegan, 1972.

Plimpton, George. *Shadow Box*. G. P. Putnam's Sons, 1977.

Pope, Edwin. *The Edwin Pope Collection*. Taylor Publishing, 1988.

Powers, Ron. *Supertube: The Rise of Television Sports*. Coward-McCann. 1984.

Rader, Benjamin G. *In Its Own Image: How Television Has Transformed Sports*. The Free Press, 1984.

Rampersad, Arnold (editor), and Roessel, David (associate editor). *The Collected Poems of Langston Hughes*. Vintage Classics, 1995.

Remnick, David. *King of the World: Muhammad Ali and the Rise of an American Hero*. Random House, 1998.

Richardson, H. Edward. *Cassius Marcellus Clay: Firebrand of Freedom*. University Press of Kentucky, 1976.

Robertson, James Rood. *A Kentuckian at the Court of the Tsars*. Kentucke Imprints, 1976.

Robinson, Sugar Ray, with Dave Anderson. *Sugar Ray*. Da Capo Press, 1970.

Ross, Ron. *Bummy Davis vs. Murder, Inc.: The Rise and Fall of the Jewish Mafia and an Ill-Fated Prizefighter*. St. Martin's Press, 2003.

Rudd, Irving, with Stan Fischler. *The Sporting Life: The Duke and Jackie, Pee Wee, Razor Phil, Ali, Mushky Jackson and Me*. St. Martin's Press, 1990.

Schaap, Dick. *Flashing Before My Eyes: 50 Years of Headlines, Deadlines & Punchlines*. HarperEntertainment, 2001.

Schecter, Leonard. *The Jocks*. Paperback Library, 1970.

Schulberg, Budd. *Loser and Still Champion: Muhammad Ali*. Doubleday & Company, 1971.

Schulian, John. *Writer's Fighters*. Andrews & McNeel, 1983.

Schulke, Flip, with Matt Schudel. *Muhammad Ali: The Birth of a Legend, Miami, 1961–1964*. St. Martin's Press, 2000.

Sheed, Wilfrid. *Muhammad Ali*. Alskog, 1975.

Sklar, Rick. *Rocking America: How the All-Hit Radio Stations Took Over*. St. Martin's Press, 1984.

Smiley, David L. *Lion of White Hall: The Life of Cassius M. Clay*. University of Wisconsin Press, 1962.

Spence, Jim. *Up Close & Personal: The Inside Story of Network Television Sports*. Atheneum, 1988.

Sperber, A. M. *Murrow: His Life and Times*. Freundlich Books, 1986.

Stern, Bill, with Oscar Fraley. *The Taste of Ashes*. Henry Holt & Company, 1959.

Strother, Shelby. *Saddlebags: A Collection of Columns and Stories*. Altwerger & Mandel, 1991.

Torres, Jose. *Sting Like a Bee: The Muhammad Ali Story*. Contemporary Books, 2002.

Tosches, Nick. *The Devil and Sonny Liston*. Little, Brown, 2000.

Tyler, Bruce M. *African-American Life in Louisville*. Arcadia, 1998.

White, Vibert L. *Inside the Nation of Islam: A Historical and Personal Testimony by a Black Muslim*. University Press of Florida, 2001.

INDEX

ABOUT THE AUTHOR

DAVE KINDRED is a winner of the Red Smith Award, sports journalism's version of a Pultizer Prize for lifetime achievement, chosen by the Associated Press Sports Editors. He has been a newspaper columnist at the *Louisville Courier-Journal, Washington Post, Atlanta Journal-Constitution,* and *The National.* He is a native of Atlanta, Illinois, and graduate of Illinois Wesleyan University. The National Sportscasters and Sportswriters Association named him its National Sportswriter of the Year in 1997. Author of nine books, contributor to ESPN television, and commentator for Sporting News radio, Kindred is a senior writer at *Golf Digest* and back-page columnist for *Sporting News.* He lives in Locust Grove, Virginia.